LIFE OF A KARMA YOGI

LIFE OF A KARMA YOGI

Memoir of a Civil Servant

M. Gopalakrishna

GYAN

Published by

Gyan Publishing House
5, Ansari Road
Daryaganj, New Delhi-110002
Phone: 011-47034999, 9811692060
E-mail: books@gyanbooks.com

Distribution Network
gyanbooks.com
India, USA, Canada, UK, Australia, France

ISBN: 978-93-6433-428-0 (HB), 978-93-6433-314-6 (PB)
978-93-6433-689-5 (E-book)

First Published, 2025

Printed at: Gyan Press, Delhi.

LIFE OF A KARMA YOGI
Author: M. Gopalakrishna

Contents

Preface

Born in colonial India but living in Independent India, I was a ringside spectator of India's struggle for freedom, economic growth, and development. I was fortunate to join the Civil Service and do my duty objectively like a Karma Yogi, irrespective of the results.

The book 'Life of Karma Yogi' gives a bird's-eye view of conditions and life in India over three generations. It shows the values and ethos of the Civil Services, acting as the 'Steel Frame' which have kept India together and laid the foundations of growth for development, modern India. What drives it forward is the ancient belief of 'Vasudhaiva Kutumbakam' 'One Earth, One Family' and a better Future for succeeding generations.

My life story gives an idea of the duties of a Civil Servant in bygone days, events and efforts shaping India in its quest for peace, social development, economic growth, and world prosperity.

Maintaining a diary helped me recollect details of past events while Photo Albums provided vivid reminiscences. Some incidents were the near death experiences, ranging from a natural phenomenon like a Thunderbolt at Aizawl and gunfire in Mizo Hills in 1967, a Car accident at Delhi in 1987, as a passenger in the Air Crash of a Russian TU-154 flight at Palam Airport, Delhi in 1993 and near-fatal Fire Accident at Kolkata in 2006. Minor tremors and earthquakes in Assam fell on paths in the hills and plains and in slippery, treacherous roads were common. I was destined to live and tell my tale, thanks to God's grace.

The book provides civil services aspirants a glimpse of an exciting career, its immense scope and wonderful opportunity to serve our country and make India, Bharat, the third largest economy in the world very soon. As part of my post retirement phase, I continue to mentor, give lectures, and conduct Mock interviews to guide Civil service aspirants. I notice that successful Civil Servants are educationally, technically, and experience-wise, more qualified, versatile, and suited to analyse, advise, and lead our development efforts. India is safe in their hands.

Preface

Born in colonial India but living in Independent India, I was a ringside spectator of India's struggle for freedom, economic growth, and development. I was fortunate to join the Civil Service and do my duty objectively like a Karma Yogi, irrespective of the results.

The book 'Life of Karma Yogi' gives a bird's-eye view of conditions and life in India over three generations. It shows the ethos and ethics of the Civil Services, acclaimed as the 'Steel Frame,' which have kept India together and laid the foundations of growth for a resurgent, modern India. What drives it forward is the ancient belief of Vasudhaiva Kutumbakam:' 'One Earth, One Family' and a better 'Future' for succeeding generations.

My life story gives an idea of the duties of a Civil Servant in bygone days, events, and efforts shaping India in its quest for peace, social development, economic growth, and world prosperity.

Maintaining a diary helped me recollect details of past events, while Photo Albums provided vivid reminiscences. Some incidents were life and death experiences ranging from a natural phenomenon like a Thunderbolt at Aizawl and gunfire in Mizo Hills in 1967, a Car accident at Delhi in 1987, as a passenger in the Air Crash of a Russian TU-154 Flight at Palam Airport, Delhi in 1993 and near-fatal Fire Accident at Kolkata in 2006. Minor tremors and earthquakes in Assam fell on paths in the hills and plains and in slippery five-star hotels were common. But I was destined to live and tell my tale, thanks to God's grace.

The book provides Civil Services aspirants a glimpse of an exciting career, its immense scope, and wonderful opportunity to serve our country and make India, Bharat, the third largest economy in the world very soon. As part of my post-retirement phase, I continue to mentor, give lectures, and conduct Mock Interviews to guide Civil service aspirants. I notice that successor Civil Servants are educationally, technically, and experience-wise, more qualified, versatile, and suited to analyse, advice, and lead our development efforts. India is safe in their hands.

Foreword

Dr. C. Rangarajan

Former Chairman, Economic Advisory Council to the Prime Minister
Former Governor, Reserve Bank of India

Chairman
Madras School of Economics
Gandhi Mandapam Road, Kottur
Chennai 600025

I am happy to write the foreword to this interesting book titled, "Life of a Karma Yogi".

This is a narrative by Mr. M. Gopalakrishna who joined the IAS in 1962 and held many important positions in Andhra Pradesh, Assam and at centre over the next four decades and more.

In the administration of the country, IAS has played a critical role. The scope of government administration has itself changed over time. From a purely 'law and order' maintenance role, officers belonging to IAS have been called up to play a 'developmental' role. Developmental role has itself two dimensions, one in purely initiating and managing programmes directed towards improving the health, education, water supply and other similar activities, and the second dimension is to manage enterprises owned by government. Thus to be successful as an officer of the IAS cadre, one has to have multiple capabilities. As one reads through the memoirs of Gopalakrishna, one is impressed by an array of positions he has held and how successful he was in handling all these diverse positions. Gopalakrishna was good at handling on the one hand the policy makers who came from the political side of our society and the public at large for whom the services are to be provided.

The narrative is thick with details. Gapalakrishna must have kept detailed notes of his actions all through his career. Or he must have extraordinary memory. May be he has both. Another interesting aspect of the narrative is what we get to know about the social and family life all through the last eight decades. The insights offered into the functioning of a joint family are both interesting and revealing.

The book will be an eye opener to policy makers at the political level and administrators who have to implement decisions. Also, the public at large will get to know how decisions are made and implemented in government. There is no doubt that the book will have a wide appeal. My hearty congratulations to Gopalakrishna.

C. RANGARAJAN

Res: F-1, Rangavilas, 23/12 III Main Road, Nanganallur, Chennai 600061
Off. : 044-22300301 Res. : 044-48522310 Mob. : 9445183385 Email: c.rangarajan@mse.ac.in

Justice M. N. Rao, Former Chief Justice of Himachal Pradesh & Former Chairperson, National Commission for Backward Classes (GoI)

I have gone through with considerable care and interest my esteemed friend Sri Gopala Krishna's autobiography.

It is often said very realistically that in a democracy where the Cabinet system of governance is in vogue, if the policy fails, the Minister (Political Executive) goes and if the implementation fails, the blame falls on the permanent Executive (Civil Servant). The political Executive being represented by the Minister has no permanent interest in the administration since the tenure is limited but the permanent executive has no such choice. Bearing in mind the legal regime that governs the administration, the views of the Minister, and the policies of the party in power, the civil servant has to steer through a difficult path. In this arduous task. Sri Gopala Krishna came out with great success. Indeed, he is what an ideal civil servant should be.

The historical events to which Sri Gopala Krishna was a witness and had an important role as a civil servant have been depicted so well that as one goes through the book, a feeling is inescapable that it is more a "Drisya Kavyam" than a record of events. In solving difficult problems concerning the influx of refugees from East Pakistan, Sri Gopala Krishna played a pivotal role.

The saying that a civil servant is capable of discharging multiple duties including commercial activities of the State fits perfectly to Sri Gopala Krishna. During his tenure as the Commissioner of Commercial Taxes in the composite State of Andhra Pradesh, the administration was streamlined so well that the revenue of the State had considerably gone up. He served the State with total commitment, devotion and dedication.

Seyed Ehtesham Hasnain, *D.Sc (h.c.), DMedSc (h.c.), ML, FAAM, FTWAS, FNA*

(Former Member (2004-14), Scientific Advisory Council to the Prime Minister of India (SAC-PM), National Science Chair, Indian Institute of Technology, Delhi (IIT-D), Formerly Invited Professor, IIT-D; Former JC Bose National Fellow; Former Vice Chancellor, Jamia Hamdard, New Delhi; Former Vice Chancellor, University of Hyderabad, Hyderabad; First Director, Centre for DNA Fingerprinting & Diagnostics (CDFD), Hyderabad; Distinguished Professor, Sharda University.)

"Gopala Krishna Naidu's autobiography is a remarkable documentation of the journey covered by this very illustrious, multifaceted down-to-earth member of the Indian Administrative Service. His portrayal of his immediate family's spread over a few generations, his services to the nation, including the then much disturbed north-eastern parts of the country and also important departments within his cadre as well as in the centre and more recent association with public enterprises and financial institutions are not only worth reading but a great inspiration. My acquaintance with him has been personally a learning experience for me during our long association with the Suven Life Sciences Board of Management. A Graduate in law as well as Science, Naidu Garu's depth and understanding of varied areas of governance and human management goes far deeper and comprehensive - some matter to envy about. I'm confident given the anecdotal as well as personal notes he has been able to provide, this autobiography will be destined to become a class apart for generations to come."

M.V. Bhaskara Rao I.P.S
D.G.P (Retd.) of the combined Andhra Pradesh

He is one of a rare breed of officers who is impeccably upright and minutely just. A persuasive speaker who could disarm anyone with his logical arguments. His contribution to the economic development of the combined AP state is unique. As MD of the Godavari Fertilizers, he operationalized the plant in a span of three years as against the normal time of five years, which at the time was a record achievement. This project helped the economic development of Kakinada and the East Godavari district in particular.

M Gopalakrishna is a natural leader of men and matters and as a civil servant, he proved it to the hilt when he led the Assam Civil Service team into Bangladesh during its liberation war. His liaison with the Indian Army officers and the Mukti Bahini of Bangladesh as the head of the civil services team speaks volumes about his high level of competence in coordinating with various types of organizations in crucial times.

He is a distinguished and fluent public speaker and influencer. He is a mentor par excellence and after his retirement, he used his mentoring and motivating skills to help civil servant aspirants. To sum up, he is a great gentleman and a great officer.

Dr. S. Chakravarthy IAS (Retd).

I call him Gopal, as many of his friends call. I met him for the first time when I was Assistant Collector, Guntur in 1962. On my first tryst with him, I came to know that he was giving a shot at the IAS Examination, which brought him to the fraternity of IAS in 1962.

I have heard his lectures and presentations many times. He always delved into great detail, the disparate vignettes of the subject matter. For me, it was a learning experience, whenever I attended his unravelling of different subjects.

He was a specialist in Public Sector Enterprises Management. He was bestowed with awards for exemplary work, both academic and professional. He was associated with International Organisations like UNO and National Organisations like the Institute of Public Enterprises. An Expert in Public Administration, Industrial, and Corporate Management, he was the recipient of the LifeTime Achievement Awards, galore.

A couple of the traits I noticed in him merit mention. When he expresses his thoughts, there would unfailingly arise a sudden flash which one may say is his coruscating trait. One last trait I would like to mention is that he always observed the discipline of not criticizing the Government when he was participating in a public function. In short, he follows the principles.

G. P. Rao, IAS (Retd.)
Former Secretary to GoI and Chairman, ERC, AP.

I have known Shri M. Gopalakrishna since 1964 when he was Asst. Commissioner, Guwahati, Assam where I was posted as an Army Officer. We used to meet often. He was posted as SDO, Goalpara where he handled the large influx of refugees from East Pakistan during the Indo-Pak War of 1965. He was instrumental in setting up the Assam Sainik School at Matia. At the time of the Mizo Hills insurgency, he was posted at Aizawl where he played a major role in restoring normalcy in the district.

He was Secretary, Industries, Commissioner, Visakhapatnam Steel Plant, and Managing Director, Godavari Fertilisers. The Plant was built ahead of schedule and within the estimated cost - a rare event in the Public Sector.

He is a very good friend who is helpful and is a good speaker who quotes copiously from Sanskrit. A polyglot, he speaks quite a few languages. Post-retirement, he is active in Social work. Aspirants to the IAS and youth constantly seek his guidance and advice. He is the President of the All India Services Pensioners Association for Telangana and AP State. Our families are also in constant touch with him and his wife.

K. Sreedhar Rao, IAS Former CS of Sikkim Government.

Even as Assistant Commissioner he was the full-time officer running the Department of Relief and Rehabilitation of refugees who were streaming into Assam from the then East Pakistan. Gopal during his career had to deal with every type of crisis which was during that time so frequent in the entire NE region.

The Mizo Rebellion, the border issues with Nagaland, the conduct of

Elections in Assam in the teeth of the sustained agitation by the students are but a few of the crises that Gopal handled with efficiency and dispatch.

He was a competent leader in every post he held both in Assam, AP, and in the GoI. Throughout his career, he operated with a value system that attached immense importance to high standards of integrity, efficiency, pragmatism, and timely delivery of service.

R Vaidyanath Iyer, IAS (Retd.),
Former Secretary to GoI, Min. of Education

I am extremely happy that my colleague and friend Sri Gopalakrishna had decided to write down his memoir; any well-written memoir is a documentation of the life and times of the memorialist and hence would be of interest to contemporaries and posterity. Such documentation would be all the more interesting if it is that of an IAS officer who held top positions in the Central and State governments and as such is a participant in momentous events and decisions.

I had the pleasure of being the neighbour of Sri Gopalakrishna in the Tilak Lane government quarters in Delhi for several years; both of us were moving to the top positions available normally for an IAS officer in the Government of India. There were many occasions when during conversation we shared the agony and ecstasy of moving up the greasy pole.

I had many occasions of visiting Assam where Sri Gopalakrishna started his career in the IAS before moving on to Andhra Pradesh. Even decades after leaving Assam I was pleasantly surprised to find that he was still being remembered by many people in Assam.

Sri Gopalakrishna held many senior managerial positions in Central and State public sector undertakings and had won many accolades as a distinguished manager. As President of the All India Services Pensioners Association at Hyderabad Sri Gopalakrishna had been doing yeomen service to pensioners.

Writing a memoir is a voyage of discovery of oneself. I wish Sri Gopalakrishna a pleasant and enchanting voyage of discovery.

Dr. Mohan Kanda, IAS (Retd.), Former Chief Secretary of United AP

It had always been an ardent wish of mine, to find a person, who combines in himself, the three equally rare qualities of being a distinguished Civil servant, an erudite scholar in several languages, and a wonderful human being. My wish was more than fulfilled, when I came to know M. Gopalakrishna. I have rarely come across persons with such clarity of thought, crispness of expression and an engaging manner of conveying ideas.

I had the honour, and privilege, of working closely with him when I was the Registrar of Cooperative Societies of Andhra Pradesh state, and he was the Managing Director of the Godavari Fertilisers.

Gopalkrishna not only belongs to the threatened species of upright civil servants who value the virtues of rectitude, hard work and public spiritedness but also can give, the most eloquent of orators, a run for their money while, simultaneously, demonstrating what true friendships are made of. Having a long, enduring and educating relationship with him is probably one of the best things that ever happened in life.

Shri Ratan P Watal IAS (Retd). Former Finance Secretary GoI, Currently, Chairman, Central Vista Oversight Committee, New Delhi

I was the MD of the AP State Finance Corporation from 15/07/2003 to 03/03/2005; a part of the team that you headed as Chairman. It was my last and very significant posting in erstwhile Andhra Pradesh. I then left for Delhi to seek my destiny and my future as an administrator. I carried within me that I had assimilated in the APSFC posting, from its experienced Board members, from the advice of highly qualified staff members, and above all the counsel of a Chairman who was a friend, philosopher, and guide.

Your helmsmanship gave clarity and continuity to the mission objectives of the organization, and your empathy with the needs of the clients and aspirations of the accomplished staff was admirable. Your wisdom and sagacity as an experienced elder helped me to continue what you and Jatish had embarked upon when so many had given up on the organization.

From Dr. J.C. Mohanty, former MD of APSFC.

M. Gopalakrishna became the Chairman of the Board of Directors of Andhra Pradesh State Financial Corporation when I was the Managing Director. He guided me with sound advice for almost a year till I was transferred in December 2002. He was specifically chosen by the SIDBI and the Government of Andhra Pradesh to utilize his expertise for revamping the corporation and bringing back its past glory.

He is an outstanding and accomplished civil servant having 4 decades of experience both in government and in the industrial sector. He also worked as Chairman of the Rural Electrification Corporation where he took many initiatives in the field of the Power Sector.

During his tenure, the Corporation attained Numero Uno position in the country. It was a pleasure working with such a matured and understanding professional. In my career, I am beholden to a few senior colleagues who effectively channelled my potential and stood like a rock in support of my initiatives. Mr Gopalakrishna was one among them. I am extremely grateful to him.

Ajeya Kallam, IAS
Principal Advisor to Chief Minister, AP

I first met Sri Gopala Krishna, one of our distinguished civil servants when I was undergoing district training way back in 1984. He has been a role model in service for many junior officers like me. His no-nonsense attitude in getting things done, be it in secretariat or in project execution at field level is a lesson to watch and emulate. The way he executed a Greenfield fertilizer project like GFC right from its conception to commissioning and subsequent management is exceptional not only in the public sector but even when we compare projects in the private sector. I was fortunate to work as MD, SFC when Gopala Krishna was Chairman of SFC. The way he used to conduct meetings and scrutinize project proposals has made me learn many things that I always cherish.

SP Tucker C S, Andhra Pradesh

As a 2nd generation Civil servant in Independent India, I was fortunate to be associated with some of the prominent officers who created a path-breaking approach toward growth and poverty reduction in the Country. Mr MG was foremost among them in becoming a role model for so many of us officers. His nurturing of the Institute of Public Enterprise is a big contribution. He supported so many young enterprises through the only profit-making State Finance Corporation in the country. He also managed the most efficiently run REC in the country!

MR. MG was always the role model and service senior who mentored many of us with a realization towards time management, efficient decision-making, and the role of the competitive public sector, a precursor to reforms in the '90s.

K. Satyanarayana,
President Emeritus, Hyderabad Chapter of National HRD Network

As President of the Hyderabad Chapter of the National HRD Network in the years 2000 to 2007 and as Regional President of South India, he has contributed immensely to the growth and development of the Hyderabad chapter. The chapter has seen all-round development in terms of activities and growth in membership. Out of 30 chapters of the National HRD

Network, the Hyderabad Chapter is the only one that was privileged to have an IAS Officer as its President.

Shri Gopalakrishna Garu used all his contacts and personal influence to meet the Chief Minister and officials to get a piece of prime land in Banjara Hills on a 30-year lease for building the National Headquarters of the National HRD Network and the office of the Hyderabad Chapter. National HRD Network will remain indebted forever to Sri Gopalakrishna Garu for this selfless service for the development of Human Resources in India.

DR G. Pakki Reddy of Biotech Unit of IPE

Sri Gopalakrishna as Director of IPE was deeply concerned with the redressal of the immediate problems of farmers. He used to advise us to categorize 1) research projects that have long gestation periods, but once it succeeds, it will yield long-term benefits, and 2) projects that have short gestation whose results will help farmers in solving their immediate problems.

Sri Gopalakrishna had wide contacts and a good image in society. BTU took advantage to establish contacts with Krishi Vigyan Kendras and farmers in villages. He used his contacts with the Governor's office and involved the then Governor Dr C. Ranga Rajan in an International Conference on Biotechnology in July 1998 and through him sent a strong message on the advantages of new technology.

Dr Ravi Kumar Peesapati, [PHD], MBA [Mktg.,] MA [Pub. Admin.,] & LL.B., HMA`s Life Member and Former President of HMA

The Hyderabad Management Association [HMA] is a 'not-for-profit' Society of Management Professionals and affiliated to the All India Management Association [AIMA] – An apex Management Body in New Delhi.

Shri Gopalakrishna is one of the role model Senior Members of the HMA and contributed to the growth of the association in several dimensions. He chaired the HMA Constitutional Amendment Committee, He is a recipient of HMA's Manager of the Year Award, HMA`s Lifetime Achievement Award, and HMA`s Member of the Year Award.

Shri Madan Bezbaruah, IAS (Retd.), Former Secretary to Govt. of India, Tourism

Much before the AASU took up the problem of the illegal migrants in Assam, he had drawn the attention of the government to this menace. His commitment to Assam has been total and respect for culture and tradition endeared him to local people. I am from Jorhat, a rather conservative place and I know how the local people appreciate today his knowledge of and respect for the culture and history of the place. He is held in great esteem by Assam civilians.

Gopalakrishna Naidu has a store of anecdotes and stories of those days—of people, seniors, and public figures as well as his deep perception of issues and events of his days in Assam. If he recounts them, it would certainly be a great treasure for the administrative history of Assam.

R.K Sharma, Secretary General, FIMI

In one's career, one comes across many people from different walks of life. And if after a gap of almost 30 years, a person is as vivid in one's memory as he was when one used to meet him in an official and personal capacity, that person is remarkable. That person is Mr. M. Gopalakrishna. I have innumerable fond memories about him which I even now narrate to my colleagues. His in-depth knowledge of the subject, the clarity with which he explained beautifully and cogently both verbally in extempore (with words flowing in torrential sequence) or in beautiful handwriting was mind-boggling. In my entire life, I have never met a person as gifted as him.

As head of the Federation of Indian Mineral Industries (FIMI) which represents the entire mining industry – coal, non-coal, critical, and atomic minerals in public and private sectors – my visits to him were quite frequent. He would listen to me with an open mind, discuss and understand, and find solutions that would mostly be in the interest of the mining industry. His decision would be clear and precise. I wish the officials today were as accommodating and bold.

Shri Manoharan, then Joint Secretary Home Department, Govt. of Assam

M. Gopalakrishna, IAS was the Commissioner and Secretary to the Government of Assam in the Home and Political Departments, during the utmost turbulent times and volatile situation in the State of Assam.

He was affectionate, absolutely straightforward, candid, categorical and very pleasant and transparent in his very first interaction with me and subsequently as well as dime-a-dozen interactions with me throughout his brief, extremely challenging and toughest assignment during that short period. I would also like to mention that he was polite, courteous and business-like and had interacted with me and other senior and junior officers and staff members wearing his infectious smile on his face always with a cool headed approach and composure.

I had learnt from him the nuances of the art of governance and literally followed his footsteps in the learning curve of my administrative career in my later years in the Indian Administrative Service.

Acknowledgment

I owe a debt of gratitude to many individuals and life experiences that have made me who I am. My mother was my Guru and compass of my life. My brothers and sisters, wife, and extended family stood by me through thick and thin and made my tasks easier.

I held jobs that were risky, difficult, and not in the ordinary course of service. My colleagues, bosses, secretaries, and employees enabled me to do well. But for their support, I would have chased a mirage. I was associated with Educational and Training institutions and several social and Cultural organizations apart from professional Corporate and statutory bodies. In the process, I became a speaker, debater, narrator, tutor, and advisor to many Non-Government Organisations. They conferred on me titles and awards.

My friends, colleagues, and well-wishers have urged me to chronicle my service experiences and post-retirement activities. One of them is coaching Civil Services aspirants and conducting mock interviews. Civil Service aspirants bridged the generation gap and made me feel young! They taught me the latest mores they follow. Helping them achieve their aspirations means leaving the service legacy in good hands. I believe that my life and career could help young aspirants face competition and gain entry into Civil Services. It would also help me face and negotiate the many turns of my career and life. Readers, Civil Servants, Civil service aspirants, and their parents could benefit from reading the book. I welcome suggestions, advice, and criticism to make the book more useful.

All mentorship is about the alchemy of turning one's doubts of 'Can I Do' into confidence of 'I Can Do'. The Mantra for success is simple: Homework, Hard work, Smart work, Teamwork, and Networking.

My autobiography was made possible by the efforts of many people, all of whom I thank. Many friends and editors have helped me with suggestions, advice, and critical comments. The Publishers have produced a neat and attractive book. I thank all of them. I must especially thank my colleagues, Shri K. Sridhar Rao and Shri K. N. Kumar, and the Editors,

Mrs. Manjiri Ganu and V. Rishi Kumar, who spared no effort to make it a simple and lucid narrative. I must thank Dr PVVS Murthy and Dr Col. VRK Prasad and M. Swaminathan and Shri N. Madhusudana Rao, who painstakingly typed out the scripts and gave useful suggestions.

PART - I

1

Bellary – My Hometown

Bellary town in South India, where I was born, has an interesting history. It was part of the Vijayanagara kingdom ruled by the Rayas. After their defeat and decline, it was part of the Qutb Shahi kingdom. Later, the Asaf Jahis of Hyderabad, calling themselves Nizams, took over. During their period, the Mughal rule declined while the Marathas from Western India rapidly expanded their territory. The Nizams feared that they might not be able to withstand an assault of the Marathas and turned to the British, who had established themselves in the eastern part of India with Madras as their headquarters. During that period, the British were regarded mainly as a trading concern called the East India Company but had started to harbour territorial ambitions. With a well-equipped army to support their actions, they commenced expanding their sway.

The Nizam of Hyderabad, fearing Maratha expansionism, requested the East India Company to locate a British Garrison at Secunderabad Cantonment and agreed to pay for their upkeep and services. In 1800 AD, unable to pay the agreed maintenance cost in gold or cash, he decided to 'Cede' the four Rayalaseema districts of Bellary, Anantapur, Cuddapah, and Kurnool (BACK)districts to the Company with full rights of land administration and collection of revenues, to meet their garrison upkeep. East India Company took over the ceded districts and made Bellary the Headquarters of the four districts. It appointed Thomas Munro as Collector of Bellary. He later shifted as Collector to Anantapur and introduced land rights for farmers, known as Ryotwari Reforms.

This proved beneficial to the residents of the Rayalaseema area, as the British, while exploiting India's Resources, introduced laws, rules, and regulations that were non-discriminatory in nature and ensured that justice was dispensed after due process of law.

Bellary was considered important as it had a well-built Fort on the top of a single massive rock 250 meters in height, with a water moat all around and enclosed land in the fort area. The British considered Bellary a geo-strategic location for a Cantonment, as the Nizam's Territories were in the north and the Mysore State to the south. To the west was the Maratha Kingdom. Around the 1820s, Bellary Cantonment housed one company of English troops and two native battalions of the Madras Regiment.

Many of the soldiers in the Madras Regiment at Bellary were Telugu-speaking Naidus from Madras State and Mysore. After retirement, they wanted to settle down in Bellary. They requested the Collector to assign them land with Pattas, waive or lower land and municipal taxes, and give many concessions to enable them to build their own houses, amenities, and temples to settle down. The administration agreed to lease the locality along with a Bazaar called Cowl Bazaar. 'Cowl' was an English corruption of the Telugu word 'Kaulu' or land lease. Naidu families dominated the area around Khalasi Street, while in the Bazaar and the adjacent regions, Marathas, Muslims, other backward classes, and skilled workers lived.

The new locality had about 200 Naidu families, some Tamil Purohits, Mudaliars, Pillaiyars, goldsmiths, and Tamil harijans who were Sykes looking after the horses. The Naidus were Telagas, a subgroup of the Telugu-speaking generic Kapu (soldier-farmer-protector) community. They had held senior military and administrative posts under the Vijayanagara rulers and, later on, with the Nayaka rulers of Tanjore and Madurai. They were literate in both Telugu and Tamil. They were mostly employed in the Army, Police, Railways, Post offices, or the Public Works Departments and Revenue Department. They were 100% literate as community-sponsored street schools taught children the 3 "R"s and "Bala Siksha '' a manual for children's education in Telugu apart from Missionary and Government Schools.

The settlers built a Shiva temple with an attached step-well that has a copious flow of underground water. They also constructed a "Ramalayam," a "Jagannath Alayam," a "Vigneshwara Alayam" (Pillaiyar temple), and a Kali Temple where the 'tonsure' of hair and piercing of children's earlobes are performed.

There was a VyayamaShala or Akhada with an enclosed area where boys were taught Wrestling, Lathi drill, and Sword use. I learned weightlifting, wrestling, and sword use there. The Naidus were good at games and sports and excelled in their hallmark game, Hockey. The Naidu youth were feared because of their physique and tendency to pick up a fight.

MY GRANDFATHER - DR. GOVINDARAJULU NAIDU

My maternal grandfather, Dr.Injeti Govindarajulu Naidu, a Licentiate Medical Practitioner (L.M.P), was an Army Doctor. His father, Narasimhulu

Das Naidu, was a saintly person and singer of Bhajans, hence called Das. He used to meditate and go into trances, Samadhi. While on his deathbed, he wanted to see his beloved youngest son, Govindarajulu, before leaving his mortal coils. The army rejected his son's application for leave. In anger and disgust, he resigned from the army and met his father, when the latter took both his son's hands and put them on his head and said, "I am bequeathing all my spiritual powers to you and will gladly leave this world" and expired. We were told that my grandfather's hands were almost scorched as his father's life evaporated from his head. At that moment, he felt the need to practice meditation, activate the Kundalini, and seek a Guru in the quest for realizing God.

Bellary had a General Hospital and a TB Sanitorium. It was a growing town with a municipality and aspiring to become a city. Dr.Govindarajulu started a private practice in Bellary and set up the Panduranga Pharmacy (clinic).

He took a guru called Niranjanaswamy, who initiated him to the practice of Samadhi through Kundalini awakening. Niranjanswamy was habituated to taking Ganja, smoking Beedies, and was fond of non-vegetarian food. My mother, Bramaramba, the eldest daughter of the house, used to serve him food and give money to meet his needs for Ganja. My mother, who had extra sensory perception and could foresee events in advance, believed that the Guru's blessings and good karma from her previous birth gave her these powers.

My grandpa had miraculous healing powers, and his practice flourished. He used to get foodstuffs like Bread, English brands of biscuits, chocolates, and English medicines from Spencers of Madras. We, the children, would go by our Tonga (Horse cart) to collect the package from the railway station. Once a week, we would get a basket of fruits and vegetables from Bengaluru. Vegetables like Cauliflower, Cabbage, Beetroot, Turnips, Squash, and Strawberries were called 'English as they were not grown locally.

When his grandson Madhusudhan fell ill at the age of seven with ulcers in the stomach, the boy's father, Dr. Chalapathi Naidu, a surgeon, wanted to operate on his son. My grandfather forbade the operation and said that he would cure him by prayer. He closed the Puja room to pray and reportedly asked for an X-ray to be taken. The ulcers had healed. The boy was renamed "Markandeya," the lad whom Lord Shiva saved from death.

My grandpa became a famous Doctor in Bellary and was reputed to have a healing touch. Burqa-clad Muslim women and men would come to him for treatment, as he was considered a "Valli Saheb," or saintly person who could cure the most serious diseases with his mere touch. He was recognized as a "Raja Yogi" who performed his duty with equanimity and unselfish love. He was a linguist who could speak English, Telugu, Kannada, and Urdu, and he knew Sanskrit.

My grandpa used to be invited by the District Judge and the District Collector for tea. He offered to take me to the Collector's bungalow when I was about 7 years of age, provided I was of good behaviour. I was taught to say Good Evening, Sir, not to sit down unless offered a seat, and not to grab any refreshments provided without being asked to take them. This was my first contact with British officers.

The Collector's bungalow was very big with well-maintained gardens, many trees and flowers. There were police guards at the entrance of the bungalow. The liveried servants served us snacks and tea. I was very impressed by the Collector and his bungalow. My grandfather later told me, "***You can also become a collector if you study well***." I connected this with what my mother used to tell me about my uncle, who had joined the Army and then became an IAS Officer. I think it imprinted on me and inspired me to pursue my future career.

My grandfather used to give lectures in the Kanyaka Parameswari Temple at Brucepet on the Bhagavad Gita for about 3 weeks, covering all 18 chapters of the Gita. He had a Ford car, and I took every opportunity to accompany him to his lectures in Telugu and English and collect the garlands and fruits given to him. I subconsciously absorbed the art of speaking through the art of hearing. On the return journey, we would buy sweets, fruits, and flowers for Puja at home. I relished many bonus sweets offered by shopkeepers.

Our family used to celebrate Gita-Jayanthi at home and prepare a lot of laddus and savories for distribution. We had a horse-drawn cart, and it was the duty of my elder brother and me to distribute it to all our relatives and friends at Cowl Bazaar according to the number of persons in each family. The process of distributing laddus made us quite popular.

During holidays, I used to walk to Cowl Bazaar, about 2 kilometers away, to play in the morning with friends. At lunchtime, hunger pangs would be gnawing, and home was 2 Km away. The goodwill garnered by Laddu distribution was put to good effect as I would drop in at lunchtime at any one of our relatives' homes, make kind inquiries, and convey my mother's good wishes to them. Invariably, I would be welcomed by the ladies and given a good, hearty lunch. Good relations do matter a lot, particularly when you are hungry.

Apart from the bungalow, we owned four or five houses in Cowl Bazaar and three houses in Brucepet. The house where we lived earlier was in Cowl Bazaar. After we shifted to the Cantonment to stay in the bungalow, our house in Cowl Bazaar used to be rented out for weddings hosted by our relatives. It was a spacious residence, well-suited for large families and conveniently located near the Sri Rama Temple in Cowl Bazaar. Ramaswamy Iyer, who served as the Headmaster of St. John's Boys School in the Fort area, became our tenant under the condition that, during any family wedding, he would confine himself to a couple of rooms while allowing the rest of the house to be used for the event. He was offered the house at a very nominal rent.

During the holidays, when all the other grandchildren gathered at our bungalow, the barber would be summoned to give us haircuts. My grandfather would purchase fabric not by the yard, but by "thans" of 22 yards in length to sew clothes for all the grandchildren. A master tailor, Hayath Saheb, would take our measurements and sew the garments—each one loose, over-sized and poorly fitted. Our protests were in vain, as his standard reply was that loose clothing is beneficial for growing children, as they would soon outgrow them and ensure that the clothes would fit perfectly later on! Hayath Saheb's son became the in-house tailor for Raj Bhavan, for the then governor of Andhra State in Kurnool, and later for the AP Raj Bhavan in Hyderabad.

As English was the language of instruction at St. Philomena's High School, Mr. Krishnamurthy taught me Telugu and Sanskrit at home. I owe a great deal to him for my proficiency in both languages. When I joined Wardlaw High School, Sanskrit was my second language instead of Telugu.

SAMADHI OF A RAJA YOGI

When my grandfather passed away, our elders consulted with relatives and decided to cremate him in accordance with our customs. Revered as both a doctor and a saintly figure, many of his patients, particularly Muslim men and women, came in large numbers to implore us to bury him instead of cremating him, as he was a Pir Saheb. They believed he should be buried to allow his patients and followers to visit his grave and seek solace in his healing and curing powers. The then District Medical Officer, Dr. Chettur, along with the Collector, the Superintendent of Police, other officials, and relatives, came to offer their condolences to the family. Upon witnessing the assembled crowd and their demand for a Samadhi for the people's doctor, they advised the family to construct a Samadhi rather than proceed with cremation.

It was decided to construct a Samadhi in honour of the Raja Yogi. An open plot of land that we owned in the cantonment was chosen for this purpose. The plan was to lower the body in a seated cross-legged Yogic posture (Padmasana) within the pit. As a young observer, I witnessed the meticulous process of layering salt, camphor, sandalwood chips, and fragrant paste over the body until it reached his face and covered his head. Flowers were then placed on his head, prayers were offered, and a large granite slab was placed over the Samadhi and consecrated. It is now a place where people of all faiths gather to pray. A Municipal Park has been developed around it, which Samadhi, I renovated in 2024.

After the passing of my grandfather, it became challenging to manage his bungalow and the staff. Our family moved to Cowl Bazaar, one of our smaller residences. Eventually, my elder brother secured a position as a doctor in the A.P. Medical and Health Services and served as an assistant civil surgeon in Warangal. I was appointed as a Deputy Collector in the A.P. Government and I was posted for training in Guntur. My two sisters secured MBBS admission at Guntur Medical College and moved into the hostel. I visited them frequently. My aunt stayed with me and took care of me in the Deputy Collector's bungalow in Guntur. While I was attending Law College, I enrolled my younger brother in the then Regional Engineering College in Warangal. Consequently, our family relocated from Bellary to Warangal.

MY GRANDMOTHER – PUSHPAVENI OF THE SIKHA FAMILY

The 'Sikha' family, into which my grandmother was born, were landlords of Kodagal village, located about 6 miles from Bellary. They owned over 600 acres of land. My grandmother's bachelor paternal uncle, Kodandaram Naidu, was an avid gun and rifle enthusiast and a big-game hunter. His nickname was "Puli Tatha," or "Tiger Grandpa," as he had hunted many tigers. He trained several renowned hunters, including the Raja of Sandur and G. Babu Naidu, whose residence in the cantonment resembled a veritable museum filled with stuffed tigers, striped tiger skins displayed on the walls, and antler heads. A life-sized stuffed bear, holding a plate in its paws and positioned in the drawing room with a "Welcome" sign, was so lifelike that first-time visitors would often be startled. Guests would make a hasty exit from the veritable wild jungle despite the "welcome" beckoning sign.

The Sikhas provided us with good horses for riding, Tongas, cows, and buffaloes for milk, as well as loyal domestic servants. They persuaded my grandfather to purchase some land in the village, which they would cultivate on his behalf. My grandmother endorsed this decision. He bought over 120 acres of land in the village.

My grandmother's elder brother, Ethirajulu Naidu, served as the traditional village Munsab, or HeadMan, known as Reddy in the Rayalaseema region. As a Naidu and the Reddy responsible for collecting revenue for Kodagal Village, he was referred to as 'Reddy-Naidu.' His residence was quite expansive, covering more than 2 acres and extending from one street to another. The front porch served as a place for settling disputes and collecting land revenue for the Government. It also had a raised platform for the safe and secure storage of jowar, bajra, pulses, and paddy, which could last for one to two years. There was a large courtyard where cows and buffaloes were tied at one end, while plough bullocks were kept at the other end, with arrangements for fodder and water. Behind the living room and the women's quarters, there was a vegetable and flower garden.

We used to accompany our elders in the village to hunt deer, wild boars, rabbits, partridges, and pigeons, which often destroyed crops. While the meat from rabbits, boars, and pigeons was consumed quickly, there was typically a surplus of venison (deer meat). The venison was cut into small pieces, marinated with yogurt, spices, and salt, then strung on a twine cord and sun-dried for preservation. Whenever needed, the sun-dried pieces would be fried in ghee and served to older people who had lost their teeth, allowing them to enjoy the pleasure of chewing soft venison throughout the year as it dissolved easily in their mouths.

My mother used to manage our agricultural lands by appointing tenants, collecting rent, and maintaining accounts. I would accompany her to the village during the harvest season. At the threshing ground, known as "Kallam," the grains would be winnowed and packed into gunny bags for use at home or for sale in the market. As per practice, grains would be distributed to village workers, such as washermen, barbers, Harijans, weavers, and others, based on the services rendered and the size of their families. The grains served as their annual wages, referred to as "Kadavas," which were earthen pots holding approximately 33 kilos of grains.

2

Birth of my Mother

NASTI – MATRU SAME GURU

(None better than a mother as a Guru)

My grandfather was posted in the Nallamala Forest in A.P. on malaria duty at Srisailam when he received the news that he had been blessed with a baby girl born in Bellary on July 1, 1912. She was the second child, the eldest of his four daughters, and had a younger brother named Janakiram. She was named Bramaramba after the consort of Lord Shiva, also known as Mallikarjuna Swamy, the renowned deity at Srisailam. She received her education in Telugu at the local school in Bellary until the sixth grade. Her mother, Pushpaveni, was in poor health, and as the eldest daughter, my mother had to care for her and the family. At the age of 17, she married Muddusetty Narayanaswamy Naidu, a forest officer working in Burma, and moved to Rangoon to live with her husband, his mother, and younger sister.

She had eight children - five sons and three daughters. The first two sons died young in Rangoon. The third son, my elder brother Sunder Rajulu, was also born in Rangoon. Fearing for his survival, she moved to Bellary to raise the child and stayed at her father's house while my father visited Bellary on leave. Events indicated the onset of the Second World War; my father sent my mother, who had returned to Rangoon, along with his sister, to India for their safety. I was born on January 12, 1939, during a time when the likelihood of the Second World War was looming large.

There was an old prophecy made by Venkatamma, who was born into the Muddusetty family but married into the Beerala family before committing Sati in anticipation of her husband dying young. She prayed and prophesied that only sons should be born in the Muddusetty family for seven generations. She is venerated in our families, as only sons were born as per her prophecy! My paternal aunt, Kanthamma, was the first girl to be born into the Muddusetty family after seven generations. As my aunt's birth nullified the no-girl prophecy, my parents were also blessed with three girls, my younger sisters born after me.

As World War II erupted, my mother remained at Bellary with her father to look after her ailing mother and raise her children. Her elder brother, Chalapathi Naidu, was enrolled at Andhra Medical College in Visakhapatnam, while her younger brother, Janakiram Naidu, attended Loyola College in Madras. A younger sister, Lalithamba, was married to Kamatham Suvacha Naidu, an advocate in Bellary, and two other younger sisters were still in school. My mother was, in fact, the materfamilias (mother) of the family.

My elder brother, Sunder Rajulu, completed his Intermediate from Loyola College in Chennai. Following that, he enrolled in Andhra Medical College in Visakhapatnam, earning his MBBS degree. He began his career as an Assistant Surgeon in Warangal and later pursued his M.S. at Osmania Medical College. He served as R.M.O. in K.E.M. Hospital, Secunderabad, and later worked as a professor of surgery at Warangal Medical College. He retired as the Superintendent of M.G.M. Medical College and held the position of Director of Medical Education.

My younger brother, Vijaya Kumar, earned his B.Tech from R.E.C. Warangal and completed his M.Tech at I.I.T. Bombay. He served as an Assistant Professor at R.E.C. and later as an Associate Professor at Osmania Engineering College. Tragically, while pursuing his Doctorate at I.I.T. Bombay, he lost his life in a local train accident, leaving behind his wife, Dr. Lakshmi, and their two children, a son and a daughter. Their son, Shridhar, completed his B.Tech at CBIT, Hyderabad, worked at Wipro and subsequently secured a position as a consultant in the U.S. Their daughter, Sunitha, earned her M.S. in the United States and is currently a software engineer at a U.S. bank in Hyderabad. She is married with a son.

My younger sister, Dr. Mythreyi, completed her MBBS at Guntur Medical College and earned her Diploma in Gynaecology from Osmania Medical College. After retiring from the A.P. Medical Service, she established the Maruthi Nursing Home in Secunderabad. Dr. Mythreyi is philanthropic and offers free treatment to the poor.

Another sister, Sukanya, completed her MBBS at Guntur Medical College and obtained her M.D. in Pediatrics from Andhra University. She retired as a government professor of Pediatrics and is currently working at a private medical college in Hyderabad.

My mother had dreams in which she could foresee events affecting our family. Some of these dreams were vivid and easily interpretable, while others required deeper unravelling and interpretation. Her dreams, likely stemming from anxiety or concern, varied in clarity; some were explicit, while others needed careful analysis. At birth, my head was relatively small compared to the average size of new borns, which led her to worry that I might be mentally deficient. During one of her moments of concern, she dreamt of Lord Shiva and bemoaned about this to the Lord. In her dream, Lord Shiva chastised her for speaking without knowing, forbade her to say so again, and hurled his Trident at her leg. Despite this warning, she continued to fret about the size of her son's head.

In a subsequent dream, she saw Lord Ganesha driving a huge car into our compound and parking it in the garage. He took out three white sheets and wrote, "Elephant, elephant, elephant. "He then locked the garage door and left. This cleared her doubts, and she believed that Lord Ganesha would bless me with wisdom.

In 1960, while I was awaiting the results of my IAS examination, I mentioned to my mother that I was becoming anxious about the results. In a couple of days, she rang me up and recounted a dream she had. In her dream, she saw her sister, Rukma Bai, arriving at our bungalow in a beautiful horse-drawn carriage, holding a crown. Rukma Bai climbed the stairs where my mother was waiting and presented the crown to her, saying, "This is for your son." My mother was confident that I would be selected for the IAS and advised me to visit Tirupati to fulfil her vow that, if I were selected, I would pray there. I followed her advice to honour her vow.

After my training at the National Academy of Administration at Mussorie was over, I spent some time with my family in Warangal when I received my posting as Assistant Commissioner at Guwahati. I told my mother that I was posted to a faraway place in Assam to begin a new career. She smiled and said, "As a bride, very much younger than you, I had to go to Burma, another country. You are posted to a part of our own country, though distant. The next morning, she told me that she dreamt of me walking with another person up the steps of a bungalow with a thatched roof located on the banks of a river. It happened exactly like what she predicted. The DC's bungalow at Guwahati is located on the bank of the Brahmaputra River and I report to the DC with my predecessor AC Parthasarathi. I do not know whether it was telepathy, soothsayer instinct, ESP, or uncanny foresight that could predict so accurately and vividly.

While at Goalpara in 1966, I told my mother over the phone that I was posted to Mizo Hills district on promotion as Additional Deputy Commissioner and that Mizo Hills was in a state of insurgency with large-scale disturbances and destruction of bridges, disruption of communication, and looting of Government properties. She just said that your father stayed back in Burma during the Second World War and did not desert or resign from his job, "I expect you, my son, to do your duty. When we were in Rangoon, we heard about Mizos in Burma also. You need not be worried". Strangely, at Aizawl, we had a Sikh family named Bhumras who had moved from Burma during the Second World War. One of their sons had even joined the Indian Air Force. Later, I met many people who worked in Burma, and they knew my dad.

Being practical, we moved to another smaller bungalow in the cantonment area, and my mother sent word to her maternal uncle's family to locate some good servants from the village. During this time, there was a severe drought, and our tenant farmer of Kodagal village visited my mother with his four sons. He said that he was unable to feed them and requested her to look after them. My mother looked after the children with love and care. The following year, as the monsoon turned favourable, the farmer-father came home to take his sons back. However, one of three sons, Shivaram, refused to go back with his father and desired to stay with us. My mother agreed to take him under her fold and looked after him like her own son. She got him married to a girl, Parvathi, who was his relative from the village. My mother would always say that Lord Shiva had blessed her, and in the guidance of Shiva, Parvathi was serving her!

It is said that as God cannot be everywhere, he created "Mothers" on earth. It is indeed true. Through the ages, we have believed in "Manyata sa Matha," that is, Mother teaches us to love and respect one another. In Mahabharata, when Yaksha asks Yudhishtir, "Who is greater than the earth," Yudhishtir replies, "Matha Guru Thare Bhume," that only Mother is better than the earth as she has a great deal of patience like a tree and despite suffering, dearly loves her children. My mother probably had such a personality.

In addition to educating her children, my mother also educated the children of Parvathi and Shivaram. Subsequently, Bhimakka, Shivaram's sister, was cared for and also her son Veera Reddy and his wife Veeramma. When it was my turn to thread the needle, I educated Veera Reddy and got him a job. Their children are now software engineers and are doing well in life.

The average lifespan in India was less than 45 years. There were several young widows in the community. My mother cared for their welfare by helping them financially to look after their children and educate them. My mother was stout but had a good personality and cheerful demeanor. She had a reputation that her hand was indeed as large as a serving spoon (Ladle) used at marriages.

My mother was a born manager and confidently handled multiple roles. Always cheerful, she would liven up the home. A good cook, she single-handedly catered to the whole family and guests and even hosted a marriage, as she did in the case of my elder brother's marriage. All members of our extended family appreciated her non-vegetarian dishes. Many of our relatives and poor people often sought her advice and, sometimes, financial help. As she managed her father's earnings, she always assisted those who sought her help. Poor brides were given golden Mangalsutras and new clothes besides monetary help; our tailor, barber, dhobi, carpenter, and maidservants looked up to her as a Godmother.

My mother trained all her own children, including her nieces and nephews, to get up early in the morning and study the class lessons for the day at school. Around 5 a.m. every day, we would hear the whistle of the train that halted at Cantonment Railway Station for a couple of minutes before proceeding to the Bellary Main Railway station. She inculcated the habit of rising early in the morning to concentrate on studying in a quiet environment, and it has become a routine of my life.

At home, coffee beans were roasted and freshly ground, with a nice aroma all over. The brewed decoction in brass filters was adequate for the whole family. Children, however, drank milk. Buttermilk was kept in a large earthen pot near the verandah with a ladle for every Visitor. Anyone could visit the house to slake their thirst with fresh buttermilk and refresh themselves in the hot summer season.

My youngest sister, Dhimathi, began feeling unwell. She had contracted a lung disease when the family went to Tirupati. She was named Thirumali at Tirupati. During the diagnosis, we were advised that she be taken to Madras General Hospital where Dr Sadashivam, an eminent doctor and my uncle's dear friend, would treat her as an in-patient and, if necessary, operate and remove the affected part of the lung. In Madras, Thirumali was operated, and a part of her infected lung was removed. Once she was discharged, she came to Warangal for recovery, where my brother was working as an Assistant Civil Surgeon. She joined Fatima Convent and topped her class. Unfortunately, she died after a couple of years.

Living in a joint (collective) family, one realizes the eternal truth and ethics of life—as expounded by Kautilya (Chanakya): Matha (mother) is Satyam (Truth); Pita (father) is Jnanam (wisdom); Bhrato (brothers) represent Dharma; Sakha (friends) teach us Daya (compassion), while Patni (wife) is peace, and Puthra (children) teach us Kshama (forgiveness).

According to Chanakya (Kautilya), there are seven mothers (Sapta Matrikas) who should be respected. They are:

Adou Matha - Our mother
Guru Patni - Wife of the teacher or the spiritual master
Brahmini - Wife of the Brahmin (Priest)
Raja Patnika - Wife of the King or your Superior

Dhenu - the Cow which gives milk – the Amrith for life
Dhatri - Nurse who takes care when we are ill
Prithvi - the Earth that feeds us

If I were to have a Punar Janma, I would like to be Reborn to my mother and lie on her lap, listening to the old lullabies she sings. As my Guru Dakshina, I have instituted an Award to be given to ideal mothers called the Muddusetty Bramaramba Naidu Mathru Murthy Award and Prizes in her name at Bellary and Hyderabad for meritorious students.

KANTHAMMA, MY FOSTER MOTHER

My paternal aunt Smt. Kanthamma had an unhappy married life due to ill-treatment and harassment by her husband, a postmaster in Burma who had a mistress, a roving eye, and an unholy liaison with other women. My father saw her suffering and brought her home. She vowed not to live with her husband or marry again and has since stayed with us. She was literate and could speak Telugu, Tamil and Burmese.

As my mother was busy looking after her parent's own siblings and managing our properties, it was my aunt who cared for and looked after us.

If my mother got angry with me or my other siblings, we would rush to my aunt to complain to find solace. She was an excellent cook and served us hot and tasty food from the kitchen.

When my mother had to stay in Chennai to look after my hospitalized younger sister, Kanthamma was our mother at home. My mother used to always address her not as sister-in-law; but as 'Pinni' or mausi (mother's sister) which strengthened the bond of relationship between them.

When I was Deputy Collector, my aunt came to Guntur to look after me as I was her favourite child. My two younger sisters were then in the Medical College hostel at Guntur. On Sundays, all of us would have a hearty lunch, good banter, and occasionally see a movie.

When I was posted in Mizo Hills, I got a message that she was seriously ill. On route to Warangal to see her, I had to halt for the night at Assam House, Calcutta. I received the sad news by telegram that she had passed away. I could not attend to the obsequies but visited the cremation ground to pray for her soul. My elder brother and I later immersed her ashes in the Krishna River at Vijayawada.

To me, Kanthamma was a real heroine and an epitome of a selfless foster mother with great compassion and love. She believed in service as a means to finding fulfilment in life and securing Punya for a better Janma. I prayed that God should give her a better life, if she is reborn, as she was an embodiment of selfless service to everyone who came in touch with her. No visitor went without having a meal in our house. She never felt tired or hesitated to serve us, even when we requested her to feed us at odd times or to give us tea or refreshments even at late night. For her, guests and children were God's children visiting us. She would take particular care of our guests, our servants, and more importantly, our buffalo and three cows which were tethered in our bungalow compound. The mute animals probably missed her much more than all of us, because she took such good care of them. For her, we were like calves to be looked after till we could take care of ourselves. All the children prayed to God to grant peace to her soul and Sadgati in her next life.

Naasti maatru same Chaaya, Naasti maatru same gati
Naasti maatru same traanam, naasti maatru same prapaa"

None excels a mother in providing shade and shelter
None excels the mother in providing direction and way
None excels the mother in providing protection
None excels the mother as a Life-giver and supporter.

In school, I realized the importance of having two motherly figures—one at home and one at school. At home, I was fortunate to have two mothers as well: my biological mother and Kanthamma, my foster mother. Even if one of them was absent, we never felt a lack of maternal care.

We owe our growth and success which are largely attributed to their immense love for us, a debt we feel we can never repay in this lifetime.

3

Our Family and my Birth

I was born on 12th January 1939, the night before the Bhogi-Sankranthi festival, as the fourth son of Srimathi Bramaramba and Muddusetty Narayanasamy Naidu, a Forest officer in Burma (Myanmar) when it was part of India. The horoscope was cast. The birth star was Chitra" in the third padam (part), and the Rasi, Thula (Libra).

My father, an ardent follower of the freedom fighter Gopalakrishna Gokhale, the founder of the "Servants of India Society," wished that I be named after him. My mother liked the name Gopalakrishna but did not approve of 'Gokhale.' My maternal grandmother Pushpavenamma wanted a shorter name like Gokul, Gopal, or Krishna, whose childhood was at Gokul. My grandfather said that Lord Krishna was the 'Raja' of Gokul and that I should be called Gokul Raj. My uncle suggested that my name be Gopichand, the beloved of the Gopis! In the records, my name is Muddusetty Gopalakrishna Naidu. Among relatives and friends, I was better known as Bramaramba's son or Gokul. In Cowl Bazar, I was Bungalow Gokul since we lived in a bungalow in the Cantonment area. In official circles, as M. Gopalakrishna, M.G. Naidu or plain Naidu or Nayudu in Assam.

Bellary was well known for its educational institutions. Wardlaw High School was established in 1845 by Reverend Wardlaw, a missionary, and was run by the London Mission Society at Brucepet. St. John's High School was located in the Fort area. St. Philomena's High School for Girls was an English convent set up in 1885 and located in Bellary Cantonment near our Bungalow.

My mother, keen to provide her children with the best possible education, admitted me to the Kindergarten class at St. Philomena's High School. An English nun, Mother Teresa, was my class teacher. She gave me Chocolates and assured my mother that she would take good care of me. I was excited to visit the school and meet students with nice white shirts and blue pants or blue skirts. The school had large classrooms, an Assembly Hall, a Church, gardens, and a shop that sold chocolates, toffees, and Chikkis during the afternoon recess. My class had about 20 girls and three boys. Parents of many Anglo-Indian girls at school were residing in the cantonment and were mostly employed in the Railways, Police, or Schools.

Mother Teresa was very fond of me and wanted me to stand first in the class. Her fondness led to a lot more homework for me! She taught me writing, studying, and listening skills and to speak like an Englishman. She believed in homework and often said, "The work of the day must be completed that same day." She expected me to 'excel' in my studies and any work I was asked to do. I was unhappy that my Saturdays became homework-day of writing essays, compositions, and précis- writing. I was left with only Sunday for my fun, games, and sports. When I cribbed about it, my mother would sing her song "Homework, hard work, smart work, and Teamwork" alone leads to success. Do your homework, and you can Play.

As part of the moral study, I had to read the Bible, Panchatantra, Aesops' Fables, and Ramayana and tell short stories in class. Mother Teresa would tell us to learn to 'do one good act every day,' which would then become a habit and make us very good. My mother would say that doing a good act was easy, but being good all the time was difficult. Instead, do a good act every day. She said, "**Do Good to Become Good**" and to "**Feel Good**". I tried to follow it in my work and life.

Bellary had an Army Recruitment Office. Many of our relatives were recruited into the army, served in the First and Second World Wars, and rose to high ranks. The British and Indian soldiers in the Cantonment, along with Sikh soldiers with colourful turbans, would march on the streets of Cantonment with arms. There was, however, a ditty in Telugu, quite popular at that time, which said

"Alas, though my father and mother forbade many a time, I joined the army; the army gives us heavy boots and puts a knapsack on the back and makes us run with them – If we slip and fall, they pick us up, only to kick us on our bottom. And make us run again. Alas, I did not listen to the good advice at my home!"

At school, I used to doubt whether I had two mothers or one mother - My teacher at school was called mother, and at home, I also had a Mother! When I posed my doubt, my mother laughed it off by saying that I needed a mother at home and also in school to look after me and keep me from mischief. Mother Teresa was my "**Teacher-Parent**" in school. At home, my mother was my "**Parent-Teacher**." From them, I learned that a student should have a teacher both at school and at home.

I topped my KG classes and was promoted to the first Standard. I got a double promotion from I Standard to III Standard. While I was in the V standard, Independence Day was celebrated on 15 August 1947 with the hoisting of the Tricolour at the school in place of the Union Jack by a Minister in the presence of the assembly of parents, mothers, teachers, and students. That scene is sharply etched in my mind and comes alive on every Independence Day.

I was appointed as the class monitor and given a 'Prefect' badge to help maintain discipline, ensuring that students stayed quiet and listened attentively during lessons. It was then that I probably imbibed the art of 'listening,' which later became a boon and monitoring, a habit.

A memorable event at the convent was the arrival of the Raja of Sandur SY Ghorpade to the school, with the carcass of a just-killed large striped tiger spread out on the bonnet of his Rolls Royce Car. He shot the tiger in the Nallamala Forest. We all looked at the dead tiger, the hunter, and his gun with awe and wonder.

MY FATHER

My father, Narayanaswamy Naidu, used to come home on leave by steamer from Burma during summer every year for about two months. We, the children, eagerly looked forward to his visit for the varieties of chocolates and goodies he brought for the family. He had gifts for everyone in our joint family, including sarees, trinkets, gemstones, bead garlands, and good silk carpets called 'Rathna Kambali". My unmarried aunts used to eagerly await their Rangoon Baava (brother-in-law) and sing the chorus of a popular Telugu song whose refrain was "Vacchade maa baava, Rangoon baava; thechade cheeralu, nagalu". Welcome to our brother-in-law, who has come all the way from Rangoon carrying lots of sarees and jewels for all of us. My father used to look like the model on the Gillette razor packaging. I asked him about it. He laughed and said that only his moustache was like that of the man on the Gillette Blades packet.

My father was respected both at Bellary and in Burma as an honest, upright officer who was compassionate and helpful. He was closely associated with the Indian Association of Burma at Rangoon and involved in social and cultural activities and the upkeep of Hindu Temples in Burma. During the Second World War in Burma, he was more worried about his family at Bellary and bravely bore the hardship of the war.

My father would take us to Brucepet, the main Bazaar at Bellary, and buy us Bata shoes, Ready-made pants and shirts, books, and costly pens, pencils, and sharpeners. He would take us to the Amba Bhavan Hotel on Brahmin Street. There, we used to have masala dosas, puris, and sweets topped with delicious ice cream. Just before his retirement, he came home on leave but suddenly passed away in 1947 due to a severe heart attack.

After obsequies, my elder brother and I went with our grand uncle (grandmother's brother), Ethirajulu Naidu, to the Tungabhadra River at Hampi to immerse the ashes of my father. We had Darshan of Lord Shiva at Pampapathi temple and received blessings from the Matadhipati. We saw the ruins of the Vijayanagar empire, reflecting its past splendour and glory through its magnificent buildings like the Vittaleswara Temple with the stone chariot and musical pillars, the Hazara Ramaswamy temple, Lotus Mahal, Elephant stables and the Ugra Narasimha, a massive stone statue badly disfigured by the invaders.

Pilgrims to Hampi used to carry a copper vessel with attached rope to draw drinking water from wells with pulleys. On the way back, as we were thirsty, we stopped to draw some water from a well using our vessel with rope. A couple of farmers who came to the well to draw water without a vessel and rope said in the Kannada language, "Ma Thadappa." My elder brother remonstrated saying, "That is our rope, and dare you to say that it is yours." My granduncle laughed and told us that "MaThadu-appa" means "please speak" in Kannada, while in Telugu, it means" it is our rope." We apologized to them, exchanged greetings, and gladly gave our vessel and rope for drawing water. Later on, I had bitter experience of using Tamil without knowing its meaning. The lesson is that we must understand the meaning of words before we speak in other languages.

4

Happy Days

During the summer holidays, my elder uncle and aunt's children at Bellary would stay in the bungalow. We used to have lots of fun playing games and visiting neighbours. My mother would sometimes ask us to collect the tender leaves of the tamarind tree used to make delicious dal. We also used to gather Badari or Ber fruits. Some were big and fleshy, while some were small and grew on thorny shrubs. With the surfeit of ripe Ber fruits, Vadas from its paste would be made and sun-dried, which were sour and sweet and liked by children very much. Eating all types of fruits and eating more food many times and at odd hours often upset our stomachs. My grandfather would scold us, and he would not give us any medicine, and we would have to suffer. My grandmother would come to our rescue and administer a dose of castor oil (laxative). We would be back to normal in a couple of days.

We, boys, would play war games with bows and arrows in the compound or play tops or marbles and try our skill at slingshots and tree climbing. We also played Gilli Danda, an indigenous form of cricket and spinning of tops. Girls would play Pallam Goti, Carroms, Snakes & Ladders, or Ludo and learn dancing. When more friends joined, we used to play cricket and some form of kabaddi with no concern about the injuries, sure that my grandfather would apply iodine and then patch up with benzoin.

During summer, all my cousins would come and stay at the bungalow. We took a family group photo at the famous Babu Studios in the Fort Area. It is now a precious possession in our families. The summer holidays were welcome but soon became boring. The mornings would be spent playing marbles and Gilli danda. The afternoons would be spent swimming in the Shivalayam Big Well or in the Fort Moat (Kandakam) or reading books at home while reclining on an easy chair - like my grandfather eating peanuts and jaggery. This luxury continues even now!

HUNTING FUN: AIR RIFLES AND DUCK SHOOTING

When some neighbour's children were shooting birds and pigeons with an air gun, my brother and I convinced our mother to buy us two air rifles with lead slugs to practice. We practiced with the air rifles, but our real interest was to go for duck shooting with our elders with shotguns (12-bore guns).

SWIMMING CLASSES

I wanted to learn how to swim. An elder cousin, Govindanna, was asked to coach me who wanted me to first get triangular "Langotis" (Loincloths) stitched. I was then taken to the Shivalayam Temple stepwell (PeddaBavi) down the steps to the lower pavilion level, touching the water level. A few logs of the moringa (drumstick) tree were tied into a neat pack and strapped onto my back. I was led into the water, step by step by my coach, to waist level to make me feel comfortable with the backpack and asked to keep paddling. I was lying on the water, and he was beside me, holding me afloat with his hand under my stomach and taught me the basics of breathing and swimming. In about a week, I was able to swim on my own with the strapped backpack. When my coach felt that I was ready, he taught me how to hold my breath, dip under the water, and come up with a held breath. I was asked to jump and, later, dive into the water with the backpack from the side pavilions. After a few trials, I felt comfortable, so the log pack was removed. Thus, I learned the basic techniques of swimming, jumping, and diving into the water.

My coach took me to the moat adjoining the Rock fort called Kandakam along with two senior swimmers. He asked me to swim in the moat water close to land to familiarize me with the water spread and its waves. While the water at the Shivalayam stepwell was sweet and clean, the water in the moat was anything but clean and lovely. I was told not to swallow that water. In a couple of weeks, I could cover a distance of about 100 meters from the land end of the moat to the gigantic rock face, touch it, and come back. It was quite an arduous swim. After a few days, I was a swimmer, capable of taking care of myself in deep water. I was pleased as punch, and so was my coach and mother. Later on, I learned "Savasana" as part of my Yoga classes and could easily float in the water lying on my back whenever tired. It proved useful for long-endurance swims.

DWADASHI BHOJANAM

During winter, on the day following Vaikunta Ekadashi, many relatives would gather to take part in the Dwadashi feast. A huge number of curries with vegetables greens, including some tubers and fruits, were made into a sour dal, which was very tasty and nutritious with many vegetables and greens. This Dal would last for 2 to 3 days and serve as a side dish for breakfast. About 22 different greens were required to prepare the special dal dish. Boys were tasked with the duty of collecting some of the greens and leaves available in the neighbours' compound.

TIRUPATI PATRA- YATRA

The tradition in many Telugu families is to keep a vessel called 'Tirupati Patra' in the Puja room to drop silver rupee coins or loose change and spare currency. The money accumulated in the vessel could be used to meet the expenses of the journey to Tirupati Temple and back. The remaining amount, if any, along with the contribution, would be dropped in the Hundi of Lord Venkateshwara. When our vessel was nearly full, my mother asked Grandpa to allow all of us to go to Tirupati. Our entire family, including my aunt and some relatives, went by train from Bellary to Renigunta Junction near Tirupati. Since the entire family was traveling for the first time, there was a lot of eating, chatting, relating anecdotes, and great fun during the journey.

A friend and college mate of my uncle, I.J. Naidu, was Kannayya Naidu (Jovial Naidu). He was a bus owner and landlord at Nagari Town near Tirupati. He received us at Renigunta Railway Station with a bus. We went by bus to Tirumala. In those days, in the late 1940s, there was no decent accommodation at Tirumala and not much of a rush. Except for a TTD-run small tiffin center, there was no arrangement for food. Pilgrims are used to carry food and utensils to cook food. There were a large number of jackfruit and mango trees at Tirumala Hill. There were some common washrooms and good drinking water. C Anna Rao, the then E.O of TTD temple, arranged accommodation in one of the better chatrams (choultry) at Tirumala, and we had a good Darshan of Lord Venkateshwara. We learned at Tirupati that temples are constructed in inaccessible places to make people know that arduous, hard, and sincere efforts are required to reach God and secure his Grace. Many Telugu songs praise the endless steps leading to the temple of Lord Venkateswara at Tirumala. The lyrics express the journey of climbing those numerous steps, longing to see the divine presence, and asking for blessings, saying, "I climb and climb, but you remain unseen. Please shower your Grace upon me."

My uncle, Dr Chalapathi Naidu, invited my mother and me to spend some part of the summer holidays with them in Chennai. He arranged for a local guide called Munuswamy to show me around Chennai. I was taken to the famous Madras Zoo, the Government Museum, the Kapaleeshwarar temple in Mylapore, and the Parthasarathy Swamy temple in Triplicane.

I was also taken to see Kalakshetra at Adyar and Marina Beach. I was impressed with Madras, which had stately buildings like the High Court, wide roads, and the Tramway, in which we had a joy ride. I had enough material to write a dozen essays on what I saw and did in Chennai! My mother, aunts, and I visited the Flower Market, Moore Market, and a market where brass and copper utensils were purchased for the family. My uncle took me to a big tailor shop and got me and my elder brother four pairs of pants and shirts stitched.

5

Relatives and Festivals

Festivals were celebrated at home and by visits to temples. Children would enjoy Holi, Ugadi (Telugu New Year Day), Dusserah, and Deepavali as it meant new clothes, houses alight with oil diyas and lamps, bursting of firecrackers, and hearty repasts. The pulling of the chariot (Ratham) during Vaikunta Ekadashi around the main streets of Cowl Bazar was eagerly awaited. At every house where the chariot stopped, Harathi was given, coconuts broken, and sweets offered and distributed to children. The Dusserah festival was the occasion for a procession of elders and grown-up boys with weapons demonstrating their display of skills up to the Shammi tree in Babu Naidu's compound to relive the episode of the Pandavas retrieving their weapons before the epic Mahabharata battle.

DOLLS SHOW – BOMMALA KOLUVU

Children, especially girls, enjoyed the Bommala Koluvu (display) during Dussehra, where every household displayed its heritage collection of old dolls and toys arranged neatly in rows and thrown open to visitors. Sweets and savories made according to their family recipes would be offered to visitors. We, children, would form small teams of two or three to go from house to house to see the display of dolls on different dates and to relish the variety of boiled pulses, sweets, murukkus, and savories.

MARRIAGES

Marriages were celebrated for a week but later on, trimmed to three days, and now it is two days or just an evening. The bridegroom would arrive on horseback at the bride's house with his baraat, procession in the traditional dress of silk dhoti, kurta, and turban with zari and a sword or a dagger dangling at his waist as a mark of valour. When the Gemini Circus was playing in our town, the manager lent the caparisoned circus elephant to a Bride groom for the marriage procession. We witnessed the unforgettable and unique scene of a relative arriving in real royal splendour on elephant

Howdah to marry! A flashback to the era of Rajas! This became the talk of the town.

Bellary is well known for the Bellary Ram and quality mutton, and Bangalore is a major market. I used to be sent occasionally to purchase mutton and eggs from the Cowl Bazaar. I learned the art of testing eggs and selecting the correct portions of meat required for different non-vegetarian dishes. A Mopla (Muslim) dealer from Kerala would come on Sundays on a pony cart to our house to sell other varieties of dried fish. We, the children, would detest the unpleasant smell and stay away, while the elders would happily buy different varieties of dried fish.

MY UNCLE Dr. I CHALAPATHI NAIDU

He was well-built and a good hockey player who represented his school and college. He was a classmate of N. Sanjeeva Reddy, the CM of A.P. and later President of India. He had leftist views and was chummy with many communist leaders. He passed his M.B.B.S. in Visakhapatnam with flying colours, standing first in all five years of the medical course, and won the ***Andersons Gold medal***. He later did his M.S. under the eminent surgeon M.S. Kini at Madras. After Operation POLO in 1949 in Hyderabad, he was posted as District Medical Officer in Nalgonda District. Later, he was Superintendent of the Osmania Medical College and Superintendent of Guntur Medical College Hospital, and he retired as Principal of Osmania Medical College.

MY UNCLE I. JANAKIRAM NAIDU (I. J. NAIDU)

My younger uncle, I.J Naidu, did an M.A. in both Physics and History from Madras Presidency College with 1st Class Honours. As recruitment to the I.A.S. was suspended during the Second World War, he joined the Army as a Civilian Officer. He was recruited to the I.A.S. in 1948 as part of War Service Recruitment, with 1944 as the year of allotment. He served in the Madras Government and later in Andhra State. He did outstanding work in Vizag as a Collector during the floods. He was an expert in agriculture and was the first Secretary of the Department of Rural Development in the Indian Government. He retired as Chief Secretary in Andhra Pradesh in 1979. He also served as Advisor to the Governor of Tamil Nadu, which was under President's rule in 1980. After that, he lived in the Satya Sai Ashram in Puttaparthi and was the treasurer of Satya Sai Trust. He passed away in 2004. He has three sons and a daughter. One of his sons, Srinivas Injeti, is an I.A.S. officer of the Orissa cadre who later became the Secretary of the Ministry of Company Affairs.

My mother would often tell me that she used to carry around my uncle when he was a child and had taught him to speak and write. She would say,

"If your uncle, whom I taught to read and write, could get into the I.A.S., my son can also do so. I think you are no less intelligent than him and perhaps better. I am sure you will make it to the I.A.S. if only you make it your goal". These words became my goal with my mother's constant reminders. To succeed, you need both internal aspiration and external inspiration. My mother amply provided both and became my life coach, mentor, and motivator.

My uncle I.J. Naidu was allotted to Madras State and worked as Sub-Collector of Karur and Chenglepet and was later posted as Under Secretary in the Home Department of Madras Government. He had two friends, Mr. G.G. Naidu in the Secretariat and Radhakrishna Naidu, a Judge. My uncle's marriage was fixed with Venkata Ratna Devi, daughter of Rajah S Y Mallu Dora of Chintaluru and Thotapalli Estate in East Godavari District. The marriage was celebrated in 1951 on a grand scale at Chennai in the bungalow called Mercury House on Pantheon Road, Egmore, Madras.

A GRAND MARRIAGE

The bungalow and garden were lent to the marriage parties for a week – courtesy, a Mudaliar family who owned it. The marriage was a grand affair with bright illumination. The evening garden party with a lot of refreshments was graced by the then Governor of Madras, the Maharaja of Bhavnagar state. A dance recital by Kum. Vyjayanthimala, then an upcoming star of the film industry who had acted in the film 'Jeevitham.' The Governor of Madras presented her with a gold medal while an uncle read the citation.

After my uncle, I.J. Naidu's marriage, we stayed in his house in Aminjikarai at Madras for a week. During our stay, D. Raghuram Naidu, Deputy Secretary, invited us to his residence in Mint Street, where we met a Muslim Baba called Swami Oliullah and returned to Bellary.

In 1952, my aunt Subhadra married C Ranganatham at Tiruchanoor near Tirupathi. Ranganatham was a journalist who later joined the Information and Public Relations Department in the A.P. Government and retired as Joint Director. That was the last marriage in the family that my grandfather attended.

On 1st October 1953, Andhra State was inaugurated at Kurnool. My uncle, I.J Naidu, was posted at Kurnool. I visited him during the summer holidays. Due to the paucity of accommodation, many officials were staying at Kurnool in tents known as Camp I, Camp II, etc. The Collectorate had become the Secretariat. CM Trivedi, I.C.S., was the Governor, while O Pula Reddy, I.C.S., was the first Chief Secretary.

6

School Days – convent and Wardlaw High School

While in Standard VI in the Convent, the test for admission to 3rd Form in Wardlaw Boys High School was announced. Without informing at home, I took the test and was selected. My mother and elders were angry that I had appeared for the test without telling them. My grandfather pacified them by telling them that Wardlaw High School was a good school with English medium and close to his clinic, Panduranga Pharmacy. I joined the school and paid the fees. My nickname, Gokul Raj, was entered in the records and later corrected to M. Gopalakrishna, my full name.

I opted for Sanskrit as my second language. There were only five students in the class. We had to sit cross-legged on a carpet (dhurrie) on the floor like in a Gurukul. The teacher, Lakshmi Narayana Sharma, would sit or lie down under the fan on the carpet, as there was no table or chair for him! He made us commit to memory the Shabda Manjari, Amara Kosham, and Bala Ramayanam. He would recite some verses and tell us the meaning. He emphasized that correct pronunciation was important. We were taught to read and write the Devanagari script, but the books had Sanskrit verses in Telugu script! We had to read Sanskrit in Telugu script and write the answers in English or Telugu!

The District Collector's Office, Judges' Courts, Divisional Forest Office (DFO), the Imperial Bank of India, and the Main Railway Station were close to the school. I was taken to the Imperial Bank (this became the SBI bank later) to open a bank account. The cashier with a turban and a Tilak received us. Money was deposited, and an account was opened in my name. Some amount was drawn, and I was given a Passbook. The Bank Manager kept the money in my pocket and closed it with a safety pin. He told me not to touch the pocket till I reached home and showed it to my mother.

The school had three sections in each class: A and B, which were Telugu medium sections, and C, for Kannada. Our regular classes in school began with the bell at 9 am. The interval was between 11 and 11.15 am, and morning classes would close by 12.30 pm, followed by lunch for an hour. Afternoon classes would start at 1.30 pm and close at 3.30 pm on three days of the week. Twice a week, we would have 'crafts and skills' practice classes. We were taught drawing and painting, fretting and saw-work, carpentry, woodwork, and much more. We were taught different types of knots, like Reef, Sailors, Fishermen, and Clow Hitch.

We had physical training and games from 4 pm to 5 pm. The school had large playgrounds for football, hockey, tennis, volleyball, and basketball, as well as facilities for long jump, high jump, and athletics. There was a separate area for gymnastics and physical training with parallel bars and related equipment. Games were a great attraction, and we would play till 5.30 or 6 pm. We learned to play games of our choice and to compete and enjoy ourselves. I joined the School Hockey Team. I was then stout and could not run fast, so I had to play as a 'goalkeeper.' After some time, I started to play full back and Center half. I continued to play Hockey and was captain at the college level and even when I was SDO at Goalpara.

PINCHING LUNCH

The lunch brought from home in tiffin carriers by students would be placed on the shelves in the room where water was served from big earthen pots by an attendee. During lunchtime, we could take our tiffin boxes, sit and have lunch under the shade of the trees, and hand over empty tiffin boxes for safe custody till we picked them up before going home. We noted that some outstation boys got tasty food in big tiffin carriers with roti, curd, rice, and rich vegetarian and non-vegetarian dishes and sweets. We would make a note of such tiffin boxes, arrive a little earlier at lunchtime, filch and finish them quietly, and place them back on the shelves. However, we were soon caught and produced before the class teacher and admonished.

I was the youngest student in class but had many friends. I was good at English elocution and debates and was the Literary Secretary in the Vth and VIth Forms. My bugbear was mathematics. We had well-trained teachers in the school. Many of the English and Math teachers were Tamil Iyers or Iyengars, while others were Telugus. Most teachers were bilingual.

The school's Annual Sports day was a big event and eagerly awaited. Our school used to win many awards in Inter-School competitions and did well at the Grigg Memorial Championships, held in rotation among the big Towns in the District. I attended the championship games at Adoni, the first overnight stay outside our house, along with friends.

AS A BOY SCOUT

I joined as a Boy Scout at school and learned many useful skills, played games like Treasure Hunt, Rock-Climbing, and Lassoing, and attended campfires and excursions. I learned the meaning of the three-finger Scout salute and the motto "Be Prepared." In the Vth form, we went to Siddapur village, where we saw the southernmost Ashokan edict in India. We also spent a night at a Hanuman temple in the vicinity. The school took us to see the newly constructed Hagari River Aqueduct and the reservoir from which Bellary was supplied piped water. We also went to the riverbed and dug a small hole in the sand. Lo and behold, much water filled up the holes. We understood that river sand holds much water for future use.

Some students had a hobby of collecting stamps and matchbox labels. We learned from them that Sivakasi in Madras State was known for the manufacture of matchboxes and firecrackers.

THE ROCK FORT

We went on excursions with packed lunches and water bottles to the Bellary Rock Fort from the morning until the evening with our History, Geography, and Scouting teachers. They explained the importance of the fort, its fortification, ramparts, turrets, gun positions, and the arrangements for water supply on the hill. They also explained the rearing of crocodiles in the moat to scare intruders. We noticed different types of trees, creepers, lizards, and snakes in the fort. The visit was a learning and enjoyable experience.

A LESSON ON THE POWER OF WORDS

While I was at school, a mischievous boy taught me some swearing and slanderous words, calling it the Tamil language and asking me to use it. While I was going on foot from Cowl Bazaar to our house at Cantonment, I saw a few Tamil boys playing near a tree. I tried out my newly learned Tamil on them. The boys became furious. They caught hold of me, tied me with a rope to the tree beside the road, and left the place. I later learned that the words taught to me were obnoxious and slanderous. I was scared, worried, and at my wit's end on how to free myself. Luckily, a horse-cart driver passing by recognized me and freed me. He dropped me at our bungalow. I learned a life lesson: one should not talk or use words without knowing their meaning.

TORN PANTS

One day, a classmate and I bunked school and went to the Fort area. We climbed onto the hillock where age-old rainwater flows caused a long and steep natural rock slide and repeatedly slid down the rock, enjoying the fun while relishing peanuts. After getting down, we picked up our cycles when another playmate shouted that our half-pants were torn and our bottoms exposed. We had not felt or noticed that the rough surface of the slide had torn the seat portion of our pants. We were in a jam and panicked that if noticed, we would be chided at both the school and home for cutting classes and ruining our pants. A brilliant idea flashed in our minds. Instead of the usual tucked-in shirt expected at school, we untucked the shirt so that it could cover our exposed bottoms. We managed to get through the ordeal in school. On the way back, I thought that at home, if my mother noticed, she would scold and chide me. After I reached home and hesitatingly related the incident, instead of beating me, she laughed aloud and related the incident to her mother and my aunts. All of them had a hearty laugh and would often tease me about the incident. I dare not repeat such an adventure.

I was quite mischievous, hiding books purposefully as an excuse for not studying. My mother would reprimand me, sometimes using a cane. On occasions, it would be quite painful. My aunt(s) would support and console me.

I had a few friends. Some were classmates, and the rest were from Cowl Bazaar, where I used to go to play. They were Naresh, Ramesh, Suresh, Narayanamurthy, Chitti, Ramamurthy, Seetharam, and Bhaskar. I maintained contact with them and attended family functions like marriages and the like.

FILMS

We used to watch English and Telugu films in Prabhat Talkies, close to our High School. The manager was a relative named "Cinema Naidu". He had one glass eye because he had accidentally shot himself while tinkering with a gun. Ironically, his family name was 'Thupakula' or Guns! We watched films like Keelu Gurram (Flying Horse), Jeevitham, Pathala Bhairavi, Maya Bazaar, and some English matinee shows.

I enjoyed many classic films with my brothers like Thomas and Hardy, Charlie Chaplin, and MGM historic films like Samson and Delilah, Ten Commandments, and Hindi films like Awara, Shree 420 and Parichaiyan, etc. at Royal, Mubarak, and Prabhat talkies. Telugu movies were popular and would play for 100 days or more. I still remember the immaculate dialogues of S.V. Ranga Rao and comedians like Peketi, Relangi, and Shiva Rao. Pathala Bhairavi and Maya Bazar were popular.

On 30th January **1948**, my brother and I were watching an English film called Captain America in Star Cinema Hall. Suddenly, the film was stopped, and a person came on the stage and announced that Mahatma Gandhi was shot dead in Delhi and that we must hasten home.

BELLARY – THE BIRTHPLACE OF TELUGU DRAMAS

Bellary was the birthplace of Telugu plays and memorable performances. They were spearheaded by playwrights like Kolachalam Srinivas Rao, Dharmavaram Krishnamacharya, etc. There was a drama hall opposite the Municipal High School where English and Telugu plays were staged. Bellary Raghava, the famous Shakespearean and Telugu actor, honed his skills in this Hall, which is now called Raghava Hall. M.R. Radha's plays used to attract large crowds due to his acting prowess, satirical dialogue delivery, and humorous slant. We used to attend puppetry shows as well.

CAUGHT PANTS DOWN!

There was a one-time posh but abandoned swimming pool near the Rock Fort moat with cement benches. The pool was enclosed by a thatched fence with a hole at the ground level - probably made by dogs to creep in and creep out. Some of my friends wanted to swim in it. We thought that all of us could sneak in through the hole and have a free and joyful swim in the pool. When we all crept inside, we found that the water was not clear and looked dirty with a lot of twigs, leaves, frogs, and tadpoles. I was not particularly eager to swim in such water but volunteered to keep their pants and shirts and watch out for danger while they swam. My friends happily swam in the water completely naked.

Unexpectedly, the watchman entered through the regular gate. There was utter chaos and confusion. Some of my friends ran away naked and hid behind bushes. However, a couple of them were caught. I meanwhile escaped through the hole with all the clothes entrusted to me. The boys who escaped got their clothes from me. All of us got dressed and approached the watchman, pleading with him to release our two friends who had been caught. We apologized for the lapse and pointed out that if the parents came to know, they would get a thrashing and caning at home. We promised the watchman not to visit the pool again. After making us promise not to see the pool again, he freed the two hapless boys. They dressed quickly, and we all left. None of us dared to share our adventure and the subsequent lucky escape at home or elsewhere—a well-kept secret for over 60 years.

CAUGHT BY THE POLICE AND RELEASED

On another occasion, my cousin brothers Raghupathi and Ramu, my younger brother Vijay Kumar, and I went on two cycles to watch a hockey match in Brucepet. On the way back, Raghu, Ramu, and Vijay left a little earlier triple - riding on one cycle. I followed them a little later on my cycle. A constable from the Cantonment Police outpost saw them triple-riding and asked them to stop. As they did not stop, the constable had to do some fast running behind the cycle to catch them. Annoyed that the boys had not stopped and made him run fast and pant for breath, he caught them and the cycle and took them to the Police outpost. He insisted that unless an elder came or they called their parents, they would remain in police custody. They were in a predicament since they could not communicate their detention and were afraid to do so as they would be taken to task at home as well. However, one boy was allowed to go home to call an elder.

Fortunately, as I was following them a little later, I saw them waving their arms and hailing me from the outpost. I went to the outpost, understood the situation, and told the constable that we were residents of a bungalow on Infantry Road from a respectable doctor's family. I asked him to release my cousins, or else I would complain to his superiors. He poo-pooed and laughed it off. In the meantime, my cousin's sisters landed at the outpost, plaintively pleaded, and started cursing the constable for his hard-heartedness and detention of innocent young boys.

Realizing that the constable would release the boys when their parents came, and we dared not tell them of the incident, I went straight to the S.P.'s residence and rang the bell. He was an Englishman. I greeted him respectfully and told him about the incident while assuring him that my cousins would not make such a mistake again. He asked me where I was studying. I told him that I was a student of Wardlaw High School and earlier of St. Philomena's convent. He appreciated my bold action in meeting him. He called his wife, and both accompanied me on foot to the outpost, much in the manner of their usual evening walk. The S.P. gave a dressing down to the constable for neglecting his duty to guard the outpost and its weapons and instead running after the boy cyclists. The constable was downcast, profusely apologized, and released both Raghu and Vijay. When I reached home with my cousins, and they related the story to our elders, I became an overnight hero with my collar up.

COMMUNITY FEASTS

The "Pankti Bhojanam" or seated rows community feast at marriages or other occasions with a variety of dishes and lavish food served on plantain leaves, was an eagerly awaited event. During the lunch, we would hear elderly army veterans from the First and Second World Wars relate their exploits with varying degrees of exaggeration. One of the retired veterans who fought in the First World War, with white hair and a white moustache, was called Agha Khan, as he closely resembled him. He and other veterans would heartily eat the non-vegetarian dishes. The mutton, chicken, fish, kebabs, prawns, and delicious items of food would quickly vanish, while the picked bare bones would neatly rise in a pile beside their plates! So much for old age! We cannot forget the humorous conversations and remarks amongst young boys and at home.

I PASS THE SSLC EXAM

I secured an age exemption and appeared for the SSLC examination. I passed the examination with decent marks. In the wake of the appointment of the States Reorganisation Committee about the future of Bellary, there was a lot of speculation, anxiety, and uncertainty. The talk was about Bellary not being part of Andhra State but becoming part of Mysore State.

Many of my relatives who were officials were debating whether they should shift to Madras, Bangalore, or Hyderabad, which would become the capital of Andhra Pradesh. My Uncle, who was working in Hyderabad, felt that Hyderabad would be a better choice for our family as it was a growing city with all the facilities, good colleges, Osmania University, and many opportunities. He wanted me to study in Hyderabad.

I JOIN COLLEGE AT HYDERABAD

My mother sent me to Hyderabad to stay with my uncle's family and do my intermediate. I boarded the train at Bellary, and a relative at Guntakal Junction put me on the train to Secunderabad Station which reached Secunderabad around 7 p.m. It was raining heavily. My uncle met me at the Railway Station and drove me to his house in Marredpally. All my cousins were happy that I would be staying with them.

My elder uncle's house at West Marredpally was part of Secunderabad Cantonment. I wanted to familiarize myself with the bus routes in the twin cities of Hyderabad and Secunderabad. Hyderabad had double-decker buses. I boarded a double-decker bus for the first time. It took me to the Charminar and Salar Jung Museum. The famous museum was then at Devan Devdi, the residence of Salar Jung III. The main attraction for children was a mechanical clock where a Toy-Soldier with a hammer would appear exactly at noon, strike a bell, and go back, closing the door. It had a Statue of veiled Rebecca on one side and a figure of Mephistopheles, a bearded soldier, on the other side. It has many paintings, records, artefacts, and furniture from all over the World. It has old swords, daggers, spears, shields, and various firearms like vintage guns, rifles, and pistols. It has many valuable manuscripts and paintings as well. It has now moved to its spacious building. I also caught a tourist bus and visited the Public

Gardens, Golconda Fort, Osman Sagar Lake, Zoological Park, and Osmania University.

Theatres at Secunderabad - Plaza, Dreamland, and Tivoli exhibited English pictures. There was a Telugu cinema hall called Rajeshwari near Monda market and a small one in Chilakalguda. While we were in college, a posh new theatre called Paradise opened in 1954-55. Unfortunately, the train in which its owner, Mr. Goud, was traveling to Vijayawada died when it was washed away on the railway bridge at Alair due to torrential rains and flash floods in the Vagu.

7

Intermediate at Mahabub College, Secunderabad

Hyderabad is a big city, and I wanted to familiarise myself with it. I made friends in the Marredpally area, which helped me understand the people and culture of Hyderabad. In 1953, Hyderabad used two types of currency: the Osman Sikka (O.S.) or Hali and the Indian Government (I.G.) currency. An I.G. Rs. 100 was equivalent to O.S. Rs. 116. Locally, students would ask, “Is your word I.G. or Hali?” meaning, “Is it valuable or not?”

The Hussainsagar Tank demarcated Hyderabad and Secunderabad, the twin cities which were quite distinct from one another. Both towns had their unique ways of life, dress, language, and food. Secunderabad was modern in outlook, with good English schools and cinemas showing English films. It had no cycle rickshaws but had good vegetarian hotels like the Taj Mahal near Patny’s Corner and Anand Bhavan in Kingsway (now called Rashtrapathi Road). It had a fancy cloth bazaar on James Street (now called Mahatma Gandhi Road), many bookshops, pen stores, and stationery shops. Custard apples were sold in season in baskets in Seethafalmandi, near Osmania University.

After the Police Action in 1949 called Operation Polo, my uncle Dr Chalapathi Naidu was posted as District Medical Officer at Nalgonda. MS Naidu, a relative, was the District Treasury Officer. He was a close relative of Major M.G. Naidu, an army doctor at Secunderabad who married Sarojini Naidu, the Nightingale of India. Another relative, Admiral Ram Das Katari (RD Katari), was the first Indian Chief of the Indian Navy. He had studied at Mahbub College, Secunderabad. I was advised to make a courtesy call to both of them, which I did.

I was admitted in 1953 to the Mahbub College Science Section of Osmania University at Secunderabad, opposite the Gymkhana Ground.

The Building with twin spires was called Mahbub Manzil. It is now a Function Hall called "Royale Palais." I used to cycle to the college from my uncle's house in West Marredpally.

The college term fee was only Rs.21/-for both the Junior and Senior intermediate classes. I got a scholarship and did not have to pay any college fees. There were 60 students in both the Junior and Senior Intermediate classes. The college provided two options – Maths-Physics-Chemistry (M.P.C.) and Biology-Physics-Chemistry (B P C). I joined the M.P.C. class. The students were Telugus, Tamils, North Indians, and some Parsis. Most of the female students took B.P.C. Among them were Vasantha, who married a legal activist Kannabiran and Leela Benegal, the younger sister of Shyam Benegal, the famous cinema director.

The Principal was Mr. Jaffar Ali. The lecturers were friendly, took an interest in our transition from school to college, and helped students with laboratory work. The lecturers were Narasimha Murthy, Thatte, Afzal, and Saxena. S. Natarajan taught Mathematics in a humorous way. Prof. C. Narayana Reddy, who joined as a Telugu lecturer motivated us and instilled a love for Telugu poetry and lyrics. He later became a Jnanpith Awardee, a Cinema lyric writer, and a Padmabhushan recipient.

I had a classmate called Antony Emmanuel, whose father, Charles Emmanuel, was an architect in the Government and whose mother was a kind host. I was a frequent visitor to their house as it was nearby in Marredpally. They had a good gymnasium with weights in their basement, where I practiced with weights and did my exercise. In the evenings, I used to go for a cup of tea to an Irani joint called Khurshid Hotel, near Clock Tower. There, I met seniors from Nizam College like Vaidyanathan Iyer, a student activist who later joined the M.R.A. (Moral Re-Armament), Shyam Benegal, the future famous director, G. Kishan, a nephew of cricketer C.K. Nayudu and Amar Singh, a wrestler.

We used to play cricket on the streets of Marredpally and at the New Club, along with M.L. Jaisimha who was a student at Nizam College and then an upcoming batsman who later became a Ranji Trophy and Test player. E Aibara was our cricket coach. Two of my juniors in college, P.R. Mansingh and Dr.C. Rammohan, were avid players and lovers of cricket and were associated with the Hyderabad Cricket Association. Mansingh later became the Manager of the Indian Cricket Team, which toured overseas, and was Manager of the 1988 World Cup winning team. In the 1980s, I was elected the Vice-President of the Hyderabad Cricket Association for one term.

VICE PRESIDENT OF THE COLLEGE STUDENT UNION

I used to play hockey and do weightlifting regularly. I won prizes in inter-college elocution, quiz, and debate competitions. The Principal of the college, who was President of the Students Union, nominated me as Vice-President. We used to celebrate important events such as Fresher's Day, Independence Day, Republic Day, the Annual College Day, and some festivals. We organized dramas and cultural events on our college day and distributed prizes. VIPs like Gopalrao Ekbote, and D Sanjeevayya, the Education Minister, visited our college and addressed the students. Sanjeevayya's, brother-in-law Namdev, was my college junior. He later became an important Member of the Osmania Graduates Association and the Exhibition Society.

The Mahbub College Science section students had a joint celebration of Independence Day at Mahbub College Arts Section. C Narayana Reddy, the poet, recited his poems on the occasion. There, I met a freedom fighter student, MPV Anantha, who became a good friend. Later, he joined the Hyderabad Road Transport Corporation and rose to a high position.

The college took us on an excursion to Nizamsagar Dam and Bodhan Sugar Factory. We swam to our hearts' content at the swimming pool near the Dam, where my "Savasana"- i.e., floating without swimming (lying flat and still on my back on the water)—was applauded by my classmates.

Football was the craze in Hyderabad, and Hyderabad City Police was a formidable team. They were winners of the Rovers Cup. Mohan Bagan, Mohammedan Sporting Club, and East Bengal Club at Calcutta picked up many Hyderabad players. We would attend the Football matches at Lal Bahadur Stadium or Goshamahal Stadium.

In 1953-54, the Rangaswamy Cup Hockey Tournament was held at Gymkhana Grounds, Secunderabad. My uncle, a good hockey player, and I attended the final match played between the Services Team and Punjab Police. We were impressed by the footwork, dribbling, and speed of R.S. Bhola of the Services Team and Raghubir and Balbir Singh, then Captain of the Punjab Police Team. Balbir Singh became the captain of the Indian Team for the Olympics. When the game was getting over, a ball, unfortunately, hit the forehead of Balbir Singh, and he was injured. We took him and two other Punjab players to our house, where my uncle dressed the wound, offered refreshments, and dropped them back at their camp.

I passed the Intermediate in 1955 and joined B.Sc. with Physics as the Main and Chemistry and Mathematics as subsidiaries in the Osmania University Science College.

8

Graduation, Osmania University Science College, Hyderabad

I was impressed by the imposing Arts College building, the Landscape Gardens, the Engineering College, and the three blocks, Physics, Chemistry, and Biology, of the Science College. There were many hostels— 'A' hostel for Arts students, 'B' hostel for science students, 'C' hostel for Veterinary and other branches, and an exclusive hostel for Engineering students and women.

I used to cycle from my uncle's home in Marredpally to the college. On the way, my classmates S Vijay Kumar, an excellent sprinter and athlete; M. Ranganath, a cricketer; S.Madan Mohan, who later became a Marketing Manager; and M.Venkataramana (Chitti) joined me at Mettuguda.

As commuting from home to college, studying, and returning took much time, I joined the 'B' hostel at the university. It was a 3-seater room, and my roommates were from Marathwada. The term fee for B.Sc was Rs.28/-. The hostel charges were Rs.42 per month- Rs.26 towards food and Rs.16 towards rent and services of the dhobi and barber. I would go home on Sundays, meet my cousins, have lunch, and come back to the hostel.

The hostel mess served a good breakfast, lunch, and dinner. Tea time was from 4 to 6 pm. A young server, Sabith Ali, at the mess took special care of me as I was teaching him Telugu. He was a master cook and managed the messes later. He retired as the manager of the O.U. Guest House and supervisor of other University Hostel messes. He later on assisted at all our family marriages and functions. The Mess Committee organized the Milad-un-Nabi elocution competition, where I spoke on Prophet Mohammed and His message to the world and got the first prize.

Dr. S.Bhagavantham, a well-known Physics Professor, was the Vice-Chancellor who later on became Scientific Advisor to the Indian

Government. N V Subba Rao was the Head of the Chemistry Department, and M Sayeeduddin was the Principal of the Science College and Head of the Biology Department. Capt Ahmeduddin headed the Geology department.

Prof Ravada Satyanarayana was the Head of the Physics Department. We had many Research scholars, including Dr.Navneeth Rao, who became Vice-Chancellor of the University, and S K Iyengar, who became the Director of the Regional Research Laboratory of CSIR at Jorhat in Assam, whom I met many years later when I was Deputy Commissioner of Sibsagar District.

Dr. S Balakrishna of the Geology Department had the task of publishing the College Magazine "Scientia." I was joint editor in the first year and editor in the second year. I wrote two articles on Johann Kepler and William Johnson, which were published.

Our English and Sanskrit/Telugu common classes were held in the Arts College in Room no.126 for students from the campus colleges. Rajarathnam was our English professor, while the Telugu Professors were Ganti Jogi Somayajulu and PSR Appa Rao, who translated Natya Sastram into Telugu. AM Khusro, former Ambassador to Germany, was then in the Economics Department.

Ravada encouraged me to take part in Telugu literary meets and student activities. V R Sreenivasan of the Chemistry Department, Adviser to the Students' Union, and a bachelor was my local guardian on campus.

CO-CURRICULAR ACTIVITIES

I got involved in student unions and literary activities. Goka Ramaswamy, who later became a Minister, and I used to organize Telugu lectures and literary activities. Viswanatha Satyanarayana, a Jnanpith awardee and the author of Veyi Padagalu (1000 snake hoods), gave an exposition of the book and the Telugu language and poetry. P V Narasimha Rao, our Prime Minister, translated the Telugu book into Marathi and Hindi.

ANDHRA CULTURAL FESTIVALS

The Andhra Cultural Festivals held at Nizam College enabled us to get in touch with poets, playwrights, dramatists, and actors, and the Indian National Theatre (INT) group headed by A.R.Krishna and Mantri Srinivasa Rao, who used to enact plays. I participated in some plays portraying Chanakya (Kautilya) and Bhima characters. We got good support and encouragement from All India Radio artists like Sthanam Narasimha Rao, who used to play women roles, and poets like D Krishna Sastry, Dasarathi, etc. They encouraged and gave us opportunities to participate in student literary and drama programs in AIR. I was elected twice as General Secretary of the Andhra Cultural Festivals, which conducted one-act play competitions at Nizam College grounds for about a week every year.

I was elected as an Executive Member of the Students Union and the Literary & Cultural Association. I made many friends with student leaders on campus and outside colleges.

The Indian Science Congress session was held in 1956 in the Landscape Gardens of OU. Science college students were volunteers who helped with the arrangements and assisted guests from all over India and abroad. We got a good idea of the sweep of sciences and its cumulative impact on society and the delivery of technology to meet the country's needs.

I used to play Hockey. Our physical director, Mr. Ghouse Mohammed, would come on a big Bullet Motorcycle with a pipe in his mouth. He would encourage students to participate in at least one game. Players practicing at the Recreation Ground would be provided with a glass of milk from the dairy. Students not taking the milk were given a coupon that fetched us a biscuit and tea at Khurshid restaurant nearby.

The University librarian helped us by suggesting books and magazines to read. I won the Basalat Jah Inter-College Essay Writing, the Prof Seyiduddin Debating, and other competitions. I participated in the Inter-University Debate competitions and won an All-India Elocution Contest, receiving a cash prize of Rs.1000/-, a big sum in those days. I threw a party, got a good suit, and purchased four khaki bush shirts.

Cycles were available on hire at a rental of 4 annas or a quarter Rupee from 05.00 pm and had to be returned the next day before 8 Am. We used to hire cycles to go to Narayanguda – Koti, where we had good tiffin at the Taj Mahal Hotel and saw both the first and second shows in the cinemas and come late at night to our hostels.

There were students from all parts of India in the hostel and the University campus colleges. The students from Karimnagar, Nalgonda, and Warangal districts were politically conscious and left-oriented. Karimnagar students were fond of Telugu literature, while many students of Hyderabad and Warangal had studied in Urdu. I picked up speaking or understanding different languages and dialects of Telugu as spoken in the Telangana and Andhra regions. I used to mimic some of the accents and phrases, which were humorous. Students were leftist in orientation and under the influence of communism and socialism, especially Lohiaism. Some Maharashtrian Students from the university and Viveka Vardhini College participated in the Goa Liberation March to Goa.

Prof. Doraiswamy, then Vice-Chancellor, asked me to give a talk on Republic Day from the Osmania University Staircase landing. It was my first talk to a large gathering of students from all colleges on the University campus. Though slightly nervous, I gave a good speech about the tasks ahead for development and the role of students. This established me as a good speaker, and I became quite popular in the university.

The Bhoodan Movement of Vinobha Bhave was at its peak with a donation of 600 acres of land in the Nalgonda district by P. Ramachandra Reddy. His younger brother, Prof. P.Madhusudhan Reddy, was a Professor of Philosophy and an ardent follower of Sri Aurobindo. He encouraged me to study philosophy and gave me books on Aurobindo.

AP STATE INAUGURATION

The States Reorganisation Commission recommended the formation of Andhra Pradesh, with the merger of Andhra with Telugu-speaking areas of Telangana. The Marathi-speaking areas of Hyderabad state went to Maharashtra, while Kannada-speaking areas went to Karnataka. Elaborate arrangements were made for the inauguration of the new state on 1st November 1956 at the Lal Bahadur stadium. Tangaturi Surya Kumari, the grand-daughter of T Prakasam, the first CM of Andhra, melodiously sang the Telugu State Anthem "Maa Telugu Talliki, Malle Poo Danda" – "A Jasmine garland to our Telugu mother" – Incidentally, the Telugu anthem was composed by a Tamilian! The Indian ethos and its syncretic culture were at play.

While we were in the second year, the USSR announced its success in putting Sputnik in orbit. I wrote a poem in Telugu with the refrain, "I am a Man; I am a Victor with an insatiable Thirst for victory." It was published in many Telugu magazines.

Due to my involvement in student unions and literary activities, I should have paid more attention to my studies. I also fell sick during the exams, so I did not clear the examination. I went home and stayed with my younger uncle, I.J Naidu, who was posted to Hyderabad. I studied well and passed the B.Sc. examination.

Prof.Ravada Satyanarayana and Dr. N.V.Subbarao, my professors in College, met my uncle, Dr. Chalapathi Naidu, and advised him that I was more suited to become a successful lawyer or a civil servant and that instead of doing post-graduation in Science I should join the Law College to become an advocate or Government official. My shift from the study of science to the humanities was probably destined as further events unfolded.

9

Law College, Osmania University, Hyderabad

My uncle took me to Justice P. Jaganmohan Reddy of the A.P. High Court to seek his advice about my career. Justice Reddy inquired about my graduation and other interests, such as sports and debates, and my aim in life. He told my uncle to admit me to Law College, which would give me multiple career options.

The University Law College was located in Hyderabad at Chaderghat on Tilak Lane. The LLB course was of 2 years duration. The college was running classes in two sessions – The Morning session was from 8 to 10.30 am, while the Evening session was from 6.00 to 8.30 pm. Full-time students joined the morning session, while employees joined the evening course to improve their career prospects. The college fee was Rs.35 per term. There was no hostel for the law college, and students had to make their arrangements by renting rooms in the adjacent areas like Hanuman Tekdi or near Reddy's Hostel or Basheerbagh.

Many High Court advocates were part-time lecturers or guest speakers because there were few full-time regular lecturers. The timings enabled advocates to take classes in the morning, attend court work, and, after finishing court work, come to college to deliver lectures.

A relative, G.G. Naidu, was the Registrar of the Administrative Staff College of India (ASCI) at Hyderabad, which conducts courses for practicing managers from the government, public, and private sectors. He offered to give me a job at ASCI, which would involve light work and ample free time to study. I joined ASCI as it suited me to work in the daytime, earn, and attend college in the evenings. I took a room for rent near Law College and used to eat at hotels nearby. One of my relatives from Bellary was employed in the Income Tax Department in Hyderabad. We rented and shared a small house with two rooms at Himayatnagar and later at Basheerbagh. I used to have breakfast, go to the office, have lunch, and come back in the evening to pick up books and go to college.

The syllabus in Law covered the Constitution of India, Criminal Laws and Evidence Act, Personal laws (Hindu and Muslim Law), Contracts, including Mercantile Law, and Jurisprudence, Roman law and International Law. The Constitution of India, having come into force in the 1950s, had little case law or experienced teachers. Our Principal, Dr GCV Subba Rao, took some classes on the Constitution of India, ably supplemented by lectures from senior High Court Advocates, LLM students, and guest speakers. There was an emphasis on case laws and concepts of civil wrongs in Torts.

Advocate Lecturers supplemented regular lecturers. They created in us an interest in the legal profession through case laws and finer nuances of the law. The stalwarts were T. Anantha Babu, a senior advocate, author, and eloquent speaker, who later became the Advocate General of A.P. under both the Congress and TDP governments. GVG Krishnamurthy, Advisor to the Students Union, became the Election Commissioner of India. G Ramanujulu Naidu and A Seetha Rama Reddy, who taught us contracts, became High Court Judges.

My classmates, mostly employees, were all senior to me in age. I learned a lot about their departments and work. There were student unions for both the morning session and evening session. Many of my seniors in my Final year of Law and my classmates persuaded me to take an active interest and contest the college election as I was a bachelor with plenty of time and energy. A panel was formed to contest the election. Our panel won, and I was made the General Secretary of the Union. We conducted many Lecture Meetings, Get-togethers, and functions.

I used to play volleyball whenever I had time and other indoor games at the college. Among my classmates were Vaman Rao, who became a judge of the High Court; Chengappa, who became a Deputy Collector; and many who became leading lawyers. Among my seniors were Mr. P.P. Rao, the senior advocate of the Supreme Court, and Mr. G. Vedanta Rao, who became a Minister. Some of my friends in the morning session were Nadendla Bhaskar Rao, who became Finance Minister and later Chief Minister of A.P, P. Krishnamurthy, who became a Trade Union Leader and Minister in A.P., and Mr. T. Panchajanyam, who became MLC.

I used to organize lectures by VIPs and senior advocates for the benefit of students. CP Ramaswamy Iyer, former Dewan of Travancore-Kochi; Balwant Rai Mehta, Chairman of the Committee for Panchayat Raj; Justice

P Jagan Mohan Reddy; PVG Raju, Education Minister of A.P.; Neelam Sanjeeva Reddy, Chief Minister of A.P.; and D Surya Narayanaswamy, then Law Secretary, addressed us. We used to organize get-togethers and celebrate National days and events like the Annual Dinner.

I started acting in dramas and plays, besides participating in elocution and essay-writing competitions. I joined Hanuman Vyayam Shala at Sultan Bazar to resume weightlifting and wrestling, and I also played hockey for the college. I continued my association with Andhra Cultural Festivals at Nizam College. I attended lectures and poetry recitals at the Andhra Sahitya Sabha and Andhra Cultural Academy, which were nearby.

As I had to cycle a lot and was exercising, I used to feel ravenously hungry but could have dinner only after 9.00 pm. I used to eat at different hotels in and around Abids and Basheer Bagh, buy and eat bananas, and drink hot milk. An annual Eating competition was held by the college in the Taj Mahal Hotel to select the winner. I won the contest by eating 22 Chapathis with curry within a fixed time! T Anjaiah, Trade Union Leader and President of Hyderabad Allwyn Workers Union would come pillion riding on the motorcycle of G. Venkataswamy, another union leader, in the late evening for tea and dinner at Orient Hotel in Abids of Hyderabad. I knew them as I was occasionally having dinner at the Orient Hotel.

In the summer, I went home on a month's leave to Bellary. My younger brother Vijay had passed Intermediate in the first division and wanted to join the Regional Engineering College (REC) at Warangal and, if selected, join immediately. The REC, which was being set up, was operating from temporary accommodation. I told my mother that I would take him from Hyderabad to Warangal and get him admitted. My classmate P Janardhan Reddy (younger brother of P Uma Reddy, Chairman of the Warangal Municipality) volunteered to come with me from Hyderabad to Warangal. All three of us went by train to Warangal and stayed at their house. The next day, we went to the REC for Vijay's interview. He was selected and got admission to REC and Hostel. My senior colleague at Law College Nagasayana Rao was working as the Accounts Officer at REC and readily agreed to be his local guardian. Vijay later got a scholarship and completed his engineering studies with a first division and got an appointment as a lecturer in REC. He did his M.Tech. at IIT Powai. He was a good player in Hockey and Cricket and was captain of the REC Cricket team.

I topped the first-year law examination of Osmania University, which spurred me to try for the first division in the final law examination. In the second year of law, I was elected President of the Law College Union after a tough debate and voting. Many friends from my Intermediate and degree courses came to the law college and canvassed for me.

As I won the elections as President of the Law College Union (Evening Session), I hosted a dinner at the Orient Hotel in Abids for my college mates. At a nearby table were Mr. Maqdoom Mohiuddin, an Urdu poet and communist leader; T Anjaiah, and G. Venkataswamy, both Trade Union leaders, whom I already knew. They noted that I was hosting a dinner. Anjaiah asked me why I had not included them in the dinner and jocularly remarked that many employee-students of Hyderabad Allwyn had voted for me! I gladly requested they join us for dinner, which they did.

A two-day model Legislative Assembly sponsored by YMCA was conducted in December 1959 by the Osmania University Students under the Youth and Government program by its Chairman Gopal Rao Ekbote, M.L.A, and former Minister. In the meeting, K. Keshava Rao, later, MP was the Deputy Speaker, while I was the leader of the Communist Party. It was a thrilling experience to act, speak, and behave like the role models we played.

I was the Editor of the Law College Souvenir "Justitia" and a quarterly newsletter by the same name. These newsletters updated students about interesting aspects of law, the meaning of Latin phrases, and the importance of Fundamental Rights and Writs available for redressing grievances.

Aligarh Muslim University used to conduct an All India Debating Competition for colleges. I led the debating team from the Law College of Osmania University with T Panchajanyam as my co-debater. It was December 1959, and Aligarh was very cold and breezy. Our team won first place and a cash prize. We left for Delhi to attend the World Agricultural Fair, which opened on 1st January 1960 at Pragati Maidan. K Keshava Rao from Viveka Vardhini College was leading a team of students from Hyderabad to the World Agricultural Fair. We met in Delhi and spent three days together, sightseeing in Delhi and Agra. That was my first visit to Delhi and North India. Little did I realize at that time that I would later be working at Delhi.

The marriage of my aunt Dr. Rukmabai, a gynecologist, was fixed with Dr. V. B.S. Naidu, a surgeon at Hyderabad. My uncle, Dr I C Naidu, entrusted me with a lot of work for the marriage, like printing invitations, posting them, purchasing clothes, making accommodation arrangements, and looking after guests, relatives, and friends. In those days, the Chowki Dinner with Mushaira was popular. It was held in the Fateh Maidan Club at Lal Bahadur Stadium. Delicious Hyderabadi Non-vegetarian dishes were served on low square tables.

The Osmania University Graduates Association used to hold an Annual All India Industrial Exhibition at Hyderabad for about a month or 45 days from 1st January, where traders from all over India would exhibit their wares. The dry fruits, shawls, textiles, and wooden articles of J&K were the craze of Hyderabadis. Government stalls, particularly Irrigation,

Electricity, Forest, and PWD, were very popular. There was a toy train, a variety of food, and dare-devil games to attract children. Household goods drew women crowds. It was the 'Numaish,' the showpiece exhibition for Hyderabad shopping!

I appeared for the LLB final year examination and did well. I secured a First Class, which was a rarity in the Law College, but narrowly missed the first rank and got the second rank in the University. I had redeemed my honour as a meritorious student and fulfilled the prophecy of my teachers. My uncle and all at home were elated and started discussing my future.

AP Public Service Commission had announced recruitment for three Class I State government posts of Deputy Collectors and some Commercial Tax officers, Dy. Superintendents of Police after a long lapse of 6 years. I wanted to appear for the IAS examination but was not yet of age and had not applied. Instead, I appeared for the APPSC Examination. I did well and was called for an Interview. I was eagerly awaiting the results.

APPSC usually sends the list to the Board of Revenue for scrutiny and to be sent to the Revenue Department for the issue of Government orders of appointment. On 28th December 1960, late in the evening, P Sanjeevappa, then Superintendent of the Board of Revenue, who was known to our family, congratulated me and told me that I had been selected as Deputy Collector by the APPSC and that my appointment proposal would be sent by the Board of Revenue to the Revenue Department in Government immediately. He advised me to contact Prakasha Rao, Superintendent of the Revenue Department. I did so the next day. He told me that I was being posted to Guntur District as Probationary Deputy Collector and that I should immediately proceed to Guntur and positively report to the Collector on 31-12-1960 for a Year-long training before appointment as Revenue Divisional Officer.

I felt happy but did not understand the urgency of joining on 31st December when the New Year's Day program with friends had been fixed. I also wanted to get a new suit stitched, buy some clothes, resign from my job, vacate my accommodation, inform friends and relatives, etc. He explained to me that the Deputy Collectors post was a feeder post for promotion to the IAS and that every year, a list of eligible officers, as of 1st January, would be prepared for selection to IAS. If I joined by 31st December 1960, my name would figure in the list of the year 1960; otherwise, I would have to wait for one more year. At that time, it was all Greek and Latin, but I followed his advice. He was good enough to speak to the Tahsildar at Guntur who received me at Vijayawada Railway Station and organized accommodation at Guntur to enable me to join on 31-12-1960 (FN) at the Collectorate.

I collected my belongings and left hastily by the night train on 30th December 1960 for Guntur. I met the Collector GVS Mani on 31st December in the morning. He welcomed me and asked me to join duty. I gave my joining report as a Probationary Deputy Collector under training on 31-12-1960. The Collector invited me to attend the New Year Party at the Officer's Club and join as a member of the Club.

A new year and a new phase of life have started! The insight, foresight, and judgment of my professors at the Science College about me have proven true! I braced myself for a career in Civil Service and the future it holds for me.

10

Probationery Deputy Collector and R.D.O. Guntur (Jan 1961 – June 1962)

AS PROBATIONARY DEPUTY COLLECTOR GUNTUR (PDC)

Guntur is a large district with both irrigated and dry areas. It is famous for chilies, turmeric, tobacco, paddy, and a variety of crops and pulses. Tobacco curing, sorting, and packing offered ample job opportunities. Guntur was known for ghee and hot, spicy food. The communist and socialist philosophies attracted many youths. Andhra has a reputation of being cinema crazy. The district had 126 high schools and 3 colleges. There were a lot of literary, commercial, and industrial activities. Cattle shows and fairs were popular. For me, every day was a new learning experience.

The Collector held the first meeting I attended with all District Officers for the conduct of Census 1961. Enumeration for the census was scheduled from 10 February to 26 February 1961. After discussions, detailed instructions were issued.

The PA to the Collector, Mr. Khasim, a senior Deputy Collector, briefed me on the training for Probationary Deputy Collectors (PDCs). A camp clerk and peon were appointed to assist me. I had to write a daily diary of work done from Monday to Saturday and submit it to the Collector which would come back on Monday with the Collector's remarks and guidance.

P.V. Ramana, a Divisional Forest Officer (a widower) and a family friend had rented a big house at Arundelpet in Guntur. He welcomed me to stay with him. T.V. Rangarajan, an ACF, and C. Venkateshwara Rao, a CTO, both under training, were already lodged there. I moved to his house, and there was no dearth of company.

A 3-day District Revenue Officers' Conference was held along with the Revenue Sports Day on 5th February 1961. I gave the running commentary on Sports Day. The news spread that the new PDC was a good commentator and interested in sports. On the next Republic Day 1962, we organized 4 floats (tableaus) depicting the progress made by the district in developmental work. For the first time, Guntur witnessed a Republic Day like in Delhi.

Collector GVS Mani took a personal interest in my training and took me along with him on tours and inspections. He gave useful suggestions and advice on the correct behaviour and conduct of officers. Later, Shravan Kumar was posted as Collector, and he entrusted me with many inquiries. His philosophy was that working on the job is the best course of training and learning. I worked with three joint collectors during my probation: Narayanaswamy, Lakshma Reddy, and P K. Doraiswamy, who was also in charge of collector for short periods. The Assistant Collectors were K.M. Ahmed (1959), T. Padmanabhan (1960), and S. Chakravarthy (1961).

Being young officers, we used to meet and exchange notes often.

The first six months of training was in the Revenue Department, starting bottom-up from a Village, Taluk, Sub-division, Treasury, Survey, and Settlement, and Land acquisition and included working as in-charge Tahsildar and Revenue Divisional Officer. In the remaining 6 months, monthly or fortnightly attachments at the district level were with different Government departments. A month's training each was with the District Judge and Criminal Courts, Superintendent of Police, Development Departments like Agriculture, Cooperation, Forests, Irrigation, Zilla Parishad and Block Development Office, etc. Towards the end, there was a month's attachment with the State Secretariat and Board of Revenue to meet senior officials and Heads of Departments to study Social and Tribal Welfare. The training scheme equipped the PDC to gain magisterial experience, exercise first-class Magisterial Powers, get an overview of District Administration and be ready to take over as RDO.

CHEBROLU VILLAGE ATTACHMENT

The first month was spent in Chebrolu village, about 8 miles from Guntur town, which had two hamlets. I stayed in the Inspection Bungalow and worked "bottom-up" in the hierarchy as Karnam, or "Village Accountant"; Munsab, or "Village Headman"; Revenue Inspector; and Deputy Tahsildar. I had to study Land Records and Revenue Registers and review the collection of land revenues, water charges, and so on. Chebrolu has a village office called Chavidi. I learned Revenue work, map reading, survey, and admonish or inspection. Officers were advised to accept only

Coconut water, buttermilk (chaos), or plantain from villagers and not accept lavish entertainment. We used to carry our foodstuffs in a "Rukmini Cooking Carrier" in which rice, dal, and vegetable curry could be cooked together quickly and supplemented by fruits.

Chebrolu village has a hoary past, and through the ages, it was known as Thamravolu, Jayavolu, Jayabrolu, and now Chebrolu. The 10th-11th century AD stone inscription at Kanakadurga temple in Vijayawada mentions that Chebrolu folk would visit the Bejawada Jathra (fair). Chebrolu has an ancient Brahma temple and a Kala Bhairava idol. The local lore is that Brahma is not eligible for worship as he married his daughter, Saraswathi, and committed a sin. To make Brahma eligible for prayer, he was encrypted in stone into the four faces of Shiva. Hence, the name of the idol is Chaturmukha Brahma Lingeswara Swamy (four-faced Brahma- Shiva).

Excavations at Chebrolu revealed many finds of Roman gold coins dating from the 3rd century BC to the 2nd century AD. The soil of the ruins is rich in phosphorus. The tobacco grown in or with that soil is called Chebrolu tobacco and is highly prized. Winston Churchill was reported to be a fan of Chebrolu tobacco. Chebrolu cigars and cheroots are very popular with smokers because the ash does not fall off until the cigar is over.

I had to write the Rural Economy Report of Chebrolu for submission to the Board of Revenue. The local Deputy Tahsildar would occasionally come and help me with the statistics. The report was to evaluate the competence, knowledge, and interest taken by the PDC in the development of the village and make suggestions for its socio-economic growth. The report was well received. I had malaria for the first time in my life at Chebrolu but recovered quickly and hoped that this would be the last time! As Tahsildar of Bapatla Taluk, I visited several villages, the Agricultural College, and the ILTD (Imperial Leaf Tobacco Development) Company, which purchases, processes, and exports tobacco to the UK and Russia. I also visited a small seaside resort called Vadrevu. I met the highly respected 'Amma' of Jillellamudi village (the wife of the Karnam), who was revered as a spiritually evolved person. She had a benign presence and a brilliant glow on her face. Visitors would experience calmness and peace in her presence.

In the absence of Coaching Institutions and as part of my preparations for IAS, I used to go to the district library in Guntur in the afternoons and study till it was closing time. The librarian, Narayana Reddy, was most helpful and would suggest and get good books for study. He gave me a chair and table in a quiet corner of the library for undisturbed study. I owe a lot to him for passing the exam.

The record room in the Collectorate had many 200-300-year-old Records and Palm leaf manuscripts. Many British civilians meticulously recorded their memoirs. I read many Kaifieths (records) of Mackenzie, a historian, and Civil Service officer. There was an interesting book on "How to write judgments," which gives the format and recommends that judgments should be precise, clear, and not exceed three pages. It stressed lucidity and clarity.

I was attached to the District Judge for training in Criminal laws and to hold court. I earned my 3rd class, 2nd class, and 1st class magisterial powers. The District Judge made me sit beside him during the trial in a murder case and explained the issues and manner of recording the findings and writing the Judgement and extent of punishment. Having studied law, I enjoyed court work.

I attended a two-month-long training course in Survey and Settlement work in Visakhapatnam and Srikakulam districts. Settlements used to be done once every 30 years to update the Survey and Revenue Records, including recording of changes in ownership and particulars of the current Pattadars. KVS Suryanarayana, the Settlement Officer, explained the classification of lands according to soil composition and assessment of rating and value. The discontinuation of periodical Surveys and Settlements has led to a lot of litigation.

As the in-charge RDO of Narasaraopet Sub-division, I conducted the Jamabandi or Annual Review of Revenue Records and Revenue Collections for about a week. As Village and Revenue officers were present, petitions and representations from villages were settled on the spot. It was akin to the Gram Sabha, which focused on revenue issues. Vavilala Gopalakrishnan, a selfless Satyagrahi, freedom fighter, and MLA, was the lone person who sincerely attended for the whole week.

In the Treasury office in the Collectorate, I familiarised myself with the Accounts Manual, Rules for the withdrawal of salary bills, Pension payments, and recording of Treasury receipts from Excise auctions and the sale of opium to people with an addiction. I appeared and cleared all prescribed Revenue, Language, Accounts, Land Records, Criminal law, and other tests.

Attachment with the Superintendent of Police included working as a Sub-Inspector of a police station, caring for weapons and ammunition, and investigating a criminal case, including the disinterment of mortal remains in suspected murder cases. Rural policing, citizen contact, and informer relations were emphasized.

Attachment for a month with Zilla Parishad and Panchayat Samithi provided an overview of the functioning of Panchayat Raj Institutions

The Executive Engineer of the Irrigation department briefed me about the maintenance of Buckingham Canal, other Irrigation Canals, and Lock mechanisms for smooth boat transport. The importance of Prakasam Barrage and the maintenance of bunds along the canals, channels, and field channels was explained.

Interested in history, I took every opportunity to visit ancient places, old temples, and Buddhist relics. I visited the Amaravathi Shiva Temple, the Buddhist Stupa, and remains at Nagarjunasagar, Bhattiprolu, and caves in the Palnadu area.

The fables and ballads of valour of Kondapalli, Kondaveedu, and Palnadu were fascinating. As RDO, I completed the land acquisition for a museum to house the Buddhist remains at Amaravathi.

I got the call for the interview at UPSC, Delhi. My uncle requested P S Krishnan (1956), T L Sankar (1957), and Santhanam (1958) of the AP cadre to conduct mock interviews for me at Hyderabad. They grilled me with such a barrage of questions that it gave me confidence that I would do well in the interview. In fact, UPSC could not find any new questions, except for some queries on my experiences as PDC!

When the census was in progress in 1961, S Santhanam (1958) was Sub-Collector of Ongole Division and was under orders of posting to Hyderabad. Rajamani (1959) was to take over from him. Santhanam was keen that Ongole must be the first sub-division to report the completion of the census before handing over the charge. The only pending census report was from Chinnaganjam village, which was reportedly with village munsab. I accompanied Santhanam to the village in a jeep late at night, and at the break of dawn, we woke up the munsab, collected the records and drove back to Ongole, and gave the first complete report for Guntur district. R Rajamani took over from him. At the farewell function, I recited a small Telugu poem.

The last phase of a month's training at the Secretariat in Hyderabad enabled me to meet senior officers at the Board of Revenue and in various departments like General Administration, Home, Education, Social Welfare, Tribal Welfare, etc. During Tribal Welfare training, we were taken to tribal villages near Bhadrachalam. We went by steam launch down the Godavari River to Perantapalli via Papikondalu to Polavaram, where we boarded a train back to Hyderabad.

I met Chief Secretary M P Pai, whose advice was to "always respect the revenue officers, irrespective of rank as many of them will be older in age and more experienced than you" and that "You must command respect, not demand respect." K M Unnithan, Chairman of the Board of Revenue, said, "Do not be satisfied with the PDCs post. You are young and should try for the IAS." V Narayan Rao, who was Deputy Secretary of GAD and coordinated our visit, was very cordial and helpful.

The bus stand at Guntur was highly congested and inconvenient for passengers. Anantha, my college classmate who had joined the A.P. State Road Transport Corporation, sought help to construct a new bus station at Guntur. Suitable land was not available in Guntur town. There was a sewage cum cesspool of ten acres at the tri-junction at Guntur leading to Tenali, Vijayawada, and Bapatla. I suggested that it could be filled up with earth and levelled to become a spacious and ideal bus stand. He agreed, and Guntur now has a large APSRTC bus station. It shows that insight can sometimes become good foresight. I count this as my contribution to Guntur.

RDO, GUNTUR

My training as PDC was completed on 5th February 1962, and I was awaiting orders of posting as Revenue Divisional Officer. I took charge as Revenue Divisional Officer in Guntur on 15th March 1962 from Ghulam Jilani. I went to Tirupati to redeem a vow and was awaiting news about the IAS results. Meanwhile, the General Elections were announced, and I got busy with the Election process.

In the first week of June 1962, I received an order that I had been selected for the IAS with instructions to join Mussoorie for training immediately. I attended a farewell party given by the staff of the Collectorate and the Revenue Divisional Office. I handed over the charge as RDO, went home to Warangal, took leave of my elders and family members, packed my luggage, and left for Mussoorie via Delhi. I had fulfilled the dream of our family and redeemed my pledge to my mother that I would make it to the IAS.

11

Probationer at NAA, Mussourie (June 1962 – May 1963)

I reached Delhi and caught the train to Dehradun. I got down at Dehradun railway station on 10th June 1962 and took a taxi to the Lal Bahadur Shastri National Academy of Administration (LBSNAA) at Mussoorie. I reported to the Administrative Officer Kukreja. Many probationers who had reported earlier had already gone for Army attachment in J&K and Assam. We were told that we would also be sent to J&K shortly. Accommodation in Room No.79 in the Happy Valley Annexe, which was a 3-boarder room, was allotted for T. Cajee from Shillong and me. The other inmate, R.K. Ahuja, had already gone for Army attachment. I met Brig M.A. Sheriff, the Senior Deputy Director, who briefed me. We called on AN Jha, I.C.S., Director, who was basking in the lawn. We introduced ourselves, and he welcomed us in a friendly manner with a smile.

We purchased personal stationery like visiting cards, crested letter pads, and service ties from Hari's, a family firm. We were advised to get a blue blazer and grey flannel pants, a formal black or white Jodhpuri coat for formal occasions like dinners, etc., at Jacksons, a tailoring firm. To familiarise ourselves with Mussoorie, we went from 'CharleVille,' our Academy, to the shopping mall area and had a cup of tea at the Whisper Point, which had French glass windows from which we could have a panoramic view of the main portion of the mall and holiday crowds.

Our army attachment was with a Brigade located at Naushera near Jammu City in J&K. We went to Pathankot by train and reached in the morning. We were taken to Jammu and the 3rd Raj-Rifles Battalion mess and given tented accommodation. Mahinder Singh (Bihar) was my companion at Raj Rifles. The other 2 battalions in the Brigade were the Grenadiers and the Guards. We used to attend the morning parade and accompany patrol parties to the Line of Control along the Indo-Pak border. We saw the difficult conditions under which our soldiers had to stay in the trenches and bunkers from where they had to operate, patrol, and look out for intruders or unusual movements on the border. In the afternoons, we used to listen to the radio broadcast, and in the evenings, play volleyball, football, and hockey. I took part in a kabaddi match played between two teams and was complimented for my skills. We were given training in the use of firearms like rifles, L.M.G.s, and grenades. We were also taught about signals and the use of night vision glasses. We were taken to the other 2 battalions of the Brigade, and the commandants briefed us on the history of their battalions and invited us for dinner in the officers' mess. We used to go to Jammu City on Sundays to visit the temples, do sightseeing, and have lunch. I purchased some trinkets and beads for my sisters.

Towards the end of the army attachment, all the I.A.S. probationers posted in J&K were taken to Srinagar where the Sadr-e-Riyasat Karan Singh hosted a tea party with sumptuous refreshments across a long banquet table. Some of us got a place near Karan Singh, while other batch mates were on the opposite side of the table. An orthodox batch mate was not in the habit of taking tea. He was furtively glancing at milk jugs to pour milk into his empty teacup. But the milk jars next to him were empty. Karan Singh noticed his predicament as did I. I found a couple of milk jars near me and passed them on to Karan Singh, who was just beside me and opposite the probationer. Karan Singh glanced at me with a twinkle in his eyes and passed the milk to the probationer across the table, who happily drank his cup of milk. Later, at dinner, this episode became the gossip of the day.

At Srinagar, we visited Shalimar Gardens, Shankaracharya temple, and Dal Lake for a boat ride. We had a free day to explore Srinagar, visit the Jama Masjid, and shop. I purchased some trinkets for my mother and sisters. After the army attachment, we returned to Mussoorie for further training.

The I.P.S. and Central Services Officers used to join the Academy for the common Foundational Course of 4-5 months duration, which was intended to foster Corps-de-spirit among all Service Officers.

Our classes at the Academy began at 9 a.m. and went on until 1 p.m., with a short recess in between. We were taught subjects like Political Science, Public Administration, International Law, Constitutional Laws, the Indian Penal Code, the Evidence Act, Criminal Procedural laws, Principles of Economics and Five-Year plans, History, and General Administrative Knowledge. Our professors were retired Government officials, Academicians, and persons with practical experience.

We used to have physical training and horse-riding classes in the mornings. Horse riding was a bugbear for some probationers and the lone probationer Mrs. Mrunalini Garde. Subedar Nawal Singh, a Rajput with an impressive moustache, was our equestrian instructor. He would find fault if we were not in firm control of the horse and shout, "If you cannot control a horse, how can you control a District?" He advised us to tightly grip the flanks of the horse with the knees and shout, "Ghutno Dhabake ghode-chalaana." We were taught the basics of saddling, mounting and dismounting a horse, trotting, cantering, and, after some experience, galloping. We had to pass a horse-riding test by clearing a three-foot high fence (hedge) on horseback. It called for control of the horse and equilibrium with the momentum of the horse. Some probationers found it difficult to do so. The horse would sometimes abruptly stop, and the rider would fall on the other side and would wonder what happened! Sometimes, the rider would be thrown off before the barrier, while the horse would have jumped over the barrier! Nawal Singh would sarcastically remark to the faulting officers that he had not given the order for them to dismount! Good riders with permission could take the horses for short treks. On Sundays, probationers would go trekking or visit the Kempty Falls or a nearby Shiva temple on a hill.

We had a big hall for the mess, where breakfast, lunch, and dinner were served. For breakfast, we had bread and toast, cornflakes, porridge or oats, and eggs as per preference. The lunch would be vegetarian and dinner vegetarian or non-vegetarian. There were elections to the Mess Committee. B N Yugandhar was elected as President of the Mess Committee, G. Sundaram was secretary, and I was the Executive Committee Member. We used to go down to Dehradun once a week on holidays and pick up foodstuffs, vegetables, and other essentials, which were much cheaper there.

TELUGU "GUMPU" AND OTHER GROUPS

Several Telugu officers selected for the IAS or other Central services were attending the foundation course at the academy. I have a group photo of all of them. Other probationers would call the group "the Gumpu" or "Crowd," as we excitedly discussed happenings in Andhra Pradesh. The St. Stephens group from Delhi were high-brow, sophisticated, and snobbish. The Indian Foreign Service officers were a close-knit and exclusive group and would not mix much with other probationers. The South Indian group was down to earth. The Bengali group was talkative and noisy. The Punjabi group used to swagger a lot. IPS officers would concentrate on horse riding and physical training, while other service officers would move in clusters, depending on the service or state to which they belonged.

IAS probationers allotted to different states were given language training according to the State allotted. However, Officers allotted to

Assam had to learn Assamese only when they reported for duty in Assam.

The Academy song was in Bengali, and it highlighted qualities generally required by patriotic civil servants. The Bengali officers would heartily and lustily sing the chorus.

GUEST LECTURES

Senior officers from the Indian government and States were invited to give guest lectures. Many of them were incidentally on the lookout for grooms for their daughters! The academy would host dinner for guest speakers. A probationer had to propose the toast to the Guest. On one occasion, since the guest was from the UK High Commissioner's office in Delhi, an Oriya officer had to offer a toast to Her Majesty. In Oriya, the pronunciation and distinction between 'S' and 'Sh' are probably not very distinct and clear. The officer, while proposing a toast, instead of saying "God save the Queen" said, "God Shave the Queen!" With great difficulty, we probationers could control our laughter while the discomfiture of the guest was palpable and visible.

V S Gopalakrishnan (Maharashtra) is a very good cartoonist. Once a week, he would put out a cartoon that captured a funny incident or idiosyncrasy of a probationer or a teacher. There was an active film club run by Madhusudan Mukherji, where we watched classical English, Hindi, and Bengali films. We saw Satyajit Ray's Trilogy of Apur Sansar. Some were busy with their hobbies, such as singing, drawing, debating, and playing indoor games. There was always a rush for access to the Billiards table. Jokes about fellow batch mates and romances in the Foundation course were a staple item of gossip. Some love marriages did take place. The mannerisms of the faculty members would be mimicked.

Pathak, a retired judge from Maharashtra, was our Professor of Law. There was a discussion on the topic of Law and Order where an acceptable definition was to be found. As I had worked as a First-Class Magistrate in AP and as an RDO, Pathak suggested that I should go to Hyderabad, meet senior IAS & IPS Officers, and ascertain the distinction between law and order and maintenance of order. The Academy deputed me to go to Hyderabad, where I met the IG of Police, Ramachandra Reddy, the Director of Anti-Corruption Bureau, S. Vijayarangam, IPS, and S. Venugopal Rao, who had written a book on the Police and Academicians like Prof. G. Ram Reddy from the Political Science Department of Osmania University, who later became the Vice-chancellor of the first Open University in India and the Chairman of University Grants Commission. I wrote a paper about the phrase 'law and order' referred to the maintenance of order through the instrumentality of law and abiding by the rule of law. Pathak and the group appreciated the effort.

When the final examinations for probationers were held, I secured 100% in the Law paper, setting a new record. I received a Government letter complimenting me, saying,"Your record can at best be equalled, not excelled." Professor. Pathak wrote me a touching letter that the 'Law' subject for the first time had got 100% marks like in mathematics at the Academy during his tenure.

India suffered a severe defeat and setback on the Indo-China border with the Chinese moving troops across the Kameng Division of Northeast Frontier Agency in November- December 1962 rapidly and reached the foothills of Assam before they unilaterally withdrew.

BHARAT DARSHAN

IAS officers are taken on a tour called Bharat Darshan to different parts of India to familiarise them with the cultural and somatic unity of India. As part of Bharat Darshan, we had to call on the President of India and Prime Minister. President S Radhakrishnan told us that the Himalayas were considered impregnable, but it was not so, and that eternal vigilance and preparedness for any eventuality on our border were essential.

We called on the Prime Minister, Jawaharlal Nehru, who was feeling let down by the Chinese, and the subsequent humiliation, addressed us. We were seated on the ground while the Prime Minister spoke, sitting on a chair. In an emotional voice and tone, he lauded the valour and courage of the Rajputs throughout history and their sense of sacrifice when they donned the saffron robes and rode out to war to win or die. Suddenly, he turned towards me and asked me," What do you say?" I was caught unaware and dazed by the abrupt question. Unwittingly, I said, "Sir, the Rajputs were brave but unfortunately got defeated." There was a hushed silence as many felt that I was too blunt and foolhardy and did not realize that I was speaking to the Prime Minister of India and should have been circumspect. The PM harshly said, "Sit Down," and continued with his talk. I felt I was impertinent, foolish, and had committed a big mistake.

After the meeting was over, our Deputy Director, MAS Rajan, chided me and advised that I should learn propriety when addressing a VIP. I thought I would be reprimanded and admonished at the Academy upon our return from Bharat Darshan. However, I was greatly relieved when there were no repercussions of the incident. I was probably lucky, as the matter appeared to have been brushed under the carpet—as it often happens about lapses in our administration.

To appreciate the multilingual, multi-ethnic, and multi-religious entity called India. Officers from South India would be sent to the North and from the West to the East and the East to the West to enable them to see different parts of India. We used to travel in first-class railway coaches during the night and arrive at our destination in the morning. The coaches would be kept in the railway sidings. We got ready with the sanitary and bathing facilities of the railway station and spent the daytime visiting places of interest by bus and continuing the journey by rail at night. I was the leader of a batch visiting Rajasthan, Gujarat, and Maharashtra. However, there was one extra person in our group than the berths in the carriage. As a leader, I offered to sleep on the floor of the compartment on day one, and that one officer must, thereafter, volunteer to sleep on the floor every day. This went on smoothly, but on one occasion, a probationer refused to do so. I threatened to bodily lift him and throw him out of the running compartment. A batch mate interceded and warned the probationer of the consequences. He immediately piped down and agreed to sleep on the floor. The problem was solved; the principle of equity was upheld. The probationer, a friend of mine, would often recall the incident with a sigh of relief.

CHINA'S ATTACK IN NEFA

In the aftermath of the Chinese attack on NEFA in 1962 and their incursion up to the foothills near Tezpur in Assam, there was panic in Assam. Unfortunately, the Deputy Commissioner of Tezpur District panicked, burnt all currency in the RBI chest at Tezpur, closed his office, and shamefully boarded a flight to Calcutta with his family. Prime Minister Nehru, in a radio broadcast from Delhi, said, "My heart goes out to the people of Assam!" This was misunderstood and misinterpreted in Assam as the Central Government's inability to help Assam and to leave it to its fate. This demoralized the administration in the districts for a while, but immediate corrective action restored public confidence. Bhupen Hazarika, then an upcoming lyricist-composer and music director composed the famous lyric "Luit-or-Parore Deka Lora– Ami Mariboloi Bhay Noi," meaning, "we the young people living on the banks of the Red River (Luit-Red & Blood) are not afraid to die! According to mythology, the Brahmaputra River had turned red because lord Parshuram had washed off the sin he committed by killing several Kshatriya Kings - at Parshuram Kund, at the whirlpool pit of the river in the Easternmost portion of India where the pure snow melted waters from the Himalayas enter the plains.

The Indian Government wanted the Academy to select probationers to go to Guwahati and attend Republic Day on 26 January 1963, visit Bomdila and learn first-hand about the Chinese incursions in the Kameng Division of NEFA, and learn about Civil Defence measures.

Four probationers, deputed to attend Republic Day at Guwahati in 1963, had to board a flight at Calcutta airport. At check-in, the lady at the counter said that she could accommodate only three persons on the Indian Airlines flight. When the left-out probationer said that they were all going together for important Government work, the lady said that she could not accommodate him on the Dakota flight, but she could provide accommodation for him for friendship. The officer immediately retorted, "Madam, I am going on government duty. I want you to give me a seat "not for friendship, but for duty." He was not aware that Fokker – Friendship planes had just been inducted into the IA Fleet! The other probationers and the lady had a hearty laugh. The officer was provided with a seat in the Friendship Fokker flight later.

A British expert, Maj. General Hendricks was deputed to Guwahati to train officials about the civil defence measures to be taken. As I was allotted to the Assam cadre, I was one of the deputed officers. We were accommodated at the Guwahati Circuit house and, after Republic Day, despatched to Bomdila by jeep. We saw stark pieces of evidence of Chinese presence, burnt vehicles, tents, and rabbit burrows made by the Chinese to ward off the cold and snow and get a warm night's sleep. We saw the natural beauty of the hills, forests, winding roads, and blooming Rhododendrons.

We went to Bomdila and met an Indian Frontier Administrative Service (IFAS) officer, SN Johri, who was Deputy Commissioner, and another officer Joshi, who accommodated us and briefed us about the physical and psychological damages caused by the Chinese incursion. We were taken to a few tribal villagers to observe the way of life of the tribals and Monpas who live in the higher ranges. We, had to acclimatize ourselves before going to heights above 7500 feet. We went halfway to Tawang, but had to retreat because of snow and the lack of oxygen. An uncle of mine, Maj. Rangabashyam of a Sikh infantry battalion was killed in the war there. I whispered a silent prayer for his Sadgati and the peace of his soul. Later, I told my aunt (his wife) Savithri that I had paid homage to a martyr for India. After returning to the Academy, we had to present an account of what we saw and what we learned.

After the conclusion of our training at the academy, we were advised to report to the state Governments concerned after availing leave, including joining time. I had learnt many things, made friends, seen many places, and had to get ready for a new career in a new state and a new environment. I bid farewell to the Academy and eagerly looked forward to meeting my mother and relatives back home at Warangal.

12

Assistant Commissioner, Guwahati (June 1963 – August 1964) About Assam and Guwahati

To learn about Assam, the State to whose cadre I was allotted, I read the book "Red River and the Blue Hill," authored by Hem Barua. The Brahmaputra River, which flows through Assam, is called Lohit or Luit (red color), and the Hills are blue green (Nilachal). The colour red alludes to the Brahmaputra River as during the monsoon, due to heavy rains normal in that part of our country, a lot of mud and silt flows down, lending a reddish colour to the waters of this huge river, regarded as the only river of India bearing a masculine name.

The word Assam comes from the Sanskrit "Asama," which means uneven (unequal), Peerless, or unparalleled. The Ahoms, who came from Thailand in 1228 AD and ruled a major part of present-day Assam for over 600 years, could have given the name Assam. The word Guwahati comes from Gua, meaning cow or areca nut and haat (Bazaar), i.e., Guwahati, the market for areca nuts. It was also a marketplace for cattle (gau) trading. The Assamese call sunset time "godhuli" meaning the dust raised by cattle returning home after the day's grazing.

In ancient times, Assam was known as Prag Jyotisha, and Guwahati was known as Pragjyothishpur. The Allahabad inscription of King Samudra Gupta mentions Kamarupa as Prathyanta or an area outside the Gupta Empire. Huian Tsang, the Chinese scholar who visited Kamarupa in 743 AD at the invitation of King Kumar Bhaskara Varman, left a record of his visit. The Burmese invaded Assam in the early 19th century and reportedly cruelly treated the local population still under Ahom rule. The Ahoms, who were not in a position to defend themselves or protect people, requested the help of the East India Company, which successfully repulsed the Burmese.

They decided to incorporate Assam into the British colonial system under the terms of the Treaty of Yandaboo in 1823.

In 1962, Assam had 10 districts and a population of about 80 lakhs. The Mizo Hills district was then the second-largest district in India. Assam is the gateway to the entire North- Eastern (region) including Bhutan and Arunachal Pradesh on the north (abutting the Tibet region); Manipur, Nagaland on the east; Meghalaya, Tripura, and Mizoram on the south as well as Bangladesh. To the west are West Bengal and Sikkim. Assam provides connectivity and access to and between the Sister states of the North East and the rest of the country. The strategic importance of the state of Assam and the entire region and its economy under the current Look East policy needs to be given due importance as it has a long international border of 3200 Km with the Tibet region, Myanmar, and Bangladesh.

After completing my training as a newly minted IAS officer in the National Academy of Administration Mussoorie and being allotted to the Assam cadre, I received orders to join at Guwahati, the commercial capital of Assam with the designation of Assistant Commissioner of Kamrup district. Communication systems to the North-East from the rest of India and within this region at that time, even after some 15 years of Independence, were rudimentary. To reach Assam from any direction, one had to cross major rivers like the Ganga and Brahmaputra. This is mostly attributed to the partition of the country as earlier communication to the Northeast region was mainly through East Bengal, which became East Pakistan and later Bangladesh.

To reach Guwahati, I had to go by train from Kazipet to Vijayawada and board the Madras-Howrah mail, which reached Howrah junction the next morning. I had to catch another train to Guwahati via Barauni in Bihar. In between, one had to cross the mighty Ganga at Manihari ghat by a large ferry—a totally new experience for me—and on the other bank, get into another train for the onward journey. The journey took two days and two nights.

A Sub-Deputy Collector (SDC) received me at Guwahati railway station and took me to the Circuit House for my stay. As I was joining duty, he advised that we first visit Kamakhya temple on Nilachal hill to seek Goddess Kamakhya's blessings. According to the local folklore, if one does not do so, one would have to come back to Assam at least nine times! We went to the temple famous for Tantrik rites, which attracted devotees from all over India and Nepal. After the puja, two venerable priests asked us to be seated for the Ashirwad (blessings). The priest blessed us as "Hath-Ayurman Bhava" instead of "Shatha Ayurman Bhava," meaning – Live a 100 Years. Hatha-aYurman Bhava could mean that I would have a lesser length of life or be killed. I got the fright and shock of my life as I knew Sanskrit and was looking askance. The SDC calmly said, in Assamese, 'Sh' is pronounced as 'Ha,' which really means Shathayurman. He assured me that I would indeed live a hundred years. I had learned my first lesson in the Assamese language.

My predecessor holding the office of Assistant Commissioner at Guwahati was E.S. Parthasarathy, whom I had met earlier on Republic Day in 1963 in Guwahati on a visit during our training period. He took me to the Deputy Commissioner (DC) PH Trivedi, who belonged to the 1953 batch of the I.A.S. The DC welcomed me warmly and said that I may have to stay in the circuit house for some time till a bungalow falls vacant. He was a rotund and jovial person from Gujarat who had a fine sense of humor. His wife Pratibha Trivedi, also an I.A.S. officer of the same batch, was expecting a child and was at Shillong. The DC advised me to call on the Commissioner of Plains Division, R B Vaghaiwala, I.C.S., at Guwahati and to meet the chief secretary and other senior officer sat Shillong, which was then the capital of Assam state. It was much later that a new hill state called Meghalaya was carved out of Assam. The DC said that there was no prescribed training schedule and that he would give instructions from time to time. I would have to learn to work on the job through a series of attachments to various departments, which formed part of the system of administering the District.

The AC Parthasarathy was an ebullient, talkative, and friendly person who had a flair for relating numerous jokes and making friends. He was fluent in Telugu, having studied in Vijayawada. As an instance of his sense of looking at every situation in a novel and unusually light hearted way he described to me an incident relating to his encounter with the Indian army in the wake of the Chinese incursion. Lt-Gen N.P. Sen was to set up the tactical headquarters of the Eastern Army Command at the Circuit House at Guwahati pending regular arrangements. When Parthasarathy was showing them accommodation that could be spared for the army in Circuit House, one of the army officers said that the Circuit House would suit them but enquired of the other military officer accompanying him, "Where will Bogey go?" Parthasarathy, thinking that the officer was referring to some bogey-rail carriage, interjected, saying, "Where else can the Bogey go but to the Railway siding? If there is any difficulty, I can help as I know some railway officers". The army officers went red in the face as General N. P. Sen's nickname was "Bogey," but Parthasarathy apparently did not know it.

I was allocated the Assistant Commissioner's bungalow at Guwahati, which was close to the railway station. It was located near the Digali Pukhri

(Long lake). On one of the banks stood the Handique Girls' College, and a little further away, the Cotton College, easily the most prestigious College in the plains of Assam. Both were within walking distance from the D.C.'s office.

Parthasarathy introduced me to the Chief Engineer of Northeast Frontier Railways, a post-partition creation, Basu and his wife, who were a hospitable couple staying in a bungalow near the railway station. Parthasarathy took me to the vegetarian Rajhans Hotel and a small Madras hotel. At Guwahati railway station, we could get a good breakfast at reasonable prices. We called on Justice Mehrotra, Chief Justice of the Assam High Court, and Mr Brahmaji Rao (a Telugu), who was Head Postmaster of Guwahati, to become my local guardian. I met Parameshwar Sarma, Principal of a local college, and Sadar S.D.O. Taimur. (His wife was later the Chief Minister of Assam). We met Goswami, a tea planter and a good raconteur. Both of us went to call on the D.I.G. of Police, I.P.M. Menon, IPS. His wife's name was Parvathi, and they had a caged parrot. As soon as anyone entered the verandah or rang the bell, the parrot would shout "Parvathi Parvathi " in a gruff voice mimicking its master. It would alert the DIG's wife to respond! It was her personal calling-bell! The Menons were a hospitable couple. Within a short time, Parthasarathy was posted as S.D.O. at Kokrajhar in Goalpara District.

This association with Parthasarathy, though brief as fellow Assistant Commissioners, left a lasting impression on my mind as Partha (as he was affectionately addressed) was an extremely intelligent officer with a great memory and a fine sense of humour. It greatly pains and saddens my heart that he met a tragic end when posted as Divisional Commissioner at Jorhat. An explosive was planted right under his seat during the prolonged student agitation on the "illegal Immigrants issue" during 1979-80, which led to his death.

Vaghaiwala, Commissioner Plains Division at Guwahati was a Parsi ICS officer hailing from Bombay. He had earlier worked in Sylhet District that was, at one time, part of Assam - then in East Pakistan, and now Bangladesh. An outspoken person, he was a nationalist to the core. Jawaharlal Nehru freedom fighter and a stalwart of our freedom struggle before he became India's first Prime Minister- during his travels, was hosted by him at his bungalow in Sylhet. This raised the eyebrows of many British superiors. After the Chinese incursion in 1962, it is reported that Nehru, as PM, visited Guwahati, held a meeting, and wanted officers to speak frankly about the NEFA debacle and the way forward for Assam and India. Vaghaiwala is reported to have said in the meeting, "I admired three things in my life. The lofty Himalayas, majestic and unconquerable;

Rabindranath Tagore, who got the Nobel Prize for literature, and Jawaharlal Nehru, the inveterate freedom fighter who got us Independence and then sadly remarked that two in his list, the Himalayas and Nehru were off and only Rabindranath Tagore remained! The frank outburst reportedly took place when high-ranking political leaders and officials were all present. It used to be the hushed talk in official circles in Guwahati and Shillong. This bold and frank outburst of Vaighawala in the presence of a man of the stature of Nehru, who was venerated by almost all, was the subject of many a hushed conversation in official circles. It appears Vaghaiwala also said quite a lot of frank and nasty things about the poor state of the preparedness of the Army and the collapse of morale, but this need checking up.

I called on Vaghaiwala, who said that South Indians are brainy and good at mathematics and gave me a book called "Man the Unknown" to read. He once took me to the Kokrajhar Sub-Division in Goalpara District, where E.S. Parthasarathy was SDO. We reached Kokrajhar, and the Commissioner inspected the office. In the afternoon, Vaghaiwala proceeded to Dhubri and said that he would pick me up on his return from Kokrajhar to Guwahati the next day. That evening, I was requested to be the Chief Guest for a football match. At the introduction of players, there were many preceding initials, such as KL, RN, etc., before the names. I noticed that only two names got repeated over and again. One was Brahma, and another was Basumatary. All players were either a Brahma or a Basumatary, two common titles of the Bodo Kacharis. It reminded me of the Naidu's hockey team at Wardlaw High School, Bellary. Later, Vaghaiwala, on his request, was transferred to Bombay as Chairman of the Forward Markets Commission. I helped him by packing his goods and sending them by train. He wrote me a lovely letter, expressing his gratitude most courteously.

THE DC's OFFICE

Having seen many impressive Collector's offices and bungalows in Bellary, Hyderabad, and Guntur, the D.C.s office in Guwahati was a big disappointment. It did not have any spacious compound and was adjoining the road. It was not properly maintained, did not have a distinctive personality, and worse, it was dirty with red stains of pan spitting, disfiguring the walls. The redeeming feature was its location on the bank of the Brahmaputra River, facing a small, beautiful, verdant island with a rock temple called Umananda. It was a real climb-down from my imagination of the D.C.s office and a comparison with D.C. offices elsewhere in India. As I had already exercised the magisterial powers of the first class, during my tenure of office in A.P. as Deputy Collector, I commenced working as a Magistrate. I was provided with a Peshkar (court clerk). He is an Assamese Muslim, Rehman, fair in complexion and well-dressed. He would take much interest in grooming his hair, powdering his face, and making liberal use of perfumes. The office corridors and courtroom could smell his approaching presence. He was very helpful in teaching me rudimentary. Assamese also fixed up a lady teacher for Assamese. There was very little litigation in Assam except for minor land disputes of the nature of trespass, encroachment, and thefts. There was a lawyer or pleader called Digambar Kalita, who knew little of the law but would endlessly cross-examine and submit vociferous arguments to impress his clients. During cross-examination, he asked the opposite party about the land located 'to the north of the plot' and to its north, and it went on and on ad nauseum. I got annoyed and could stop him only by saying that we had gone so far north that we had already reached the Himalayas! And that he must confine to issues of ownership or trespass and the point of law, if any! The other lawyers in the court were happy that for once Kalita was dumbfounded, Digambar, and under control.

THE AP CONNECT

A battalion of the A.P. Special Police commanded by S. Ranganathan was posted near Guwahati. It was to strengthen Assam's efforts and that of GOI to combat the then-serious Naga Insurgency. The Nagas demanded total independence from Indian rule. Strangely, they had no complaints about remaining part of British India. He arranged for a young cook called Nagaraj, a camp follower, to work for me. He was a good cook, and I started getting homely food at Guwahati and later at Goalpara, Mizo Hills, and Sibsagar districts. He later married a Mizo girl and started a Hotel at Aizawl, which was doing well. While at Guwahati, I met Captain GP Rao in the Army Ordnance Corps (AOC) who was posted at Narangi near Guwahati. He used to invite me to the AOC mess. Sometime later, he wrote the UPSC competitive examination for army officers and was selected to join the IAS and turned out to be a fine officer who kept up the high standards of the service.

ANDHRA CULTURAL ASSOCIATION

One of the cinema halls in Guwahati used to exhibit Telugu films on Sundays, which attracted many Telugu-speaking people among the general populace and the Army units stationed in and around Guwahati. The cinemas enabled me to make friends with many Telugus, working in Indian Oil Corporation, All India Radio, Guwahati University, Railways, and other Central Government Offices and banks. They suggested that I take the lead in forming an Andhra Cultural Association at Guwahati and become the General Secretary. C.S. Nayudu, a judge of the Assam High Court, became the President of the Andhra Cultural Association, Guwahati, which used to host lectures, music, and literary meets.

As part of training, I went to Shillong and called on Chief Secretary A N Kidwai, ICS (he was Chief Secretary for Assam for 12 years), Deputy Secretary of Political, Home, and GAD: MC Narasimhan and Krishnamurthy, Secretary to the Governor. The Chief Secretary received me cordially, enquired about my background, and was surprised to know that I had undergone a year's formal training as a Probationary Deputy Collector, also worked as an SDO. He said that there was a need for a formal training program for IAS probationers in Assam and asked me whether I could attempt to prepare a training manual. I told him that I was new to Assam and its administration and had yet to experience the training of IAS officers. The C.S. suggested that after some experience in Assam, I could attempt to draft a training manual. I prepared such a manual much later, which was approved and heralded the formal training program for IAS Officers in Assam.

D. SANJIVAYYA, PRESIDENT OF INDIAN NATIONAL CONGRESS VISITS GUWAHATI

The President of the Indian National Congress, D. Sanjeevayya, came to Guwahati in 1963-64. I had known him in A.P. earlier as a Minister and as Chief Minister. GVG Krishnamurthy, my former law teacher at Delhi, had told Sanjeevayya that I was posted as Assistant Commissioner at Guwahati. When D. Sanjeevayya came to Guwahati and sent word to meet him at the Circuit House, I met him and invited him for tea at my house with a few friends from the Andhra Cultural Association. Sanjeevayya accepted my invitation and came home for tea. Sanjeevayya had a melodious voice and entertained us by reciting a few Telugu poems. The news that the President of the INC had gone over to the bachelor A.C.'s residence for tea spread like wildfire among Assam politicians. Senior Ministers and aspirants for Congress tickets for contesting in the elections began making inquiries about me and contacting me. I told those who contacted me that I had only a nodding acquaintance with the President and was too small a fry to take up any matter with the dignitary.

I informed Sanjeevayya that there were many pockets of Telugu-speaking workers in some tea gardens, Railway Station colonies like Bongaigaon, and industrial towns like Digbol, Tinsukia, Namrup, etc. It would help if children were provided with facilities for study in Telugu and Assamese, at least up to the primary stage. Perhaps he mentioned this to

Deba Kantha Barua, the then Education Minister of Assam, who wanted me to meet him in this connection. I met him when he surprisingly welcomed me in Telugu. He said that he was deputed to Andhra Pradesh during the earlier general elections and was aware of the social and caste structure in the state. He said that he would help set up Telugu teaching facilities at the primary stage in some places. The problem would be to get teachers and reading material. D.K. Barua was the person who, as President of INC, had said, "Indira is India."

Prime Minister Nehru, in a radio broadcast in 1962 after the China debacle, said, "My heart goes out to the people of Assam. "The press and people wrongly interpreted this. To assuage the feelings of Assam, Nehru sent Ms. Indira Gandhi, who visited Guwahati and Bomdila in the rainy season in 1963 to reassure the tribals and people of NEFA about the Government of India's firm commitment and support to them. As there was heavy rainfall in Bomdila with the attendant risks of traveling by helicopter, the Assam Government enquired the D.C. of Bomdilla regarding the desirability of travel in such weather and the dress Indira Gandhi should carry with her for the tour. The D.C Bomdila sent a cryptic wireless message read, "Raining Heavily. Helipad is a quagmire. Advice: bring heavy Gumboots". Very practical advice indeed!

I happened to see a somewhat similar message later in the D.C.s office at Guwahati. John Kenneth Galbraith, a celebrated economist and Ambassador of the U.S. to India, was planning to visit Manas Game Sanctuary in Kamrup district (famed for rhinos, wild buffalo, and tigers.) to indulge himself with some trout fishing upstream of Manas River. His message for help said, "I am very tall (over 7 Feet) and have learned to bend at the door before entering any room, but I have not yet learned to sleep in a bed shorter than me. I would be thankful if a long bed or at least an improvised bed can be provided for me at Manas sanctuary so that I can have a peaceful and restful night there". The district administration, resilient as it was, acceded to that request with a bamboo hut, full-length bed, mosquito net, and similar requests.

I spent my time in the district visiting different historic or picturesque places, and offices and meeting officials to learn about the way of life of local communities. I visited Sualkuchi, which is famous for its silk industry, and Pao Mecca (Quarter Mecca), a religious shrine at Hajo.

FAMILY PLANNING WORK

The Minister of State for Family Planning and Welfare from the Government of India, Dr. S.Chandrasekar, visited Guwahati to address family planning doctors and workers. The Andhra Cultural Association gave a dinner for him, during which he explained the need for family planning and that the slogan of three children for a family must move towards "We Two—Our Two" and "Hum do aur Hamare do."

I was invited by SDO Barpeta to visit the Satra of Shankar Deva, the famous philosopher and founder of the Bhakti Cult in Barpeta, Assam. He and his disciples were responsible for spreading the Vaishnava cult all over Assam, particularly on Majuli Island (one of the largest riverine islands in the world) in the Brahmaputra River. There was no idol for worship at the Satra, but Bhagavath Kirtans (songs) from the Bhagavatham were sung.

The SDO was organizing a family planning meeting and was frantically searching for role model speakers with a small number of children as Guests of Honour. He wanted me to attend the meeting and speak, which was expected to recommend vasectomy operations for men. The Barpeta subdivision, even at that time, had a large, not preponderant, Muslim population who were not in favour of family planning of any kind for doctrinal reasons. Try as he did, it was becoming well-nigh impossible to get a role model who was practicing family planning. Most of the VIPs at Barpeta and likely speakers had more than 5 or 6 children. I was in a dilemma whether to attend the meeting or not as I was a bachelor and there was a probability that in the absence of speakers, I would be asked after my talk to volunteer for a vasectomy operation!

The Government of Assam wanted to streamline the working of the Animal Husbandry Department, whose headquarters was in Guwahati. Dr. C.Krishna Rao, an eminent Veterinarian from A.P. who had worked at the National Level at Izzat nagar, was taken on deputation as Director of Animal Husbandry. He was staying with his family in a bungalow in the veterinary compound at Guwahati. I used to visit him. I was often invited for a meal at their place, and they told me that there was much work to be done in Assam by the department to improve breeding practices, increase the yield of cows and buffaloes, and upgrade the goats and sheep. Due to heavy rainfall in Assam, the minerals are washed off the soil, and hence, cattle and goats are stunted and appear much smaller than in the rest of the country. I learned some facts about dairying, animal husbandry, and its role in the agricultural economy.

LOVE'S LABOUR LOST

I had a lot of leisure on my hands and wanted to write a book on district administration. There were many bachelor lecturers from all parts of the country at Guwahati University. I used to attend their evening get-togethers and college functions. I met Prof. V Venkat Rao, an elderly bachelor who was teaching political science at Guwahati University. He welcomed the idea and suggested the books that I should read and the chapter headings. I prepared a summary of about 60 – 70 pages so that he could clear it and put it up to the university for permission to enrol as a part-time Ph.D. student. Unfortunately, Guwahati University did not consider my LLB as a Postgraduate qualification and treated it as one more graduation and turned down the proposal. I felt downcast but hoped that my efforts would prove useful on a future date. A book on District Administration has since been printed.

SURVEY CAMP

As part of our in-service training, all six IAS officers of Assam of my batch (1962) attended the Survey and Settlement training at Jalukbari near Guwahati University. This training was considered essential as D.C.s had to deal with land measurement, acquisition, land disputes, and the like, besides updating the changes in ownership. A young IAS aspirant from Assam, Madan Bezbaruah, approached me to brief him on the IAS interviews by holding a mock interview. All six of our batch constituted a "Mock Interview Board" and grilled him quite a lot. He cleared the IAS in his first attempt, which carried good press coverage in Assam. We had overnight turned IAS guides! The reputation stuck, and I am even now, after 62 years of service, chairing mock interviews in Hyderabad and elsewhere. The more things change, the more they remain the same!

DIPHU INCIDENT

I suddenly got a phone call from the Chief Secretary that I should proceed immediately to Diphu in Mikir Hills to assist Deputy Commissioner S. C. Bhattacharya, who had to tackle an important and urgent law and order problem but was down with dysentery. There was a need for a young officer to assist him and operate the RBI Treasury chest. I went by train to Diphu and called on the D.C., who was lying in bed in his Bungalow. He told me that some tribals had assaulted and killed a couple of encroachers from the Nowgong district, who had occupied some tribal land in Mikir Hills near the Kopili River. D.C., who was sick, sent a message to the local army authorities, requesting them to depute a 'battalion' to control the situation. As the Hill districts of Assam were disturbed, the army authorities promptly responded by sending two army Majors to visit Diphu, meet D.C. and the scene of occurrence, and assess the situation before deciding on the force to be sent.

After seeing D.C.'s wireless message to the army authorities, I realized the faux pas of D.C. calling for the army 'battalion' to tackle a situation that, at best, called for a section or platoon of the armed police and not the army.

Meanwhile, the Chief Secretary advised S.N.Barkataki, Commissioner of Hills Division, to rush to Diphu and restore normalcy. The Commissioner asked me to visit the site. Some tribals had already assembled there. The Commissioner, an experienced officer who had worked in Tribal areas, brought with him a Carton of Rum bottles. He opened a couple of bottles and invited the tribal elders who had assembled to meet him and join in a rum session for talks by opening a Rum bottle and inviting them. It was just before noon. After a few rounds of rum and friendly banter, the environment suddenly changed from a surcharged air of tension, revenge, and anger to one of mirth, joy, and happiness. Rum had done a miracle. After some bonhomie, the tribals promised not to attack and kill encroachers and instead report to the police or the local SDC. A few more bottles were handed over to the Tribal Chiefs to seal the oral treaty with a liquid treat! The law-and-order problem was solved satisfactorily. We must learn to understand and deal with the tribals in their tribal way of life to ensure peace.

During this brief but eventful encounter with tribal life in Assam, I recall an instance that showed their unique sense of humour. A bus service was recently introduced from Nowgong in the plains to Diphu, the district Headquarters of the Mikir Hills district. The tribals were unhappy that they had to purchase tickets to board the bus. Their argument was simple. As the bus, in any case, was going nearly empty that way, and there were ample empty seats, what was the harm or difficulty in giving a free lift to persons who wished to travel and get down en route? This is probably the way in which people think or expect of from government facilities and properties.

DARRANGA MELA

During my tenure as Assistant Commissioner at Guwahati, there was a young EAC (Extra Assistant Commissioner) called Pratul Sarma at Guwahati who was quite an authority on Assamese literature and used to write poetry. We became good friends, and he translated a couple of my poems from Telugu to Assamese and Bengali and published them in Guwahati and Kolkata.

We spent time learning about the various tourist spots in the District. On one weekend, a group of EACs led by Pratul Sarma and I visited the Daranga Mela near the Bhutan border. Bhutanese would come to sell Oranges, liquor, and other fruits and purchase clothes, spices, trinkets, and beads from the Mela. I learned the various types of home-brewed liquor in the Northeast, like Laopani, Madhu, Pacchwai, Rice beer, Bhutanese liquor, and IMFL, etc.

A CAR OR A BUS?

M.M.Chowdary was the Revenue Minister of Assam (he later became Chief Minister). He was very popular in the Barpeta area. When he was traveling by car, many passers-by on the road would recognize him and raise their umbrellas. He would stop the car and give them a lift. This would go to such an extent that very soon, the backseat of the car would get filled up and then the front seat of the car also filled up, almost pushing the driver out of the car. At one stage, it appears that the driver was so discomfited that he stopped the car and said that he was unable to drive and would not drive in a squeezed position with the danger of being pushed out of the car or the car crashed. When the Minister persuaded him to drive on, the driver is reported to have said: "Sir, a car will not su□ce. I suggest that 'we buy a bus' so that when an umbrella is lifted, we can stop and accommodate all persons on the way". I do not know if any further action was taken on his suggestion.

My tenure as Assistant Commissioner was ending, and I was expecting orders of transfer to a substantive post. I was periodically told that I would be posted either as Sub Divisional Officer Goalpara or as Under Secretary in the Political Department (Cabinet Cell). The wheels of administration move slowly, and in Assam, they seem to move even more slowly. The wait for the actual posting orders took some two months to materialize. Finally, I was asked to take over as SDO Goalpara.

Meanwhile, my successor, K.Sreedhar Rao (1963), joined as incoming A.C. He was staying at the Railway Colony in Maligaon with his elder sister, who was married to a senior Railway officer. He was fond of Tennis and Western Music. He later married the granddaughter of V.V Giri, who was then Vice President of India and later President of India. He would come to my house in the morning, and we would go together to the DC office and come home together for lunch at my place.

Sreedhar was a serious type, well-read, and exceptionally good at English. Having been brought up in a highly educated and sophisticated family, he was aghast at the leisurely and lackadaisical pace of work in Assam. I told him that in Assam, the byword was "Lahe -Lahe" or slowly and slowly. I told him that we have to adjust to the work culture shock, take things calmly, and concentrate on only relevant and important issues. We need not hurry or worry, but we need to adapt better to the environment and do our best under the circumstances.

Having got his posting orders, Sreedhar walked into my office and joined as the AC. He was very formally dressed despite the humid and steamy weather in Guwahati. He was keen on calling on the DC at his Bungalow and wanted me to introduce him to D.C, a promoted IAS Officer Kusum Kumar Phukan. We went to the DC bungalow, and the peon ushered us into the DC chamber. There were some visitors already either sitting or standing in the room waiting to obtain DC's signature. The peon asked two of them to get up to make way for us. We sat down. The DC came dressed in a lungi and a torn banian. He apologized for his dress and said that he was having heat boils on his bottom. He sat down on a cushioned chair while the peon brought a tray full of tea. There was a mad rush for the tea from the Sadar SDO Taimur, who wanted the DC to sign some papers. Tea was served in chipped or broken cups. The peon, recognizing us as Assistant Commissioners, gave us good cups and poured the tea. The teacups did not have any saucers! The visitors left as soon as the tea was finished, and the DC signed papers.

Sreedhar did not touch his cup in accordance with his notions of etiquette and propriety, and he was probably awaiting a signal from the DC to ask us to take tea. I nudged him strongly with my elbow on his ribs and said in a low tone that he better take tea, or it would get cold, or someone else may grab it. Sridhar reluctantly took the tea and asked D.C. about his training program. The DC, who was never known to be affected by anything, said that he would move the High Court to confer III Class magisterial powers for Sreedhar as the judiciary was separated from the executive branch in the Kamrup District, but in the meantime, he should get familiar with the work of executive magistracy. He asked Sreedhar to seek guidance from me and said that he would learn to work on the job and not be unduly worried about the formal training program. We came out of the DC's bungalow. On the way, Sridhar burst out in exasperation and bemoaned that his imagination and dreams about the expected training in district administration had evaporated into thin air. I advised him not to feel disheartened and reminded him that his role was "to keep his eyes open and ears alert," which is the true responsibility of the SDO or DC. Sridhar merely nodded and said that in case he had any doubts or questions, he would ask me.

The Handiqui Women's College at Guwahati used to celebrate Saraswati Puja and Durga Puja. When Sridhar and I were returning from the office to my bungalow, the girls invited us to witness the Puja and receive Prasad. When they learned that we were both IAS Officers, they requested me to give a lecture on preparation for the IAS examinations, which I did. I am not aware of the results.

RAIL CUM ROAD BRIDGE AT GUWAHATI

Till 1962, there was no road or rail bridge over the river Brahmaputra. Railway coaches and wagons would be transported from the northern river ghat on large steamer launches with rails to the southern side of the river and vice versa. After the Rail-cum-Road bridge was constructed, movement by rail and road across the river became easier and faster. Assam now has three large bridges across the river at different places, making travel between the southern and northern banks of the river faster and safer.

RIVER TRANSPORT

Assam depended on the transport of heavy goods like steel, cement, building materials, and salt from Hooghly to Assam by 2500 to 3000 tons DWT capacity steamers of the RSN Company via the sea and river route in East Pakistan to Dhubri, Goalpara, Guwahati, Neamatighat and other locations along the river Brahmaputra till Dibrugarh. The river transport cost was much lower than by rail or road; but slower. However, navigation in the Brahmaputra River, particularly during the summer season, posed problems due to the formation of 'chars' or deposits of river sand, much like small islands. The problem of navigation was ascribed to the after-effects of the great earthquake of 1950 in the Himalayan sub-ranges. A big landslide blocked the Subansiri River overnight and created a dam. When the dam burst under the pressure of the water, it swept a significant amount of debris into the Brahmaputra along with the floodwaters. The debris slowly makes its way through the river from Dibrugarh to Guwahati and then to the Bay of Bengal. Assam will have to bide time for nature's sweeping but slow clearance – and self-renewal.

13

Sub-Divisional Officer, Goalpara (August 1964 – April 1966)

I was posted as a Sub-Divisional Officer at Goalpara, a subdivision of Goalpara District on the southern bank of the River Brahmaputra. A new bungalow for the SDO was constructed atop a small hillock on the Agia- Goalpara Road on which the Additional S.P.'s residence was also located. The old bungalow for the SDO, atop a hill opposite SDO's office, had been abandoned. A steep jeep track led up the hill to the said bungalow. SDOs who wanted to be left alone used to reside there. Any petitioner who wanted to meet or give a representation to the SDO before or after office had to tread uphill on foot, an exhausting process by itself. The exertion would make the petitioner breathless, and he would merely hand over the petition and quickly be on the way back!

I met all the officers and staff of the SDO's office who briefed me on the nature of Court and Revenue work and pressing problems that required my attention. There were three Extra Assistant Commissioners (EACs) of the State Civil Service, namely H N Gogoi, L K Baruah, and N.N. Baruah. An elderly Additional S.P. rank officer, C Bargohain, was the SDPO. The Superintending Engineer was Bhattacharya (a widower) with a 10-year-old son. A brilliant Engineer, he was interested in Rural Development Works: the Executive Engineer, Irrigation Dept., B.C.Khataniar was a very competent, friendly, and hospitable person. The Divisional Forest Officer Bhowmick was a sincere officer, relatively young, and a good friend.

The main tasks were updating land records, processing land acquisition proposals and land assignments, collecting land revenue and work related to courts, law and order, procurement of paddy, maintenance of civil supplies, and essential commodities. Many items like wheat, sugar, fruits, medicines, corrugated iron sheets, which served as roofing material used in the State, cement, steel, and even several articles of daily use had to be transported into Assam as none of them were at that time produced within the State.

There was a woeful inadequacy of updated manuals, revenue maps, codified instructions, rules, and regulations for land records and revenue administration. This was in sharp contrast to the detailed manuals on every aspect of district administration in Andhra Pradesh. I was accustomed to the fixation of targets, reviews, and collections of almost 100% of revenues while serving in the state of A.P., whereas, in Assam, there was inadequate attention paid to this work.

The village revenue maps and records of Mauzas, Taluks, and Districts were generally not readily available and quite outdated. Despite such shortcomings, the district administration was run by the DCs, SDOs, and EACs with reasonable efficiency by exercising powers vested in them by law based on sound principles of good governance, precedents, and orders. Though revenue levies were not high, the collections were low due to apathy in the collection and poor supervision.

There was very little crime in the Subdivision; people had more than adequate food and fish to eat, but unemployment was rising its head. There was hardly any industrial activity except for a couple of tea gardens and rice and flour mills. Food items were quite inexpensive, such as fruits and vegetables that were grown locally. A big basket of oranges from Garo Hills cost just two rupees. With such a situation of the abundance of all essential food items, a chicken costing less than a rupee and 10 eggs for a rupee, my cook took upon himself, with missionary zeal, the task of ensuring that his lord and master were well-fed every day, specializing in a variety of non-vegetarian delicacies.

ESTRANGED RELATIONS WITH THE LOCAL MLA

Even when I was awaiting my posting orders, some of my colleagues had warned me of the troublesome character of the local MLA at Goalpara, Khagendranath Nath, a bachelor who espoused the cause of illegal Bengali Muslim immigrants from the then East Pakistan into Goalpara District, on the grounds of their poverty and land hunger but more so because they constituted his Vote Bank. The illegal influx of East Pakistan immigrants was assuming alarming proportions, leading to law-and-order problems with serious demographic and economic implications. These illegal immigrants constituted a long-term threat to the security and integrity not only of the State of Assam but the entire strategic Northeast of India. Moreover, with political support from local politicians such as Khagen

Nath, they could get themselves enrolled in the electoral rolls, obtain ration cards, and determine the outcome of elections at all levels. At the time of independence, Assam had about 15% Muslim population, and this had ballooned to over 25% during the 1950s, and at present, it is estimated to exceed 34%. Informed opinion is of the view that such a large population may create serious internal and external security problems in a strategically located region. This is the reason why the late CDS Gen Bipin Rawat talked about a two-and-a-half-front war that India has to face. Unfortunately, narrow electoral consideration had blinded many politicians of the ilk of Khagen Nath to much larger and very serious repercussions on local and national issues.

We launched vigorous eviction campaigns against illegal immigrants who had encroached on large areas of government land, followed by deportation efforts. These actions yielded positive results, which sparked the ire of the MLA, who found the SDO, another bachelor, a hard nut to crack. He was used to summoning EACs and even SDOs to meet him at his residence to discuss matters and to impress his followers about his influence with the Government officials. My officers were advised not to meet him except in the office. He invited me to his house for tea, which I politely refused. He invited me once again for lunch with a visiting VIP at his residence, where villagers would meet him and me to give representations. I said that I was always willing to hear all grievances of the petitioners at my office or my bungalow office and did not need any mediator or spokesperson. He was peeved and complained to several Ministers about my strong stance and that I was an obdurate young bachelor officer.

On one occasion, Chief Minister BP Chaliha, a fine gentleman imbued with Gandhian ideals, and Finance Minister Fakhruddin Ali Ahmed, who became the President of India, visited Goalpara on official engagements that I attended. They were invited for lunch by the MLA. I was also invited but did not attend. The MLA appears to have complained about my non-cooperation in eviction matters and that I did not participate in his lunch despite the invitation. The CM and Minister probably guessed the reasons for my absence. Later on, both the F.M. and CM called me to the Circuit house to discuss some matters and, in passing, said that they missed me at lunch. I explained to them that I was following the convention of the Civil Service not to accept hospitality from persons who may have official dealings. Both the ministers appreciated the point. The CM changed the subject and said that he was happy with my sensitive handling of the clashes between the refugees from East Pakistan, local inhabitants, and some immigrants with prompt action and redressal of their grievances.

He enquired from me about my title of Naidu, which I explained was derived from the word Nayakudu or Leader cum soldier. "Naidu" is also a title given to the village head in Andhra Pradesh and South India, which means Soldier, Farmer-Protector. He asked whether I was related to the famous Strongman called Kodi Ramamurthy Naidu, who visited Assam when CM was young and gave many shows of strength. I told him that I was not related to him.

ILLEGAL IMMIGRATION – A CONTINUING PROBLEM

Goalpara district and, in particular, Dhubri and South Salmara had, a problem of uncontrolled, illegal immigration by land-hungry Muslim Families from the then East Pakistan. The Bengali Muslim immigrants who remained in India, even after Partition, heartily welcomed the new immigrants as their brethren. In fact, given their common ethnicity, language, and physical appearance, it was very difficult to distinguish the earlier immigrants from the recent immigrants. Every immigrant would claim that the new arrivals were their relatives who had come to join them a little later. The immigrants were hard-working and good cultivators of paddy and Jute or Hemp. The Assamese villagers found them a cheap and easy source of labour and were not aware of the implications of harbouring them on the economy and future demography of the state and their sharing of wealth. District officials had reported to the Government about this alarming trend of illegal immigration into Assam and its future impact on demographic trends and economic and electoral implications.

While controls against immigration at Land borders worked fairly well, the immigrants came mostly by boat through the river Brahmaputra and first set foot in the big and small Chars (River Islands) before moving to other adjacent land areas. There was hardly any organized and determined effort by the government to stop it. The only resistance encountered was when the immigrants tried to enter or encroach lands in tribal villages of the Bodo Kacharis or Rabhas or the forest areas.

Sporadic evictions of encroachers from East Pakistan and their deportation took place. Police and Revenue authorities tended to turn a blind eye to this growing problem despite district authorities regularly reporting the nature and implications of such illegal immigration. There was resounding silence and inaction on the part of the Government. The Government issued no clear instructions on the policy to be followed and determined action to be taken. Politics and policies seemed to be one of "'willing to strike but not to hurt."

INFLUX OF REFUGEES FROM EAST PAKISTAN

Despite the Nehru-Liaqat agreement on the protection of minorities in their respective countries, the minorities in East Pakistan, mainly Hindus, were periodically subjected to large-scale oppression and deportation. Assam had to deal with the regular large-scale influx of refugees who were accommodated in makeshift, temporary Refugee camps constructed with locally available materials such as bamboo. It was indeed a sad chapter in the history of our subcontinent that Pakistan, influenced by religious considerations, inflicted inhuman atrocities on its minorities, reducing their number to minuscule proportions and forcing them to flee their country while constantly falsely and maliciously complaining about the ill-treatment of minorities in India.

A Refugee camp was set up at Harimura near Dalgoma village in the Goalpara subdivision. There were intermittent troubles between Refugees and earlier Muslim immigrants who were settlers from East Pakistan and with the local people. My batch mate, Terence Cajee, was posted as Camp in charge of this particular camp. I went to meet him. He had a tale of woe. He was from the cool climes of Shillong and did not speak Assamese or Bengali. He had found it difficult to manage in the humid and steamy environment at Harimura and was desperately seeking a transfer to Shillong.

In October 1964, refugees of the Harimura camp assaulted some Muslim villagers who had come to the Haat (Bazaar) from three other villages nearby. Frustrated and angry refugees intimidated and forcibly took away rice and dal brought for sale to the market. The local police informed the Additional SP and me. I sent the Additional SP in advance and visited the place a little later. I assured the local people that culprits would be prosecuted, and normalcy would be restored soon. A Local Peace Committee was formed. I received a phone call from the Chief Minister. As the voice was inaudible, I told him that I would call him after I reached Goalpara. I did so, and he advised me to keep a close watch and quickly restore normalcy.

The next day, the SP B.S.Babbar and ADC, UC Sarania from Dhubri, came to study the situation. The DC Hem Borah also came the following day. However, by then, the situation had been brought under control as we had arrested some refugees and assuaged the feelings of the Muslims. Two days later, the IG of Police, Home Minister, and R N Brahma, Minister for Relief and Rehabilitation, visited and were satisfied with the arrangements made and measures taken to ensure that there would be no recurrence of such incidents.

I had to go home urgently on a month's leave as my younger sister fell sick and had to be taken to Madras for treatment. A Dakota flight carrying tea chests used to operate from Gauripur near Dhubri to Calcutta. It could accommodate 4 or 5 passengers, but there was no set schedule. I took one of these flights and managed to save a lot of time compared to traveling by train.

SURPRISE VISITOR

One day, when I was in the office, my peon told me that a lady who came in a big car wanted to meet me. I asked him to let her in. She pleasantly greeted me in Telugu with a Namaskar. She introduced herself as Rani Manjula Devi of Sidli Estate in the Kokrajhar subdivision. She said that she was from the Rajah of Pithapuram family in Andhra Pradesh and was married to the Rajah of Sidli. She had heard from S.D.O Kokrajhar, Parthasarathy, that a Telugu IAS Officer was posted at Goalpara and had come to see me and that she had no requests to make. She said that in case I visit Sidli, she would be happy to host me. It struck me that the world is a small place. People want to meet and talk in their native language and get to know one another.

THE REFUGEE EXODUS FROM EAST PAKISTAN

In 1964, there was a sudden large influx of Hindu Hajong tribal refugees from East Pakistan coming into Assam through the Garo hills. The BSF outpost in Garo Hills informed us that the fleeing refugees had told them that the Government of East Pakistan was deliberately driving out Hindus and Tribals from many areas to Assam. The trickle of refugees was expected to become an exodus. The Chief Secretary called and advised me to visit the Border Outpost in Garo Hills, assess the situation, and report to him. I did so and realized that there would be a flood of refugees. It was clear that Assam would have to be prepared to handle a large number of refugees at short notice. There would be great difficulty in setting up refugee camps and giving rations in Garo Hills, involving difficult logistics and transportation problems in hilly terrain. Moreover, it could create tension with the Garos.

After hearing from me, the CS asked me to go ahead with transporting the refugees from Garo Hills and identify suitable areas in Goalpara Sub-division where temporary accommodation could be set up. The Government would issue orders and authorize expenditures to that effect. A meeting with concerned heads of departments and officers was held in the Secretariat at Shillong, which expedited sanction orders.

MATIA REFUGEE CAMP – THE LARGEST IN INDIA

When I saw the sad state of fear-stricken, ill-clad, and hungry mothers and children clutching one another's hands carrying what all they could carry in a small bundle of clothes and the forlorn looks of the menfolk, I realized the enormity of the tragedy that cruel fate had indeed lashed on the Hajongs and other tribes of East Pakistan. They had committed no crimes except that they were Hindus unwelcome in a Muslim-majority state. Leaving their hearths and homes, they had to eke out and seek their unknown future in an unfamiliar land. It was a pathetic and heart-wrenching scene. Happy and contented families had overnight become helpless, forlorn people in search of a livelihood. Only faith that fate would be kind sustained them. The enormity of the tragedy dawned on the Government, and alternative rehabilitation avenues were searched. They ranged from shifting to less populated districts in Assam to employment in the tea gardens or being sent to Arunachal Pradesh. It was not clear whether they would be welcomed or shunned. It was clear that it would add to the tensions of faith, religion, ethnicity, language, and assimilation. A lot of empathy, sympathy, and kindness was needed to find a solution.

The trickle of refugees from East Pakistan soon became a torrent, posing many problems. We had to handle emergencies with inadequate notice and resources. We had to select sites hastily, provide transportation, collect construction materials and essential commodities, including rations, and make administrative arrangements. We shifted more than one lakh refugee trucks from Garo Hills to the Matia area near an abandoned Second World War airfield, where land was available. It became the largest refugee camp in India at that time. We later reorganized it into as many as 10 smaller camps, each in charge of a Camp Officer and a Central Camp with an Administrative officer who looked after Rations, Medical supplies, firewood, and coordinated the work.

It was a colossal task to look after some 20,000 families for an indefinite period. All the officers and staff at the Sub-Divisional and district level worked with great vigour and accomplished the job of providing accommodation, arranging supplies, and medical care in record time. There were no untoward incidents as we had lodged them in different camps, each of which was under the control of a camp officer. We also built storage for essential commodities and made arrangements for fuel for cooking purposes to prevent deforestation. A temporary camp hospital and dispensary were arranged. Young children were supplied with nutritious supplements and medical attention. Rudimentary arrangements were made to teach the Three R's of Reading, Writing, and Recitation.

Rup Nath Brahma was the Minister for Relief and Rehabilitation, while B S Sarao was the Secretary of Relief and Rehabilitation. R N Brahma wanted to address the refugees and exhort them to maintain peace and goodwill in the new place. We organized a meeting that was attended by over 30,000 refugees who had nothing else to do and some press representatives. The Minister was thrilled, as he had never seen or addressed such a large gathering. After the meeting, he wanted me to issue a press release about it. I asked the Sub-Divisional Public Relations Officer, Rabha, to prepare a draft and show it to the Minister. He did so, but the Minister was not satisfied and wanted that I should see and clear the draft before it was sent to the press. I found the draft quite good but only made a small change in the title of the press release. Instead, the "Minister addressed a large gathering of refugees." I corrected it to read, "Minister addressed a Mammoth Meeting at Matia." The Minister was happy because the sentence used an alliteration of words with the letter "M" and made a good headline. He was so fascinated that he hummed the sentence all along in his car. He called the PRO and told him that he must learn to draft the Minister's Press Notes from his own - Little did the Minister know that I had only touched up the draft - Just a matter of belief that a second look by a senior is better. The Minister had become a bureaucrat.

On yet another occasion, Sarao, Secretary (Relief & Rehabilitation), asked me to draft a letter from the Minister, Brahma, to Thyagi, Minister of Relief and Rehabilitation in the Indian Government. I did so and showed it to the Minister. He asked me whether I had shown it to the secretary. I said that I had not done so. I was asked to show it to the secretary. The draft began by saying, "Minister may please consider." The secretary altered the draft by replacing "please" with "kindly," and this change was approved. This illustrates how officials often focus on minor details instead of addressing the main issues. But the Minister said that two persons approving meant that no mistakes were made. He then added that he had been Minister for nearly three decades under different regimes, and his success and longevity as Minister was due to his following the process of not signing a note unless the secretary of the Department had seen it! He said that longevity in office is secured by signing on the dotted line. Civil Service officers, no wonder, spend a lot of time on such trivialities.

B S Sarao, Secretary R&R, used to frequently come to Goalpara to oversee the refugee camp work and sort out issues. He once asked me about the route from Dalgoma to Tura, the headquarters of Garo Hills District. As I had travelled on the route, I reeled off from memory the names of villages on the route, i.e., Dalgoma– Dudhnoi – Dambu – Dainadubi – Dalu- Dawki. He was fascinated that all the names of villages on the route started with the word "D" and sounded quite musical. He would repeat the sequence whenever there was talk of Matia refugees or the way from Matia to Garo Hills.

DHAMAR FARM

I submitted a proposal to Government to set up an agricultural farm to settle some Hajong refugees at an unused village grazing reserve in Dhamar, near Lakhipur. There was a small local river that had split into two streams– one had dried up (mora) and one live (Jia) was flowing with some water. I consulted the Superintending and Executive Engineers, Agricultural officers, and experts, who advised me that it would be possible to completely block and close the nearly dead stream and deepen the channel of the live stream. This would release land and also provide adequate water for cultivation. I had read a book about Taiwan, where they had trained fast-flowing small rivers to flow only along the main channel by a clever combination of driving bamboo spikes across the streams they wished to close. If the bamboo spikes are driven at a 45° angle against the flow of water, sand or debris would quickly pile up and choke the flow of water. The remaining stream could be diverted in the desired direction. If necessary, 4 or 5 such barriers called baffles could be added to speed up the process and prevent the flow of water. Such baffles would also hold back the water hyacinth weed, which was becoming a menace by choking the water flow by its spreading root system. Agricultural experts advised us that the water hyacinth could be removed, dried, and used as either fertilizers or as mulching material between the furrows to prevent any weeds from sprouting. We received support for our proposal from the Planning Commission, Union Government in the R&R Ministry, Irrigation and Embankment Divisions of the P.W.D., and excellent advice, cooperation, and coordination from the Agricultural Department and the Sub-Divisional Agricultural Officer.

We got the reclaimed land tilled with tractors and selected good farmers from among the displaced Hajongs to settle down there. The officials and farmers wanted to name the settlement as "Gopalgaon" in my honor. I rejected the proposal, and the farm area was named Dhamar Farm, as it was carved out from the Dhamar Grazing Reserve. The families quickly settled down, became good agriculturists, and started growing two crops instead of one. I was surprised when, in 2020 (55 years later), the driver of KN Kumar, an I.A.S. officer of the Meghalaya Government, came to Hyderabad with his boss and told me that he was from the third-generation Hajong family settled in Dhamar. I was overjoyed that my efforts had given good results and rebuilt the lives of some refugees who had lost their homes and hearths in East Pakistan. A tear or two of joy flowed down my eyes. I was happy that I was chosen as an instrument of God for a good purpose.

BRAHMAPUTRA BUND

During my tenure, unusually heavy floods in the river Brahmaputra caused severe erosion of the embankments protecting Goalpara town. The Executive Engineer (E&D) wanted me to acquire some land as a backup area to strengthen and/or build suitable embankments to prevent erosion and perform a Puja. It was done speedily, and the bund was built. The embankment, I am told, is strong and serving well even after 60 years!

INQUIRY OFFICER FOR BREACH OF BRAHMAPUTRA BUND

In September 1965, there was an unusual flood in the river Brahmaputra, which had breached a recently built bund near Jaleswar. The Government appointed me as an Inquiry Officer to ascertain whether there was any lapse on the part of the Executive Engineer or his subordinates in the construction of the bund. After due inquiry and taking the depositions of the villagers, officials, and other interested persons, I concluded that the department had been vigilant and had taken all precautionary measures. They were not in any way responsible for the occurrence as the river, without any warning, had breached the bund. The concluding portion of my report said, "Nature, when in high tension, can be most unpredictable, and it was probably one of those angry moods in which she found herself an outlet to vent her pent-up fury." The case was closed.

NATIONAL DEFENCE FUND

In the wake of the 1965 Indo-Pak war, the Union Government set up the National Defence Fund to collect donations from the public. We held a series of meetings all over the Subdivision and were able to collect a substantial amount of money. Some ladies contributed gold ornaments. We received a commendation letter from the Chief Secretary for our N.D.F. efforts.

VIPS GALORE

A flood of V.I.P.s visited Goalpara during the winter to stay at the circuit house, which was picturesquely located on a small hillock overlooking the Brahmaputra River. To add to the attraction, we had a good cook. Among the V.I.P. visitors were Justice Mukherjee, heading the Commission of Inquiry into Minority Incidents, and his Secretary N Vittal I.A.S. from Gujarat. Chief Justices of Assam High Court, Mehrotra, and C S Nayudu, came to Goalpara to ascertain the availability of land to set up subordinate courts at many places. Many visitors came from the Ministries in Delhi to see the Refugee camps and supervise the transfer of some refugees to Arunachal Pradesh. Dr. Nagendra Singh, I.C.S, Secretary Transport G.O.I. (who later became a Judge of the International Court of Justice) and Chief Engineer, Inland Water Transport visited Goalpara to examine the scope for construction of a second bridge over the Brahmaputra River. The Minister for Railways, Chairman of the Railway Board, and General Manager of N.F. Railways came to examine the feasibility of linking Bongaigaon to the Ferry point at Jogighopa to speed up the movement of goods and people to Assam.

SAINIK SCHOOL AT MATIA

Krishnamurthy, Joint Secretary in the Defence Ministry (father of K. Jaishankar, India's External Affairs Minister), visited Goalpara with a proposal to start an Army Sainik School in Assam. He requested the allotment of a suitable site to accommodate the school building, hostel, firing range, and playgrounds. It will help if the area is close to an airfield. We took him to Mornoi, where there was a Second World War abandoned airfield and adjacent land. He was excited and said that he would speedily process the proposal. He deputed Lt.Col.Sahni and Majors HS Singh and Galvankar to expedite matters. I fixed up some rented accommodation for them at Goalpara and assisted them by speedily processing the land acquisition for the Sainik School. Government approval was soon received. As the Government was keen on setting up the Sainik School, it called for applications, pending the construction of their buildings. I was on the Interview Board for the selection of students. The Army officers helped me in activating the Ex-servicemen Society at Goalpara. I consider the setting up of the Sainik School my proud contribution to Assam.

I used to give motivational lectures to the students of the Sainik School harping on the Military traditions of India and the legendary heroes of Assam, and particularly Lachit Barphukan, who kept at bay repeated attacks by the Moghuls. I was Chief Guest at the first parade of the Sainik School when the Army officers lauded my role in setting up the Sainik School and seizure of a steam launch during the 1965 Indo-Pak war; the school presented me with a Ceremonial Sword at the parade, which is a proud possession of mine.

Goalpara Sub-Division covered areas on both the southern and northern banks of the Brahmaputra. I made it a practice to tour extensively to familiarise myself with the people and their problems. There were two Rajbangshi Zamindars at Lakhipur in the south and Abhayapuri in the north bank. There was an important ferry crossing on the Brahmaputra at Jogighopa near Goalpara. Jeeps, Cars, and small vehicles were transported across the river through steam launches. Bongaigaon Railway Junction on the north bank was a Municipality and a thriving business center with good communication and educational facilities. There were nice Sal forests on the north Bank. I was reminded of the Mahabharata story of the Tournament of the Princes where Karna is described as a straight, erect, and strong figure as a Sal Tree!

DALANGS - TIMBER BRIDGES

There were timber bridges over the many streams and minor rivers made of pile-driven Teak or Sal logs for stability. The Notice-cum-warning Board at the entrance of the bridge would either read as "Tek Dalang" (narrow bridge) or "Durbal Dalang" (Weak Bridge). The Executive Engineer, R&B, told me that the Quality and Safety Certification process for the bridges was very simple. An elephant would be goaded to tread slowly across the bridge to test and note its load-carrying capacity. If successful, clearance was given for jeeps. On bigger bridges, if three elephants could cross safely together, clearance would be given for 3-ton vehicles—a local ready-made Quality Assurance System!

NO WORKDAY STRIKE

One incident worth recalling is the All Assam Ministerial Employees Union call for a "no-work day" strike, which coincided with an All India strike in the month of March 1965 when payments due to contractors and officials had to be paid and Annual Accounts closed. The government had prohibited the strike. Both the ministerial staff and the class IV staff, including court clerks, were planning to participate in the strike to make it a complete lockdown. We kept a watch on the movements and activities of the staff both in the office and outside. We noted that influential leaders were from the offices of the SDO, Superintending Engineer, and the Divisional Forest Office. Senior officers tried to persuade the main leaders to call off the strike, but they were adamant. I called the main leaders and told them that the strike was declared illegal and that any person participating in the strike would be arrested and prosecuted. The court would ask the strikers, "Did you participate in the strike or not?" If the answer is "Yes, I had Participated", it would be an admission of guilt, and punishment would follow. If he said No, he would not be true to the cause and would forfeit the confidence of his followers. It led them to rethink and had some effect on older employees. Some essential staff were persuaded individually, and they agreed to attend to urgent and important matters.

There were only three hard-core committed leaders, of whom two were from the SDO office. As a precautionary measure on the day of the strike, they were arrested, brought to court, and sent to remand for three days. This happened early in the morning. When I went to my bungalow for lunch, I felt unhappy and did not want to take my lunch when my own employees were starving in jail. I asked my cook, Nagaraj, to prepare food for three people and carry it to the jail with me to give it to the jailer to feed the three employees. When I spoke to them, they initially refused but later took the food.

When the news of the arrest of the striking leaders at Goalpara spread, the striking leaders in Dhubri called off the strike. This led to the strike being called off all over Assam. Our quick and firm action triggered action for the strike to be called off. The Chief Secretary appreciated my firm and strong action and the gesture of feeding the employees. I received a Commendation letter that said that my action had averted a crisis and would be placed in my Confidential Roll. (C.R.).

KAMARAJ NADAR PRESIDENT I.N.C VISITS GOALPARA

In March 1965, Kamaraj Nadar, then President of the Indian National Congress, arrived by helicopter in Goalpara to address Congress leaders and workers and proceed to Dhubri. We planned for a helipad at the High School playground at Goalpara. A problem arose as Kamaraj Nadar did not know English and spoke only Tamil. No translator at Goalpara could translate Kamaraj Nadar's Tamil into English, Hindi, Assamese, or Bengali. The local leaders approached me to translate his speech. I told them that SDO should not attend or participate in political meetings except to oversee law and order arrangements. I did know some conversational Tamil but was hesitant to take on a task that was not in the ordinary course of work. The local MLA Khagen Nath requested that I translate the talk, saying that the presence of Kamaraj was important but not the exact translation. Soon after that, I received a phone call from the CM's office that in the given situation, I should help. I reluctantly agreed to do so.

The helicopter landed at about 3 PM. Some young girls were lined up with garlands to welcome the VIP. The Pilot was a young, handsome Swede. As soon as he stepped down the ladder, the girls mistook him to be the VIP and promptly garlanded him, instead of Kamaraj, who stepped out later. The garlands were exhausted! Luckily, there was a bouquet at the table, and a local leader handed it over to the VIP. When he came to the Dias, I greeted him in Tamil, i.e., Vanakkam. He made some inquiries about me and said that he had to visit Dhubri and get back to Guwahati before sundown and wanted a quick getaway. I knew that Kamaraj was a man of few words or monosyllables. "Paarkalam," meaning 'let us see' was his favourite reply to many loaded questions. I told him that I understood his urgency and would make my translation brief and short.

There was an Agarbatti stand on the table, which had toppled, but no one had noticed it. The tablecloth was singed and about to catch fire when I noticed and put it off. He said "Apasakunum," meaning a bad sign. The welcome address of local leaders took some time. Kamaraj began by saying "Vanakkam" or Namaskar. He then said – "I am in a hurry to go to Dhubri before dark – I will come again." With my broken Tamil and Assamese, I translated his very brief speech even more briefly. He thanked me and said he had to attend one more meeting at Dhubri and at Guwahati and left quickly. The brevity of speech can be a boon and saving grace or a curse, depending on the speaker, his translator, the time available, and the audience.

ROGUE ELEPHANTS

Goalpara had some hilly forest area. In 1965, we had a problem of rogue elephants causing damage to fields near the forest areas in Goalpara. Instead of the usual single rogue male tusker normally encountered, we had an unusual group of three rogue elephants. People were scared to go near the forest area. News spread far and wide. In the past, SDO was provided with a 0.350 Magnum Gun with ammunition to be used for killing such rogue elephants which cause human deaths after due notification. Two senior officers H.Pais (1960) and AC Ray (1959) had come to Goalpara in connection with some relief and rehabilitation work for refugees from East Pakistan. We had finished lunch at my place. Parthasarathy, SDO Kokrajhar, came to my bungalow from the Jogighopa Ferry Ghat and excitedly said, "Gopal, you are attracting not one but three rogues in your sub-division." A C Ray immediately retorted, "Partha." you are mistaken; we had 3 rogues to deal with till now, but with your arrival, poor Gopal must handle one more! We all had a good laugh.

We had a young hunter at Goalpara who was adept in the use of guns and rifles. He told me about a reputed big game hunter, Hemson Marak from Tura of Garo Hills, who was known for his hunting prowess and was called upon by the Government to shoot rogue elephants. At our request, Hemson Marak came to Goalpara to survey the area and become familiar with the forest.

In the meantime, two of the rogue elephants in the group had left the group. We had only one rogue elephant to deal with. A local hunter, forest officials, and I accompanied Hemson Marak and were at a safe distance away. We saw the elephant peacefully grazing on the other side of a flowing stream. The elephant saw us and started trumpeting and approaching us to cross the stream. Its movement was slowed down due to the undergrowth, mud, and slush beside the stream. From a vantage point on the bank, which provided a clear view, Hemson fired the lethal shot that hit the Center of the head of the charging elephant. We could see blood oozing and spluttering and the loud trumpeting and crying of the elephant. When it turned its head, the hunter fired yet another bullet, which went through the neck of the elephant just below the head. One more shot above its foreleg was fired. The elephant staggered, cried piteously, slumped on its legs, and fell dead. We felt bad to see a magnificent animal fall. We reported the shooting of the Rogue elephant to the Forest Department and Chief Secretary. The villagers were relieved. We felt a tinge of sadness for a long time for shooting an innocent animal instead of shooing it away.

If I thought about any issue deeply before sleeping, I would often dream with clues to solve it; in one such dream, I saw a Shiva temple covered by vines resembling a jungle along the south bank of Brahmaputra near the Jogighopa ferry. The word Jogighopa means "Caves of the Yogis". I requested the forest department to clear some jungle area near the waterfront, as I had dreamed. A small Shiva temple was indeed found! My dream had turned into a reality. A large number of people, including ladies of the Marwari Community, visited the temple to offer worship. There was a businessman called Birdhi Chand Chajjar who came forward to renovate the temple and lay a small path to it from the road. He kept his promise, and I am told that the Shiva temple continues to attract devotees.

PARASHURAM KUND BECKONS

In the month of January 1966, I had a strange dream: I was bathing in the river Brahmaputra in an unknown place with my batch mate CD Tripathi, SDO of North Lakhimpur, amidst many devotees. I phoned Tripathi about the dream and asked whether he would like to join me in visiting Parashuram Kund. Strangely, he told me that he, too, had a similar dream that both of us had gone to Parashuram Kund. We were astounded by the coincidence and similarity of the dream at approximately the same time. He said that he could plan a visit for both of us to coincide with Makar Sankranti, due on 14th January. I took leave and went by train to North Lakhimpur. I visited a couple of tea gardens with Tripathi and stayed for the night in his official bungalow.

He narrated an incident that had recently occurred in his subdivision. A British Tea planter had used slanderous words about Indian Leaders and Indians and had beaten up a tea garden labour in North Lakhimpur. The police arrested the Planter and, and the court sent him to judicial custody.

He was lodged in the Sub-jail. The information reached the Deputy High Commissioner of the U.K. in India, who rushed to North Lakhimpur to ascertain the facts and secure the release of the tea planter. Tripathi took him to the Sub-jail to meet the tea planter. The Deputy High Commissioner remarked that the conditions in the sub-jail were subhuman and frankly horrible. Tripathi calmly replied that it was the British who had constructed the sub-jail and laid down the rules. After that, no changes were made - even a wee bit. If the British thought it was good enough for Indians, I guess it should also be good enough for the Britishers. The Deputy High Commissioner realized that India, now a Republic, was only following and maintaining the Rules and standards they set. Equality is a constitutional guarantee, and under similar circumstances, everyone is equal in the eyes of the Law. It had just been put into practice.

The following day, Tripathi and I crossed the Brahmaputra River by ferry along with his jeep and reached Dibrugarh. We drove straight to the SP, Medini Chowdhary's Bungalow. He was known as a person with a strong belief in Tantric rites and a devotee of Goddess Kali. When we related our dream experience, he said that he would not only arrange the requisite permits for Arunachal Pradesh but himself accompany us to Parashuram Kund. The next day, we proceeded in two jeeps to Sadiya Ghat to cross the river Brahmaputra, reach the northern bank, and proceed from there to Parashuram Kund.

The scene at Sadiya was awe-inspiring, serene and overwhelming. The Brahmaputra River stretched in width to an incredible fourteen kilometers! Elaborate arrangements had been made to handle the river crossing of numerous pilgrims with vehicles who wanted to visit Parashuram Kund to have a dip in the holy water and wash off their sins. The legend is that Lord Parashuram's hands were smeared with blood due to the killing of many Kshatriya kings. He could not wash the blood smears despite his efforts in several rivers. He was advised to go and wash his hands in the easternmost part of India, where the sun rises and pure and holy water of the Himalayas enters the plains. He did so, and the blood stains were washed away from his hands, but then the river turned red! Hence, the name of the River Brahmaputra is Lohit or Luit (red).

A battalion of the Madras Special Armed Police was on duty to control the crowd and to ensure the safety of pilgrims who took a dip in the holy water. Strong barricades had also been put up. The Assistant Commandant saw the SP and made special arrangements for our stay for the night, which enabled us to take a dip in the waters at dawn. The visit was enjoyable and completed without any hitch. I returned a rejuvenated person after a joyful sojourn to the Himalayas. I returned to Goalpara and resumed my duties. I wrote to my mother about my Pilgrimage.

TRANSFER TO AIZAWL

In the first week of April 1966, I received a phone call from the I.G. of Police, Mr. Bhabani Kumar Baruah, who said that due to the insurgency created by the Mizo National Front (MNF), continuing disturbances in Mizo Hills District, and the need to restore Law and Order, the Government was proposing to post me to Mizo Hills district. The Mizo National Front (MNF), a political-cum-armed body, had declared Independence of Mizoram in March 1996, demolished many bridges on the way from Vairengte to Aizawl and disrupting communications to Aijawl. They kidnapped the SDO Lunglei, R V Pillai, my batch mate, and took him to East Pakistan. Due to disturbed conditions and the tense situation at Aizawl, the D.C. T.S Gill had shifted to the Assam Rifles Camp, which had a well-fortified hilltop campus with a helipad. He told me that I should be prepared to move to Aijawl at short notice. Soon after, a call came from Chief Secretary Kidwai who told me that there was an emergency in Mizo Hills District, and notification was issued under Defence of India Rules, empowering officers to take deterrent action. I was specially selected and would be posted on accelerated promotion as Additional DC with requisite magisterial and judicial powers to assist D.C. in the restoration of law and order and trial of cases. The Army had already been called out, and some columns had reached Aizawl. I would have to report at Silchar and move to Aizawl with a column of the army and a convoy of essential supplies. This was the least anticipated event.

A little later, the CM, B P Chaliha, called me on the phone and said that the MNF had betrayed the trust reposed by him and the government and had created large-scale disturbances and resorted to the destruction of government properties, including the kidnapping of R V Pillai, my batch mate, from Lunglei and taken him captive. He said that as a young and trusted officer of the Government, I was chosen to restore law and order in that district. A Superintendent of Police would be posted for the first time in Mizo Hills to strengthen the police and assist law and order administration. He hinted that a seasoned IAS officer would shortly be sent to the District as Deputy Commissioner, and till that time, I should hold the fort, maintain good relations with the Army and create confidence among Government officials and public, and ensure good communications and quick movement of civil supply. More officers would be posted to strengthen the administration, and firmly put down unlawful activities. I thought that the CM had personally picked me, indicating his confidence in my ability to face tough situations.

I received orders for promotion and posting as Additional Deputy Commissioner and Additional District Magistrate of Mizo Hills District with powers of a Sessions Judge and instructions to move immediately to take charge at Silchar and then proceed to Aijawl. The Government posted K.K. Sinha (1963) to take over charge of SDO, Goalpara, and relieve me. I took him to DC Dhubri, and to Bongaigaon to familiarise him with the issues and problems. I introduced him to all the officers at Goalpara. There was a spate of fare-well functions. I handed over the charge as SDO on 6th April 1966.

I spoke to my mother and sought her advice and blessings. She said, and I quote from memory, "Your father, during the Second World War, faced such situations in Burma. He did his duty as expected. I would like you to do your best in the new assignment."

My friend, Pratul Sharma, Senior EAC at Guwahati, planned for my onward travel and hosted a dinner at Guwahati. At Shillong, I met the Chief Secretary and IGP, who briefed me. I reached Silchar and took charge. I was briefed about the law and order situation, problems of transportation, and Air dropping of supplies due to severely disrupted communications.

14

Addditional Deputy Commissioner and Deputy Commissioner, Mizo Hills District, Aizawl (April 1966 – July 1967)

With an armed insurgency against the Indian State in Mizo Hills District, I was asked to rush to Aizawl as Additional Deputy Commissioner and Additional District Magistrate. I did some homework about Mizo Hills to understand the background, causes, and consequences of what amounted to an armed rebellion, the first to take place in independent India barring the insurgency in Nagaland.

MIZO HILLS

Mizo Hills or Lushai Hills, so called on account of the language, Lushai, spoken by most Mizos, was the second largest district in India, covering an area of over 8200 sq.miles. The northern area of the district was inhabited by hill tribes known as Lushais, Raltes, Kukis, and Hmars, who were educated due to the activities of the missionaries who during British rule, were given a free run not only in this district but also in the Khasi and, Naga hills. The southern portion of Mizoram was inhabited by other tribes like Pawis, Lakhers, and Riangs, etc while the southwestern and southern parts had Hindu tribals called Chakmas. The population in 1961 was 2, 66,000. The word Mizo means Highlander or Hillman. Most of the Mizos had been converted to Christianity by the missionaries. As the Mizo language does not have a script of its own, the Roman script was adopted.

The British annexed the district in 1891 and placed it under the Chief Commissioner of Assam in 1898. The Head of the district used to be called Superintendent from 1898 till the designation became Deputy Commissioner in 1952 in line with the other districts in Assam. The D.C was not only the District Magistrate but concurrently Superintendent of Police, Superintendent Engineer, and Head of all Departments in the District. The only exception was the District Medical Officer. This was in tune with the single-line command and the 'Ma-Bap' style of administration in Hills districts. Non-residents or visitors to the district had to obtain a formal permit under the inner-line regulations to enter the Mizo district.

Christian missionaries operated in the Mizo hills from the 1870s, with many denominations, such as the Welsh Mission, Presbyterian Church, Seventh-day Adventists, Calvinists, etc. Rev Roberts was the Head of the Welsh Mission. A small group of Mizos believed that they were the descendants of a sect of Israelis and called themselves the lost Israel tribe. There were also Indian missionaries from Kerala and Tamil Nadu.

MAUTAM FAMINE – CAUSE FOR MIZO UNREST

Two types of Bamboo plants grow in Mizo Hills: Mautak and Rauthing. Once every 40 years, Mautak bamboo forest flowers shedding protein-rich seeds, which leads to the proliferation of the Rat population, which devours not only the Bamboo flower and seeds but any available food crop. This causes an acute shortage of food grains for the populace, resulting in famine-like conditions called Moutam.

Similar flowering of Rauthing bamboo leads to the famine called the Thingtan. Recent research at the Jawaharlal Nehru Tropical Botanical and Research Institute, Thiruvananthapuram, in 2022 showed that during gregarious flowering, the bamboo produces large fruits, which draw rats and other predators who eat and multiply rapidly, causing a famine called Rat Flood. After the fruits are over, they start devouring standing crops and causing famines.

After the Mautam famine in 1958, there was a scarcity of food grains and consequent suffering of the people. There were rampant allegations of mishandling the famine by the Assam administration. Taking advantage of the fairly widespread dissatisfaction among the Mizos, an indigenous militant organization called the MNF (Mizo National Front) was formed under the leadership of Laldenga with the declared objective of fighting for a separate, independent homeland for the Mizos.

MNF's DIABOLIC GAME

MNF could easily enlist volunteers from young students, collect arms for training a group of volunteers, and indoctrinate them to fight for the Independence of all Mizo-inhabited areas. They established contact with East Pakistan authorities to obtain arms, ammunition, training, safe havens, and even financial support. Pakistan was only too happy to aid and abet any separatist movement in India, given its inveterate hostility towards India. At the same time, to mislead the Assam Government, the MNF promised loyalty to India but was planning to declare Independence. In 1964, when cornered by the Government with evidence of their contacts with East Pakistan authorities, MNF confessed that they had indeed established contact with the Pakistan Government and were obtaining assistance of various types even while professing its loyalty to CM Assam and the Assam Government. In the meantime, they secretly mobilized upwards of 20,000 MNF volunteers, gave them training in the use of arms, and raised the chorus of Independence.

Laldenga, as the President of the MNF, and Lalnunmuwaia, as Vice President, wanted to secure, based on ethnic affinity, a greater Mizoram covering the Mizo Hills and adjoining areas in Burma, East Pakistan, and Manipur. They were able to secure arms from Naga Rebels and Chins. They built a formidable force of Mizo National Volunteers (MNV). The MNF played a double-crossing political game with the Government by running with the hares and hunting with the hounds.

MNF wrote a letter to the Chief Minister of Assam on 14-2-64 confessing their misguided actions but professing that the MNF was not anti-state and not against the Indian Constitution but were only trying to protect their ethnic brethren in India and Burma and wanted a separate state within the Indian union. Despite such a solemn assurance, they overran Aizawl and many administrative Centres in Mizo hills on 28-2-1966. They looted the treasury at Aizawl and seized it. Denghnuna, who protested their actions, was threatened with death, but good sense prevailed, and he was released.

On 24th February 1966, MNF declared Independence, blasted the bridges on the rivers and streams on the main roads, and cut off all access and supply routes to the Hills. They took over Aizawl, the district headquarters, and all Government offices. The SDO of Lunglei, RV Pillai, was kidnapped and taken away by the MNF cadres to East Pakistan. Pillai had earlier warned the Government about his apprehensions of revolt and the likelihood of large-scale disturbances by MNF. In March 1966, the Mizo National Front (MNF) became more belligerent and threatened all non-Mizos. The district was under siege, supplies disrupted, administration almost paralysed. The Central Government had no alternative but to confront and control the open armed rebellion. The Indian Army was asked to move in aid of civil administration and quell the rebellion.

The MNF also kidnapped an Audit Team of four members from the A.G's office at Shillong from Lunglei and took them to East Pakistan. They were all subjected to a lot of torture and privation. As a result, Pillai contracted Malaria and developed a bone marrow infection in his right arm and had to later undergo surgery in New Delhi as the doctors at Guwahati suggested amputation as the only solution.

Later, a joke about the audit team was in circulation. After a week in captivity, the audit team appears to have told their captors (MNF) that they are used to working and being idle without any work was itself a big torture. They innocently asked their captors "The provisional Mizoram Government would also have to maintain accounts which were subject to Audit. As we do not have much work, we can assist in the maintenance and audit of such accounts". The gossip was that MNF authorities, shy of any probe or audit, immediately released them! The first batch to be released from MNF captivity was incidentally the members of the Audit Team!

The Central Government put a lot of diplomatic pressure on Pakistan to secure the release of RV Pillai, who had been kidnapped by MNF and taken to East Pakistan. The Pakistan Government advised the MNF to release RV Pillai. When this was done much later, he was picked up by the army and brought to Aizawl. The Cabinet Secretary and the Home Secretary came to Aizawl by Helicopter and met all of us. They took Pillai for de-briefing and medical treatment. We felt relieved and hoped that all others taken hostage would be released.

On 1st March 1966, MNF issued a Declaration of Independence signed by six persons headed by Laldenga. MNF attacked many Government offices at Aizawl and declared that the Mizo National Front Government was in control of the district and was seeking international recognition and support. The DC had to take shelter in the Assam Rifles Post at Aizawl. MNF attacked the Assam Rifles post at Aizawl, which strongly resisted, and the MNF retreated. MNF attacked a few border villages in Burma, where Mizos and allied tribes were residing. They simultaneously cut off all lines of communication to Aizawl and destroyed many major and minor bridges.

Government of Assam on 2nd March 1966, declared the whole of Mizo district as a Disturbed Area under the Assam Disturbed Areas Act 1955. On 3rd March 1966, notification was issued under Sec.10 (2) of the Criminal Law Amendment Act 1932, making several offenses cognizable under the Indian Penal Code. The Air Force planes strafed Aizawl to clear the town of MNF volunteers and restore a sense of normalcy. The Government of India in the Ministry of Home Affairs, after being satisfied that the MNF is indulging in activities prejudicial to the security of Mizo district in the Assam State and, in fact, waging war against the Indian State, declared vide Notification dated 10-3-1966 that the MNF fell under Rule

32 of Defence of India Rules 1962 and is to be treated as an enemy and dealt with accordingly.

The Government extended the Armed Forces (Assam and Manipur) Special Powers Act to Mizo Hills district, authorising any Commissioned officer, Warrant Officer, Non- commissioned officer or any other person of equivalent rank in the armed forces in a disturbed area, to fire upon or otherwise use force to the extent of causing death for contravention of any law or order for the time being in force in the disturbed area. It also prohibited the assembly of five or more persons or carrying weapons like firearms and explosive substances. It gave powers to armed forces to destroy any fortified position shelter or hide-outs. The Army quickly moved in with paratroopers and the infantry, with supporting groups, to construct bridges and culverts, restore communications, and set up the Brigade Headquarters.

SILCHAR-AIR DROPPING OF SUPPLIES

The immediate task of the administration was to ensure the flow of essential commodities into the disturbed areas to feed the people. As road communications were disrupted, food supplies were airdropped. I reached Silchar, the district H.Q of the Cachar district neighbouring the Mizo Hills, met the Deputy Commissioner, and started the process of arranging timely and regular supplies for Mizo Hills. The Transport Officer in charge of civil supplies of Mizo district briefed me. He explained the processes involved in packing and airdropping foodstuffs and essential commodities in difficult hill areas of Mizo District. The airdrop schedules were determined by the weather and advice from D.C. at Aizawl. Flights operated on fair-weather days only. He was liaising with the Indian Air Force and Kalinga Airlines for the airdrop of supplies from the Kumbhirgram airport. C D Tripathi (1962) was later posted as ADC in charge of civil supplies at Silchar.

Kalinga Airlines pilots were more experienced than the IAF pilots, having worked earlier in the Mizo area, and willing to take risks. There was a problem with the dropped packets bursting on impact on the hillsides and sometimes irretrievable. The problem was sorted out by better quality packing material and standardizing the number of bag wrappings and weight. This drastically reduced wastage, flights, and airdropping Costs Chandulal Seth (CL Seth Brothers) was the transport contractor for all essential commodities and other goods from Silchar to Aizawl on the government account. They also supplied essential commodities to private shopkeepers. With 30 years of experience, they worked with a patriotic and national outlook despite the hazards and risks.

I visited Vairangte, located right on the Inner Line Border Check Post between Cachar and Mizo Hills. It was an outpost from where convoys to Aizawl departed. There were 200 to 300 stranded trucks carrying essential supplies awaiting an armed escort party to proceed to Aizawl. Some tankers carrying Petrol, Oil, and Lubricants for Aizawl were also stuck up. Many truck drivers at the Check post were running short of money, having waited for convoy movements, which were delayed. Several bridges on the rivers and streams on the road from Vairangte to Aizawl had been blasted by MNF. Clearance of the road was getting delayed, as some transhipment arrangements at road and broken river bridges had to be made. The army did an exceedingly fast and truly admirable job of providing Bailey bridges and clearing the road wherever required. The army initially provided escort parties for convoys whose duty was later taken over by the Armed Police Battalions.

My first task was to get the convoys moving to Aizawl to meet the needs of the civilian population, government officials, and Assam Rifles personnel. I contacted the army camp and marched along with a small column of Army and Police to familiarize myself with the alternate routes on the road to Aizawl and to study the logistics of convoy movement, halting places, or holding points and security arrangements. There were imminent risks of the MNF (Mizo National Front) shooting at our convoys from vantage positions from hilltops, especially at hairpin bends and double hairpin curves and indeed anywhere on the road to Aizawl. Ambushes can be organized, and roadblocks created by the rebels who knew the territory better than anyone else. Such attacks were quite frequent, to begin with, leading to some deaths and the burning of vehicles, but it was quickly eliminated with better security coverage and control of the hilltops on the main Vairangte – Aizawl Road. The convoys with army protection after the restoration of the road initially took three days to reach Aizawl, but with good repair arrangements, we were able to reduce it to less than two days. After streamlining arrangements and road clearance patrols, convoys would start early in the morning from Silchar and reach Aizawl by late in the evening on the same day despite slushy roads and obstacles. In the meantime, IAF organized helicopter movements to Aizawl and other places for security forces and Government personnel. Helipads were constructed post haste at far flung Administrative Centres.

The MNF had a large number of well-trained armed volunteers in and around Aizawl and on the road from Aizawl to Serchhip and Lunglei. The East Pakistan Government reportedly trained the MNF for more than two years, and hence, the Army had a really tough situation to deal with. While they succeeded, as happens in an armed combat situation in jungle terrain, casualties did take place.

There were many incidents of MNF cadres firing from hilltops at the road convoys, causing casualties. On one occasion, there were three deaths on the Aizawl-Serchhip Road. We studied such incidents and decided to secure vantage hilltops and provide scouts and escorts for road patrolling. The Maharashtra Special Armed Police took over the task from the army. This improved control of the spinal road, the morale of the truck drivers, and convoy movements.

There was a severe shortage of vegetables till road supplies were restored. The populace had to depend on local greens, tubers, green bananas, and pears, which were our saviours. Green and ripe pears were used as vegetables and as fruit, while over-ripe pears were our sweet dish or dessert! With the surfeit of pears consumption, the new S.P., B Phukan and I suffered from sore throats and resorted to large cups of hot tea to get some relief, as medicines were also in short supply. Fresh milk was not available, and we had to depend on Milkmaid condensed milk. In interior regions, salt was the rarest and most expensive commodity. In 1966, salt was sold at Rs.20/- per Kg, and it was considered more precious than gold in the interior villages.

On reaching Aizawl with the first convoy, I met DC, T S Gill, who had moved back to his official bungalow from the Assam Rifles Headquarters. He briefed me on all important and urgent matters that required my attention. He said that he was expecting a transfer shortly and that a new D.C. would soon be joining. He advised me to meet the Commandant of Assam Rifles and Major M V Shastry second i/c to get a briefing on MNF. They described to me how MNF had overrun Aizawl Town and other important administrative Centres in Mizo hills like Lunglei, Serchip, Champai, Saiha, Lawngtlai, and Sairang near Dhaleshwari (Tlawng) river and how the Army was succeeding in retaking all these places. In some areas, the casualties on both sides were high as the MNF had more knowledge of the terrain, were armed, and laid ambushes, but the army had better fire power. Ambushes and counter-ambushes were the order of the day.

I went to the D.C.s office and met the officer in-charge of the Police (who was a Dy. Superintendent of Police), the Transport Officer in charge of civil supplies, and officers of the PWD etc. The Deputy SP told me that there were only five police stations in the district with a total strength of 150 policemen in one of the largest districts in India! After a few days, the first Superintendent of Police Bhaben Phukan joined duty.

Our initial assessment was that the Government would have to induct armed police battalions for the security of the roads and Government offices at several administrative Centres, which had to start functioning quickly. We had to raise the morale of the employees and the confidence of the public by restoring normalcy in the administrative Centres, improving communications and supply of essential commodities, and security of convoys. We had to strengthen intelligence gathering about the movement of rebels and put an end to their threats and depredations. I got in touch with some leaders of the Mizo District Council and the Dubashi (interpreter) of the D.C., who was an elderly and very knowledgeable person, to seek their support. I also met some Missionaries and Pastors. We realized that government publicity must be effective, reassuring, and lift the morale of the population to bring about normalcy. An AIR station was set up at Aizawl.

To control the situation, 61 Mountain Brigade of Eastern Command of the Indian Army was inducted into Mizo District. It consisted of the 8th Sikh, 3rd Bihar, and 5th Para battalions. Brigadier Kabraji, a Signals officer, was the Officer commanding the Brigade. He was assisted by Adjutant Major Narayanan and Brigade Major Brar (who later became a Lt. General). The 5 Paras under Lt. Col Thomas was an elite corps of paratroopers. They proved very useful in cordoning or rounding up groups of MNF rebels in the jungles.

I called on Brigadier Kabraji, whose first remark was that I was too young for the job and did not have much experience. He stressed the need to secure the main route from Vairangte to Aizawl and Lunglei. His limited force should not be tied up in Road security but should concentrate on rounding up or neutralizing the rebels. He wanted the Government to induct more police battalions to take over the static security and road convoy duties on the Aizawl to Vairangte road and other arterial roads. The Border Road Task Force started work on constructing or widening roads and rebuilding the damaged and destroyed bridges all over Mizo Hills. Col. Kantha Nathan was in-charge of the BRTF group. Later, Brigadier Chachi was in- charge of speeding the road construction activities of the Dantak and Pushpak groups.

After Brigadier Kabraji's retirement, a Sikh Brigadier, Jaswant Singh, took charge. 61 Mountain brigade was reporting to the 101 Communication Zone headed by Major General Shamsher Singh (whose son was killed in the 1965 Indo-Pak war).

I received a message to meet Chief Minister Chaliha and Chief Secretary Kidwai at the Assam Rifles Helipad at Aizawl. I briefed them about the Law and Order situation and the importance of restarting the Centres. We needed young and willing officers to work under disturbed conditions and man the Centres. The CS said that young unmarried

Assistant Commissioners under training would be deputed to Aizawl, who could be posted at different locations after proper briefing. The Government probably considered them - all young bachelors – eager to do district training, as spare able material for Mizo Hills!

The CM felt that the MNF should be pursued by the army and police forces and hit really hard to make them voluntarily surrender, lay down arms, and seek durable peace. I was assured of full financial and administrative support from the Government and told that the new DC would soon take charge.

Groups of two or three MNF volunteers with arms were intimidating families at Aizawl and other places, seeking clothes, food, money, and medicines. People had no choice but to oblige for fear of harm. The women folk were worried their sons or husbands had joined the rebels. Their whereabouts, welfare, health, and safety were a constant worry – information was scarce, which heightened their fears. There was fear and uncertainty about the prevalent situation, and families started gearing up for a prolonged state of strife and continuing hardships.

In the DC's office, very few employees reported for duty- Transport Officer, DSP, a couple of Magistrates, skeletal clerical staff, and peons reported. Untoward incidents were proving a nightmare for lady employees. The DC hardly attended office as he was under orders of transfer. Our immediate problem was the restoration of the morale of the government employees and the creation of a sense of normalcy.

The newly inducted Armed Police Battalions were put on patrolling duties on the main road to Aizawl and in different parts of the town. Immediate requests from officers and staff were for escorts for the journey from home to office and back. Worries were about the receipt of salaries and the availability of food, vegetables, salt, and greens. The Government raised the allowances to meet the high costs of living in the district. One of the new allowances was Disturbed Areas Allowance (DAA)!

I convened a meeting of the Commandants of all Armed Police Battalions to work out a plan for the safety of the supply chain, regularity of convoys, and patrolling of sensitive places in Aizawl. The physical presence of police with walkie-talkies and arms to infuse courage and Vans with loudspeakers assuring people that the situation was getting normal created a measure of confidence. The only lights after 6.00 PM were in the Bungalows of officers and the campus of armed forces.

The first sigh of relief and normalcy began with the arrival of the Dak (Post) at Aijawl with the first convoy after nearly 45 days, which heralded the commencement of work in the DC's office and other offices. It provided welcome work for the staff. As replies to the post had to be sent by the return convoy, there was a flurry of action for a couple of days.

The supply of petrol was resumed, Convoys brought essentials, small grocery shops started functioning, Senior Magistrates and officials started moving around the town to instil confidence, and the road from Aizawl to Lunglei and Demagiri was opened.

Christian Missionaries were contacted to impress upon churchgoers that peace was paramount. There was scope for discussions and talks, but violence should be eschewed. Rev. Roberts of the Welsh Mission and Tamil and Malayalee priests guardedly helped the administration as they wanted to avoid getting into the bad books of the MNF. Elderly pensioners of the Assam Rifles and, some school teachers supported us in ensuring relatively peaceful conditions in the towns and administrative Centres and run schools. We sought help from Mizo District Council Members, who were quite cooperative.

Gun smuggling by MNF took place mainly from Burma through the Naga rebels. As there were a large number of Mizos, Kukis, and Zomis in Burma, Manipur, and East Pakistan, we maintained good border intelligence cover. We opened a new Administrative Centre at Lawngtlai and strengthened the Champhai Administrative Centre.

Laldenga, the leader of the MNF, was good at tactics. We noticed that when the army operated in company strength, MNF operated in platoon strength. If the army moved in platoon strength, the MNF would move in section strength. This enabled them to easily escape pursuit by the army, disappear into the jungles, or merge with the villagers who harboured them. There was a constant battle of wits between the army patrols and MNF regarding ambushes and counter-ambushes. I used to think that commitment to a cause –good or bad – could infuse courage and evolve tactics that could keep a well-trained army on its toes. It was yet another test of emotional and behavioural leadership. When the game was understood, the army had the upper hand.

With the help of a couple of Extra Assistant Commissioners (EAC), who joined the DC's office, the Transport Supervisor, and advice from the Dubashi (Interpreter), we reorganized work in the DC's office. Liaison with the Army, Armed Battalions, BRTF, District Council Members, and Intelligence cover was directly managed by me. I exercised the powers of a Sessions Judge as was in vogue in the Hill districts. The police department was strengthened by appointing and deputing police officials to all the Police Stations and Administration Centres.

The biggest problem was to restore and improve the morale of the local population and officials for bringing about normalcy. The collective efforts placed the administration back on the rails in a reasonably short time. With the basic structure in place, we worked out a sound strategy to curb illegal activities, restore law and order, and keep the MNF on the run so as to bring them for discussions while making it clear that the Rule of Law must and should prevail. It took six months to resume safe travel and normal activities in the district, thanks to the support of the Government and coordinated efforts of the Magistracy, Police, and administration, newly inducted Extra Assistant Commissioners, and the opening of the roads and Administrative Centres. The army was getting a grip on the situation. No doubt, the civilian population had to face many hardships. Later, in consultation with the army, we started the scheme of Protected Progressive Villages (PPVs) by clubbing villages to deny arms and food to the MNF rebels.

Four young IAS officers, D.K.Gangopadhyay, NN Mukherjee, RN Muhuri, and Madan Bezbaruah of the 1964 batch undergoing training were deputed and reported to me at Aizawl for briefing and posting. Subsequently, S K Agnihotri was also deputed. All of them stayed with me at Aizawl for a little over a week for briefing and were sent to their administrative stations by helicopter. Gangopadhyay, a cheerful person, was sent to Champai near the Manipur border with rations for a month, a National Flag, and stationery to operate the Administrative Centre. We also gave suitable instructions to the Armed Police at that station to keep a watch on the activities of ChuraChandpur District in Manipur. NN Mukherjee was sent to Serchhip, Madan Bezbaruah to Lunglei and R N Muhuri to Kolasib. After Muhuri was released on personal grounds, S K Agnihotri was posted at Kolasib. The young officers were feeling restless for missing their usual District training and felt isolated. Keeping up their morale by talking to them daily at night became an important task. There were fervent appeals on compassionate grounds and, in a couple of cases, to relieve them to attend to pressing family problems or to get married. I had to console, comfort, counsel, infuse courage, and assure them that we would release them as soon as the situation improved, or alternative arrangements were made.

In the case of Madan Bezbaruah, who had been moved from Lunglei to Lawngtlai, an isolated and remote place, he had to go home to look after his ailing father. I had to advise him to construct a helipad on priority to avoid the movement on foot with armed police parties to a road pick-up point with attendant risks. He did so and hoisted the National Flag at the new helipad. Helicopter trips were authorized only for emergency purposes like evacuating sick personnel. I requisitioned the services of a helicopter from the IAF as I had to attend to urgent work at Lawngtlai, and a casualty was to be evacuated. A glimpse of the complications involved in discharging our duties, I quote below an extract of what Madan Bezbaruah, who later became Secretary to the

Union Government, has written about the incident. "While there (at Lawngtlai), I (Madan Bezbaruah) came to know that my father was unwell, and my presence was essential. I was informed that it would not be possible to arrange an army column to escort me back, and the only way I could come out was by helicopter. Lawngtlai did not have a helipad, so I had to make one with the help of the local people. Those days, the army-civil relationship was unfortunately not always very friendly, and getting a helicopter to lift a civilian was unthinkable. I was very worried, but Naidu told me that he would ensure that suitable arrangements would be made. I felt very reassured. True to his words, within a few days, he asked me to be ready for a helicopter lift, and he would come. It was such a great sight to see the helicopter approaching. As soon as he came out, he loudly asked, audible to the helicopter crew as to how I was feeling and if everything was alright. Before I could say anything, he signalled to me to keep quiet and come near, explained in Assamese, which he had learned fairly well – that he had asked for the helicopter to give a lift to me as I was the 'casualty" – sick person. He was also coming to see the administrative arrangements and security assessment. That is Naidu as I have known him, as Assam has known him – getting things done and not making excuses. I shall never forget what he told me – "Madan, in an atmosphere of fear and security concern everywhere, in the far interior of the hills, I was so thrilled and proud to see from the air miles away, the national flag flying in your helipad." I know it is real pride; he is a true nationalist, always thinking of the larger interests of the country".

I had to recruit porters as many had left due to MNF Action. The Transport Supervisor, Sangzuala, explained the method of selection of porters to me. The test was simple. Each aspirant had to carry a load of 20 Kg strapped to his back, walk up a hill of about 300 to 500 meters, and return within a specified time. Porters passing the test were asked to stand for an inspection of their calf muscles. The bigger the calf muscle, the better he would fit for the porter's job. It was a perfect person- position fit in today's HR language.

We had another officer, L K Baruah EAC, posted at Lunglei who had earlier worked with me at Goalpara. He desperately wanted to be transferred to Assam to enable him to look after his ailing father and was even prepared to resign. I spoke to him and said that he should hold on and that we would help him as soon as possible. Luckily, we could help secure a transfer outside the Mizo Hills district within a short time and relieve him.

Government officials had initially depended on helicopter movement to administrative Centres, which the rebels had ransacked. All these centres had to be rebuilt, personnel stationed, and the normal tasks of ground-level administration recommenced. Later, road movement began.

AIR CHIEF MARSHAL TAKES STOCK

The Air Chief Marshal and his team visited Aizawl when they were apprised of the need for and importance of more frequent helicopter trips for the transport of government officers, staff, and doctors for emergencies. The Air Chief Marshal readily agreed and made suitable arrangements. Young Air Force pilots were placed in charge of MI4 Russian helicopters plying between Kumbhirgram Airport and Aizawl and other places in Mizo Hills. Among them, Pandey and Kharbanda were the most helpful. A Sikh Air Force Officer Bhumra was a native of Aizawl who would, on occasion, visit Aizawl.

CM's PRESS MEET

On 14th May 1966, Chief Minister B.P Chaliha came to Aizawl by helicopter and addressed a press meeting, where he denounced the MNF for betraying the trust he and the Government of Assam and the Indian Government had placed in the MNF. He called on the MNF to surrender to the Government and lay down their arms and ammunition before any discussion could take place with them. The policy of the Government would be to deny food and shelter to the rebels, and the village councils and the local authorities were expected to support the Government.

R Natarajan (1957) joined as DC, took stock of the situation, and identified the priority areas for action. He was a Chartered Accountant and had already earned a reputation of being a highly intelligent, competent, and decisive officer with a fine sense of humour. He had earlier been DC of the neighbouring District of Cachar, where his work was much admired, and hence knew the area very well. His wife Nalini (Bakre-nee), also an IAS, was a Maharashtrian and a batch mate of the DC and stayed back in Shillong to take care of their two children.

Natarajan stayed alone at Aizawl. True to his reputation, he was meticulous in all that he did and result-oriented, though, to my mind, slightly reserved. He would occasionally seek my views about our intelligence collection, collation, and dissemination system. The SB officer Trivedi IPS and a small complement of officers from the Government of India had already joined. The SP had also collected some information through his network of police sources. The DC, ADC, SP, SB officials, Commandants of police battalions, and Head of AIR Aizawl Station would meet regularly at the DC's bungalow to take stock of the latest developments all over Mizo

District and decide on the action required. Natarajan and I would sit down after the meeting to review events and decide on the follow-up action. We developed our unique cypher Telephone- Talk code to pass on confidential information to the Government at Shillong. Natarajan, and I would speak on the phone in Tamil or Telugu to M.C.Narasimhan, V.Ramakrishnan, and E.S. Parthasarathy at the Shillong secretariat, all connected one way or the other with the affairs of the troubled district.

LUNGLEI CIRCUIT HOUSE

On a certain occasion, I had to visit Demagiri and stay for the night at the Circuit House at Lunglei. In those days, the toilet used to be at some distance from the main building. The circuit house had an old, well-kept bound register for recording remarks of the senior visitors. The Circuit House Engineer was expected to go through the register, note the suggestions, and act. I casually went through the register. On the issue of the inconvenient location of the toilet, one of the senior officer's remarks in the register was, "The toilet is far from the circuit house and causes inconvenience." Another officer said, "I agree with the above remark. I think the toilet must be closer". Another senior officer just remarked, "I do not agree; the officer should have started earlier"!

Keeping in view the necessity to upgrade the Government's ability to effectively and expeditiously bring normalcy, the Indian Government decided to induct Special Armed battalions like the CRPF, Maharashtra Special Armed Police, and Madras Special Armed Police in Mizo District. The CRPF and Maharashtra Special Armed Police had several ex-army officers. Kaliappan commanded the Madras Special Armed Police battalion, and the second in command was Rajaratnam. They were happy that both the DC and ADC were South Indians who knew Tamil. The battalion had never worked in mountainous areas like Mizo hills and was finding it difficult to adjust to the terrain, weather, and trekking involved. The only Mount they were familiar with was St. Thomas Mount in Madras! And they had probably never seen mountains like Mizo Hills. The battalion was stationed at Sairang, near river Dhaleshwari, and Aizawl.

NICKNAMED MACHINE GUN NAIDU

The Mizos found it difficult to remember my full name. M.Gopalakrishna Naidu or Gopalakrishna preferred the simpler word, Naidu. They used to refer to me as Pu Naidu. Some of them used to call me MG Naidu. Some of the Mizo officers, District Council Members, and the public felt that I was quick and business-like but enigmatic and brusque. They used to say that

MG was like a Machine Gun and MG Naidu was Machine Gun Naidu! I do not know whether the epithet was because I spoke as fast as gunfire, or my actions were continuous like gunfire. As I was both Additional Deputy Commissioner and Additional District Magistrate, with many names, this sometimes led to confusion as to whom they were referring to.

One day, I received a short and terse police radio message in Cypher Code from the Chief Secretary, asking me to report to him at Shillong immediately and saying that a helicopter was being arranged. I was surprised and taken aback by this message, which did not mention the purpose and was quite intriguing, as the CS would normally call me on the phone. As the situation in the district was quite normal, I was unable to fathom the reason for the message. I gathered all the papers I considered relevant, packed my suitcase, and went to Shillong by helicopter.

Dressed in my best suit and tie, I went to the secretariat with a lot of trepidation to call on the Chief Secretary. I knocked on the door and said, "May I come in, Sir?" 'Yes', was the voice of the CS. I opened the door and warily stepped in. Kidwai saw me and inexplicably burst out laughing uncontrollably with his hand on the table and holding his head. I thought that my tie was probably not knotted properly or that some coat button was amiss. While I was nervously adjusting my coat and tie, he asked me to come in. I waited till he asked me to sit down and sat down like a pussy. He again burst out laughing and asked me, "Are you Mr Jekyll, Mr Hyde, or both?"

I was nonplussed, shell-shocked, stupefied, and indeed speechless. I could not comprehend the strange behaviour of the CS and mention of Jekyll and Hyde or the reason for his laughter and for my being summoned to Shillong. I thought that he had gone bonkers. Sensing my bewildered consternation, Kidwai put me at ease by asking for some tea for us. He addressed me formally, "Mr. Muddusetty Gopalakrishna Naidu, you have created a problem for me with your transfer." I thought that I might have made some serious mistake, not performing well or not living up to expectations, hence the talk of my transfer. I gingerly told the CS that I did not comprehend what he was saying. He reassuringly smiled and said, "Your CS knows his officers like the lines of his palm. But I cannot say that of many other officers who do not know the officers or even their names". So, saying, he pulled out an official note addressed to him by the Commissioner, Hills Division, and showed it to me.

The note said, " Gopalakrishna, ADC is doing a good job and has won confidence of the people. However, Naidu, the DM, is a very tough guy who does not know the tribal mind. I recommend that Gopalakrishna may be retained in Aizawl as ADC while Naidu, DM may be immediately transferred out of the district. After I had read the note, Kidwai said, "Boy, only you can help me to solve the dilemma. Tell me what should be done now. Whom should I transfer?" He laughed, and I felt relieved.

Kidwai smiled and said, "The Civil List of Assam is my Bible. I know the names and full particulars of all my officers—Muddusetty Gopalakrishna Naidu is from the 1962 batch. Muddusetty is your house name, Gopalakrishna is your name, and Naidu is your title. After seeing the note, I knew that the Commissioner was out of touch, and you were possibly under considerable strain. I thought that you needed a break from Aizawl and that a short holiday at Shillong would do you much good and help sort out pending matters of the district at the Secretariat. The problem is satisfactorily solved – you go back as DC to Aizawl after a two-day stay at Shillong for relaxation and recreation".

That evening, he invited me to his house for tea, where I met Mrs. Kidwai, her son Baba, and her daughter Shahnaz. Late at night, when I went to bed, I thought, here was an officer with a heart of gold who was truly a father for the civil servants in Assam. Our generation will remember him as an affectionate Godfather who really cared for and shared the joys and tribulations of the officers, staff, and people of Assam.

During my tenure in Mizo Hills as ADC and ADM, Natarajan, DC, went on short leave for 45 days. I was expecting to be posted as in charge or officiating DC, which is the norm, but was posted as regular DC on promotion to hold the fort. CS told me that this was an exceptional case and was being done as the army was very protocol conscious and the Brigadier at Aizawl should know that I was of the rank of DC. He advised me to function like a full-fledged DC and not as an ADC. This pushed up my morale and ego as well!

I received a letter in May 1967 from Major M.V. Shastry, who retired from Assam Rifles at Aizawl, to congratulate me on my promotion as Deputy Commissioner of Aizawl and to compliment me for the work in Mizo Hills in capturing many senior MNF leaders during my tenure. He hoped that with continuous pressure on rebels and surrender of arms by them, peace would soon return to Mizo Hills.

MEETING WITH GENERAL MANEKSHAW - PROTECTED, PROGRESSIVE VILLAGES SET UP

The Army authorities wanted MNF to be denied food, shelter, or support from the villagers. General Maneckshaw wanted Mizo Hills to follow the example of Malaysia, where, under General Gerald Templar, the Gurkhas effectively put down the rebels in the dense jungles of Malaysia. He wanted the civil administration to re-group the small villages into manageably large-sized villages located on the Main Road where good communication and peaceful life and development were possible. These villages could be properly barricaded, and passes would be issued to the residents who would be required to come back to the village after cultivation by sunset. Accepting this advice and under orders from the Government, such villages named Protected Progressive Villages (PPV) were set up.

The movement of inhabitants from over 100 villages with a population estimated to be around 50,000 and their re-grouping into 18 PPVs was a colossal task. We had to photograph all residents and issue Identity Cards. We had to shift building materials, people with their granaries, live-stock agricultural implements, and household materials. Villagers had to bring their household articles to the main road, where trucks would pick up people and their household materials and take them to the designated villages. We had the task of organizing regular supplies of building materials, food, essential commodities, and medicines for the villagers. They also helped build barricades around the village to prevent any hostile acts. To manage the PPVs, a large number of officers from Assam and Mizo Hills were inducted to set up the PPV Centres and manage them.

Lt Gen SHFJ Maneckshaw, Commander of the Eastern Command at Calcutta, visited Mizo Hills to review the situation and give instructions to senior army officers. The Brigadier requested that I provide Gen Maneckshaw with accommodation for a night in DC's bungalow. I readily agreed and hosted High tea to which senior army officers were invited. After the army officers left, Maneckshaw asked me whether I had good relations with the army officers and whether they were cooperating. Even though there were pinpricks on protocol issues now and then, I told Gen Maneckshaw that we were having cordial relations and there was no difficulty in coordinating with the army. Before leaving by helicopter, he seems to have remarked to the Brigadier Commander that I was all praise for the Army. Lo and behold, after seeing off his boss, the Brigadier came post-haste to my residence and thanked me. He said, "You could have listed out all the pinpricks that the army gave you, but you chose not to do so. I must thank you." It was an unexpected compliment and, therefore, more than welcome.

GENERAL OFFICER COMMANDING-IN-CHIEF EASTERN COMMAND

Lt Gen SHFJ MANEKSHAW, MC

DO No 401004/GOC in C
HEADQUARTERS
EASTERN COMMAND
CALCUTTA-21
29 Oct 66

Dear Mr Nayadu.

It was a pleasure meeting you at AIJAL and I am extremely grateful to you for your charming hospitality. You have a difficult job, but I am sure everything will go fine.

With my kind regards,

Yours sincerely
Sam Manekshaw

Mr M.G.NAYADU,
District Magistrate
AIJAL (Assam)

General Maneckshaw wrote me a nice letter from Kolkata thanking me for the hospitality and hoping that things would go well.

My batch mate C.D. Tripathi was functioning as ADC Mizo Supplies at Silchar. He wanted to visit Bhairabi in Mizo District on foot with me to study the scope of sending supplies by road on an alternate route or by mules. We organized a police escort-cum-patrol party and trekked from Vairangte to Bhairabi. We marched and reached Bhairabi in the evening. We had an early dinner and relaxed on the lawn. It was a full moon-lit night when we heard melodious songs in Mizo being sung by a small group of three boys. It was the season of oranges and the fragrance of orange flowers, the moonlight, and the melodious songs that cast a magic spell, evoked romantic and ecstatic thoughts, and had a mesmerizing effect on us. After the transfer of C D Tripathi, ADC at Silchar as DC Nowgong, R.P. Sinha was posted as ADC in charge of Mizo supplies at Silchar.

BUILDING BRIDGES OF FRIENDSHIP

We had a group of Mizo officers who did not like the violent, and misguided activities of MNF. They were unhappy that the MNF had singled them out as non-cooperative Mizos. Among them were Pu Denghnuna, the Public Relations officer, Sangzuala, the Transport officer, Sangliana, and the PS to D.C. a lady, Lal Remi. Conversations with them and my personal staff enabled me to learn and speak simple sentences in Mizo. I studied a Mizo Primer, took the tribal language test in the Mizo language, and got a cash reward of Rs.1000/- from the Government of Assam. I used to be in touch with Pu Bawichuaka and Pu Pahlira of the Mizo District Council, who did not like the violent ways of the MNF. Some of the Christian missionaries did not approve of the MNF taking up arms against the Government. They tried to persuade the leaders to see reason and start a dialogue to secure peace in Mizoram. One of the pastors suddenly went missing. We traced him with the help of trained sniffer dogs and were able to locate the pastor and the MNF camp to which he had been taken.

The MNF used to collect illegal taxes and forcibly secure food and medicines from the villagers. They would harass Government servants who were getting Special Disturbance Allowances to part with some of it. Emboldened by the presence of the army and Armed Police forces and relentless pressure on MNF, a large number of Ex-servicemen from the Assam Regiment and Assam Rifles, including Mizos who had settled in different parts of Mizo District came forward to help stop such depredations by the MNF. In consultation with S P (Special Branch, etc.), we utilized some of their services.

Our intelligence network became reliable and fairly accurate about the movement of MNF in the jungles and the location of their hideouts. This enabled the army to drop paratroopers and round up many MNF leaders. In one such action, Major Bisht of the 5th Para captured five top MNF leaders, including Pu Sainghaka, the self-styled home minister of the provisional Mizoram Government. With their capture, there was much jubilation in government circles, and demoralization among the MNF ranks. We hosted a party for Major Bisht and his Group.

Based on reliable sources, we received information that top MNF leaders, including Laldenga and Lalnunmowaia, were secretly visiting their families and that some families at Aizawl had even joined the MNF camps in East Pakistan. Family members of some MNF leaders were arrested for aiding and abetting the MNF, which was declared an unlawful organization. Their arrest had a demoralizing effect on the MNF cadre. Some Mizo Ex-servicemen also advised MNF that it would be foolish to take up arms against the Government. A wiser option would be to discuss matters and arrive at an agreeable truce and solution.

With the pressure of the Army and Police battalions, there were quite a lot of desertions from the MNF ranks and more so in the northern areas, which was then controlled by J F Manliana, who was lame in one leg. He sent feelers to the Special Branch and an emissary to the CM, saying that he was willing to lay down arms if amnesty was provided. When this was conveyed to the Government, CM Chaliha and IGP Barua came to Aizawl to discuss this matter. We told the CM that the back of the rebellion had not been broken and that MNF, by professing and pretending surrender, would get time and opportunity to re-group themselves. The surrender of arms may be nominal and not total and complete. Premature acceptance of surrender would minimize but not eliminate trouble till an acceptable political solution is found. We told the CM that just as the Government must follow the Rule of Law, MNF should also follow the Rule of law. Law and Order must be enforced through the instrumentalities of law. Since MNF had violated the law, they must get the deserved punishment. Moreover, MNF had not been hit hard enough for them to surrender all the arms and ammunition in their possession. The consensus was that the operations in Mizo Hills would continue till the MNF voluntarily disbanded and surrendered substantial quantities of arms, created conditions for a truce, and agreed to hold discussions to find an acceptable solution.

Towards the end of September 1966, I received the tragic news of the death of my youngest sister at Warangal. I went on leave and returned to duty on 9 October 1966. I was touched by the gesture of many Mizo employees in the D.C. office, who, as per their custom, consoled and gave me small token amounts to share my sorrow and help me meet expenses. I donated the sum received to the Salvation Army in Aizawl.

THUNDERBOLT INCIDENT

The weather in the hill areas is quite unpredictable, with heavy, incessant rainfall accompanied by thunder and lightning. I took this in my stride, but an interesting incident happened. The kitchen of the ADCs bungalow was about 5 meters away and had CI sheet roofing. On a rainy day of thunderstorms, a thunderbolt fell on the roof of the kitchen with a piercing, bright, blinding light and, like a white ball of fire, went through the corridor of the bungalow - which separated the dining hall from the living rooms onto the open veranda in front where a trusted sentry Dhan Singh, a retired Havildar was guarding the bungalow with a rifle with fixed bayonet. The thunderbolt passing through the passageway hit the steel bayonet, and Dhan Singh fell with the impact of the thunderbolt while the rifle he was holding also fell on the other side. Hearing his cries, my cook Nagaraj and I came out to the veranda. We saw that Dhan Singh had fallen down, and the rifle with bayonet was also thrown some 3 feet away. The bayonet had blackened and turned dark. I realized that it was God's grace that my cook Nagaraj, who was in the kitchen, and myself in my office room, and Dhan Singh on the verandah were not hurt or injured. It was particularly fortunate that Dhan Singh did not suffer any injuries. I was probably destined to relate this episode.

OUR JONGA JEEP FIRED UPON

I used to travel in a Jonga Jeep vehicle with an armed escort in and around Aizawl at dusk to check whether the curfew was being enforced effectively. On one occasion, our vehicle was shot at from a hilltop in Aizawl town itself. As soon as the shots rang out, the driver, me, and the escort party got down and crept under the Jonga near the hillside. Except for bullet damage to the windscreen and the body of Jonga, none of us were hurt. We intensified house searches and sent patrol parties to cover hilltop points in Aizawl town.

Entitlement to the Government supply of water in Aizawl was based on the rank of officers. The D.C, in whose bungalow there was a large water cistern, had the highest allotment of 5 tins (buckets) of water per day. The ADC and SP were allotted 4 tins. The number of tins decreased based on the rank of the officer. Most of the house roofs were of CI sheets. The rainfall on the rooftop was collected through a pipe and connected to a big cylindrical ground cistern enclosed by CI sheets with a cement floor with pipe outlets at different levels for tapping the water. The women folk jealously guarded the water. Clean water from taps on the tank would be used for cooking and for washing clothes that were not soiled badly. The once-used but saved water after filtration would be used for washing dirty clothes. The decanted water would again be used for washing dirtier or grease-stained clothes. The remnant water would finally be diverted for gardening. It was a fine example of water conservation and water-use efficiency practice, which is effectively "waste not - want not"!

THE MIZO DHARMA – TLAWMNGAIHNA

While I learned some very interesting facts about the Mizo way of life, particularly the high regard for the womenfolk, one of the most interesting was the sense of social cohesion and mutual assistance in times of need and crises. I learned about "Tlawnghaina '' the Dharma or ethics of Mizo society. It was the duty of the tribal youth to help elders and people in distress. The unmarried youth would stay in a dormitory called Zawlbuk and carry out community work. If a person fell ill and had to be shifted to the nearest hospital - a two-day march away- the youth of the village would make a make-shift cot for the sick person, and a team of four persons would carry the cot to the next village. A runner would be sent in advance to keep a similar group ready in the village to take it to the next village. This was their fast human courier system! I was amazed to see the spirit behind the action and the sense of fellow feeling among the youth. It reminded me of "Dharmo Rakshati Rakshitah," a Vedic exhortation meaning Dharma, if protected, protects.

FLASH AND LIGHT SIGNALS

I also observed their method of sending signals from one village to another village- both during day and night - During the daytime, they would go to the hilltop and place a mirror. The flashes of the mirror under the sun's rays would indicate signals to the next village about important news like death, marriage, childbirth, or danger. During the night, they would light a fire or a beacon on the hilltop, and two persons holding a blanket would alternatively lift or lower the blanket to allow the light to give short or long flashes. The periodicity of the movement worked like Morse code signalling.

JHUM CULTIVATION

Mizos did "Jhum," or shifting cultivation. They would cut and slash trees and shrubs, burn the remains, level the ground, and after a short while, plant the crops, mainly paddy and maize, and wait for them to ripen. The natural fertility of the soil, adequate rains, and drainage would result in a good crop. They would move from one area to another area and leave the cultivated area as fallow for 3 or 4 years, by which time the forest would have re-generated the soil. Where necessary, small bunds were made to hold water.

Another notable feature of the Mizo village economy, which was based mainly on agriculture, was that there were no individual land holdings. After clearing the land using the 'slash and burn method, the whole community worked together during the entire sowing to harvesting operations. The village chieftain took it upon himself to distribute the total produce according to the needs of each family. There cannot be a better example of a participatory form of Governance or even socialism in its true form.

I also observed another strange phenomenon in the district. There were hardly any birds in Mizo Hills! All the birds had been killed or eaten!

The women were good housewives who kept their homes tidy and clean and took care of their children. They stored grains to last for a year or more. Mizo girls were pretty and fond of coloured dresses. Women wore Puans (skirts). They were fond of ivory bangles, bead necklaces, and fanciful rings. Women would weave colorful Puans. They liked blue, red, white, black and purple colours. The boys and men prefer Western dress. Mizos wear a special type of sturdy hat made of bamboo, which is popularly known as the Mizo Cap. Many of our officers had acquired this quite attractive headgear and jauntily walk around.

Mizos are fond of Western music and are skilled at singing and playing the guitar. The All-India Radio Station set up at Aizawl provides opportunities for Mizo youth to exhibit their skills in the arts, music, and singing.

GUNFIRE VOLLEY

In the last week of December 1966, a little past midnight, we heard a continuous volley of gunfire and grenade blasts from the Sairang valley not far from Aizawl. The DC rang me up in the night and wanted to know if I had any idea about the firing in the valley. I said I was not aware and had not received any report, so I presumed that MNF might have tried to attack the Madras Special Armed Police Camp. D.C. asked me whether we should send any reinforcements. I told him that we had no report or message from the Police. The Army would take action as needed.

Early the next day, we were able to contact Rajaratnam Dy, Commandant of the Madras SAP Battalion, who told me not to worry and that he would meet us at Aizawl. He reported to me. I asked him the cause of the volleys of gunfire at an odd time and whether MNF had attacked the outpost. To my surprise, Rajaratnam said, "Sir, you are an IAS Officer who is surely aware of the rules of the Madras Police Manual that all 'practice ammunition' should be exhausted before the end of the year (31st December) and a report of compliance given in the first week of January. Sir, that is why we have exhausted all our ammunition and have now opened the newly supplied ammunition boxes". He grinned happily and added, "Sir, if MNF hears the sound, they will think that even before an attack, if they can fire so much and for so long, how much more they would fire if in case we attack them and therefore refrain from attacking us"! I thought it was quite a novel way of looking at a situation that only seasoned Government Babus, accustomed to writing replies to explanations called for, could think of.

I was invited to a Barakhana in the Madras SAP Battalion on a Sunday afternoon as the Chief Guest and requested to address the policemen after

Lunch. We asked the constables if they had any problems or difficulties that ADC could solve. I began my talk by thanking the Madras Government for deputing the battalion to Mizo Hills and the men for having done a good job in their new location. I said that I would be willing to hear grievances, if any, other than requests for leave and try to help. I heard many requests, most of which related to the difficulties in adjusting to the weather, lack of recreational facilities, or obtaining leave to attend to important domestic problems. However, there was an unusual request – A constable almost sobbing in his tremulous voice, said, "Sir, my elder brother contacted me and also wrote me a letter saying that his wife had eloped with some person in our village." I asked what his problem was. He said, "Sir, my brother is staying in our village, but his wife has eloped. I am staying far away in Mizo Hills. I do not know what will happen to my wife. I request you to kindly grant me one month's leave on compassionate grounds so that I can go to my native place, console my brother, and ensure that my wife does not elope." – Such are the fears that haunt people in unfamiliar surroundings.

In 1967, the Government appointed senior IAS officer from the Maharashtra Cadre B C Cariappa as Commissioner for Mizo Hills and the nearby District of Cachar. He was stationed in Silchar. He had earlier worked in Vietnam along with the Indian Peace Keeping force under the

U.N. He had the reputation of a tough administrator. He had just arrived and was staying in the Circuit House at Silchar, which served as his office as well. He was keen to visit Mizo Hills to acquaint himself with the problems and guide the district administration.

A WRONG PHONE CALL

Meanwhile Natarajan rejoined as DC after returning from leave. He did not know about Cariappa's posting as Commissioner or had met him. The DC, a stickler for protocol, was unhappy with the Commandant of the Madras Special Armed Police, Kaliappan, who had gone to Silchar without informing him. Natarajan wanted to talk to Kaliappan and give him a piece of his mind, so he tried to contact him over the phone. Unfortunately, the Circuit house phone call was received by a junior functionary, who, instead of connecting it to Kaliappan, the Commandant connected it to Cariappa, the Commissioner, who responded by saying, "Cariappa speaking." It probably sounded like Kaliappan speaking. Natarajan, not aware of the situation, thought that Kaliappan was putting on airs, and started berating Cariappa for dereliction in his work. The bewildered Mr. Cariappa could not follow the conversation. Cariappa calmly told Natarajan that he was speaking to the wrong person and that he was not Kaliappan but Cariappa, the newly appointed Commissioner of the Hills Division. Mr. Natarajan realized his mistake, paused for a minute or two to regain his breath and composure, and profusely apologized and heartily welcomed the Commissioner. I used to often relate this joke about Natarajan to junior officers, cautioning them that we should ascertain who the person on the other end of the phone was before we start a conversation or, worse, a tirade of abuse or praise.

BC Cariappa wanted to visit Aizawl and other important places to acquaint himself with the area, the officers, and the problems. He chose to come by road convoy from Vairangte to Aizawl. I accompanied him on the road from Aizawl to Serchhip and Lunglei. He met the DC and senior officers at Aizawl and assured them that he would visit Mizo District quite frequently and act as a bridge between Mizo District and the Assam Government. He would often remark that the attitude of the Mizo people was quite similar to that of the Vietnamese people who had seen the horrors of war in Vietnam.

REFLECTIONS ON THE MIZO HILLS

Due to disturbed conditions, Mizo families had to undergo a lot of hardships, uncertainties of communications, and constant fear of action from the Army and police forces. If they refused to provide food or shelter to the rebels, they would be harassed by MNF cadres. Many families had to live in a state of anxiety with their husbands or sons as MNF volunteers or forced to work for them as carriers of information, rations, and medicines.

A peaceful place with happy and contented people had to face famine due to Mautam, a natural cause and thereafter deprivation due to political ferment and ambitions of the MNF and its leaders. The worst affected were the womenfolk and children with anxiety written large on their faces and behaviour. Their privations were ascribed to the MNF or Government actions. As a civil servant and magistrate cum judge, I should lessen their sorrows and increase their joyful days. I visualized my role as one of calming the frayed nerves of the people and reassuring them that the process of restoring normal conditions of life for a better life had begun and peace would soon return. I believed that showing the humane face of the Government to the affected Mizo families and assisting them to lead normal lives for the sake of the health and education of their children and the family's economic development was a pressing need.

That was indeed the concept of the Collector or Deputy Commissioner as the Ma Bap of the people. Normalcy had to be first restored in the minds of the people and then on the ground to carry on their lives as best as they could. We wanted the education of children not to be affected. We prioritized ensuring the availability of civil supplies and rations in all

Administrative Centres and surrounding areas. We intensified airdropping of rice with prior intimation to the villages.

We provided good housing, rations, and health facilities in the PPVs, where over 50,000 people lived. We photographed the residents by hiring teams of photographers and issued identity cards to all adults. In a way, it was probably an early precursor version of the electoral identity or Aadhaar card!

We advised the womenfolk to prevail upon the menfolk to surrender arms as the fight between rebels and government forces was an unequal fight. Holding discussions and surrendering arms could prepare the ground for a satisfactory solution. The more the fight continued, the more would be the hardships and tribulations of the innocent people. Printed leaflets and Radio announcements from Radio Aizawl carried the message. Normalcy could bring in songs, games, and joyous events with less sorrow and more joy.

My priorities were the morale building of the Mizo people, employees, and their families, closer coordination with Army and Armed Police forces, restoring peace and trouble-free travel along the main lines of communication from Silchar to Lunglei and Dhaleshwari and Aizawl to Champhai for supplies of essential commodities and rations and the benefits of economic development.

Keeping a vigil on the border with East Pakistan and Burma was essential to prevent the smuggling of arms, gold, and other contraband stuff, including narcotics. Action on building new lines of communication through the good offices of the Border Roads Task Force and helipads at all the administrative Centres and an Airfield near Aizawl were our priorities, which could benefit all and break the isolation of the district.

As there were many Mizo IAS and Government officers, Traders, and Teachers, as well as retired Army personnel, we sought and secured their support in building bridges of Trust, Faith, and Brotherhood. We used to often talk to them about the virtues of Nonviolence, truth, and peaceful approaches are the sole means to accomplish our objectives. The Government wants Mizo rebels to abdicate the path of violence and start the dialogue process for a peaceful and acceptable solution within India, which could foster economic development and ensure peace, progress, and prosperity for Mizos as proud Citizens of India.

The situation in Mizo Hills was a classic case of conflict between the Rule of Law and the Rule of the Jungle – My refrain was that the Rule of Law binds both MNF and Government and cannot take the law into their own hands. If they did so, they would have to face the consequences. Dharma should prevail by upholding order in society and bringing people closer. I found the task difficult as both parties stuck to the viewpoints of their aspirations. It takes a lot of patience and perseverance for peace to prevail and create an environment for negotiations towards a solution. I learned that time and patience can solve many problems.

Mizo Hills District has since undergone many changes. With the implementation of the North Eastern Reorganisation Act in 1972, it became a Union Territory. After a settlement between the MNF and the Indian Government in 1986, Mizoram became the 23rd State of the Indian Union. The accord was initialled by Pu Lalkhama, a Mizo IAS officer.

In July 1967, I received orders posting me in the Finance Department of the Assam Secretariat at Shillong. KK Sinha SDO Goalpara was to relieve me. I paid farewell visits to Lunglei, Demagiri, Serchhip, and Champai. The 61 Mount Brigade, Assam Rifles, CRPF, Maharashtra Special Reserve Police, Madras Special Armed Police gave me farewell parties at Aizawl. I thanked all the officers and staff of the DC's office for their tireless work in restoring normalcy and their cooperation and support for the speedy progress of the district.

The Mizo Hills tenure during its most turbulent, dangerous, and risk-prone period is an unforgettable part of my life, which taught me the need for equanimity of the mind when making decisions. Patience, empathy, and compassion can heal disturbed minds and calm palpitating hearts. I rejoice when I see the progress of Mizoram and its outstanding achievements and progress in myriad activities like music, sports, football, & Hockey. I wish Mizoram and its people continued success and a happy life – Let their music and songs enliven the north-east and India.

15

Deputy / Joint Secretary to Assam Government (Finance) Department, Shillong (July 1966 – Sept. 1968)

After my tenure in Mizo Hills, I was posted as Deputy Secretary in the Finance Department at Shillong. Many of the employees were Bengalis whose exquisite English language was impeccable. Many of them were graduates of Calcutta University and prided themselves on their handwriting and prowess in usage of idiomatic English.

Khasi girls were permitted to move into the Secretariat and sell hot cups of tea, which we drank in fairly large quantities in winter. The atmosphere was quite informal, unlike the Central Secretariat in Delhi and, in many other states. I thought that this was because Assam and the neighbouring areas came under formal British control only by the middle of the 19th Century, and the rigidities of bureaucracy had yet to take root in the Northeast.

Quite a few colleagues in the Secretariat were from South India. I could meet H Pais, V Ramakrishnan, MC Narasimhan, and Krishnamurthy, Secretary to the Governor. Due to the paucity of official quarters, I had to search for rented accommodation and stayed for some time in the Circuit House, which was purchased from Dr. B C Roy, CM of West Bengal. It was located on a small hillock beside the main road and had some good fruit trees. During the cherry blossom season, it was a pleasant scene that was reminiscent of Japan. I rented a small house in Bishnupur. Being compelled because of the lack of a vehicle, Pais, who was Joint Secretary, and I would walk in the mornings to the Secretariat and in the evenings from Secretariat to the Police Bazaar, which had good restaurants for some snacks. The vegetable and flea market in Police Bazaar were dominated by Khasi women.

Khasis and Jaintias have a matrilineal system of society, where property is inherited by the youngest daughter, whose duty is to preserve the name of the family and the tribe. The bridegroom was expected to stay with the bride's family. It was both a surprise and an object of admiration for me to see the independence that women- folk enjoyed in this society and the way they all ran businesses with considerable elan and knowledge of the finer points of business even though they may have never heard of Harvard, IIMs or even the word Business Management. I got the impression that apart from the inheritance rights and control over the family's material resources, the women had full rights to choose whom they wished to marry and divorce the husband if they felt like doing so. In fact, to divorce or dismiss the husband, all that the lady had to do was to keep his shoes outside the door, which amounted to his dismissal orders, and the husband was prohibited from entering the premises.

I called on the CS, A. N. Kidwai, who treated me as if I was a valued colleague, and the Finance Secretary, R Paramasivan, who was a very sharp and intelligent officer but a man of few words. He invited me to tea at his house, where his wife, Madam Jaya, served us really good South Indian dishes.

My batch mate Temen Aonok, who was from Nagaland, was posted at Shillong in the Relief and Rehabilitation Department. He was familiar with the town as he had studied there. He told me that an Italian Catholic Priest who was teaching at Saint Edmunds College was an excellent tailor who used the best tailoring materials from Italy. He wanted me to get a smart suit stitched. At that time, synthetic and blended fabrics were quite popular. I got a stainless and crease-resistant suit stitched. It was one of my well-cut prized suits, which I wore on special occasions.

Parthasarathy was posted in the Appointments Department, in which he was kingpin for all postings and transfers of I.A.S officers. He took me along to call on senior officers at Shillong like P.H. Trivedi, Mr. Ramesh Chandra, SML Bhatnagar, BS Sarao, SJ Das, and BK Bhuiyan. All their wives were very hospitable, particularly to bachelors. We had an unwritten pact amongst bachelor officers at Shillong that if any one of us was invited for tea or dinner by senior officers, we should invariably mention that I had another bachelor friend. The host would then invite the friend also to join. There is a saying in Telugu, "Alludu tho Patu Gilludu," meaning if you invite the son-in-law, he will not come alone but will get another one, a near relative or friend, Gilludu which also means 'pinching' in Telugu. As we had T. S. Gill as Secretary in Shillong, Parthasarathy would revel in telling the meaning of the Telugu saying since the word Gilludu for TS Gill rhymed well with Alludu.

The British called Khasi and Jaintia Hills Scotland of the East. On Sundays at Shillong, I used to go for long walks to the Race Course ground, where many Archery competitions were held among the Khasis. I used to visit the golf course to see the game and players, but I never joined the club or learned golf, feeling that it was an old man's game. Nearby, there was a steep climb with steps up the hill called Jacob's ladder named after Jacob, a well-known Forest Officer. It was an arduous climb, but it was worth it for the panoramic view of Shillong, which is at an average height of 4500 feet.

The monsoon is from April to September, and the weather is very pleasant from October to November, with flowers in full bloom. It becomes very cold in winter, and the night temperature on some days dips from 0% to -2% when the water in the pipelines freezes. In winter, we wore warm clothes, a Wool cap, and gloves. It reminded me of our stay at Mussoorie and Srinagar. Some officers used coal-fired Chimneys to live in comfort. The Secretariat itself was centrally heated, but this system could, at best, be described as unreliable.

The Secretariat of North East Frontier Agency – NEFA (which later became Arunachal Pradesh) was located at Shillong. The Indian Frontier Administrative Service then administered the NEFA. The DCs of the then four districts of NEFA were mostly IFAS officers. In the initial stages, and view of the harsh conditions of life and the border disputes with China, Ex-army officers were sent as administrators or Lt. Governors of Arunachal Pradesh. Subsequently, IAS officers were posted to Arunachal Pradesh.

CHERRAPUNJI – A WET SPOT TO REMEMBER

Out of curiosity, I made a trip to Cherrapunji, some 30 miles from Shillong, which had the reputation of having the highest annual rainfall in the world at 542 inches. It overlooked the plains of then East Pakistan. There was a Ramakrishna Mutt High School where Dileep Singh (1961), a Jaintia officer, had studied. During my stay, late in the evening, I experienced the intensity of the rainfall at the Inspection Bungalow, which was falling in torrents and battering the CI roof. The sound was like that of a railway engine hose pipe discharging water on a tin roof. The noise was so loud that I found it difficult to sleep. It also became cold, and we had to light a small fire in the hearth. The used towels would go damp due to nearly 100% humidity. The towels had to be hung on an iron stand near the fireplace to keep them dry for reuse!

I was soon promoted to joint secretary in the finance department. GC Phukan took over as Finance Secretary from Paramasivan. He placed me in charge of Economic Affairs, Taxation, Budget, and Policy matters and processing of all proposals for financial sanctions. I prepared the Budget for

Assam for the financial year 1968-69. It was my first exposure to estimates from departments, formulation of Budget estimates, revised estimates, and final estimates. I learned the basics of GDP, per capita income, taxation, and ways and means advance. In short, Budget formulation, its presentation, and approvals in the Legislature Assembly.

I was asked by the Chief Secretary to attend the Cabinet Meetings called to clear the Budget. The Cabinet had illustrious personalities like Fakhruddin Ali Ahmed (an alumnus of Oxford and a hockey player to boot) as Finance Minister, MM Chowdhary (Later CM) as Revenue Minister, and D K Barua as Education Minister (later INC President). CS wanted me to record the Minutes of the Meeting, probably to test my attention, comprehension, and correct recording of the decisions taken.

In the meantime, I worked on the Training Manual for IAS probationers and submitted it to the Chief Secretary. It was adopted, and the Government issued relevant orders.

I had to occasionally drive down from Shillong to Guwahati and Borjhar airports to receive Government officials and VIPs from Delhi and escort them to Shillong. It used to take a little over 3 hours of travel from Shillong to Guwahati and likewise for the return journey. The view on the way was wonderful. The pine trees, variety of flowers, houses on the slopes, halting points for vehicles, and quaint tea shops were a sight to behold! It reminded me of the roadway in Kashmir, which no doubt had much more green cover and many brooks and streams. Midway between Guwahati and Shillong is a place called Nongpoh Gate where vehicles moving from Guwahati to Shillong had wait to enable vehicles from Shillong to Guwahati to reach Nongpoh and park there and wait for the safe crossing of upgoing vehicles from Guwahati. This was essentially a gate system to ensure that the vehicles going up or down did not collide on the single road. We used to have about a half-hour break at Nongpoh, where good tea stalls served bread and omlettes, snacks, and hot cups of tea and coffee. A small bazaar was run by Khasi women, selling fresh pineapples, flowers, vegetables, ginger, and turmeric.

The army had a medical unit-cum-field hospital in the Khasi hills on the way to Nongpoh from Guwahati. I met my brother's friend, Major Venkat of the AMC, and a dental surgeon, Major Sriranganath, who were stationed at that unit. I used to drop in and have lunch or tea at their unit when going to the Airport.

Air Vice-Marshal Krishna Rao, who was from Andhra Pradesh, was posted in the Eastern Air Command at Shillong. I called on him and his wife. A hospitable couple, they would occasionally invite me for dinner.

AS SECRETARY OF IIPA

I was nominated as Honorary Secretary of the Shillong Regional Branch of IIPA (Indian Institute of Public Administration), which had been dormant for some time. We organized Lectures by senior officers working in the Secretariat on contemporary issues like Organization and Methods (O&M), Program Evaluation, and implementation, review, and evaluation of the Five-Year Plans in the States.

Senior officers like S J Das, Trivedi, B K Bhuyan, and BS Sarao were very hospitable and would invite us. One of the notable features of the Assam bureaucracy is the general atmosphere of camaraderie, informality, and less emphasis on protocol, a far different situation from many other States and the Central Government.

16

Deputy Commissioner & District Magistrate, Sibsagar District (Sept 1968 – Oct 1970 {2 Years})

I was Joint Secretary in the Department of Finance when Chief Minister Chaliha called and told me that I would be posted as DC to Sibsagar district in upper Assam. I thought that posting as DC in the district from where the CM hailed was a sign of his confidence in me. The CM said that as DC, I must see that peace prevails on the Nagaland border with Assam and work for the district's all-around development. He was concerned about the recurring floods that afflicted the district and the safety of Majuli, the largest river island of India, where river-induced erosion had become a serious problem, rendering many people landless and homeless. I thanked him. I told the Chief Secretary about it. He congratulated me and told me to do well in Sibsagar District. I received orders posting me as D.C and District Magistrate of Sibsagar District.

I reached Jorhat, the headquarters of Sibsagar District. I met S D Phene, DC, who briefed me on the situation prevailing along the Nagaland border, the skirmishes in the reserve forests, and the encroachments in areas bordering the State of Nagaland. He introduced me to senior officers and the personal staff of the D.C. at the Bungalow. He handed over the charge on 17 September 1968 and left the same afternoon to join his family in Shillong. I paid a courtesy call to the District Judge, Mr. Sen, and met the members of the Sibsagar Bar Association. The ADC, Sadar SDO, and senior officers briefed me about their duties. The District Medical Officer, the Superintendent of Police, the Chairman of the Jorhat Municipality, and some prominent local persons called on me.

My personal staff were the Confidential Assistant-cum-Stenographer Bora and Peons Sarukhan and Ghafoor. I had six armed constables on

Shift duty. A personal security officer would accompany me on tours to the interiors. On special occasions, the Dafedar, wearing a colourful shoulder cross fabric with a brass badge (Daval), would also accompany us.

The next day after taking charge, I received a notice from the Central Government Employees Association informing us about the All India Strike in the Railways, Telephone Exchanges, Banks, and Post offices on 18-9-68. I reviewed the arrangements for maintaining law and order with the S.P. My concern was that the daily lives of the people should not be affected even if they are deprived of the services provided by the Central Government Departments. All vital installations had to be properly protected. The non-availability of rail services would not matter much as there were other alternative services in the district. The SP informed me that static guards had been deployed to protect vital installations and that we could always promulgate and enforce orders under Sec 144 of the Cr PC, for which adequate forces were available.

POLICE FIRING AT MARIANI

On 19th September 1968, Railway trains between Guwahati and Dibrugarh were stopped by demonstrators near the Mariani Railway Junction about 12 Km from Jorhat. At about 11 AM, S P came rushing to my office and told me that there was trouble at Mariani Railway junction and requested me to accompany him to Mariani Town in his jeep as he had received information that there was a tense situation and that my presence would be useful. I went with the SP to Mariani Town and asked my vehicle to follow. When we reached Mariani, the railway gate on the road was closed. Crowds were shouting that two persons had been killed in the police firing and dense smoke was coming from the other side of the road.

T K Bora, Senior EAC, had been deputed to Mariani to maintain law and order along with a police party. Apparently, due to the forcible shutting down of shops, the menacing posture of the crowd, and the destruction of some public property, the Magistrate had ordered the firing of teargas shells, but to no avail. As the situation was tense and had to be brought under control by using necessary force, he had ordered firing by the Police. Unfortunately, two persons were killed in the firing, and a couple of others had minor injuries. We realized that the small police party needed reinforcements for effective action as otherwise, the situation could go out of control. I immediately announced, through megaphones, the imposition of 144 Cr PC orders and curfew. The crowd quickly dispersed, and in a few hours, normalcy was restored.

We inspected the railway track with the help of the Railway Protection Force and satisfied ourselves that no tampering had taken place and would be safe to resume rail movements. With the cooperation of the local railway authorities, who were presumably in constant touch with their control room, we were able to get the trains moving. We returned to Jorhat in the late evening.

On 20th September 1968, I ordered a magisterial inquiry into the firing by the ADC. We relaxed the curfew hours to enable people to purchase essential items. In a couple of days, complete normalcy was restored. I reflected on the event and realized that intelligence gathering, and dissemination were not adequate and that advanced preventive steps were lacking. I advised the SP that we should strengthen our intelligence machinery and send adequate force whenever we anticipate serious incidents and keep the rapid strike force ready for action at short notice. I also advised that mock drills must be conducted at trouble-prone areas at frequent intervals. The SP readily accepted these suggestions and acted upon them. I reflected on the incidents of the last two days and thought that I had received a warm welcome and been geared for a variety of events in the district.

On 21st September 1968, there was a fire at Jorhat town. The fire tenders arrived at the spot along with equipment to deal with the situation, but with very little water in the tanks! This was highlighted in local press reports and caused avoidable embarrassment. I realized that a lot of upgrading and fine-tuning of the law-and-order machinery and fire services was required. I conveyed this to the SP (Mishra), and he made some improvements.

We received information that the CM would be coming to Jorhat and Sibsagar on 28th September 1968. I had to receive him on the National Highway at Baguri near Kaziranga Game Sanctuary, which was the border between the Districts of Nowgong and Sibsagar. As per convention and protocol, according to the head of the Government, I had to accompany him to Jorhat. The SP followed me. The CM's car stopped when he saw me. The CM asked me to get into his Benz car and sit beside him in the back seat. He asked the SP to follow us in his car to Jorhat. The driver and Security Officer occupied the front seat of the CM's car. Since I was receiving CM for the first time during his visit, I wore my new suit stitched at Shillong. The CM asked me about the situation on the Nagaland Border and other important matters that occupied his mind.

The CM used to carry a small basket of loose jacket oranges in the back seat. He would break the oranges into two parts, eat the orange slices, and spit out the seeds in a wastepaper basket kept at his feet in the car. He offered me a couple of oranges. I did not want to eat it because the waste basket was far away at the CM's end. A little while later, CM offered 2 more oranges. Both my coat pockets were full of oranges. I was also worried that my suit would be spoiled if the oranges got squeezed. It suddenly dawned on me that my batch mate Aonok had so thoughtfully got a stain-free coat stitched for me at Shillong!

As Jorhat was about an hour's drive, I had ample time to brief the CM on important matters and the nature of representations he might receive from the local people when he halts at the Circuit House before proceeding to his home in Sibsagar. After lunch at Jorhat, the CM would, as was his practice, proceed to Sibsagar. On the return journey to Shillong, if necessary, he would call me to meet him at the Circuit House.

The district is the most important tier of area administration in India, where the policies and programs of all government departments and agencies converge and are in direct contact with the people. It is the principal point of contact between the citizens and the government functionaries. It is a fundamental feature of district administration all over India and has an ancient lineage. It covers a wide range of activities and touches the lives of millions of people. Its efficiency and integrity determine its utility as an instrument of good governance.

Indian Administration has an ancient and rich historical tradition. Kautilya's Artha Sastra of the 2 - 3rd Century ,Akbar Nama and Ain-e-Akbar of Moghul times in the 15th Century AD and the Daftar of the Marathas in the 15th -17th Centuries have chronicled the history of the district. During the Mauryan age, village or gram was the basic unit and the 'little republic' of India. Manu, the ancient lawgiver, ordained the king to appoint a Lord for each village, for 10 villages, 100 villages, and 1000 villages called Adhipathi. In Assam, the titles of Bora, Barua, Saikia (100), and Hazarika (1000) probably echo the continuation of that tradition.

Etymologically, the word District is derived from the Latin word 'Districtus,' which means both territory and the exercise of Justice for the people. Some authorities believe that the British borrowed some principles of district administration from the 'Prefect' system of France and applied them to the British Indian Public Administration. District Administration can be considered the art and science of management applied to the affairs of the state within a defined geographical area.

Just as the district is the most basic compact geographical and territorial unit of administration, the Collector of the district is the most crucial figure in the process of administration at the district level. He is the 'eyes and ears' of the government. For the people, the Collector or DC is "The Government" and is considered the "Ma- Bap" (Mother and Father) for people in need of succour. He is responsible for the well-being of about one to three million inhabitants in the normal district.

The DC or Collector is responsible for the collection of revenues for the government (hence the name of Collector), maintenance of law & order, and land administration, including the acquisition of land and maintenance of land records. He is responsible for civil supplies, the conduct of elections, the census of people and cattle, and all work of the Government not specifically allotted to a Department or functionary apart from protocol duties. He organizes relief and rehabilitation during disasters, floods, and famine times. In short, a Disaster Management Officer. His role has changed over time with the concept of the welfare state, the creation of urban bodies, and Panchayat Raj Institutions. Several changes in political, social, and economic spheres over the last 75 years of India's Independence have impacted the office and functions of the District Collector. With several welfare programs of the State and the Centre, the work of the collector has become heavy, varied, and multi-faceted and often needs multi skills as the job is undefined but important.

The Collector has been provided support by way of Additional or Joint Collectors and Additional Deputy Commissioners or District Revenue Officers in charge of Land Acquisition and Land Revenue matters, Civil Supplies, Panchayat Raj, and liaison work with Municipalities and urban authorities. But people still look up to the Collector for Justice and fast redressal of grievances at the local level. The district is primarily concerned with the implementation of the policies laid down by the Centre and the State. The district has Subdivisions, Taluks, Tehsils or Circles, and now Mandals.

The principal function of the Collector is to coordinate the activities of all departments in the district and be responsible for the total functioning of the government in the district. In a way, the district is not merely a convenient area for administration but a miniature government operating in the local area with its ears and eyes close to the ground.

Two Assistant Commissioners, CNS Nair (1967) and Jomin Tayeng (1968) were sent to Jorhat for their training in District Administration. While Nair was from Kerala, Jomin was from Arunachal Pradesh, married, and had his ways of keeping himself busy. I made it a point to take both with me during my tours and inspections. Both maintained a diary, which was submitted to me every week for my comments. I would indicate in the diary the work they should do in the following week and the reading material, such as Acts, Regulations, etc.

During my tenure, there were three SDOs at Golaghat: Prabir Sengupta (1965), CP Mishra (1966), and Ashok Pradhan (1967). Golaghat was a peaceful Subdivision with many tea gardens, and the general standard of living was quite high. Government offices, tea gardens, local businesses, and educational institutions seemed to provide adequate employment opportunities.

All three sub-divisional officers during my tenure did commendable work and managed the Subdivision successfully and left a mark and favourable image of themselves as young dynamic officers with a great future ahead.

I made it a point to learn all that I could during my tours about the way of life in the villages, towns, tea gardens, and forest areas in Assam. The Special Branch under the SP kept me posted on activities in the district that may require countermeasures through daily and weekly Situation Reports from the Police stations. The Block Development Officers, Sub- Deputy Collectors, Forest officials, and District Medical Officer also kept me informed of all important developments. This enabled me to anticipate and take preventive action when needed.

I adopted the practice of regular inspection of the Revenue Circle offices and monitoring of revenue collection, which resulted in sustained improvements in the collection of land revenue in the entire district. The district received a Government appreciation letter for the highest collection of revenues in Assam in 1969-70. I inspected a few police stations to note whether FIRs were regularly recorded, and action taken in a reasonable time. I do not know whether this system continues or not.

BS Sarao, a Sikh officer from Punjab, was Commissioner of the Plains Division. He wanted to inspect the DC office. He sent two officers in advance to go through the registers in the DCs office and prepare relevant points for the Commissioner who came but did not conduct any inspection. When I reminded him, he asked me to accompany him in his car and proceed towards Sonari, a small town in the District. Sarao was earlier Dy Commissioner in the Sibsagar district, and many farmers recognized him because of his turban and beard. We stopped at a couple of villages in the evening. He asked the farmers whether they had seen or knew the new Deputy Commissioner. They said that I had visited the village earlier and had sorted out long-pending problems with encroachments in the area. In other villages, we did not receive many petitions or applications from the villagers who had been informed about our program. On the way back, I reminded Sarao about the inspection at the office. He said that the inspection was over! I did not understand and asked him again. He said that when the villagers said that they knew the DC, it was clear that DC was quite active and had visited even interior villages. Since the number of petitions received was few, it meant that I was passing orders quickly. He said he was satisfied with the work of the DC, and there was no need for any formal inspection of the office. Our visit to the villages was adequate proof of my work! Sarao was known throughout his career for his innovative and unorthodox ways of examining and solving problems. He later became Chief Secretary of Assam and was also the Chief Commissioner of the Union Territory of Chandigarh.

When our office staff learned that the inspection ordeal was over, they hosted a High Tea for the Commissioner and his staff. Sarao, addressing the staff, said there should be only three trays for files on an officer's table. They should be labeled as "Abhi-Abhi" – Just Now for immediate action; "Abhi-Nahi" – Not Just Now, indicating that some more thought has to go into the decision and "Kabhi-Nahi" –Never to be decided as they are tricky issues, not amenable to quick solutions and need proper attention and care for disposal– It was probably the system of file disposal as practiced in the olden days and the unorthodox ways that Sarao was known for.

Writing the CRs (Confidential Reports) of the officers and staff is quite a big task and should be done in a proper frame of mind to record them objectively. I used to take such and other important files, proceed to a good Forest Rest House nearby, and spend two or three days there writing the CRs objectively and in a calm mind and mood.

Sometimes, after ordering the preventive arrest of some notorious or undesirable persons, I would become untraceable, ensconced as I was in a forest rest house for a couple of days, making it difficult for them to obtain bail. This was a typical bureaucratic ruse.

The DC bungalow had a large compound with over 5 acres of land. Four of the Jail prisoners used to be sent to the DC's bungalow to clear wild plants and assist Mali in gardening. I wanted the prisoners to learn some useful skills to help them in rehabilitation after release from jail. I cleared a large portion of the unused land and ploughed it with a tractor to make it suitable for cultivation. Paddy and maize were grown. We had a good crop that was sold, and proceeds were put into the bank accounts of the 4 prisoners so that on release from prison, they would have some money in hand. They worked happily, feeling that they were useful citizens.

A NOSTALGIC VISIT

Mr. Tom Hayley, an ICS officer, was the last British D.C of Sibsagar District at Jorhat in 1946. I received a request in September 1969 from Anne Hayley, his wife, and her daughter, who had arrived in Jorhat from the United Kingdom and wanted some accommodation for a week to ten days there. We provided them with accommodation in Circuit House and helped them visit Sibsagar, Joysagar, some tea gardens, and the Kaziranga Sanctuary. At the time of their departure, I presented them with a gift of tea packets. I received a nice letter from Mr. Hayley from London, thanking me for the comfortable and nostalgic visit of the family to Jorhat after 20 years.

The foothills of the Himalayas are an active Seismic zone. It has a history of frequent earth tremors, with a big earthquake occurring once in 40 years or so, as Assam is also in the seismic zone. Buildings are made of light construction materials like timber, wood, and bamboo. The walls had timber frames with splintered bamboo plastered on both sides with cement or lime to make it light. The roofs were of CI sheets or thatch. The PWD had good experience in constructing buildings that could withstand earthquakes.

Jorhat used to have occasional tremors. In 1970, when I was holding Court in the DC's office, around noon, we found the entire building tilting and all of us rushed out of the office. We could see the whole building rocking for about half a minute and then stabilizing as the energy of the quake dissipated. We resumed work in the office

DERGAON SUGAR FACTORY

A Cooperative Sugar factory in Dergaon that was running profitably later got into problems. Adequate sugarcane was not available, the sucrose content was not high, and molasses sales did not get good prices. The farmers and employees were agitated as there was a proposal to shut down the sugar factory. The Government took over the factory and made the DC Chairman of the Sugar Factory Board. This matter was heatedly discussed in the Assam Assembly at Shillong. I was requested to visit Shillong and be available to give correct information and help the Minister to answer questions raised in the Assembly. The Minister in charge of Cooperation said that the DC has been made Chairman, and it is hoped that the factory would resume operations quickly and be turned around. Debeshwar Sarma, MLA (former Finance Minister) from Jorhat, made a scathing attack on the incompetence of the factory management and Government to run the sugar factory profitably. He castigated the Government and quoted an Assamese proverb that said, "If the pumpkin goes bad, call the Brahmin, and give it to him as a gift." It would get rid of the unwanted pumpkin and gain some Punya or merit for the gift made! For the Government, the DC seems to be the Brahmin to whom the difficult sick and crying baby can be handed over". We did turn around the factory and prevented its closure. The DC (Brahmin) had indeed become the saviour!

ASSAM STATE ELECTRICITY BOARD STRIKE

In August 1970, a section of workers of the Assam State Electricity Board (ASEB) went on a strike, jeopardizing the supply of power in Sibsagar district. The District Administration mobilized personnel from ONGC, RRL, and Defence Establishments to prevent disruption of power supply and ensure the availability of power. The ASEB Chairman Dharmendra Das (later became CS) conveyed appreciation to the ASEB for the services rendered by the district administration to restore and maintain vital power supply to the public and industry so quickly. We circulated the letter to all who helped in the effort.

POLLUTION IN THE NAMRUP RIVER

The Namrup fertilizer factory was located on the border of Dibrugarh and Sibsagar districts. The factory was releasing its effluents without proper treatment into the Namrup River. Due to the pollution caused by the discharged chemicals in the water, fish died in large numbers, and there was an uproar from nearby villages and fishermen. The DC of Dibrugarh got complaints about chemical pollution of the river and wanted to visit Namrup and requested me to join him for a joint inspection and work out measures to prevent future pollution of the river in consultation with the Namrup fertilizer factory officials. The M.D. was Mohini Phukan, an IAS officer of the Assam cadre. We saw the fertilizer factory, noted the cause of the pollution, and wanted better effluent treatment facilities to be set up in Namrup to prevent pollution of the river. We suggested that the polluted water should be sent to a pond in which fish were kept. Only if the fish survived should the sewerage be cleared for letting out into the river. It was not a scientific or technically sound arrangement, but it helped reduce pollution in the river and allay fears. The plant authorities were harping that "the only solution to pollution is dilution," and therefore, they had let out the pollutants during the rainy season when the river was full. We had to remind the fertilizer authorities that if pollution continued, the Government would have to impose monetary fines based on another maxim called "Polluter Pays" for the damage caused.

REVENUE COLLECTIONS INCREASE

We introduced the practice of giving gold rings on Republic Day to Mauzadars (Revenue Agents), who exceeded the collection targets with respect to current and arrear dues on Republic Day. A Mauzadar with consistent 100% revenue recovery was Saikia, a respected landlord of Titabar. His son Ashok Saikia, who attended the function with his Mauzadar father and later got into the IAS, would often cite me as his inspiration to become an IAS officer. He was later secretary to the then PM AB Vajpayee and executive director of India at the Asian Development Bank in Manila.

MAJULI – THE ABODE OF THE SATRAS

Majuli, an island in the Brahmaputra River, between Sibsagar and North Lakhimpur district, is the largest river island in the world. It is now severely eroded due to flooding and riverbank erosion and has affected the lives and livelihoods of its people. Majuli became a district in 2016 and has seen some development in terms of better communications and tourism.

The Vaishnava movement, which spread from lower Assam to upper Assam, found Majuli - naturally isolated and protected by the river Brahmaputra - a haven for the location of ***Satras roughly equivalent to the mutts in Southern India established by the great Acharyas such as Adi Shankara, Madhva,*** and ***Ranmanuja,*** and ***Namgarhs*** were prayer halls where kirtans were regularly sung. Shankardeva's message was carried forward by his successors, Madhavdeva and Damodardeva.

There were doctrinal differences between Shankaracharya's Advaita Vedanta and the Vaishnavite syncretic tradition of Srimanta Sankaradeva, which, to my mind, was more akin to the Madhwa and even Ramanuja's Philosophy. Adi Shankara's emphasis was on Gyana Yoga, whereas Madhwa's was on Bhakti Yoga, which was also the philosophical doctrine of Srimanta Shankardeva. It is truly wonderful to witness how great an influence and a benign force Sanathana Dharma was and the unifying role it played in every part of Bharatha Varsha.

The more prominent Satras were Dakshinapat, Auniati, Gormur, and Kamalabari. The Satraadhikari or Matadhipathi was in-charge of the Satra. He had a group of Sishyas or disciples and an Upa-peetadhipathi, an apprentice Brahmachari being trained to take over the functions of Satradhikar in due time. Some Satraadhikaris were well-read and helped their followers to solve their problems. They used to explain many philosophical matters through Lord Krishna's stories in simple language, based primarily on the Bhagwath. I was particularly impressed by the Satradhikaris of Gormur and Auniati Satra, who were revered scholars able to explain intricate questions pertaining to Advaitha, Dvaita, and Vishishtadvaita philosophies lucidly and comfort and console devotees and help them solve their problems.

SATTRIYA DANCES

The Satras have a tradition of generosity and hospitality and feed all disciples and visitors. I was keen to understand the Rasa Leela Sattriya dances of Majuli, as they are famous. After many delays and a great deal of effort, the Sattriya form is now recognized as a classical dance form along with Bharatha Natyam, Kuchipudi, etc. I visited Majuli and spent four days learning about the Satriya dances in the Auniati, Dakshinapatha, and Gormur Satras. I took photographs of the Rasa Leela performances for my record and wrote an article for the Telugu press.

In many South Indian traditions, the dances relating to Lord Krishna and his consorts Radha, Rukmini, and Satyabhama were performed earlier only by males who donned the roles of women. But this has changed over time, and women are honoured participants in all forms of dances all over India. The Satriya dances appear to closely resemble the Kuchipudi dance tradition of Andhra Pradesh. I told the Satradhikari about Kuchipudi dances and their evolution and that time and events had allowed girls and women to take part in the dances and play the female characters instead of only males doing female characters. In Kuchipudi dances, women's roles are being performed by girls who are now also playing the role of men! The ancient traditions were being tuned in line with current trends. I also told them about Kalakshetra Dance Academy in Madras. As Chief Guest, I witnessed two dance performances at Jorhat by two Assamese girls trained in Kalakshetra, Madras, which was highly appreciated and lauded by the local people. It should be noted that changes first start in the mind when cross-fertilization of ideas takes shape and then happens on the ground.

SIBSAGAR - A TEA DISTRICT

Sibsagar District has many tea gardens, some of which are located on the border with Nagaland. I visited tea gardens to learn how the industry was organized, the various processes in making the green leaf into a marketable commodity, and the issues of labour welfare and housing problems of the tea garden labour. I was informed that the yield of the tea bushes was falling as most of them had been planted during British times and were old. The bushes needed replanting with application of organic or inorganic fertilizers and adequate shade. Pest attacks had to be prevented. Most of the gardens were privately owned and managed. Reinvestment and replantation of the tea bushes was the responsibility of the owners. Assam tea was highly rated in the international market, and most of the tea companies were making handsome profits. The Tea Board of India, located in Kolkata, was assisting the tea garden management.

Fresh tea leaves are plucked and collected by the women early in the morning, weighed, and sent for drying to a large shed called a "withering shed." The top two leaves of the plant, along with the bud, were considered high-quality, particularly the second flush tea. This has given rise to the epithet of "two leaves and a bud" for good tea.

Tea leaves are plucked during the sprouting, which happens as soon as the rain starts after the end of the dry winter season. Leaves plucked in the second flush in spring command the highest price. The leaves are taken to the factory, the juice extracted, and the leaves sun-dried or oven-baked to speed up the process. They are later made into CTC (Curl Tear Crush) or Orthodox tea with full leaves. After the processing, the teas are graded into leaf grades and other varieties before being packed for use. The tea factories used to burn a lot of Assam coal with high Sulphur content, causing pollution. Much later, when I was CMD of Assam Gas Company (AGC) in 1977, we provided piped natural gas to the tea garden factories by laying pipelines that eliminated sulphur contamination.

There were Bank branches only in the District, Subdivisional towns, or some important commercial places, whereas the tea gardens were in remote or isolated rural areas. In every tea garden, there were one or two Marwari shops supplying rations, soaps, oils, and daily use commodities to the labour. The money given by management as wages to the labourers would go to the shopkeepers, who, in turn, lent the money to the tea garden management, completing the cycle of money circulation in the garden. Many labourers also borrowed from the Marwaris and fell into debt. Sadly also, many among the labourers fell into the habit of drinking locally brewed alcohol or spirits which were adulterated and harmful. This led to several problems like crime, theft, and violence against women.

TOCKLAI TEA RESEARCH STATION

To solve the problems of the tea industry, the Tea management and Government collectively funded the Tocklai Tea Research Station at Jorhat. A group of qualified research scientists—biochemists, agricultural graduates, agronomists, and soil physicists—worked in Tocklai. The Tea Board of India at Calcutta relied upon Tocklai for guidance on the uprooting of old bushes, replantation, and scientific plantation of tea bushes to secure higher productivity in small gardens and the curing processes of tea.

The group of tea gardens owned by Birlas started the experiment of plucking leaves not only during the rainy season but throughout the year which they called 'perennial plucking'. Tocklai Tea Research Station was studying the long-term viability of this practice. Tocklai collected information on yields of tea bushes based on age, soil, shade, moisture, and other parameters from many gardens and was doing a series of experiments to improve the productivity of the tea bushes.

TEA TASTERS

The taste of tea, in terms of flavour, smell, lightness or strength (pungency), and fragrance, determines its demand and price. Tea Tasters predict its acceptability and price. Tocklai developed special expertise in Tea Tasting to advice about the price range of teas from different gardens. Tea samples in water without milk would be made and twirled in open cups. The tea taster would take a sip, swish it in his mouth, and throw it out. His tongue and palate were so sensitive that they could distinguish the taste, flavour, thickness, and pungency of different grades of tea. He could also, with experience, say which tea garden the tea leaves had come from. Tea Tasters were the highest-paid officials in the industry and had to take care of their valuable assets– their mouths, tongues, and palate! Many tea tasters took Insurance cover. To maintain their value as reliable tea tasters, these individuals, though well-paid, had to forgo smoking and alcohol consumption, which I guess is a price worth paying.

During my tenure at Jorhat, I got acquainted with experts at Tocklai and learned from them some finer points. Satyanarayana, a biochemist; Ram Mohan Rao, a soil physicist; Rehman, an Agricultural Scientist; Bezbaruah and his wife, both scientists who were working in Tocklai. They were knowledgeable on all aspects of the tea industry. Assam, at that time, was the world's largest producer of tea, contributing some 60% of India's tea production. I learned a lot about tea auctions at Calcutta, where prices were determined for both internal and export use. Later, Guwahati also became an Auction Centre for Tea.

PLYWOOD INDUSTRY

The huge demand for tea chests led to the development of the Plywood industry in Assam. However, it led to large-scale deforestation. Though the State Government Forest Department planned to reforest, this did not diminish the rate at which forest cover was being lost.

TEA PLANTATION INDUSTRY

Sibsagar District had over 250 tea gardens and was the venue for several events concerning the tea industry. The headquarters of Assam Tea Company was at Jorhat. The Tocklai Tea Research Station was world-renowned. Many of the tea garden managers were still British, while the Assistant Managers, Supervisors, and Labour were all Indians. Some Assamese families owned smaller gardens. The garden labour was mostly from Chota Nagpur, Bihar, Orissa, and M.P. and some refugees from Burma from the Second World War.

The British brought the tea plantation industry and culture to the State of Assam, understanding that the climate, rainfall, and soil character were suitable for large-scale cultivation of this camellia plant. They did face many privations, given the fact that the area was malaria-infested, and the climate was far different from what they were used to in the British Isles. There are records to show that many an Englishman lost his life and wife in this venture. Some fell prey to marauding elephants and tigers.

The Indian Tea Association (ITA) members owned many Tea Gardens controlled by British interests. Mr. Courtney, a British national, was the Secretary of the ITA, who used to meet me quite often in connection with the problems of the tea industry and invite me to their annual and special events. Tea Association of India (TAI) was in the hands of Indian Tea planters. The planters were quite comfortable with good bungalows, well-manicured lawns, and tennis courts, and they led a very luxurious life with a plethora of servants. There was an ITA Racecourse- cum-Pavilion near Jorhat where functions would be held. There was a posh Planters Shop at Jorhat where we could obtain the choicest English biscuits, chocolates, and other British goods. I could get Huntley-Palmers and Peek Frean biscuits and Cadbury chocolates imported from London, which I had not eaten since childhood.

I made friends in the tea industry from among the Indian and British Managers. One of them was Charles Emmett, who represented India in Hockey at the Olympics. Among the Indian managers were two Telugus Subba Rao and Siram Ranga.

JUDGE AT A TEA GARDEN COOKING COMPETITION

On one occasion, tea garden ladies invited me to be a judge at a cooking competition. I was expected at 11 AM (Garden time) for the function. I went at 11.00 AM (Indian Standard Time), which is one hour later, i.e. noon in Garden Time. At that time, I did not know that Assam followed both Garden and Indian Standard Time. The sun rises in the east in Assam at least one to one and a half hours earlier before it crosses the middle of India. The tea garden management starts work early by plucking tea leaves at dawn and closes operations by late noon as it gets dark in Assam by about 4.30 PM. I apologized for the delay due to my ignorance, and the ladies understood. They not only pardoned my misunderstanding but also rewarded me by giving me a boxful of select cookies, biscuits, and eatables made for the competition and some choice tea packets. It was a surprise reward. On the way back, I believed my need for tea-time snacks had been covered for a while. Two such gracious ladies were Mrs. Nag and Mrs. Chitra Dutta, wives of Garden Managers. They helped me a lot in connection with the visit of the President of India, Dr Zakir Hussain, and other VIPs by suggesting menus or supplying snacks and good tea and the décor of the circuit house.

ASSAM OIL INDUSTRY ORIGINS – ELEPHANT BATH AND DIGBOI

Crude oil was discovered in Dibrugarh district in 1898. The story goes that an elephant had gone into a swamp, and when it came out, its body was completely covered in crude oil. An enterprising tea garden manager saw the elephant and realized that crude oil was probably available in the area. Drilling for oil started, and to speed up the operations, the manager, to encourage the operators to continue digging, seems to have said "Dig-Boy," "Dig-Boy." The place is now called Digboi and is considered the first strike of crude oil in India.

OIL INDIA TOWNSHIP

Oil India was set up as a private company to investigate, explore, and drill for crude oil. They developed Duliajan as their model headquarters on the lines of Jamshedpur, with a good township, wide roads, and avenue trees providing shade and flowers. It is really a colourful township and a pleasure to behold.

ONGC EASTERN HEADQUARTERS AT NAZIRA

The Indian Government set up the Oil and Natural Gas Commission (ONGC) to investigate, explore, and invest in the discovery and recovery of oil and natural gas. An ICS officer, Johnson was the Secretary to the Union Government. He came to Sibsagar to discuss land acquisition for ONGC in Sivasagar Subdivision. They were negotiating to purchase some land near Sibsagar town. I told Johnson that a tea garden called Nazira` was not doing well, and management was thinking of selling it. I told him that it would be a worthwhile proposal to purchase the tea garden outright, which could come cheap, providing ONGC not only ample land but also bungalows, offices, etc., and give ONGC a quick start. This was agreed upon, and Nazira became the Headquarters of the Eastern Region of ONGC.

ONGC – GAS FLARES

ONGC speeded up work on drilling wells for oil and natural gas in the Sibsagar and Tinsukia areas of the Dibrugarh district. On many occasions, large volumes of oil and gas at high pressure would gush out of the bores.

COLLEGE GIRLS CAUGHT IN THE RAIN

Assam and the NE region is a heavy rainfall area. One evening, when I was in the bungalow office, it started raining heavily. A group of college girls returning home got caught in the rain just in front of the DC bungalow. Realizing that the rain would not stop quickly, and they would get drenched, they rushed to DC's Bungalow. The rain was relentless and furious, and some more girls came to the bungalow and waited on the porch. Soon, the group spilled over to the veranda. The sentry came and told me that 8 to 10 girls who were caught in the rain had taken shelter in the veranda were standing. I asked him to let them into my office room and be seated. They sat at the end of the room.

My cook came down the stairs as usual with a cup of tea and a couple of biscuits for me. I felt embarrassed to take the biscuits, so I started sipping the tea and asked the cook to get some tea for the girls. He became extra gracious and told me loudly, "Sir, shall I bring biscuits and cookies also?" I quietly called him aside and asked him, "Do we have so many biscuits?" He replied, "Sir, we have got the box of biscuits and cookies sent by the Tea Garden Mem Sahibs." I realized that the cookies and homemade biscuits, which I thought I could leisurely savour over several evenings, would be all consumed by the girls seated in front of me and the entire stock exhausted in a jiffy. I felt it would not be fair to deprive the girls of the goodies, who were already quite nervous and distressed. Regaining my composure, I asked him to serve tea with biscuits and cookies. The girls, who were pleasantly surprised to receive not only tea but also delicious homemade cookies and biscuits, were very happy. The ice had been broken. The girls started whispering, giggling, and talking amongst themselves. I could not hear them but guessed that they enjoyed the unexpected hospitality.

The rain was still pouring, and it was getting dark. My driver, Raju, came to my room for instructions regarding my program for the next day. One of the girls happened to know or recognize Raju, as they were from the same locality. She said, "Sir, it is getting dark and Raju knows my house. "Another girl said, "It is getting late." Other girls said, "Rain is not stopping – What do we do?" Another girl said, "It is getting very late. Our parents will be worried". My driver, Raju, said that he knew one or two girls and offered to drop them in my car if permitted, as it was still raining.

My mind went dizzy for a minute. There was a bevy of girls stranded in a young bachelor DC's bungalow at a late hour in the dusk when it was heavily raining. To send them off in the DC's car with a red light on top in the dusk or dark could present quite a few problems and many questions later on and be easily subjected to misinterpretation. If any person notices, and, worse still, a journalist, and if the event is reported in the newspapers the next day, this could easily lead to misunderstanding and misrepresentation. I feared that my image would be sullied. I called Raju aside and whispered in his ear to ensure that the red light on top of the car was not switched on, the nameplate of the DC's car was fully covered, and without using the horn or anything else that may invite the attention of others, quietly drop the girls at their respective places, and return to the Bungalow post-haste, park the car and go home and not talk about it. Luckily, there were no reports in the local press. A lone parent thanked me. Probably, the parents of the other girls had blessed me with my concern about the safety and security of the young college girls. I do not know what the girls thought about my hospitality. Anyway, it spared me a dozen explanations.

THE KAZIRANGA SANCTUARY

Kaziranga Sanctuary is a perennial attraction for tourists because of the variety of wildlife, natural habitat, and big mammals like elephants, water buffaloes, rhinos, etc. It had the unique distinction of being the home of the largest number of **one-horned Rhinoceros**. The African rhino has two such smaller horns. The other wildlife in abundance were swamp deer, boars, pygmy hogs, snakes and pythons, birds, and some elephants. Some tigers have also been sighted in this reserve. It was picturesquely located beside the Brahmaputra River in Sibsagar and part of Nowgong District on the south and Darrang District on the north bank.

I had to accompany VIPs and visit Kaziranga Sanctuary so often that the forest officers would remark that I probably knew more of the Kaziranga terrain than they did. Frequent visits enabled me to understand wildlife, their nature, and their habits. I witnessed some poignant scenes while I was on an elephant back in the sanctuary. There was an old blind rhino that had either lost its sight in a fight or due to old age. It was depending on a small pygmy hog to guide its movements in the sanctuary. Rhinos have a habit of grazing everywhere but would go to a specific spot to drop their excreta. The pygmy hog used to circle the front legs of the blind rhino, move some distance, and grunt, thus guiding and leading him to the correct grazing points and to the defecation area. It made me think of God's mysterious ways of helping humans and animals in distress.

There used to be heavy floods in the Brahmaputra, and the elephants, wild buffaloes, and rhinos would move from low-lying areas to higher ground. The forest department had earmarked a 'safe corridor' for the animals to move from the sanctuary and cross the national highway to safer, higher level forest areas available in Mikir Hills. The Forest Department would stop trucks driving on the National Highway to ensure the safe passage of the animals. The intelligent elephants sensed an opportunity. When the trucks with goods were waiting on the highway on either side of the safe corridor, two or three elephants would stand on the road to prevent the movement of the trucks. Some enterprising drivers started carrying bunches of bananas in their trucks. Once the bananas were offered, the elephants would take them and allow free passage to the trucks on the national highway. In fact, it became an elephant-manned banana check post!

POACHING FOR RHINO HORNS

There was a lot of poaching for rhino horns as it is considered an aphrodisiac (like Viagra) in China and Southeast Asia and was in great demand and highly-priced. The horn is, in fact, not a muscle or bone but only an agglomeration of hair on the head (held by a glue-like substance) that gives the hair a solid profile. This was the only defensive weapon for the Rhino, which by nature was slow-moving and short-sighted. No doubt, the thick skin resembling the armour plating of a tank was also a deterrent. The horn is highly valued and used in Southeast Asia and in many parts of the world as medicine. There is no scientific basis for this belief, and it was nothing more than a superstition. This led to indiscriminate poaching and killing of rhinos. The forest guards of the sanctuary were inadequate in number to guard a big area, not mobile enough, and did not have appropriate firearms to prevent the poaching activities. The forest department, over time, has been able to prevent poaching and killing of rhinos to a very large extent. Credit must go to the Forest Department for their work to prevent poaching and to bring poachers to book. There was an enterprising DCF called Deb Roy who brought about much-needed changes in the sanctuary. He secured the support of the villagers bordering the sanctuary, which increased the rhino population. This sanctuary has been converted into a national park, which has resulted in good funding, the augmentation of personnel, better supervision, equipment, and mobility. The number of tourists has also increased. Latest reports indicate that the Rhino population, which had been reduced to a dangerous level, has now increased significantly.

INFLUX OF DIPLOMATS

A large number of foreign diplomats, national and international tourists visited Kaziranga Park during the fair weather. Many of them would stay for a couple of nights or more at Kohara Guest House which was subsequently renovated. Due to the strategic importance and natural beauty of Assam and Northeast India, many foreign diplomats from Australia, Canada, and New Zealand, and Ambassadors from the U.S, EU, and Russia would visit Assam to see the Sibsagar monuments, Tea Gardens, etc. I often had to take care of them during their stay and arrange local programs.

With the sustained increase in visitors to Kaziranga Sanctuary, Kohara Guest House proved inadequate and was enlarged and reconstructed. There was a bachelor, Dr. Rabin Banerjee, who worked as a doctor in a tea garden in Golaghat Sub-division. He was a good wildlife photographer and nature conservationist. He made educational and entertaining small documentary films, which were projected at night at Kohara's guest house for the benefit of visitors. Several wildlife films on Kaziranga Sanctuary were made subsequently. Kaziranga has now become an internationally recognized National Park for wildlife-cum-adventure tourism.

KAZIRANGA AS A NATIONAL PARK

In early 1970, the Assam Government wanted to send a proposal to the Union Government to make Kaziranga Sanctuary a National Park. BS Sarao, who was Commissioner of the Plains Division, was requested to prepare a report for submission to the Indian Government. He camped in Kohara and requested that I assist him with the history, facts and figures, flora, and fauna of Kaziranga, as well as help in the drafting of the report. We worked on the report seriously and nearly finalized it. Sarao wanted the recommendations to be presented informally to the Forest Minister and the Advisory Committee of the Forest Department to incorporate their views in the report.

A two-day meeting was organized at Kohara Guest House. The first day was for discussions. The next day, all of us went to the Kaziranga Sanctuary by jeep and on elephants to see the important features, understand issues, and prepare a plan for development. Lunch was organized in a select spot near an observation tower beside a small brook in the sanctuary. Members of the Committee who saw the brook and water spread beside it, teeming with a variety of fishes that had grown temptingly big, wanted to have delicious fish dishes - boiled, curried, and fried to be part of the menu. The Advisory Committee members enjoyed the fish repast and were in a happy mood. They wanted such meetings to be held more often, fully endorse the report, and assure support in the Assembly and other fora.

The Report on Kaziranga set the ball rolling and with the Union Government's approval, Kaziranga is now India's prized, world-recognized wildlife National Park for single-horned rhinos and other wildlife.

NAGALAND BORDER

In the 12 -13century, Ahoms, under the leadership of "Sukapha" from Thailand, occupied the plain areas of Assam. They delineated the border of the hill areas inhabited by the Nagas (scantily dressed), who were fierce warriors and who used to come to the plains to sell salt and buy essential needs. The Nagas are of Indo-Mongoloid origin and occupy the hill areas abutting Assam, Arunachal Pradesh, Myanmar, and Manipur. There are 16 tribes among the Nagas with their distinctive dress, customs, and habits. The prominent tribes are Angamis, Aos, Chankasangs, Kukis, Konyaks, Lothas, and Zeliangs. The Tangkhul Nagas live in both Nagaland and Manipur and across the border in Myanmar. While each tribe has its own dialect, inter- tribal communication is through a simple form of Assamese known as Nagamese, which is a mixture of Assamese and Naga tribal dialects.

The Ahoms used to pay an annual fee to Nagas to prevent them from raiding the Bazaars in the plains and harassing the local residents. They also built a barrier or border road to prevent the Nagas from entering Ahom territory. This was called "Dodar Ali," as it was built by conscripting lazy persons as punishment. The remnants of this road are still visible in various parts of the district.

The Nagas were considered head-hunters. They were warrior tribes that fought among themselves and with other tribes. In some tribes, a bachelor could get married only if he had killed a person to prove his martial prowess. The Nagas used spears and a sword or dao to slash the jungle. When the Japanese invaded Burma and came to Kohima in Naga Hills, the Nagas supported the British Indian forces.

The women folk looked after the children and assisted in agricultural operations. Nagas like colourful dresses and women weave their own clothes. Both men and women performed Naga dances. A National Festival called 'Hornbill' is celebrated and has now emerged as a big tourist attraction.

The British, who annexed Assam in the 19th century, gradually extended their control over Naga Hills. They encouraged missionary activities, which led to the spread of Christianity and educational facilities. While most tribes accepted Christianity, the 'Heraka' group led by Rani Gaidaliue, honoured as a freedom fighter and remembered with pride among some tribals, was a notable exception. However, their effort to resist spread of missionary activities was not successful.

Kohima is the capital of Nagaland, but the commercial centre and gateway is Dimapur, which has a Railway Station and Airport in the plains. Nagas used to come to Dimapur for trade and commerce. The town is inhabited by the Dimasa Kacharis, who hold the view that the Dimapur town and adjoining areas were unfairly made part of the State of Nagaland.

A British delegation under Clement Atlee, who came to India to consider the demand for India's Independence, also visited Nagaland. When the British conceded the demand for India's Independence, it triggered a demand from the Nagas for an independent Nagaland called 'Nagalim' for uniting all ethnic Nagas resident in India, Burma, Arunachal Pradesh, Manipur, and other adjoining areas. They formed the Naga National Council (NNC) under the leadership of Angami Zepho Phizo, who collected a band of young people, procured arms, trained and indoctrinated them to launch an armed insurrection to attain an independent Nagaland called Nagalim. Prolonged negotiations took place, both with the officials of the Indian Government and the Assam Governor, Naga National Council, and other groups, when it was agreed to make Nagaland a State within the Indian Union. While some Naga groups felt that statehood in India with requisite powers could be accepted, as they would get better roads, communication facilities, and educational and employment opportunities in India, the NNC was not agreeable. Jayaprakash Narayan, the socialist leader, and BP Chaliha, Chief Minister, tried to convince the Naga factions to accept Naga statehood within India. The Central Government formed Nagaland as a State in 1961. Access to outsiders was through Restricted Area Permits, to prevent migration by plains people to settle in Nagaland. Despite full statehood granted to Nagaland, this solution was not accepted by some sections of the Nagas.

A new body called the NSCN (National Socialist Council of Nagaland) came into being under the leadership of Isaac Swu and T Muivah (both Tangkhul Nagas) whose presence is significantly more in Manipur and across the international frontier in Myanmar who stick to their demand for total independence and unification of all Naga inhabited areas in Nagalim. In 2018, the GOI signed a Framework Agreement with the NSCN (IM).

Very few details of this agreement have been made available so far, but it appears to reinforce the idea of peaceful negotiations and the avoidance of armed conflict.

ASSAM – NAGALAND BORDER DISPUTE

After the formation of Nagaland, the CRPF was deputed to Nagaland as the state's armed police and to guard its border. The Nagaland government raised an issue by disputing the Assam-Nagaland border, which was delineated under Notification in R 302 in 1925 by the Indian Government. The notification was basically a reiteration of the inter-district boundary between the Naga Hills district and the districts of Assam, mainly Sibsagar. Nagaland contends that the Hill areas and Reserve forests adjoining the hills belonged to the Nagas as per custom and tribal laws. They did not honour the 1925 notification on the grounds that the consent of the Nagas was then not taken and, therefore, not binding on them. It was a classic clash of Roman and Tribal Law triggered by Naga expansionist ambitions. Even after the grant of separate statehood, the problem of Naga tribes raiding the forest areas on the boundary in Assam, carrying away the grains cultivated and harvested by the people of Assam, and committing crimes, intimidation, and looting continued. It was difficult for the Reserve Forest staff to guard against the sudden raids of the armed Nagas and protect the agricultural produce of Assam farmers.

The Assam Government implemented a scheme of settling an area of half a kilometer width on the border with landless Nepalis and Assamese who could protect themselves from the raiders. The Assam Government deployed the 3rd Assam Reserve Police along the half km border to prevent Naga incursions and protect the lands and their agricultural operations.

As a countermeasure, the Nagaland Government deployed CRPF in Border Out-Posts along with some Nagaland Civil police. The old claim that bordering forest areas were part of Nagaland was kept alive by officially backing Naga raids and aggressive patrolling by the Nagaland Police.

To protect areas within the legitimate territory of the State of Assam, the Government established a series of armed Border Out-posts manned mostly by trained Assam Police battalion personnel. Despite these measures, the Naga tribesmen continued their raids to destroy the huts and homes of settlers in the half-km belt and forcibly harvest paddy crops grown in the Assam area and carry them away. Stronger measures and intense patrolling were taken on a continuous basis, and the raids came down but did not stop. There are many notified Reserve forests like Geleki, Dissoi, Merapani, Kakodonga, Rengma, Nambar, Diphu, and Doyang in Assam, all along the Assam-Nagaland border. It was difficult to patrol the forest areas all along the Assam-Nagaland border. There were confrontations between Assam police and CRPF quite often. With frayed tempers on both sides, cases of firing between Assam Police and CRPF took place. The Assam Government was concerned about the likely repercussions. Discussions at the district and state level did not result in workable solutions and was remitted to the Indian Government level.

NAGA GAONBURA'S ADVICE TO D.C

During the evictions on the Assam-Nagaland Border, a group of Nagas under the leadership of a Gaonbura (Head of the village) in Nagaland came to protest the evictions in the Assam-Nagaland border areas. He enquired with the Assam Police about who the D.C was and wanted to meet him to discuss important matters. The 3rd A.P. Police Border Outpost Officer escorted Gaonbura and his four followers to meet me at the Outpost. Gaonbura asked me in crude Nagamese (a local form of Assamese spoken by Nagas), "Toi, DC, Na ki?" – Are you the DC? I said, "Hoi – moi – DC" – I am the DC. He said, "Toi DC ya DC r Lora," meaning, are you DC or the DCs son? He thought I was far too young to be a DC, whereas, in his view, the DC would be an elderly person. I affirmed that I was the DC. He said you look very young – "Puwali lagise". A child to be a DC or are you AC? (Assistant Commissioner). He protested our police actions and said he wanted to give some advice as I was young and inexperienced. He said, "Sai Sinti order di bi," meaning 'think carefully before giving an order.' "Jadi order dibi – manibi, order na bangibi" meaning "if you give an order, follow it, don't break it, but enforce it". I told him that I agreed with his advice but that he should also tell his people to follow my orders in my area and not break my orders. I told him that I was always open for discussion but would not allow illegal harvesting by Nagas of the paddy grown by someone else who had toiled in my district and raised the crop. If they did so, it would become 'theft,' and the law must take its course. Luckily, he agreed, and the incidents did decrease in that particular area.

Maintaining peace on the Nagaland border remains an important duty of the D.C. Continuous vigil and watch had to be kept, and timely intelligence was collected on the Nagaland border to prevent encroachments and provide protection to the Assamese villages. With a lot of effort and care, we could prevent the crops from being cut and taken away by Naga intruders. We procured the latest Survey of India contour maps as well as Restricted Area Maps to pinpoint trouble spots, mark the incidents in Assam and Nagaland, and tighten security.

GOVERNMENT COMMENDS MY ACTION

A major operation was mounted to prevent Nagas from entering the Plain areas, illegally harvesting paddy crops on the border and evicting encroachers in the reserve forests. We combined the efforts of different departments. This operation, which was effective, had to be sustained over a long period to prevent re-encroachment and Naga raids. The Assam Government commended me for ensuring peace on the Nagaland Border, enabling farmers to harvest their crops without fear of Naga raids, with effective coordination and leadership shown in enthusing the district administration with a sense of responsibility and setting an example to be emulated.

Frequent meetings were held by the Chief Secretary, IGP, and senior officers at the Secretariat to review the action for maintaining Law and Order and peace on the Nagaland border. The Nagaland government would often complain to the Union Government about the Assam Government's actions. Senior officers of the Central Government used to visit Shillong and Kohima to understand the viewpoints of both States and find an acceptable solution. The Government would call for reports and ask me to be present at the discussions at Shillong to explain to senior officers of the Indian Government. K C Pant, Minister of State for Home and LP Singh, then Secretary in the Home Ministry, came to Shillong to understand the ground-level situation on the inter-state border. I used to give them a detailed presentation with maps of the latest situation.

SUNDARAM COMMISSION

As the border delineation on the ground as per the 1925 notification continued to be unacceptable to the Nagaland Government, the Indian Government constituted a One-man Commission consisting of KVK Sundaram, then Chairman of the Law Commission, to study the border issue and suggest a solution. The Sundaram Commission is reported to have submitted its report, which did not accept the view of the Nagas. Possibly due to this reason, the report has been kept in cold storage all these years. A separate Commission was also set up, assisted by a senior Forest Officer, to study the border issues and re-demarcate the border based on the current ground situation. The former Principal Chief Conservator of Forests of the AP Government, the late K Kamal Naidu, was a member of the commission.

D.C MOKOKCHUNG EVACUATED AND LIFE SAVED

Though the relationships between the Assam Government and the Nagaland Government were strained, the Deputy Commissioner of Mokokchung district, S C Dev, and I had cordial relations and were good friends. In May 1969, SC Dev suddenly fell ill and had to be immediately evacuated to Jorhat for emergency medical treatment. At the request of Khating, CS, Nagaland, I used my good offices with the Jorhat Station Commander and an Air Marshal of IAF and arranged a Helicopter to lift Dev from Mokokchung to Jorhat. The Jorhat doctors informed me that he would have to be shifted urgently to Calcutta for treatment.

I contacted the West Bengal CS at Calcutta and requested that he send an ambulance with a qualified doctor and equipment to the Dumdum airport at Calcutta to transfer Dev straight from Calcutta airport to the hospital. The ambulance was made available at the Airport, and Dev was taken to a hospital, and his life was saved. The CS of Nagaland wrote a letter to the CS of Assam requesting him to convey the appreciation of the Nagaland Government for the services rendered by Nayudu (me) to save the life of SC Dev, which had created a better understanding and sense of comradeship among our officers. The letter, along with the Assam Chief Secretary's endorsement, was sent to me.

SOCIAL AND CULTURAL ACTIVITIES - ASSAM SAHITYA SABHA

The people of Sibsagar district are very sophisticated in their language, dress, and manners compared to lower Assam. Their language is soft, respectful, and sweet to listen to. They are courteous to a fault and very hospitable. The District represented the glory of the Ahom Empire and had magnificent temples, lakes, pagodas, pavilions, and palaces.

Jorhat had many respected citizens, including Neelmani Phukan, an Assamese litterateur, AC Baruah, President of the Assam Sahitya Sabha, Handique, former VC of the Guwahati University, Debeshwar Sarma, former finance minister of Assam, Sadulla Khan, (former premier of Assam) whose son Imdad Ali was DGP in Gujarat. When Sadulla Khan passed away, we assisted the family with his burial ceremony.

Wonderstruck by the natural beauty of the District, its rivers, scenery, flora, and fauna, I continued my habit of writing poetry in Telugu. I composed quite a few poems. Some of the poems were translated into Assamese and published in local papers and Guwahati. A C Barua, the President of Assam Sahitya Sabha at Jorhat, noticed this. He used to invite me to some Sabha functions. I had a fairly good grasp of the Assamese language, could speak fluently, and gave simple lectures in the language. The Assam Sahitya Sabha made me an Honorary Member of the Sabha. I was the first non-Assamese person to be given this rare honour. I was presented with a set of publications of the Assam Sahitya Sabha and a framed Felicitation Address. It is one of my treasured possessions.

I felt at home in Jorhat because of the love and affection people showered on me. There were a number of Telugu officers working in the Air Force station at Rowriah, the RRL, Tocklai, Namrup Fertilizer factory, ONGC, and other Central Government offices. I had no dearth of company. The Director of RRL, Dr S.K. Ayyangar, was a Research Scholar at Osmania University when I was a student in the B.Sc class. He would often invite me to their functions. The Air Force station had a cinema hall in which Telugu films were screened on holidays. I used to attend the movie and got acquainted with many Telugu officers. They used to request that I arrange visits to Kaziranga Sanctuary, Majuli Island, tea gardens, and the drilling sites of ONGC.

BIHU FESTIVALS

Assam celebrates with éclat the Magh Bihu festival in mid-January and Bohag Bihu in mid-April as a thanksgiving festival for the rich harvest of paddy and other crops. Special sweets made of til and jaggery were the hallmarks of Magh Bihu, while Bohag Bihu had varieties of sweets as it heralded the advent of spring and Orchids. Young girls and boys in colourful traditional Muga or Eri silk clothes would joyfully dance with pipe music and drums and enjoy for 2 to 3 days. It was like a national get-together all over the State. We used to deploy home guards to serve refreshments and maintain peace during the festivals. The DC's large office compound was the favourite ground for Bihu activities. We encouraged the festivities, also gave away prizes to the best dancers and music composers.

It was during such festivities at Jorhat that I first met Tarun Gogoi and Bijoy Handiqui, both student leaders at Jorhat. Gogoi, who was very active and popular, later became the Assam Chief Minister for 15 years. Handiqui became an MP and Minister of State in the Indian Government. Whenever Gogoi visited Hyderabad, he would always call me and enquire about my welfare and that of other Assamese families in Hyderabad. He sent Assamese patients to Hyderabad for medical treatment and asked them to contact me for local help.

Tilak Gogoi, a hulk of a man and MP, invited the CM and me for lunch at the time of harvest to his extensive farm in the district where he had organized a lunch for over 1000 guests. We sat down on the ground, and food was served. I was sitting on the left of the CM, while Gogoi was seated to the right of the CM. Young girls were serving us food, and there was some friendly banter. The CM jocularly remarked that Assamese girls were pretty and reputed to have allured many a non-Assamese person, married him, and made him settle down in Assam. With a young, eligible bachelor DC here, I would like to see how nicely our girls serve him food and their parents so that DC can get married quickly. The girls became very shy, and I was quite embarrassed and wanted to get away as quickly as possible.

In February 1969, Shivratri was celebrated in a big way in the Sivadol at Sibsagar. Our Public Relations officers were keen to publicize development activities in the district relating to Agriculture, Rural Development, and Industry. On Shivratri day, unmarried girls all over India and in Assam visit the Shiva temple and pray to God to get them good husbands. An over-enthusiastic PR Officer put up banners advocating Family Planning near Sivadol. This was brought to my notice by a professor at a local college. I noticed the incongruity of advising family planning at a time when young maidens were seeking the blessings of Lord Shiva to get married! We took off the banner. There was no mention of Family Planning on that day.

ASI - CULTURAL AND HERITAGE ACTIVITIES

The Superintending Archaeologist of the Archaeological Survey of India for Assam State, Dr. S.C.Ray, used to visit Sibsagar and other temples regarding their protection, preservation, and upkeep. Though ASI had put up a Board giving details of the construction of the temple, its upkeep was poor. Wild plants had grown in all the crevices of the temple spires. We discussed the matter, and with the help of Sibsagar College Principal Parag Chaliha, we talked to the students and, with their help, were able to clear the spires of the temple and, wherever possible, erect a fence around the temple.

We visited the Negheriting Shiva Temple, which is located in a tea garden. We met the garden manager and convinced him that the temple was an ancient one and required better maintenance and protection. The villagers near the garden wanted that daily puja should be performed in the temple, which would also help the garden management and its labour. We got puja started in the temple by persuading a Brahmin priest near the tea garden to take charge of the daily puja and rituals. Within a short period, the temple became active and well cared for by the tea garden management, its labour and local villagers. It also built a bond of kinship among them.

Ray invited me to visit Calcutta to see the Durga Puja on my way home on leave. I visited the Durga Puja Pandals in Kolkata with him. He explained many details of the Pujas in Kolkata, including the art of making images of Goddess Durga. The most important aspect is the painting of the eyes and weapons of the eight-armed Goddess.

REPUBLIC DAY CELEBRATIONS

After securing the full cooperation of all the Heads of Departments, we organized the All India Cattle Life Show with prize-winning cows, buffaloes, and other animals to educate the farmers and the public and entertain children. We also introduced Floats and Tableaus on development and social activities during the Republic Day celebrations along the lines of the parade at New Delhi for the first time in Jorhat. Students enthusiastically participated in the conduct of exhibitions and witnessed All India Sporting events like Football and Cricket matches. We started the District Rifle Club as well.

PETROL COUPONS

Due to frequent incidents on the Assam-Nagaland border, I had to go to Shillong quite often to brief the Government. We had also to attend the SDOs, DCs, and other conferences in Shillong. As I had to visit Guwahati and Shillong frequently, I requested Mr. Saraogi, owner of a chain of petrol bunks, to give me a coupon book to enable me to draw petrol from his bunks on route to Shillong and back. He obliged, and I had no difficulty drawing petrol on my journeys within the district and all over Assam. I made payments once a month. This was probably 'the 1960s precursor' of today's prepaid petrol coupons and drawal of petrol on debit or credit cards!

As winter in Shillong was quite cold, Saraos and Trivedis would send their children to Jorhat for a week or two to escape the cold winter of Shillong, enjoy the climate of Jorhat, and accompany me on some of my trips. I became popular with them, and they used to call me Nayudu Uncle.

CENSUS OPERATIONS

We had to conduct the census in 1971. The Census Commissioner of India issued detailed instructions and the proforma for securing the requisite data. A K Saikia (1960) was the Census Commissioner in Assam. He visited Jorhat, and we decided on the training and deployment of personnel for the census. Though I had handed over charge as DC, I was pleasantly surprised to receive the Government of India's Census Silver Medal for my work in the Sibsagar district.

"RABI-WHEAT CROP EXPERIMENT"

Heavy floods used to erode Majuli Island, causing loss of land, crops, and income for farmers. In consultation with Dr. DN Barthakur, a Research Scientist on rice crops, we experimented with raising a wheat crop during the Rabi season. This was unprecedented as wheat was not grown in Assam. Wheat seeds were procured with the help of FCI, Regional Manager Arif Ali, and disbursed to farmers in Majuli. They were persuaded to sow wheat. As compensation for the loss of paddy crop in the Kharif season, we gave farmers an ex-gratia relief amount as an incentive - we reaped the first crop of wheat in Assam - a historical event, although the yields were not good-Experiments and experiences go hand in hand - Innovation sharpens our practices.

FLOOD INFORMATION MONITORING CHARTS

We used to receive information from Tibet warning us about floods in the River Brahmaputra. The floods in the Himalayan region would take about three days to reach the plains in Assam. The Irrigation department at Dibrugarh would also warn us about the floods. We devised charts indicating the time taken for floods to reach Sibsagar District at Niamatighat, the ferry point to Majuli in Sibsagar District. These chats gave ample time to organize and arrange relief operations. Forewarned is forearmed! Experiments in Relief operations became less stressful and more helpful due to prior warnings. Administration must consciously develop unique practicable applications using knowledge, technology, productivity, strategy, and competence to tackle local problems.

BLIGHT OF HISPA

About 2000 acres of paddy crop were affected by the Hispa Pest in the District. Individual farmers' attempts to control the pests through spraying pesticides did not work as the pest was widespread. With the help of the Agricultural Research Station and Tea-garden managements, we could arrange aerial spraying by a plane over the entire area, which effectively destroyed the pests and saved the crop. The Agricultural Department Officials and the farmers were jubilant. The press gave good coverage, terming it as "modern science proves a saviour of the paddy crop" and "Pests effectively controlled".

CHILDREN'S PARK

There was a nice plot of land opposite the Circuit House and adjacent to the DC's office compound. I used to feel the need for a well-equipped Children's Park at Jorhat. I mooted this subject to our officers and some tea garden managers. All agreed to cooperate, and we were able to construct a good children's park with all the necessary facilities and equipment for exercise and play. I consider this my humble contribution to the future citizens of Jorhat and India.

The Gandhi Centenary Train, which shows pictures of Mahatma's life, came to Mariani Junction. Many Parents and children saw the train and understood its message of Nonviolence, Truth, and Justice.

The US, which had a strategic partnership with Pakistan, and particularly the military dictatorship, chose to completely ignore the horendous suffering imposed on the hapless people of East Pakistan. It was only in late April and May 1971 that India seriously considered active military action in support of the Mukti Bahini. As stated by the then COAS Gen Manekshaw himself, who argued before the Cabinet and the PM that if operations were truly to be conducted, he would have to arrange for the movement of forces, weaponry, and supplies also strengthen his defences on the border with China as a threat from the border on the NE front could not be ignored. Further, given the rivers and terrain in East Pakistan and the monsoon weather factor, tanks can be bogged down, which is an eventuality he would like to rule out. He said that a great deal of coordination with the Railways, various Army formations, was required and that we would be in a winning position after the monsoon was over by late November of 1971.

The PM appreciated these arguments and asked the COAS to proceed according to this timetable and keep her updated continuously. As predicted by the Chief of the Army Staff, the monsoon broke out in April 1971 when communications to and from East Pakistan were affected, and the terrain became difficult to negotiate. It thwarted any moves to provide support or assist the Liberation Movement.

The Indian Army's Eastern Command, under Lt. Genl. Sagat Singh and two Major Generals in Assam-Meghalaya, in coordination with the Directorate of Military Operations, were ordered to make plans and arrange all the logistics and supplies on a war footing. In Silchar, there was an Army Division commanded by Gen Gonsalves, and this was supplemented by one more division with an armoured Brigade under Maj. General K Krishna Rao, who was then in Silchar.

In November 1971, all available forces from Nagaland, Mizo Hills, and Meghalaya and Eastern Command at Calcutta were moved for military operations in Bangladesh. Pakistan started air raids on India on the western front, signalling a full-fledged war. The Indian Army, Navy, and Air Force launched coordinated attacks on East Pakistan by Road, River, and Air. The Mukti Bahini provided intelligence cover and information on the Pakistan Army's locations, ammunition dumps, bridges, and major movements. The armed police battalions were asked to be ready to move and to hold the areas liberated by the Army.

ASSAM ARRANGEMENTS

The Chief Secretary in the Assam Secretariat set up a control room to coordinate action between the Civil Administration and the Armed forces, exchange intelligence information, and coordinate the movement of civil supplies. The members met every day in the morning and evening for reviewing the situation. Representatives of the Armed Forces also attended the meetings. I was a member of the committee.

To facilitate the smooth transition to civilian administration, areas in Bangladesh that the Indian Army or Mukti Bahini had liberated, certain officers from Assam were appointed as Civil Administrators. Their roles included restoring normalcy, organizing the transport of civil supplies, maintaining law and order, and ensuring effective governance until the regular government could take over. S.J. Das, the Commissioner of Assam, was tasked with coordinating these civil and administrative operations from the border regions of Assam. I was selected as Civil Administrator by the Assam Govt. to move with a segment of the army and BRTF to re-establish Civil Administration in the liberated areas of Rangpur District and the nearby regions, based on the progress of the operations. Some select officers were entrusted with the work of movement of essential commodities, restoration of communications, and re-manning of the police stations, jails, and hospitals. Civil Administrators prepared draft orders for promulgation, publicity, and implementation in the liberated areas. We had visualized that as and when some area is liberated, the Mukti Bahini and local staff could work under the Civil Administrator till the Bangladesh Government is installed and makes its regular arrangements.

I visited the Garo Hills district and met Dy. Commissioner KK Sinha and PV Sumanth, IPS, Superintendent of Police. Later, I moved with the Mukti Bahini inside Rangpur District to study and assess the situation and chalk out a program of action concerned primarily with the priorities as assessed to reassure the people that conditions are returning to normalcy.

The Bangladesh operations were carried out by the Indian Army swiftly and decisively from three directions. The Army, with amazing coordination and strategic moves, advanced rapidly, and the Pakistan Army was confused and dispirited. The antagonism of the local populace demoralized the army and their civilian supporters of Urdu- speaking citizens, while students of Bangladesh fuelled their antagonism towards Pakistan. They could not comprehend the rapid multi-pronged attacks and rapid advances towards Dacca. The Indian Air Force destroyed almost the entire Pakistan Airforce planes located in Dacca and attained total air superiority within three days of the commencement of operations. The Indian Naval ships operating in the Bay of Bengal blockaded Chittagong port. They sank a Pakistani submarine called Ghazi in a historic Manoeuvre near Visakhapatnam in the Bay of Bengal. The dispatch of the submarine Ghazi by Pakistan was

FAREWELL FOR KIDWAI CHIEF SECRETARY

Chief Secretary Kidwai was posted as Secretary in the Ministry of Works and Housing in Delhi. He undertook a farewell visit to the districts with his wife. He came to Jorhat and spent a couple of days there. We organized a grand farewell party for the CS, and a memento was presented to him on behalf of the District Administration. A batch mate, R K Ahuja, who was then posted in Arunachal Pradesh (NEFA), and R Natarajan, who was D C in Dibrugarh, joined us for the farewell meeting.

ASSAM AGRICULTURAL UNIVERSITY AT JORHAT

The Assam Government wanted to set up an Agricultural University at Jorhat by acquiring a tea garden. The site was selected, and construction started. The VC designate, S R Baruah, took up the construction activities to set up the Assam Agricultural University. His wife, Prameela Pandit, was a Maharashtrian fond of children's stories, songs, and lullabies. She asked me to give her some Telugu lullabies along with their meaning. She remarked that the lullabies all over India seemed to refer to the upbringing of children in Lord Rama's stories. President Zakir Hussain inaugurated the Assam Agricultural University, which the Governor and Chief Minister of Assam attended.

Shri R.V Pillai was posted as D.C Jorhat in October 1970. I handed over the charge to him after briefing and introducing him to the prominent citizens and senior officers.

I received a letter of appreciation in April 1972 from the Chief Secretary for achieving remarkable land revenue collection for the year 1969-70, when I was the Dy. Commissioner!

17

Joint Secretary to Assam Government, Personnel Home & Political Departments and Transport Commissioner, Shillong (Oct 1970 –March 1971))

I was posted as Joint Secretary to the Assam Government in the Personal, Home, and Political Departments and concurrently as Transport Commissioner till a reliever was posted. The post of Joint Secretary was considered important as it dealt with the postings of IAS Officers and Cabinet papers and reported directly to the Chief Secretary. We had a Parsi ICS Officer, NK Rustumji, an officer of the Assam Cadre, as the CS. He had earlier worked as India's agent in Bhutan and was considered an expert on Bhutan who maintained good relations with the king of Bhutan. As he did not follow Assamese, I had to explain many matters in English to him. I used to accompany him to the Cabinet meetings to record the minutes and get them approved by him and the Chief Minister.

He would hand over all important files and disciplinary cases to me for study and suggest a further course of action. I found it embarrassing to point out the lapses, moral turpitude, and violations of the code of conduct by Senior Officers. More so, as the Chief Secretary would ask me to suggest the framing of charges and the extent of punishment to be given. It was like exercising disciplinary cum judgemental powers over seniors. As the C.S. only knew a few officers in Assam, I used to submit to him a list of suggested transfers and postings, which he would usually clear after discussions.

I was due for promotion and posted as Secretary of Health and Family Planning and Public Health Engineering.

18

Secretary, Health and Family Planning and Public Health Engineering Department, Shillong (March 1971) – March 1972

In March 1971, I was promoted to Secretary in the Health and Family Planning and Public Health Engineering Department. My previous exposure to family planning and health-related activities in the Sibsagar District and in the tea garden areas helped me. The tea garden managements welcomed family planning to reduce future problems of providing employment and housing. However, the non-adoption of FP by illegal immigrants was a cause of friction and law-and-order troubles in the Lower Assam districts.

All Top officials reviewed all aspects of the health department's functioning to take steps to improve its responsiveness, efficiency, and effectiveness. The Ministry of Health and the Governor appreciated the Assam Government's efforts in Family Planning.

BUDGET CONSTRAINTS

We had the problem of inadequate budget and delays in the supply of medicines to the PHCs to give essential medicines to rural patients who could not access or afford them. We placed special imprest amounts of Rs.1000/- to Rs.5000/- depending on the size of the PHC, with the medical officer in charge of the PHCs purchasing medicines locally for the patients to supply and recoup from the imprest amount. This helped many poor and sick patients to get medication in time. The unusually large number of cancer patients due to habits of betel chewing with lime and tobacco, smoking cigars, and gastro-enteric cases due to untreated water use were the main health problems.

The constraint of funds in the department was affecting its work and performance. The repair works in the government Hospitals, upkeep of equipment, and maintenance suffered. If the government is unable to fund the requirements from the budget, the alternative would be to levy a small health cess or charge patients who can afford to pay. The proposal was considered premature, though some increase in funding did take place. In the absence of extensive medical facilities and medical insurance coverage, health services were inadequate in the case of chronic patients who required a regular supply of medicines.

MINISTER, C.S TERON

C.S. Teron from Mikir Hills was the Health Minister. He was an honest and amiable man who wanted to learn and earn a good name. I briefed him on the department's work and listed a number of steps to improve the health infrastructure, like building scientifically designed PHCs and hospitals with all medical facilities and the latest equipment, including diagnostics. Essential equipment and treatment practices were upgraded to meet changing needs.

We suggested to the Minister a visit to the nation's capital, Delhi, as well as some advanced states to see the Hospital buildings, facilities, equipment, and operating procedures to handle patients and aid the Doctors in both the diagnostic and treatment aspects. I recommended a visit to the All India Institute of Medical Sciences (AIIMS), Delhi, as it had emerged as a truly world-class institution with advanced medical facilities and highly qualified medical professionals. Its Medical College and attached hospital were considered the best institution for medical education and treatment in India. The Minister readily agreed.

A Meeting of the Health Ministers and Health Secretaries from all States was scheduled to be held in Jaipur (Rajasthan), to which we were invited. We were lodged in an erstwhile Palace Hotel in Jaipur. The Minister was impressed by the opulence and architecture of the palace and the way of life of the rulers before Independence. We visited the Sawai Madhopur Hospital. It was an eye-opener for the Minister, who wanted something similar at Guwahati in Assam. The hospitality and conducted tours of the Rajasthan Government to Primary Health Centres (PHCs) and places of tourist interest were eye-openers, and he noted that Rajasthan was attracting tourists from all over India and international visitors. The Minister remarked, 'I wish that Assam can also showcase the state for its medical facilities and attract visitors and tourists.'

There was a medical college and hospital in Pan Bazaar near the Brahmaputra River. It catered to local patients but had no space for and learn first-hand about the Chinese incursions in the Kameng Division of NEFA, and learn about Civil Defence measures.

Four probationers, deputed to attend Republic Day at Guwahati in 1963, had to board a flight at Calcutta airport. At check-in, the lady at the counter said that she could accommodate only three persons on the Indian Airlines flight. When the left-out probationer said that they were all going together for important Government work, the lady said that she could not accommodate him on the Dakota flight, but she could provide accommodation for him for friendship. The officer immediately retorted, "Madam, I am going on government duty. I want you to give me a seat "not for friendship, but for duty." He was not aware that Fokker – Friendship planes had just been inducted into the IA Fleet! The other probationers and the lady had a hearty laugh. The officer was provided with a seat in the Friendship Fokker flight later.

A British expert, Maj. General Hendricks was deputed to Guwahati to train officials about the civil defence measures to be taken. As I was allotted to the Assam cadre, I was one of the deputed officers. We were accommodated at the Guwahati Circuit house and, after Republic Day, despatched to Bomdila by jeep. We saw stark pieces of evidence of Chinese presence, burnt vehicles, tents, and rabbit burrows made by the Chinese to ward off the cold and snow and get a warm night's sleep. We saw the natural beauty of the hills, forests, winding roads, and blooming Rhododendrons.

We went to Bomdila and met an Indian Frontier Administrative Service (IFAS) officer, SN Johri, who was Deputy Commissioner, and another officer Joshi, who accommodated us and briefed us about the physical and psychological damages caused by the Chinese incursion. We were taken to a few tribal villagers to observe the way of life of the tribals and Monpas who live in the higher ranges. We, had to acclimatize ourselves before going to heights above 7500 feet. We went halfway to Tawang, but had to retreat because of snow and the lack of oxygen. An uncle of mine, Maj. Rangabashyam of a Sikh infantry battalion was killed in the war there. I whispered a silent prayer for his Sadgati and the peace of his soul. Later, I told my aunt (his wife) Savithri that I had paid homage to a martyr for India. After returning to the Academy, we had to present an account of what we saw and what we learned.

After the conclusion of our training at the academy, we were advised to report to the state Governments concerned after availing leave, including joining time. I had learnt many things, made friends, seen many places, and had to get ready for a new career in a new state and a new environment. I bid farewell to the Academy and eagerly looked forward to meeting my mother and relatives back home at Warangal.

12

Assistant Commissioner, Guwahati (June 1963 – August 1964) About Assam and Guwahati

To learn about Assam, the State to whose cadre I was allotted, I read the book "Red River and the Blue Hill," authored by Hem Barua. The Brahmaputra River, which flows through Assam, is called Lohit or Luit (red color), and the Hills are blue green (Nilachal). The colour red alludes to the Brahmaputra River as during the monsoon, due to heavy rains normal in that part of our country, a lot of mud and silt flows down, lending a reddish colour to the waters of this huge river, regarded as the only river of India bearing a masculine name.

The word Assam comes from the Sanskrit "Asama," which means uneven (unequal), Peerless, or unparalleled. The Ahoms, who came from Thailand in 1228 AD and ruled a major part of present-day Assam for over 600 years, could have given the name Assam. The word Guwahati comes from Gua, meaning cow or areca nut and haat (Bazaar), i.e., Guwahati, the market for areca nuts. It was also a marketplace for cattle (gau) trading. The Assamese call sunset time "godhuli" meaning the dust raised by cattle returning home after the day's grazing.

In ancient times, Assam was known as Prag Jyotisha, and Guwahati was known as Pragjyothishpur. The Allahabad inscription of King Samudra Gupta mentions Kamarupa as Prathyanta or an area outside the Gupta Empire. Huian Tsang, the Chinese scholar who visited Kamarupa in 743 AD at the invitation of King Kumar Bhaskara Varman, left a record of his visit. The Burmese invaded Assam in the early 19th century and reportedly cruelly treated the local population still under Ahom rule. The Ahoms, who were not in a position to defend themselves or protect people, requested the help of the East India Company, which successfully repulsed the Burmese.

POSTINGS OF DOCTORS

There were many requests for the transfer of doctors to places with the scope of lucrative private practice. Doctors would jostle for postings at such places. The Health Minister was flooded by requests from such doctors. He thought that he could do the posting of the doctors and asked me for my advice. I told him that if he took on the task, he would have to spend a lot of time on it and would receive many requests for postings, cancellations, or a review of the order. The Minister should be the final authority for appeals against decisions and should not himself become a party subject to criticism and face awkward moments for the initial posting and subsequent cancellation. Worse still, he would have to withdraw or cancel his orders! I suggested to him that the better course would be for the Secretary, in consultation with the DHS, to decide the postings of civil surgeons and superintendents of the major government hospitals and medical colleges. Appeals against such orders could be heard by the Minister. The Minister saw the logic and accepted the suggestion. Later, he would tell me that my advice had spared him the trouble of postings and avoiding controversy or allegations of graft in postings.

TRAINING IN LAPAROSCOPY

Government was keen to improve the qualifications of doctors by deputing them to specialized courses in India and abroad to help introduce new or advanced methods of training for surgeons and anaesthesiologists. The Government of India wanted our doctors to adopt the latest and tested medical practices from across the world. At that time, Laparoscopy or pin-hole surgery was introduced in Brazil and was successful as it was safer with minimum blood loss. The patient recovered quickly and could be discharged early. In consultation with the DHS, we decided that Dr Zaman, a well- known surgeon at Dibrugarh Medical College, should be deputed for this course. He attended the course, mastered the operational techniques, and trained several surgeons to undertake Laparoscopy operations in Assam.

We maintained good liaison and contact with the Madras Cancer Institute and CMC Vellore to send patients from Assam for treatment. Long after my retirement, Assamese patients who have cancer would come to Hyderabad to meet me, seeking admission to the MNJ Cancer Institute at Hyderabad in addition to the Cancer Institutes at Madras and Vellore. The Chief Minister, Late Tarun Gogoi, and other senior officers would often refer Assam patients to me for help and local assistance at Hyderabad.

THE NEED FOR FAMILY PLANNING

The birth rate in India was far higher than in many countries in Southeast Asia and China, where the mortality rate was falling. It became clear that urgent nationwide steps were necessary to control the growth of the population. With limited land and water availability and other facilities for ease of living amid high poverty levels, it was argued that efforts to increase the country's growth rate by itself could not lead India to prosperity. South Eastern Asian nations have shown that the acceleration of economic growth must be clubbed with the reduction in total fertility rate to achieve rapid progress and prosperity, which can enable Governments to take up welfare measures and provide distributive justice.

The Indian Government launched a major family planning program to keep the population in check. Though this program began during the time of Jawaharlal Nehru, it was during Indira Gandhi's tenure that the Government started taking strong and even coercive measures to bring about a substantial and sustained decrease in the birth rate. The Indian Government created a separate Department for Family Planning. In the initial stages, vasectomy operations were recommended, but the response was not good. On the other hand, there was a much greater response to the hysterectomy operations. At that time, it was a sociological problem as people felt that children were God-given and that more children would be beneficial as infant mortality was high. The Government started with a family slogan of three children, and over time, the slogan changed to "Hum do, Hamara do," meaning "We two-Our two." The success of Family Planning in the Tea- garden areas in Assam was the silver lining in the grim situation.

The large-scale immigration of Muslim Bengalis, initially from the Mymensingh District of East Pakistan and later from other parts of East Pakistan, caused concern. The demographic, electoral, and democratic turmoil it was likely to create agitated the minds of the Assamese intelligentsia. This gave the necessary impetus for the official machinery to implement this program with the required diligence and commitment. But it did not take off.

STATE HEALTH TRANSPORT ORGANIZATION (SHTO)

The Indian Government set up a Central Health Transport Organization (CHTO) in the Ministry of H & FP. S N Yechuri (father of late Sitaram Yechuri, the Communist Party Leader) was the officer in charge of the CHTO. He came to Shillong and explained the details of the scheme to us. The objective is to ensure that vehicles in the health sector are in good condition, particularly equipped for medical emergencies, and ready For use at a moment's notice. The Health Transport Organization was charged with this specific responsibility in every State, and if necessary, the private sector's resources could also be tapped.

The Health Department uses various vehicles for different purposes, such as ambulances, hearses, ferrying staff, and transporting equipment and medicines, depending on the vehicle's payload. SHTO intended to design different types of bodies to be built on standard chassis to suit the department's specific requirements.

A State Health Transport Organisation (SHTO) was set up at Guwahati, and a qualified automobile engineer, N. Ahmed, was appointed along with a couple of junior engineers on deputation from Assam State Road Transport Corporation. Vehicles of the health department that were off the road would be sent to the SHTO, where they would be repaired very quickly and sent to the respective indentors. I arranged a visit for the officials from Assam SHTO to Hyderabad to visit the A.P. SHTO, which was then considered one of the best SHTOs in the country. Assam state made a significant impact in designing vehicle bodies to suit the varied requirements of movement in plain areas, hilly areas, and swampy places, including four-wheel drive vehicles.

PUBLIC HEALTH ENGINEERING DEPARTMENT

The Public Health Engineering (PHE) Department was part of the Department of Health and Family Planning. The major concern of the PHE Department was to provide a protected water supply after proper filtration and treatment to the district headquarters, other towns, and urban areas. They attended to problems of drainage in the municipal areas. During the rainy season, floods in the Brahmaputra River made drainage arrangements redundant or difficult. During winter, Brahmaputra virtually becomes the biggest drainage system of Assam. The PHE Department was required to take care of the upkeep of the water supply and sewerage arrangements in the district headquarters, towns, and other municipal areas and create such facilities in areas where there were none. Malaria control was also part of their mandate.

The Indian Government realized that control of water pollution and air pollution was assuming alarming national dimensions. The concept of green earth was also being debated the world over. The Indian Government was holding discussions with the State Governments to obtain their views before finalizing Acts for the prevention and control of Air and Water pollution. Experts like Prof S. Dave and Ministry of Health officials would visit Assam to seek our views and comments for incorporation into the provisions of the Act.

Having spent quite some time in the State Secretariat and contributed to the efforts of the State in the field of Health Management, the time had come for me to explore new avenues of experience. Administrative Service officers must have a wide repertoire of experience and skills in management. I requested the Assam Government to sponsor my name to the Government of India for a deputation to the Central Government for study abroad under the Colombo Plan or other such programs. I was earlier selected for a year's training in Australia, but the Government did not release me on the grounds that my services are required in the public interest. I was selected as Under-Secretary in the Cabinet Secretariat, also as Special Assistant to the then Health Minister Karan Singh. The Assam Government did not release me on both occasions in the interest of public service and told me that my request would be kept in mind and that I would be released at a future date. I still feel that an opportunity to widen my range of experience at the All India level was not provided to me in time, though I deserved this as much as anyone else.

BIRTH OF BANGLADESH

A brief discussion of the origin, reasons, and causes of the struggle of former East Pakistan to seek and create a new third country in the Indian Subcontinent, which I had occasion to witness at close quarters, could serve as useful background for understanding the problem and its repercussions.

The British left India in August 1947 but acceded to the demand for a separate homeland for Indian Muslims by partitioning the country into India and Pakistan. Strangely, the demand for a separate homeland for Indian Muslims came mainly from the Muslims from some parts of north and central India. Many people of Punjab or Sind or the North West, including a substantial number of minorities, wanted a United India and did not fully support this demand. In fact, Khan Abdul Gaffar Khan, the Frontier Gandhi, actively opposed this move. It is, therefore, an accident of history that those who vociferously and indeed violently demanded a separate homeland did not benefit much, while West Punjab benefitted the most.

The theoretical, philosophical underpinning of such a demand was provided by Sir Syed Ahmed Khan, an alumnus of the Aligarh Muslim University and the Deoband Seminary, both located in UP. The argument articulated was based on the teachings of religious scholars and the texts they relied upon. They believed that Muslims are a separate and distinct worldwide community with a distinct culture, belief system, and social norms. They believed that their religious system was superior to other beliefs and that such a community could not be expected to live under the rule of non-believers.

The founders of Pakistan, who belonged to the Muslim League, strongly believed that a common faith could create a united nation-state. The Western wing of the new country consisted of Sindh, Baluchistan, Punjab, and the NWFP each of which had separate languages, cultural mores, ethnicity, and historic backgrounds. Even at the time of the Partition of British India on the basis of religion, the Eastern Wing of the country East Pakistan accounted for 54% of the population of the newly carved-out country. To create a sense of commonality and unity, apart from religion, the solution pursued was to impose Urdu as the sole language of administration. After about five years of existence, when the English language continued to be the official language, the Government in the western part of Pakistan made a unilateral decision to declare Urdu as the sole official language of Pakistan. The people of East Pakistan who were used to speaking and using Bengali and its dialects such as Sylheti, Chittagongi, etc., for ages were against this imposition of Urdu, which was and continues to be mainly a language of the Muslims of UP, and some other places in undivided India. The Muslim immigrants from India to the newly created nation of Pakistan, called Mujahirs, use Urdu, and it is a language compulsorily taught in all schools. Despite this, the State of Pakistan was constituted by integrating areas where languages such as Punjabi. Sindhi, Baloch, Pashtun, are spoken by the residents of these parts. There was considerable resistance to the imposition of Urdu even in these parts.

It is well known that ethnically, linguistically, and culturally, there are many similarities between the people who live in West Bengal, a State of the Indian Union and the people who inhabit what was constituted as East Pakistan. This was purely based on religion. Still, the underlying cultural and linguistic bonds and unity between the two parts could not be obliterated despite the Pakistani Government's strong-arm tactics.

In the elections held in 1970 - after a long period of military rule, the Awami League Party, a new political entity in East Pakistan led by Sheikh Mujibur Rehman, won the majority of seats in Pakistan's National Assembly, i.e., 165 seats out of 300 and consequently Mujibur Rehman should have been elected as Prime Minister of Pakistan. This was unacceptable to the army and people of West Pakistan, who looked down upon the people of East Pakistan as they were of a darker complexion, shorter in stature, and no match for the tall, light-skinned Punjabis and Pathans. The Army started belittling the Bengali language and Bengalis and committed many cruel atrocities on the hapless Bengali population. Agitation on a large scale led by the students of Dacca University started and assumed grave proportions.

West Pakistan interpreted this movement as a serious threat to the unity, sovereignty, and integrity of the State of Pakistan and its control over the Eastern wing. Mujibur Rehman was imprisoned and taken away to the Western part. The Army, comprised mostly of Punjabis, let loose a reign of terror, rape of women, and unheard-of atrocities in East Pakistan, leading to the migration of a large number of refugees, estimated at 2 million, to India to escape the loss of lives and honour of womenfolk.

AWAMI LEAGUE DECLARES INDEPENDENCE OF BANGLADESH

The Awami League leaders in East Pakistan declared the Independence of Bangladesh in early 1971 and announced the setting up of Bangladesh as an Independent Country with a Government in exile led by one Tajuddin and supported by leading intellectuals and the Communist party. Repression of the people by the armed forces and administration intensified, leading to the migration of the affected population and Liberation fighters to border areas of Assam and West Bengal in India for refuge. India had to host more than nine million refugees at the peak of the atrocities and influx.

MUKTHI BAHINI – FREEDOM ARMY

The Awami League set up Mukti Bahini (Freedom Army) of dedicated volunteers to free Bangladesh from the yoke of Pakistan. They procured firearms, formed intelligence cells and self-defense parties within Bangladesh, and trained in the border areas of India. Some Mukti Bahini volunteers organized raids on isolated administrative offices and police stations in Bangladesh to obtain arms, release prisoners from jails, and enlist volunteers for the liberation struggle. The Mukti Bahini requested Indian armed police forces like BRTF, CRPF, and SSB in West Bengal, Assam, and Meghalaya for training and support. The growing influx of refugees from East Pakistan due to turmoil and its likely adverse impacts on socio-economic conditions in India was causing concern.

INDIA SUPPORTS THE AWAMI LEAGUE

Prime Minister Indira Gandhi announced her support for the Awami League and its demand for independence. In the initial stages, India was more interested in the safe return of the refugees to East Pakistan than in supporting the struggle for independence. India was also concerned that the refugees might fall into the trap of the Naxalite movement, which was still strong in the State of West Bengal.

intended to find and destroy the Indian aircraft carrier stationed at the Vizag naval base. The navy, which had advanced intelligence on the intentions of the Pakistani submarine, took electronic warfare measures and managed to eliminate the submarine.

GENERAL NIAZI OF PAKISTAN ARMY SURRENDERS

The futility of facing the multi-pronged entry and attack of Indian Armed Forces from Assam and West Bengal, the antagonism of the local people and the students, and the inability of Pakistan to help the forces in East Pakistan dawned on Lt General Niazi. Faced with popular resistance from the local population and the likely annihilation of its forces without any likelihood of reinforcements from the Western wing, and certain defeat, the Pakistan Army in East Pakistan under the command of Lt. Gen AAK Niazi conceded defeat and surrendered with 90,000 Pakistani soldiers with arms to General Arora of the Indian Army. With the formal surrender of the Pak army to the Indian Armed Forces, Bangladesh operations were over in just 18 days. A new State and Country, Bangladesh, was born, and democracy triumphed. After the Shimla accord, the Pakistani Prisoners were released.

Many nations acknowledged India's role and the swift advance of the Indian Army with the least loss of life and property as a great strategic and military victory. It was a shot in the arm for India after the 1962 NEFA debacle. Trade and commerce with India and Bangladesh were expected to be restored, and Assam's isolation was mitigated with the restoration of rail and river communications between the two countries.

CIVIL ADMINISTRATION

The Civil Administration played an exemplary role in supporting the army by keeping the supply chain moving both by road and river routes. The Assam Government and Meghalaya Deputy Commissioners at Dhubri Silchar, Tura, as well as Shillong, played a stellar role and fully supported the armed forces. They admirably handled the myriad tasks while keeping up the morale of the people and handling the refugees. JK Bagchi and KK Sinha DCs of Meghalaya received Padma Shri Awards.

19

Regional Iron & Steel Controller, Hyderabad (States of A.P. and M.P. (July 1972 – Dec 1976 {4½ Years})

On deputation as Regional Iron & Steel Controller at Hyderabad

My request for deputation to the Government of India was approved. I was posted as Regional Iron and Steel Controller at Hyderabad under the Ministry of Steel and Mines to regulate and oversee the allocation and utilisation of Iron and Steel, which was then in short supply. I had to report to the Iron and Steel Controller at Calcutta, Tejoymay Ghose. I took charge on 1st July 1972 as the First Regional Iron & Steel Controller at Hyderabad for the States of Andhra Pradesh and Madhya Pradesh.

I had to establish a new office in Hyderabad, recruit staff, and start my work. I reached out to a Deputy Accountant General in the AG's office there, who assigned a Superintendent-level official, MA Khader, and an Accountant, S. Krishna Rao, to assist me. Khader was resourceful and hired office accommodation, a typewriter, and some stationery to get the office going. I received from the Iron and Steel Controller's office at Calcutta copies of the Iron & Steel Control Order, K N Raj Committee Report on steel control, and instructions on the duties and responsibilities of Regional I& S Controllers.

In August 1972, we received financial sanctions for the office of the Regional Steel Controller at Hyderabad. I called on the Andhra Pradesh CS, VK Rao, ICS, and the Chief Minister J. Vengal Rao, who, as Minister for industry, had spear-headed industrial development in A.P. I met Anil De, Secretary Industries and Commerce, and the two Joint Secretaries Krishnan and Balakrishnan. I called on N Luther, Director of Industries, M V Ratnam, CMD of AP Industrial Development Corporation, and CS

Sastry, MD of APSSDC, to understand their requirements of iron and steel for development projects.

GENESIS OF THE IRON AND STEEL CONTROL ORDER

As the bulk of the production of Iron & Steel was diverted to the Second World War efforts, it led to shortages in the country. Licensing of I&S products was introduced in 1941. Another Order was promulgated in 1943 to control scrap that could be recycled. At the end of the II World War, a quota system was introduced, and steel produced in the main steel plants was distributed to the State Steel Controllers for distribution within the State. This arrangement did not work well as demand was rising faster than production, which could not keep pace.

STEEL PRIORITY COMMITTEE – KN RAJ COMMITTEE

The Central Government appointed a Committee on Steel Control in 1963, headed by KN Raj, an eminent economist. It recommended regulation of production, consumption, distribution, and prices. It fixed quotas for imports and exports and priorities in distribution. It suggested that a Steel Priority Committee (SPC) should decide on the quantum of steel to be allocated based on the demands projected by the Centre and States under five main heads of demand of (a) Agricultural, (b) Non-agricultural, (c) Governmental development schemes, (d) Steel processing industries and (e) Small Scale Industries. The Steel Priority Committee, in which the State Governments were represented, would assess the requirements of each state and allocate the available steel products as equitably as possible while giving priority to the National and important State projects. Requisite changes were made to I &S (Control) Order 1956 to give effect to the recommendations. I&S (control) Order 1956 was amended in April 1973, which was our guidebook.

JOINT PLANT COMMITTEE (JPC)

A Joint Plant Committee (JPC) comprising all the six integrated steel plants viz. Bhilai, Rourkela, Durgapur, TISCO, Indian Iron and Steel Company (IISCO), and Bhadravati Iron and Steel Company (Mysore) - the prime producers of steel, were set up. Nominees of the Steel plants, the Union Government, and State Governments represented by the Secretaries, Directors of Industries constituted the committee, which calls for requisitions for the allocation of steel on a quarterly basis. Taking the steel demand and availability into account, the JPC would equitably distribute the material. As steel was in short supply, there was much pressure on the members of the JPC. The Regional I&S Controllers' views were considered before allocating the material to the end-users in their jurisdictions. Since JPC collected nationwide demand for steel, the main steel plants could plan their steel rolling schedule to match the demand. The main steel plants deputed qualified engineering and IT officers to man the JPC setup. In fact, JPC introduced computerization to compile and forecast demand and allocations in accordance with policy.

REGIONAL STEEL CONTROLLERS AS VIGILANCE OFFICERS

The Iron & Steel Controller's office at Calcutta was not able to control and reduce malpractices in the allocation and distribution of steel products due to a lack of staff and a vigorous vigilance setup. Six Regional Iron & Steel controllers' offices at Madras, Hyderabad, Bombay, Delhi, Lucknow, and Calcutta were set up. They were expected to be the eyes and ears of the I&S Controller and Vigilance officers to ensure orderly allocation, distribution, use, and disposal of steel materials. The Regional offices were small outfits for surprise visits and inspections. Qualified engineers and officers from the Governments of A.P. & M.P. who had local knowledge of the Iron and Steel industry in the States were taken on deputation.

I visited the stockyards of Hindustan Steel Ltd (SAIL) at Hyderabad and Visakhapatnam, the TISCO stockyard at Vijayawada, and the Branch Sales offices of HSL and TISCO at Hyderabad, Visakhapatnam, and Vijayawada to familiarize myself with their work and method of satisfying demands cleared by JPC. They also allocate small quantities of steel, one to two tons, to individual housebuilders.

MINISTER FOR STEEL, MOHAN KUMARA MANGALAM

Mohan Kumaramangalam was the Minister for Steel. He selected M Wadud Khan as Chairman of HSL. I received instructions from the I&S Controller at Calcutta T Ghosh that I should meet the Minister Mohan Kumaramangalam at Chennai along with the Regional I&S Controller of Madras, K.Seshadri(1958), an Assam Cadre officer. We met the Minister, who indicated that the Government would like to nationalize the basic industries like Coal and Steel and increase production so that there are no Shortage of steel or coal. S R Sankaran of A.P. cadre was appointed as Special Assistant to the Minister.

All the files pertaining to A.P., earlier dealt with by the Madras office, were separated and handed over to us. The Delhi office sent the files of M.P. After returning to Hyderabad, I visited Bhopal. I met the C.S., Industries Secretary, Director of Industries Behl, and a dynamic Additional

Director of Industries A. V Singh. All the State Industries Development Corporations were running Raw Materials Service Centres (RMSCs) to cater to the requirements of Small-Scale Industries. They were dependent on allocations received from JPC.

A meeting of all the Regional Steel Controllers was held by the I&S Controller at Calcutta, who advised us to visit the main steel plants to familiarize ourselves with their production plans and allocation methodology. We were given a demonstration of the methods followed by the JPC at Calcutta to collect indents for steel allocation and match it with the production as projected. We attended meetings of the JPC and SPC along with the Directors of Industry and MDs of Industrial and Small Industries Development Corporations.

We drew up a program of inspections, including surprise visits of units in receipt of large steel allocations and consuming industries to assess their proper utilization. We intended to prevent the stockpiling of steel by large units, including public sector undertakings, and disgorge the surplus stocks for distribution to other needy consumers. The private sector hoarded steel as the open-market price of steel was much higher than steel procured through regular government allocation. We were required to keep a watch on the stocks and regular consumption. We kept a watch on the steel market at Ranigunj in Hyderabad, Vijayawada, Visakhapatnam, Indore, Bhopal, Dhar, Raipur, Ujjain, and Ratlam, which were major consuming areas. Many units managed to get the allocation of steel but did not consume it; they sold it in the open market. This tempted many units and individuals to secure allocation, not use it, and instead sell it in the market for high prices and earn profits without running the industry!

I&S Controller wanted to inspect and study the functioning of the newly created Regional Steel Controller offices. I was asked to meet him at Madras. The Regional Steel Controller Madras and I accompanied him on tour in Tamil Nadu and Karnataka states, which provided an opportunity to interact with the industry and officers of the Tamilnadu Government and Karnataka Govt. We went by road from Madras, visiting many steel- consuming units in Tamilnadu and then on to Bangalore, where we met the Industries Minister S M Krishna and the Director of Industries Zafar Saifulla. After visits to the Karnataka State Electricity Board and the Karnataka SSIDC, we proceeded to Hyderabad. On the way, we visited Puttaparthi and inspected some steel rolling mills at Hindupur and Anantapur before reaching Hyderabad.

The Steel Controller used to hold a Half-yearly meeting of the Regional Controllers at Calcutta to take stock of the developments and ensure uniformity of action in the areas of inspection of stockyards, allocation of steel to small house builders, vigilance, and prosecution. Regional Controllers laid down a policy to be followed by the branch managers of the steel plants for the allocation of steel material to allotees and small house builders.

I attended the Joint Plant Committee Meetings and became familiar with the process of collection of demand from indenting authorities, rolling programs for different varieties of steel from the main steel plants, recommendations of the state governments and the Directors of Industries before deciding on the allocations based on availability and demand. Later, an officer of the JPC, an engineer from Rourkela Steel Plant O A Seth, was posted as Dy .Regional Controller at Hyderabad to assist me in collation of the demand from Rerollers in A.P. and M.P. to improve the technical efficiency and productivity of re-rolling mills and secondary processors. This enabled them to achieve higher norms of efficiency.

MADHYA PRADESH – BHILAI STEEL PLANT

I visited the Bhilai steel plant and spent a week studying the rolling programs of the plant and the variety of rails, Z sections, and wire rods they produce. Numerous steel units had come up around Bhilai and Raipur close to the steel plant. They were mostly electric arc furnaces, induction furnaces, sponge iron and ferroalloys units, small wire drawing units, re-rolling units, cold rolled strips units, and pig iron foundries. I got a good idea of the downstream industries of a steel plant. I noticed that many of the units in the medium-scale sector were adopting modern production techniques and were managed professionally.

ORISSA – ROURKELA STEEL PLANT

I visited the Rourkela plant, which was built with Germany's technical assistance and produces flat products. My batch mate, P.C. Hota, was the Chief Administrative Officer of Rourkela Township. He introduced me to the General Manager, DP Agarwala, a steel expert who later became Chairman of SAIL. I also saw the manufacture of high-quality electrically oriented materials and thinner-quality materials, including steel strips.

However, unlike the ancillaries at the Bhilai steel plant, there was less industrial activity or downstream industry near the Rourkela steel plant.

Most of the steel-consuming industries in MP were in and around Indore, Dhar, Ujjain, Ratlam, Bhopal, Jabalpur, Gwalior, and Raipur. BHEL had a very big plant in Bhopal, which spawned a few entrepreneurial units and ancillary industries. At Bhopal, I met my batch mates and took their assistance as required. I visited the Regional Research Laboratory at Bhopal, which concentrated on mineral ores, dressing, beneficiation, and treatment. As I had a lot of leisure time, after inspecting the few units in M.P., I travelled extensively across the state. In my little over four years as Regional Controller, I was able to visit as many as 32 districts out of the then 54 districts in M.P!

MP was a very large State and a microcosm of India. Each region had its own natural, socio-economic development, distinctive culture, dialects, and way of life. There were several former princely states and Zamindaris. The Scindias of Gwalior, the Holkars of Indore, and the Singh Deos of Bastar were revered by the people. The development activities were mostly confined to the urban areas and industrial regions. Due to abundant natural, mineral, and agricultural resources, several big factories like Bhilai Steel Plant, the BHEL Plant at Bhopal, Bharat Aluminium Company at Korba, some power plants, and medium-scale industries were set up in Raipur, Jabalpur, Indore, and Gwalior areas. The three districts of Morena, Bhind, and Shivpuri, in the Chambal ravines, were dacoit-infested and faction-ridden. Notorious dacoits like Malkan Singh, Phoolan Devi, and others had made it their domain.

VIDISHA – BHIMBETKA

MP has a hoary past. The Buddhist stupa at Vidisha was well preserved and attracted national and international tourists. Ancient and famous Temples dotted the State and the banks of the River Narmada. The earliest cave rock paintings in India are at Bhim-betka. The famous Khajuraho temple is in Chhatarpur District in the Bundelkhand region. The old city of Bhopal, with a big lake, was progressive under the rule of Begums. Hockey was popular in and around Bhopal. The government built the new capital, Bhopal, on modern lines. MN Buch is credited with its concept and construction. The Secretariat, High Court, Legislative Assembly, MLA Quarters, Bungalows for officers, and quarters for the staff were of good design and well-built.

I could visit many temples and places of scenic interest, as well as my work of inspection and promotion of steel-based industries. I realized that shortage of steel was over, and there was a need to promote medium and small-scale steel-based industries. I visited the Panna diamond mines and the Panna Forest reserve, famous for white tigers. I visited Bilaspur and Korba, where Bharat Aluminium Company is situated. I visited holy places on the banks of the Narmada River, including the place where Shankaracharya contemplated. I visited Dewas, the historic Mandu Fort, and the Narmada River Shrines. I saw the famed marble rocks of Jabalpur. I visited the Ordnance factory and could meet some of my relatives who had settled down at Jabalpur.

The Director of Industry and MDs of Development Corporations helped me visit industrial clusters, steel units, and important places of historical and tourist interest, which enabled me to get a good idea of the State. A lot of infrastructural activity, including roads, minor irrigation works, and large-scale electrification, was in progress. Jagathpathy and

B.D Sharma, both IAS Officers, were living legends at that time. I had a ring-side view of the industrial development in MP and the people-friendly policies followed by the Government.

Small-scale industries in different parts of MP were producing quality agricultural implements at low cost suitable for local needs. They used alloy steels, including vanadium steel, to produce job-oriented implements like sickles, harrows, tractor attachments, mini-iron ploughshares, and seed drills. I persuaded some MP small-scale industries to start agricultural implements manufacturing units in Hyderabad. Vijayawada, Gudivada, Vizag, Warangal and Nizamabad.

STEEL MINISTER DIES IN PLANE CRASH

On 1st July 1973, an Indian Airlines plane with Minister S. Mohan Kumaramangalam and other passengers crashed at the Delhi airport, leading to his death and many others. We held a condolence meeting.

ANDHRA PRADESH

I visited the Singareni Collieries Company to check the utilization of steel allocated to them and saw coal extraction in both open-cast and underground mines. B N Raman was the CMD. He briefed me about the company's expansion programme. I also visited the APSEB power plant at Palvancha and Nav Bharat Ferro Alloys, which was constructing a power plant.

VISIT TO CESS – SIRCILLA

I visited Ramagundam coal mines and the Fertilizer Corporation of India's Urea fertilizer unit. I was invited by the Collector of Karimnagar District, VK Srinivasan, to visit the Cooperative Electric Supply Society (CESS) to see the good work done and to assist them by allocation of steel. My classmate P. Janardhan Reddy, MLA of Huzurabad, the Collector, and I went from Karimnagar to Sircilla, where we switched on the lights and inaugurated the electrification of four villages. CESS was experimenting with the construction and use of cement poles instead of metal poles for stringing the electric lines. Members of the cooperative society were themselves curing and erecting the cement poles, fixing the cross-arms, and laying the electricity wires. I visited their Pole- manufacturing area and found that they were doing a good job. The Executive Engineer Rajalingam was active and dedicated. The cement poles required a supply of steel. On return to Hyderabad, I sanctioned a special quota of steel rods to meet their current demands.

Long after, in 1996, as Chairman of the Rural Electrification Corporation (REC), I accompanied the Union Minister of State for Power, Mrs Patel, to the CESS Unit, a successful electricity cooperative. She was impressed at the progress achieved. REC sanctioned a special grant of Rs.5 crores to CESS.

VISAKHAPATNAM - STEEL-BASED INDUSTRIES

Visakhapatnam has a number of major, medium, and small-scale industries. The Visakhapatnam Port Trust, Hindustan Shipyard Ltd, Hindustan Zinc Limited, Bharat Heavy Vessels and Plates Ltd, and Coromandel fertilizers were large industries. There were medium-sized re-rolling and wire drawing units as well as structural fabricators in Visakhapatnam. Among the upcoming industries were Andhra Steel Corporation and L.N. Steels, which were managed at that time by the Mittal Brothers. One of the brothers, LN Mittal, is now one of the world's biggest steel producers in the world.

A number of small-scale industries had come up at Vizag due to work offloaded to them by large industries. During the construction of the Vizag Steel Plant, the small-scale industries got a fillip, and the state government set up an industrial area for the location of small-scale industries in Visakhapatnam.

A N Kidwai, CS of Assam, who was posted as Secretary of Works & Housing at Delhi, came to Hyderabad to attend a Program for Secretaries at the Administrative Staff College of India (ASCI). I received him at the Airport, accompanied him to ASCI, and hosted a dinner at the Secunderabad Club.

In April 1974, Stanley Nichols Roy, Minister from Meghalaya, visited Hyderabad to study Industrial Development in AP. I accompanied him to meet the Minister for Industries and the MDs of Industrial Development Corporations.

I used to visit Vijayawada and Rajahmundry very often as they showed promise of becoming industrial areas. Singareni Collieries had set up a Heavy Machinery industry on the border of the Krishna and Khammam districts. Several industries had come up in Nandigama, and industrial estates were set up in Guntur and Vijayawada. The packaging industries for the tobacco industry also received a fillip. At Rajahmundry, A.P., Paper mills spawned many small Kraft paper mills based on agricultural residues and wastepaper. Jute factories came up in Guntur, Eluru, and Srikakulam. I had a ring-side view of industrial development in A.P., and the government gave me local support and facilities to visit the units.

SPONGE IRON PLANT AT PALVANCHA

President's rule was imposed in AP when H.C Sarin, former Secretary in the Steel Ministry, was posted as Advisor. I called on him. VK Dhar (1955), who was Joint Secretary in the Steel Ministry, came to Hyderabad and told me that the Ministry was setting up a Sponge Iron plant at Palvancha in Khammam district with UN assistance as an experimental venture. I was appointed as Director of Sponge Iron India Ltd. In the meantime, Dhar was transferred as MD of the Indian Iron and Steel Company at Burnpur in West Bengal.

VISAKHAPATNAM STEEL PLANT

Though the Vizag Steel Plant was formally inaugurated in January 1971 by PM Indira Gandhi, it was not making headway due to lack of finances, infrastructural, and technological support to commence the work. The AP State Government was keen on pushing the project.

There was a lot of pilferage of steel from the Visakhapatnam Steel Yard of SAIL. Vigilance by Police and Revenue authorities was strengthened to prevent pilferage. AP became a big producer of milk by setting up the AP Dairy Development Corporation and district-level milk cooperatives. A local unit, Unicorn Industries, wanted to fabricate stainless steel tankers to transport milk from Hyderabad to places in Maharashtra and Karnataka. We helped them to secure the requisite gauge of standard steel sheets for fabrication purposes.

I used to visit Vijayawada quite frequently because of the growing demand for steel and the setting up of many industrial units in and around Vijayawada and Guntur. GP Rao was then the Municipal Commissioner of Vijayawada, who did excellent work in urban development. S Narayanan was the Joint Collector.

I VISIT VIJAYAWADA

KGR Iyer, Additional Secretary in the Ministry of Steel & Mines, visited Hyderabad in February 1975 for discussions with the South Central Railway and Secretary of Irrigation and Power to ascertain the government's priority requirement of steel for allocation under special projects. I was advised to assess the steel requirements for the Pochampad Project and submit a report to the Ministry of Steel and Mines. Iyer was subsequently posted as Chief Secretary to the Assam Govt. Unfortunately, he passed away in July 1975.

ROLLING OF Z-SECTION FOR DOWLESWARAM ANICUT

There were heavy floods in the river Godavari, and a portion of the more than 100-year-old Dowleshwaram Anicut collapsed due to floods. The breach had to be filled quickly to prevent the outflow of water, save the standing crop, and prevent future breaches. There was pressing demand for a particular Z steel section, which, with its counterpart section, could become a temporary but effective wall. Since the demand for such a section is not high, the only plant that rolled out the Z section was the Indian Iron and Steel Company at Burnpur. The campaign for rolling Z sections is planned once in two years as the off-take of Z sections is low. The Indian Iron and Steel Company expressed its inability to roll new stock and that the meagre stock they had could be given. That stock was insufficient to meet the requirement for quickly building a buffer dam to block the breached portion of the Anicut.

CM and CS of AP requested that, in view of the urgency, I somehow manage to get the steel sections rolled and dispatched immediately. I contacted V K Dhar, MD, and visited Burnpur. I told him the urgency and purpose of my visit. Dhar called a meeting of the plant engineers and, despite their reluctance, convinced them to keep other work on hold and immediately commence rolling Z sections. I stayed at Burnpur for more than a week to ensure that the Rolling of Z sections started and arrangements for dispatch were made before I left for Dowleswaram and Hyderabad. The Superintending Engineer at Dowleswaram R Chalapathi was overjoyed that an almost impossible task had been achieved. The breach was closed, and the Paddy crop was saved. He became a good and fast friend. His nephew is R Subramanyam, IAS, and his wife, Pushpa, is also an IAS Officer.

Chandrajit Yadav, Union Minister of State for Steel and Mines, visited Hyderabad and addressed a meeting of local industrialists regarding the supply of steel materials. Ghosh, I&S Controller, visited Hyderabad in March 1975, met the CM and Minister for Industry, and assured them adequate supply of steel for all government projects. He reviewed the progress on the cases registered under I&S Control order and the Indian Penal Code and visited the raw material supply centre in Hyderabad.

MISUSE OF STEEL MATERIALS IN A.P.

We had some interesting cases. The Rayalaseema Steel Rolling mills at Guntakal would indent and get large quantities of billets allotted. They did not use it for re-rolling but directly disposed of it for profits in the open market. We laid a trap and caught a lorry with billets moving out of the factory, which was seized, and a case was filed under I & S Control

Order. A nominated Anglo-Indian MP met me to secure the release of the confiscated stocks. I did not agree to release the seized steel and lift the suspension of further allocations till the case was decided. She used to ring me often but to no avail. She managed to get a Deputy Minister in the Ministry of Steel and Mines to speak to me for the release of the seized stock and to lift a ban on further supply to the unit. I politely told the Minister that we would expedite the hearing of the case but could only release the stock once the case was decided.

We received information that big units viz. Shriram Refrigeration Industries and Hyderabad Engineering Industries were indenting large quantities, much beyond their needs, and selling the surplus stock in the open market for a huge profit. We caught the trucks moving out of the premises and impounded the stocks. The aggrieved parties wanted the cases to be dealt with by I &S Controller at Calcutta. However, the I&S Controller informed them that the powers of the Steel Controller had been delegated to the Regional I&S Controller, who was seized of the matter, and the parties would have to approach his court. The cases resulted in references to the CBI, and the law took its own course.

THE CASE OF CI SHEETS

An MP from A.P. was indenting steel materials and CI sheets allegedly for poultry farms, and houses for SC & ST people for roof construction. An unusually large request for scarce material was received, and we examined the matter. He had secured heavy allocation and sold most of the material to steel traders and in the open market at high prices. He applied for 200 tons of GCI sheets for roof purposes. Roofing material commanded a premium in the market. We asked for the list of applicants and details on the use of roofing material. There was no reply, but the MP turned up and requested sanction for the requisite quantity, as he was an MP and could get orders from the Steel Ministry. When I politely told him that it was not possible to allocate the material without relevant details, he said that he was having financial problems. There were a few court decrees against him that he had to honour. He had fixed up the marriage of his daughter and was badly in need of money. If an allocation is made of CI sheets, he will get over his problem and present a car to me. I firmly told him that government rules and orders did not permit the violation of orders regarding the assessment, allocation, and distribution of steel materials. He walked out, cursing me for being stone-hearted and wooden. I felt that rules for politicians and expected propriety must precede rules for bureaucrats. A code of conduct for politicians is as important as that for civil servants. The gentleman was subsequently removed from his post in a political party.

RATLAM CASE

The Nagpals at Ratlam in M.P. had a near monopoly on securing steel allocation and controlling the steel market in that area. They were high-handed and would not permit our inspectors or the staff of the Director of Industries to inspect their mill or other rolling mills run by him. After securing ample evidence, I suspended the allocation of steel materials to him. He appeared before me in a case against him. He mentioned his contacts in Delhi and that he would get my orders reversed by the Steel Controller or the Ministry of Steel and Mines. I just remained silent. He did try but was stone-walled by the Controller and the Ministry. This had a salutary effect in the Ratlam area. The local industry department officers complimented me for disciplining the Nagpals.

I had to visit Bombay and meet the CBI officials regarding some cases of A.P. and M.P. I visited Guwahati and Shillong to depose some Court cases in Assam.

OTHER ACTIVITIES

I was an active member of the Hyderabad Management Association (HMA), the All India Manufacturers Organisation (AIMO), and the Indian Institute of Public Administration (IIPA). I was a frequent speaker at the Institution of Engineers (India) in Hyderabad. I was associated with the AP Weightlifting and Wrestling Associations and was the vice president of the Hanuman Vyayam Shala in Hyderabad, which ran a modern gymnasium with the latest equipment at Sultan Bazaar. I also conducted wrestling matches. I helped them to secure some land adjacent to their premises for constructing a small stadium to hold events.

I was invited by the Administrative Staff College of India, Engineering Staff College of India, Management Colleges, and Rotary and Lions Clubs to deliver lectures on varied topics related to Management, Industrial development, Ethics & Values, and socioeconomic problems and solutions. This built my reputation as a good speaker. I used to deliver lectures in the Federation of AP Chambers of Commerce and Industries. At their request, I was the honorary editor of their magazine for two decades. Even now, I am on their editorial board.

20

What I Learnt as a Speaker

MY EARLY DAYS AS A SPEAKER

When young, I was fond of talking with friends on various topics. My first fascination with a speech began when I attended one of my grandfather's discourses on the Bhagavad Gita. I liked it a lot and probably subconsciously noted the manner of the delivery of the speech, its speed, and its modulation. The pauses during the talk made me listen, think about, and learn the key message of the talk. The narration of parables, stories, and lessons from daily events helped me to understand things easily and clearly. I was impressed by the rhythm and in-depth meaning of Sanskrit verses and the mellifluous Telugu words, which were song-like. At home, I would try to repeat what my grandfather had said to my mother to show her that I was attentive and a quick learner. I used to repeat the keywords of the talk to remember the message of the speech.

In the convent, my teacher, Mother Theresa, noted my talkative nature and made me the class monitor (Leader) to stop my chatter. She took a lot of interest in making me speak good English with the correct pronunciation, punctuation, speed, and pauses. I was often called to talk to the class on the subject just taught. This helped her to know how well we had understood. As the only boy in the class of 20 girls, I dare not make a mistake while speaking. My teacher would write in my notebook on Fridays different topics to study during the weekend and speak on Mondays at the school's attendance-cum-prayer meeting. This made me desirous of becoming a good speaker, like my teacher, who was my role model. I learnt that one has to speak pleasantly, convey a good message clearly, and teach something new.

As my studies in school were in English, I was taught Telugu and Sanskrit at home. In the initial stages, I had difficulty talking fluently in Telugu and mixed up Telugu for Sanskrit words as many words sounded similar in both languages, but I did not always. 'Siksha' in Sanskrit means 'education,' while Siksha in Telugu means punishment or 'imprisonment,' while Sikshana in Telugu means education. I noticed and learnt the nuances of correct usage and pronunciation. Despite my best efforts, I would often mix up the Sanskrit words for the Telugu words. This made the audience chuckle, and ripples of laughter would follow. I then adopted a system of first reciting Sanskrit verses or quotations in Sanskrit and later explaining the meaning in Telugu. This helped me to remember the Sanskrit verses and polish my Telugu! This spared the audience the agony of my malapropism! I was nominated as Secretary of the English Literary Association at Wardlaw High School, which gave me the chance to introduce speakers, give concluding remarks, and write a summary of what the speaker had spoken. This made me listen attentively and gave me the confidence to later on boldly deliver lectures in my Intermediate, Graduation, and Law courses. In college, I attended the Mock UN Assembly, Mock Assemblies, and Mock Parliament at the University. My oratory helped me to win the Students' Union Elections at college. I won several prizes in college, such as the Basalat Jah Essay Writing Competition, Prof. Syed Uddin All India Debating Competition, and the Elocution competition of the Osmania Graduates Association (OGA). I have won many inter-university competitions conducted by local colleges, like Osmania University and Aligarh Muslim University. The ability to listen, think clearly, and speak well in a measured tone with appropriate speed, pauses, and a good voice are essential for a speaker. Such practice probably helped me to score in the IAS interview.

MY MAIDEN PUBLIC SPEECH

The Vice-chancellor of Osmania University, Prof. M.S. Doraiswamy, selected me to address the gathering of students from all the colleges and Hostels in the O.U Campus on Republic Day in 1956. It was the first large public meeting I addressed. I was slightly nervous in the beginning but soon got into my stride. It established my reputation in the University as a good speaker. This trend continued when I was in Law College and helped me in the interview for selection as Deputy Collector in the A.P. State Civil Service and later in the IAS examination. I learnt that in an interview, candidates should be Prepared, Poised, Polite, Pleasant, Positive, Punctual, Patient, and attentive by listening intently and answering truthfully and audibly. It's better not to guess or bluff an answer. Instead, being honest of not knowing the answer will enhance your credibility and integrity. Satya Meva Jayathe!

Becoming a good speaker entails quite a lot of homework. I had to refer to books and magazines, and I often went to the library and noted down important points. The introduction, relevance, importance of the topic, the pros and cons, the concept, context, content, and communication must be clear, as well as the conclusion. The lecture must be purposeful, topical, relevant, and intelligible to the audience. It should be simple and narrated confidently. The speaker-teacher in you has to awaken, educate, empower, and help the audience to understand the lecture and make an impact on their life and society. This involves making the talk lucid, simple, and, more importantly, euphonious and pleasing to hear. Assessing the level of education of the audience, their age and preferences, and the time given for the lecture is equally important.

I found that the audience likes to remember the keywords of the talk and use them when needed. I used to highlight the words in an alliterating and rhyming fashion, making it easy for the audience to recollect and remember the words and gist of the speech. My audience, after the speech, would usually compliment me by saying that I had made a difficult task easy to understand and to remember. This is, I believe, a unique characteristic of my talks and speeches.

With many organizations inviting me for a lecture on the same topic, I would prepare the talk to suit the particular needs of the organization and audience and never use the old script. Instead, we can convey the various views and different interpretations of the same subject. I would often quote from Sanskrit and Telugu proverbs, poems, and sayings. The audience loved to hear the similarity and continuity of Indian thought and its relevance even in modern times. Audiences enjoy hearing old verses, cinema songs, proverbs, and local idioms but want them interpreted to suit modern situations and made easy, like in Guide Books.

PREREQUISITES FOR A PUBLIC SPEAKER

Every speaker has to do homework by reflecting on the subject, determining the sequence of points, and reconciling various viewpoints. Mental visualization of the lecture, along with written notes of the main points, keywords, or sentences, is useful. The exercise is to gather and organize the points in order of importance sequentially and in accordance with the time given for the lecture. The title and opening sentence must be catchy, hold attention, and capture the imagination of the audience. Similarly, the short and pithy conclusion should enable the audience to carry home the key message of the lecture. Often, the name of the lecture itself indicates what the audience prefers to listen to. Starting a lecture with a couple of quotations, along with relevant take-home messages and concise content, can be very effective. Adding a few jokes and summarizing the key points at the end also helps reinforce the material.

ART OF SPEAKING FROM EPICS

Ancient epics emphasized the art of listening, which is called 'Sravanam.' This requires intention, attention, and eagerness to listen. Sravanam leads to 'Mananam,' which means thinking, reflection, or remembrance for easy recall. Mananam must lead to Dharanam or introspection and 'Dhyanam' to meditate and understand more deeply. Such a process of learning leads to the linking of thoughts in a simple manner. It can be embellished with good quotations. Such linking enables us to maintain the continuity of the lecture. This helps in leading the expectations of the audience towards the likely conclusion of the talk and thus holds the attention of the audience. This is the practice I followed. There are other speakers who follow better approaches. Audience expectations must be respected.

A good speaker must quickly interest the audience and make them listen attentively to what is being spoken, observe the mannerisms of the speaker as well as other listeners, and memorize good keywords of the lecture. Many listeners who are bored try to imagine who the speaker is and guess about his life, family, and career instead of listening to the lecture. A good lecture should lead the listeners to think and take appropriate action on the advice given. If done effectively, the audience will not talk among themselves and distract the speaker. Instead, it will allow for a more fruitful interaction with the speaker during the question-answer session after the lecture.

ABOUT THE AUDIENCE

A word about the audience may be appropriate. The attention span of young people is short. The speaker should engage with young people using their own language and idioms, drawing from everyday experiences to capture their attention effectively. This is particularly true of senior school and college students. Even though science and engineering subjects are taught in colleges, humanities and arts should be given more importance. The speaker should catch the attention of the young by talking about the need for personality development, confidence building, and becoming a job-ready and life-ready person to make the audience interested.

In the case of an adult audience, emphasis must be on personal relations, aim in life, harmony, and the need for a spirit of give and take, and not to hold rigidly any dogma, but find acceptable solutions and go ahead with mutual understanding. Some examples from everyday life and the need for compromises and harmony in life can be cited.

In the case of female audiences, it would be appropriate to talk about gender equality and sensitivity, as well as humorously about wife- husband relations and the need for compromises. The hard work (unpaid) done by the housewife and the need for leisure activities catch their attention. **Ladies** prefer talks where religious thoughts, responsibilities, and happiness in serving others can be adopted and reciprocated by the audience as they relate to everyday experiences. In the case of elderly women, I found that the stories and parables from epics and day-to-day life instances are appreciated as they provide some solace, advice, or guidance to them.

In the case of **senior citizens,** they usually like to be reminded of the "good old days" and how things are changing too rapidly and, hence creating problems. Lifestyles, food habits, the need for good health, support in old life, healthy recreation, and advocacy of regular habits could be sure-shot calls for applause. It is advisable to ask the organizers to suggest the topic for the lecture so that the talk meets their needs. In all lectures, it is important that the introduction and conclusion are crisp and euphonious and can easily be remembered and recalled.

PREPARATION FOR TALK AND QUESTION-ANSWER SESSION

The time required for preparation of a talk normally takes as much time as is required for the speech. It also depends on the speaker's familiarity with the topic and the audience. Compliments received for my speeches were usually about delivery, no fumbling while speaking, the sequencing of the points in the lecture, and the manner of extempore talk with apt quotes and good life examples. My quotes of Sanskrit Shlokas and proverbs were an instant hit with Telugu audiences as they helped them to remember the gist of the talk. If the audience asks no questions, it could be a sign that the lecture was lucid and cleared the doubts in the minds of the audience, or it just flew over their head! i.e., when the audience was dozing during the lecture, were not interested, or it was delivered in a monotonous tone or at the wrong time, after lunch or siesta time. I did receive many complaints that I spoke too fast and that my lecture was long. My standard reply was that I had so much material to talk about that I had to speak fast and long to provide reasonable coverage of the subject.

Many problems arise not during the talk but afterward during the Question-and-Answer session. Some ask the question in a very low or mumbled voice and tone – as if they themselves were perhaps not sure of the question they wanted to ask - it was often difficult to even hear them clearly. Some would ask mischievous and personal questions, while only the persons who listened carefully would ask relevant questions, which are usually hard to answer due to inadequate time and test the patience of the audience, who had just heard a fairly long talk. I found that, frankly, confessing that I did not know the answer or that it was late for the audience, who may not have been interested, would reduce the number of questions.

DURATION OF THE LECTURE

The normal duration of a lecture is 40 to 45 minutes. I found it too short to do full justice to the subject within that time. The audience's attention span is often challenged when it extends beyond what is usual. However, suppose the topic is complex or a lot more information is to be conveyed, then the speaker should have a lot of relevant information and important messages for application in life. Above all, the speaker should be experienced and hold the audience by making it a dialogue and discourse with some humour and not a lecture. I would take approximately an hour or an hour and a half to cover difficult topics in a wholesome manner, giving the history, background, pros, and cons of the topic, and the suggested course of action or the way forward to the future. Since the lectures were slightly longer, I had to make sure that the matter was interesting and humorous, with interesting anecdotes and common human experiences thrown in. The 'spice' of the lecture is good quotations that aptly and succinctly convey the meaning. If the audience is young, the lecture must cover every day experiences and modern idioms to drive home the point. In case the audience is middle-aged, we must bring out common feelings and thoughts when they face some problems and issues. The older audiences enjoyed stories of the past and quotations from classical texts like MahaBharat, Ramayana, and Bhagavad Gita, etc., and felt happy that the more things change, the more they remain the same. A speaker should have the requisite knowledge, experience, and communication skills to succeed. Mastering one science is not enough, and we should know many related subjects before speaking.

GUIDELINES FROM THE TEXTS

I could get a lot of advice from our classics regarding the requirements of a good speaker. A good speaker should not talk in a screechy voice or elongate words, speak very fast, speak with odd body gestures like swaying of the head, or use uncivil or foul language. The worst speaker is the one who reads out from a written speech, which is not at all interesting. Similarly, those who speak with a very 'low and inaudible voice' are the worst. In fact, the audience will be tempted to leave the venue! There are other defects as well. People show fear while talking or talk without clarity and certainty and indicate that they themselves have doubts. Some talk in a very loud tone, while some just murmur. Some speak with a nasal twang, while some talk as if they are crying. Some speakers speak in a disjointed manner, without connection or link to the lecture. Some speak without interest or dispiritedly, while some wrongly split words, use inappropriate words, and talk as if they are in a disturbed mind or mood. These failings should be corrected as early as possible, or they will become long-term liabilities.

SUBJECTS AND INSTITUTIONS I DEALT WITH

I used to address to audiences of Retired pensioners, Young students, Sports, Rotary & Lions Clubs. I also received requests from Bhajan Mandirs and religious or spiritual gatherings like the Sri Ramakrishna Math in Hyderabad. The Administrative Staff College of India regularly invited me as well as the Hyderabad Management Association, Dr. MCR Human Resources Development Institute, the College of Defence Management, National Thermal Power Corporation, Institution of Engineers, National Institute of Nutrition, Indian Institute of Materials Management, several MBA colleges for Induction or Valedictory functions and also general lectures. I delivered some Memorial Lectures on "Role of Non-Government Organizations in Social Development," "Human Capital for Excellence," "Technology and Innovation for National Development," "Energy Security A National Priority," and "Ethics and Values for National Development," and many more.

I have spoken on various subjects, such as Human Resource Development, Ethics and Values, Strategies for Corporate Excellence, Industrial Development, Leadership, Project Management, Entrepreneurship, Motivation, Innovation, Governance, Vigilance, and Corporate Social Responsibility, and so on.

I have edited three books written by Shri T. Anantha Babu, Former Advocate General of A.P. Government, and was Editor of FAPCCI Monthly Reviews. I attended many Book Release functions and wrote some Book Reviews. While in Delhi, I was invited to give talks at the Delhi Management Association, MBA colleges, and organizations involved in Industrial Development., Delhi Telugu Academy and FICCI would often invite me to give talks in English and Telugu.

I have given over 1200 lectures in different organizations on various topics. As I usually spoke extempore, I have hand-written short notes for about 600 lectures, but only 80 lectures have type scripts. Some friends have advised me to get some lectures printed as they would be useful for

Professionals, MBA students, Civil Services Aspirants, general readers, and Public Libraries. The selected Lectures are under print.

At a time when internet facilities were not available, lectures were tape-recorded if they were under the aegis of a large professional body. Later, when internet facilities were introduced and became commonplace, some members of the audience used to video-graph the lectures and put them on YouTube. I am told that there are about 20 such lectures of mine available on YouTube.

A speech creates knowledge for the audience, disseminates knowledge through them, and advocates the application of knowledge and skills in their careers and lives for success. It connects to the audience and makes them think. A speaker must be conscious of the content, pace, and tone of the speech. The message must reverberate in the minds of the listeners— it must bring about change in the listener and for the betterment of society.

A speaker has to function like a Transmission Tower - The vibration of the speech arising from the mind must touch the hearts of the listeners, arouse courage, and motivate them to go forward with greater vigour. It is like the classic example of the two charioteers, Lord Krishna and Shalya, in the Mahabharat. Both were charioteers, Lord Krishna for Arjuna and Shalya for Karna. Lord Krishna enlightened, encouraged, and motivated the despondent Arjuna, who had abandoned hope and did not want to pick up weapons against formidable foes and win the war. On the other hand, Karna, a doughty warrior eager to fight and win, was effectively demotivated for the fight and, at a crucial moment, made to make the wrong move of changing the wheel of his chariot, which gave Arjuna his golden chance to kill him.

Sports and Games teach us that Skill, Speed, Stamina, Strength, and endurance help win the trophy. So does the speaker win his spurs and get acknowledged.

I was often invited to give lectures in English or Telugu, or, in fact, a bi-lingual lecture, to meet the needs of both educated men and women who preferred talks in Telugu. I used to sometimes speak in Hindi or a mixture of Hindi and Urdu in Hyderabad. I learned that a speaker should know 360 degrees about the subject, the pros and cons, and be able to take a 180-degree position to either advance arguments or demolish them like a debater.

As my talks-cum-speeches began in the 1950s, I saw a big change in technology development, which made the talks more interesting with visuals, illustrations which acted as an aide-memoire for the speaker. Seeing the speaker is better than merely listening to a voice for understanding. While the voice may itself be a good awakening call, if the visual aid supplements it, the impact is more durable and can be recalled, as visuals get embedded in the mind and cannot be easily erased. In the initial years, I used to use audio tapes, voice recorders, slides, and transparencies. After that, videos, YouTube, and other materials became handy for distance transmission. Such developments are making lectures universally available, so there is no need for the physical presence of the speaker. Still, the speaker transmits the lecture to the audience, like in distance education. Engineering and MBA Colleges are now taking advantage by tying up with IITs and IIMs for direct transmission and distance teaching by expert Professors.

Belonging to the old school, I believe that personal interaction has a long-lasting impression and brings the teacher and the students together in a better manner than the faceless transmission of knowledge. Knowledge transmitted face to face is probably 'Prathyaksha' leading to 'Vada' and 'Prathivada' - argument and counter-argument that strengthens the bond between the teacher and the students and helps introspection and clearer perception. Also, the lecture must be supported by - Sambodhana (Dialogue) and Bodhitam (Teaching) - Teaching through dialogue, deliberation, discussion, and decisions. All learning has to be internal and reverential if it is to be relevant and useful at all times.

Many listeners have asked me what my best lectures were and on what subjects. It is difficult to recall a past lecture as I have spoken on several subjects to different audiences. My favourite subjects were related to Human Resources Development, Leadership, Ethics & Values, Management, Governance and Vigilance. Other topics were usually related to my work experiences in a long career of 60 years. Some of the lectures I delivered on Infrastructure and Investment for economic development, prospects for the mineral industry, and the need for energy conservation and energy use efficiency are quoted quite often. Both Indian and foreign professional bodies appreciated them. Some of my lectures led to more requests for lectures from both Indian and foreign audiences. After retirement, I found that I continue to receive many requests for lectures from Training Institutions for Practicing Managers. Just as the audience appreciates a good lecture, the speaker remembers speeches that reverberated with the audience, gave him a feeling that he excelled, and got him a standing ovation or good press coverage. Some lectures that enthused me were those that were delivered with a good deal of study. These lectures were delivered at International Conferences, Ramakrishna Mutt, Birla Institute of Technology, Army Institutions like College of Defence Management, National Defence College, Administrative Staff College of India (ASCI), National HRD Network (NHRD), National Institute of Rural Development

(NIRD), National Academy of Administration (LBS-NAA), Confederation of Indian Industry (CII) and National Police Academy (NPA). In a lecture delivered at the ITC Hotel, Calcutta, for NHRD, I was overjoyed when President Abdul Kalam complimented me by saying that it was the best lecture he had heard.

The then Chief Secretary of Sikkim, requested me to address Civil Servants on Good Governance, Human Resources, Management, and the Code of Conduct to be followed by them. The talks were appreciated. I was later invited by the Manipal University, which was set up at Gangtok, to address their Engineering and Medical Colleges. Many public sector undertakings like Bokaro Steel Plant, BHEL, HAL, ONGC, and IOC would invite me for talks on different topics. I was invited by Telugu Associations in the USA, like TANA and APTA, for talks in Chicago, New Jersey, Pittsburgh, Miami, and Dallas on investment opportunities in India and A.P.

Speaking requires a lot of effort and tests your stamina, strength, skill, speed, and the soundness and suppleness of the lecture. The speaker's smile, if it elicits smiles, laughter, or claps, is a sure sign of a good speech. Approbation and a standing ovation are real recognition.

I learned a lot since I had to prepare to speak to well-informed, educated audiences who used to raise points not covered in the speech and difficult questions, which had a humbling effect and showed my inadequate preparation or knowledge. My talks helped me later on, after retirement, as I was requested by UPSC to be an Expert Member on the Board for the selection of Civil Service Officers and to undertake consultancy work for national and international organizations. Leading coaching institutions even now call me to conduct mock interviews for UPSC aspirants and guide students on different ways of preparing and answering in the UPSC interviews. I continue to regularly lecture to students selected as Civil Services Officers at the MCR HRD Institute Hyderabad.

I was born on 12 January, Swami Vivekananda's birthday. Many people from religious institutions in Hyderabad and some colleges, if they liked my talk, would remark that it reminded them of the power of Swamiji's speech in 1893 in Chicago to spread the message of Hinduism, its Catholicity, and universal appeal. That was the greatest compliment I received, and my Guru-Dakshina to my role model, Swami Vivekananda.

21

My Marriage

When I was posted in Hyderabad, many marriage proposals were received. I told my mother that she should screen and select a suitable bride, and I would go by her advice. In those days, offering and taking dowry or Sthreedhan given to the bride at the time of marriage was quite common in AP. However, the Naidu families of Bellary did not take or give dowry. The girls' parents would mention the Jewelry and land gifted to her for her personal needs, which is called "Pasupu Kumkuma" or Sindhoor. The search started by contacting many relatives and friends for a suitable bride.

My to-be wife Sujatha's Uncle Chittharanjan was working as a Scientist in the Soil Conservation Center at Bellary, my hometown. His wife Ramanamma, the maternal aunt of Sujatha, appears to have made inquiries at Bellary about a suitable bridegroom for Sujatha, who was then at Bellary on a holiday. My relatives who had seen Sujatha suggested to her aunt that Gokul (my nickname), an IAS officer from a respectable family, would be a good choice. Sujatha's father, Shrimannarayana of Rajahmundry, contacted his relation, Raja Venkata Rayulu (Kumar), the brother-in-law of IJ Naidu, IAS (my uncle) at Kakinada, with the marriage proposal, and that our family was welcome to see the girl. He contacted us. I went with my mother and maternal aunt to Rajahmundry to see and meet Sujatha informally. Her family arranged a meeting to see her and her parents and for me to have an informal talk with Sujatha.

Sujatha is the eldest daughter of Muttangi Shriman Narayana, a landlord at Rajahmundry, whose father and three paternal uncles owned large extents of land at Gowridevipeta near Bhadrachalam in the then East Godavari District. They also had Cashewnut, mango orchards, and coconut gardens in and around Rajahmundry.

Sujatha's paternal grandfather was a Brahma Samaj leader at Rajahmundry. Her great-grandfather was Muttangi Ayanna Naidu, a legendary Subedar-major of the Madras Regiment who fought valiantly in the battle of Prome in Burma in 1823-24 and was awarded the Sword of Honour by the British for his courage in battle.

My mother and aunt went to see the bride along with me. Sujatha was quite shy at the informal meeting, and I was probably a lone peeping tom amongst the ladies. When my mother signalled to me that I could speak to her, I asked a few questions to know her hobbies, knowledge of English, interest in further studies, cooking skills, and willingness to move and live with me anywhere in India, including Assam which was then considered a far-off place! Seeing the visible embarrassment of the shy bride at my many questions at the very first meeting, my mother cut short my cross-examination. My mother said that she would check the relevant details separately. The interview ended mercifully quickly for the bride but was too fleeting for me.

My mother later asked me whether I liked the bride. I said yes. My mother then expressed her belief that Sujatha would provide the same level of care and support for me as she had over the years, based on her intuition. My mother and elders at home discussed and decided that Sujatha would be a suitable match for me. In retrospect, it was a personal choice backed by the collective approval of two families and the consensus of elders. Marriage is not only a Union of two hearts but a communion of two families!

ENGAGEMENT

The bride's party was keen to secure an early date for the formal engagement and to agree on the date of marriage and the process of invitations for the marriage. The Muhurtham was fixed on 11th March of 1974 at the bride's place, at Rajahmundry. In those days, the bride and groom's families would meet the bride at the engagement ceremony and exchange gifts. The groom was excluded, and the suspense and anticipation on the part of the groom would continue till the marriage date. Our family sent gifts for the bride's engagement day through my doctor, aunt Rukma Bai Naidu. It was customary to send gold ornaments, clothes, and a variety of sweets, fruits, dry fruits, coconuts, flowers, and auspicious turmeric powder and kumkum (Sindhoor) – all arranged colourfully and packed neatly in traditional cane baskets with transparent covers. My aunt had thoughtfully presented, along with such traditional sweets, a multitude of Parry's sweets, Lozenges, lollipops, and chocolates, a later selection. The marriage commitment and invitations were exchanged between the parties.

My aunt, Dr. Rukma Bai Naidu, represented our family and handed over Gold ornaments, Mangalsutra design, colourful clothes, and gifts from our family to the bride. It seems my aunt jocularly remarked to the bride that she should commence counting the days till the marriage day by daily tasting one sweet or lollipop and weaving dreams till the "M" day. My aunt and family would pull my wife's legs with those sweet remarks and her anxious anticipation of the day, whenever such an occasion arose or demanded.

Sujatha's family used to stay in Rajahmundry in their ancestral 200-year-old building called "Dutch Bungalow," built by Dutch Traders. It was located close to the river Godavari when trade was transacted through river and sea routes. It was a two-storied building with four-foot-thick walls and verandahs to keep the house cool during the humid summer. It had large windows, allowing the free flow of the river breeze. Beside it was the Gauthami Grandhalaya (Library), which housed old Telugu and Sanskrit books, Palm-leaf Manuscripts, and Holy Books

My wife has two younger brothers – Lakshmipathi (Shah) and Butchiram. She was brought up by her maternal grandmother, whose husband was the late Kandula Veerabhadra Rao, a respected Circle Inspector of Police at Rajahmundry. They had two daughters but no son, and they adopted Butchiram. They had a big house on Meraka Street where many Telaga families resided.

Sujatha's mother had a younger sister, Ramanamma, whose pet name was Chellakka. She was about 10 years older than my wife. They were more friends than aunt and niece. Sujatha used to stay mostly in her grandparents' house, studied at Schade Girls School, and earned a BA in Government Arts College at Rajahmundry. She had some close school and college friends like Lalitha Tonk (a Gujarathi girl), Sitha, Lakshmi, and others. As her grandmother's house had a lot of open space with a vegetable and flower garden, Sujatha developed an interest in gardening.

THE MARRIAGE RITUAL

The marriage was to take place over three days. Our family got busy printing invitation cards and purchasing Jewelry and clothes for the bride and their close relatives, as well as for our family, relatives, and friends. My aunt and I went to Kancheepuram to purchase silk sarees notably, a gorgeous marriage saree for the bride. We visited the famous– Varadarajaswamy, Ekambareswarar, and Kamakshi Temples. The sacred thread for the bride's Mangalsutra and bridegroom's forehead Basika, as per our custom, had to be obtained from the Srirangam temple near Trichinopoly. Mangalasutra had to be made to our family design in line with our custom.

The marriage card carried the meaning of the Saptapadi or the 7 steps (Saath Pheras) around the sacrificial fire, commencing with Step 1 – "Nourish each other"; Step 2 – "Remain friends for life"; Step 3 – "Be together forever"; Step 4 – "Grow together in strength"; Step 5 – "Care for children"; Step 6 – "preserve wealth" and step 7 – "Share joys and sorrows." The groom says that with these thoughts, "I tie the Mangal sutra to stay together for life." The bride says, "Naati Charami" or "So do I follow."

A couple of railway coaches were reserved to transport all the family members and servants to Rajahmundry from Secunderabad and back. My mother carefully brought out the turban purchased in Jaipur along with Sarpeech for the occasion. Tying a turban is an art that must be done correctly. S.Ranganatham, Commandant of the AP Special Police Battalion (who had given me my cook Nagaraj in Assam), was a former Lt. Col. of the Jat Regiment. He tied the turban in the right royal fashion. Many of my classmates, friends, and Government officials, including CS Sastry, then MD of APSSDC (and a Padmasri), and several IAS Officers, including G.P. Rao, attended the marriage.

The bride's party made elaborate arrangements for refreshments and sumptuous dinner following the marriage. There were more than 1,000 guests, including bride and bridegroom invitees. I was then President of the AP Weightlifters Association, the AP Wrestling Federation, and the Hyderabad Kabaddi Association. I had invited office bearers and important players from Hyderabad, Vijayawada, Eluru, and Visakhapatnam. They came in four buses. All of them had good physiques, were sturdy, had strong appetites, and ate large amounts of food. Food was served separately on tables for my guests. The servers had a tough time serving a lot of rice, chapattis, vegetables, and sweets, but my wrestler and weightlifter guests would never say no or ask them to stop serving. The steel vessels in which heaped rice or vegetables or other dishes were brought and served were soon exhausted. The servers had to run back and forth with more food and dishes to satisfy the insatiable appetite and please the guests who would "never say stop" as item after item was served! Very soon, it became clear that the cooks had not considered or reckoned with the more than-normal appetite and consumption of food by my special friends. The cooks had to urgently bring out the reserve vegetables and quickly cook ample rice and dishes to meet the needs of other guests. My mother, referring to this incident, later told Sujatha that I was the Bhima of the family and had won eating competitions in college like my wrestling and weightlifting friends. My aunt would taunt Sujatha that she would have no spare time for herself as all her time would be spent in the kitchen rolling Chapatis for me or cooking rice, vegetable and non-vegetarian dishes!

The bride's party usually prepares sweets at home to serve the guests. It was getting exhausted in a jiffy, thanks to the guests and my special friends. Luckily, as per custom, the bride's party also prepares sweets of bigger sizes to be sent along with the bride to the bridegroom's house. All such sweets called 'Sare' were consumed by my friends at the dinner table! As there was one more day before our party was to leave for Hyderabad, my father-in-law re-engaged cooks to prepare double the "Sare" or sweets to be taken by us to Hyderabad. The marriage rituals, the journey, the effort and strain involved, and the feeding of the guests are indeed a Yagna for both the parties, guests, and the beneficiaries. No wonder marriage is described as a Samskara, a transformation and reformation ritual. In Telugu, there is a proverb "*Pellichesichudu, Illu Katti Chudu*" which means "Perform a marriage; Build a house" You will know what difficulty is.

HOMECOMING

Sujatha, her aunt Ramanamma, and I proceeded from Rajahmundry to Hyderabad by Car, while our relatives went by train. On the way, some friends at Vijayawada hosted lunch for us and blessed our marriage. We reached our home in Banjara Hills, Hyderabad, around 7 PM. Our house was well-lit with floral decorations to welcome the young bride. After the traditional Harathi was given, we both were asked to enter the house with the right foot forward. A few close relatives had assembled to wish us well. Quite a few of them who could not attend the marriage at Rajahmundry were curious to see the bride and wished us well. The house was a three-storied one, and we were given the large bedroom on the third floor, which had an open terrace. The only problem was that we had to climb a long flight of steps. My doctor-brother remarked that it would give us sufficient exercise to keep fit as we have to come down for breakfast, lunch, and dinner!

RECEPTION AT HYDERABAD

The reception party was organized one evening at Sarovar Hotel Lawns near the Secretariat in Hyderabad. I had requested CM J.Vengal Rao, Finance Minister Ramachandra Reddy, the CS, and other relatives and guests at Hyderabad to grace the function. In the morning, I rang up the PS to the CM, BVS Prakasa Rao, to remind the CM. I was taken aback when he said that a Cabinet meeting was scheduled in the afternoon. I requested that he remind the CM about his having agreed earlier to visit the reception and bless us. He did so. Vengal Rao postponed the Cabinet Meeting and seems to have said, "I must attend the Reception. It was Gopalakrishna who arranged the Z sections for Dowleswaram Anicut and saved a crop in the Godavari Delta". CM Vengal Rao postponed the Cabinet meeting and attended the reception. I remain ever grateful for the CM's gesture and Ramachandra Reddy, Finance Minister. The CS and senior officials attended the reception and blessed us. I do not know whether such relationships between politicians and bureaucrats still exist or not.

My two uncles, aunts, relatives, our in-laws, and their relatives and friends attended the marriage. My mother gave Sujatha a big red rose and fixed it on her hair. My wife and I did Pranam to her, my uncles, aunts, and elders – Their blessings have sustained us to date.

At Hyderabad, Sujatha quickly settled down in our Joint family of educated professionals. My mother put her at ease and guided her in household duties and related tales of her childhood and how she had brought up the joint family. She used to tell her that I was an intelligent but stubborn and mischievous boy and how she used to manage me. Sujatha spoke Telugu in the East Godavari dialect, which is sweet and melodious to listen to and spoken honorifically, while we spoke Rayalaseema Telugu, relatively brusque and akin to written Telugu. Sujatha became busy looking after my elder brother's children and supervising household chores. She had some relatives in Hyderabad and school and college friends from Rajahmundry who would occasionally drop in to meet her.

We used to have many relatives dropping in and staying for a meal or guests who stayed for a couple of days. The reputation of the husband depends on the hospitality of the housewife, care of the family members, and remembering their food preferences. Sujatha learned to cook but was better at managing the manifold chores of the household and taking care of my two brothers' children. She was fond of shopping for all festivals and the purchase of clothes and jewellery for marriages in the family. She quickly transitioned from the role of the only daughter of her parents to that of one among two other daughters-in-law, both doctors. Her friends from Rajahmundry would often drop in, and she would spend time showing them around the city.

She is fond of children, but we do not have children of our own. She brought up all the children in our joint family like her own children. After my younger brother Vijay Kumar lost his life in a train accident in Mumbai, she doted on the children of my brother, whom she brought up. I admitted all my brother's children to good schools; Boys went to Hyderabad Public School, and girls studied at St. Ann's High School in Secunderabad. My elder brother's son Muralidhar studied at the All India Institute of Medical Sciences and did his MBBS and MS in Surgery. He later specialised in Oncology and is working as a Professor at MNJ Cancer Hospital in Hyderabad. His Sister Geetha did her MS in gynecology and has set up an

Infertility Clinic besides looking after our Maruthi Nursing Home along with her mother, M Govardhini, also an MS in gynecology who was a professor of O & G at Gandhi Medical College at Hyderabad.

It is a Telugu tradition to invite the son-in-law to the mother-in-law's house for the first Sankranthi or Ugadi. The custom and intention were to familiarise the son-in-law with the father-in-law's family and for the young bride to make much of the groom and invite her relatives and friends to meet the groom. It helped the groom know his wife's close relatives.

My brother-in-law Butchiram, who was then a student, came to see Sujatha. While boarding a bus in Hyderabad, he fell, broke his arm, and was in excruciating pain. My brother Sundar Rajulu took him to Gandhi Hospital Secunderabad, where an operation was performed, and a steel rod was inserted in the forearm. He was soon well and hearty. Sujatha wanted to see him in the hospital, so I accompanied her. Seeing her brother bandaged, she got frightened and fainted but quickly regained consciousness. After some time, her mother, who was a diabetic, had a cardiac problem. She was admitted to Care Hospital in Hyderabad. Sujatha used to spend a lot of time with her mother in the hospital and took care of her needs. I realized how patient she was and the care and compassion she showed towards needy people. Her mother, after a long stay of six months in hospital, passed away.

SORTING OUT FAMILY DISPUTES

My wife's family had disputes regarding the division of property, and a case was filed in the year 1923 in the Supreme Court of India, which remained undecided. After my marriage, my father-in-law and his brother Sri Krishna brought it to my notice and sought my advice. I studied the papers and suggested that they be amicably settled within the family and avoid the costs, uncertainty, and delays of a court decision. One of their High Court advocates was M Jagannadha Rao at Hyderabad, whom I had known earlier. With his advice and a series of meetings at Rajahmundry, the family was able to arrive at an amicable settlement and the case before the Supreme Court was withdrawn. M Jagannadha Rao later became Judge of the AP High Court, Chief Justice of Kerala and Delhi High Courts, and retired as Judge of the Supreme Court. I used to meet him when I was posted in Delhi. He used to mention that with my law degree and revenue and administrative experience, I had sorted out long-pending cases and lessened the burden of the courts. I found my knowledge of law an asset in matters of land, collection of Taxes, and revenue work.

Whenever possible, I used to take Sujatha on tour with me. Our family used to have the opportunity to attend the marriages of relatives in

Bangalore and Bellary and do a lot of sightseeing in and around Bangalore. We visited the Shravanabelagola, Halebidu, and Hassan temples. We went to Ooty on two occasions as she was keen to see the famous Flower Show and Rose Garden.

My wife had a problem with her eyesight and had to undergo an operation. Dr Rangareddy of Sarojini Devi Hospital operated on her, which relieved the pressure in her eyes, and she was cured.

When I was in the Ministry of Mines, I was involved in an Air crash in Delhi, where I had a miraculous escape. I went home and told her that I had miraculously survived but that her diamond earrings had been lost in the air crash. She told me to forget about the loss of her diamond earrings in the crash. I was her biggest diamond alive, and she could purchase any number of such diamond earrings with me. She arranged a puja in the house after the air crash for my well-being. When we were staying in Tilak Lane (former Hardinge colony), she became the chairman of the Hardinge Colony Health Dispensary, which was receiving some financial assistance from the Delhi Municipal Corporation. She successfully ran it for four years. She was very fond of reciting Vishnu Sahasranamam and Lalitha Sthothrams, which was being held by some South Indian ladies and convened by the wife of the then-Election Commissioner Shri T.N Seshan. They used to meet at the recitals regularly, have refreshments, and probably exchange a lot of gossip and tips on household management.

She was very fond of visiting the Lajpat Nagar, INA, and Sarojini Devi markets for household requirements. She liked going to Paharganj near Connaught Place to Lajpat Nagar Market every Saturday to buy fresh vegetables. Our ground-floor flat in Tilak Lane had a lot of land, and my wife grew a variety of vegetables in the backyard. The front yard had a good lawn with a lot of flowers and flowerpots.

She used to exhibit her collection of dolls for Dussehra/Deepavali and invite her friends for tea and refreshments. This was appreciated by all her friends, particularly South Indian families. She would also give potted plants on the occasion. My job involved travel on official duty to various countries. She accompanied me on a couple of such visits to the UK, France, the US, and Europe.

While in Delhi, she learned to drive. We used to visit Pragati Maidan, which hosts many exhibitions. Several relatives from Hyderabad and elsewhere would visit Delhi and be our guests. This enabled us to visit Agra, Fatehpur Sikri, Mathura, and Vrindavan quite often.

We visited Himachal Pradesh, Uttarakhand, and Char Dham in the Himalayas, as well as Haridwar and Badrinath. She accompanied me abroad to the UK, France, Brussels, Germany, Copenhagen, and Geneva. After retirement, I worked as an Advisor in a few IT companies, which enabled me to visit Japan and the US. Later, since my nephew and niece were working in the US, we visited them.

Sujatha never asked about my salary, my remittances to charity, or my help to other people. She was most happy when I accompanied her shopping and attending marriages and family functions. She looked after me very well, and after my mother's death, she took on the role of a foster mother. It is said that "a wife halves the sorrow, doubles the joy, and quadruples the expenses." This is perhaps true of all marriages, and our marriage is no exception.

After my stint as Regional Controller of Iron and Steel, I was posted to Assam. It was the first time that she was staying away from A.P. at Guwahati, and she had to set up our house with the guidance of my mother. We received good support from the wives of South India IAS Officers at Dispur, particularly Saraswathi, wife of K Sridhar Rao. She is the daughter of OK Murthy, a classmate of my uncle, I J Naidu. He was the son-in-law of VV Giri, former Vice-President and President of India.

My wife used to accompany me on my visits to Duliajan when I was CMD of Assam Gas Company. On the way, we stopped at Jorhat. The D.C of Jorhat invited us for tea at the DC's Bungalow when she saw how big and spacious the bungalow was. She was more interested in the flower garden in front of the DC's bungalow and remarked that one could experiment with different types of plants like creepers, Bougainvillea, and any number of flower pots and how the bungalow could be better decorated with hanging potted plants in the verandah on the first floor of the bungalow. She must have mused that if she had married me earlier, she could have stayed in the bungalow. We visited Kaziranga and saw the abundance of wildlife. We had a pleasant joy ride on the elephant's back. The staff in Kaziranga who knew me well wanted the former DC and his wife to see different areas of the sanctuary and take back happy memories. We visited the Sibsagar, Joysagar, and Negerhting temples in the district. From Guwahati we went to Shillong, Cherrapunji, and other places of interest in Khasi and Jaintia Hills. She was surprised to see chic Khasi women in bead finery and good dress running the Shillong Bazar in a colourful yet commercial manner. She learnt about the matrilineal system obtained among the Khasis, where the youngest daughter is heir to the ancestral property, and the son-in-law must stay in the bride's home.

Many officials, particularly from AP and Southern States, would drop in at our house in Guwahati on their official tour to Assam or to participate in All India Chess or Sports Tournaments conducted at Guwahati or Shillong. We used to entertain them by inviting them for lunch or dinner.

When we were in Guwahati, we received the sad news of the death of her father. She was stricken with great sorrow and transmitted it to me. I suffered a myocardial infarction; but did not notice or realise it at that time, as I was busy applying for leave and making plans to attend the funeral at Rajahmundry. After we reached Hyderabad, my brother took my blood pressure, which had gone up, and took me for a check-up of my health when the infarction was noticed. However, since I have been regularly taking medicines, my BP has become normal.

With an inter-state deputation from Assam to AP, we returned to Hyderabad. My mother welcomed us and was happy that all the brothers and sisters were together again in our new house in Secunderabad. Sujatha got busy looking after the house and, in particular, bringing up the children. She enjoyed packing lunch boxes and getting them dressed properly, and ensured that all the books were in the school bag. In the evenings, the children and Sujatha used to accompany me for a walk. The precocious children would suggest that we go on a particular route they liked during the evening walk, which led to a nice food joint called "Gokul chat," where the children enjoyed eating different varieties of chat and cooling off with a variety of ice creams. They preferred taking ice cream cones and licking them on the way back home. That scene is so etched in my mind that when I see them grown up and married, they are still children to me.

Sujatha's immense patience, unflappability, not getting flustered, and cheerfulness always made life hassle-free and peaceful. Her patience was admired in our family, which is really a virtue that should be practiced. Sahanam Eva Sanskrithi, meaning Tolerance, is real culture.

All her relatives at Rajahmundry and her friends invite her to all their functions, considering her importance as an elderly lady. She looks after the servants and also helps them bring up their children. Our family educated many servants who served us and are now holding good positions in life. As an heir to her father's landed property, she has handed over the lands to one of her brothers for management, saying that she believes that her husband does not need her property and has given her a good standard of living. I guess she has made her choice of need over greed.

Since Sujatha looked after the house and my health and welfare, I had no worries on the domestic front as she would take care of all the small issues and irritations of the family. This enabled me to lead a well-regulated life with ample time to continue my habit of walking, reading, glancing through newspapers, meeting friends, learning many new things, and attending social and cultural functions at AP Bhavan and Delhi Telugu Academy, etc. I found pleasure in doing my work; rather, I enjoyed it and was happy to keep learning something new every day. That was perhaps her best contribution that she has made to me and my life. Quite a lot of my progress in life and achievements were probably due to her patient service, thoughtful advice, and counsel. This made me feel humbled that though I belonged to an All-India Service with service as a creed, she had really done "Service with a smile and service above self".

In the words of wisdom and according to an ancient lore, a wife embodies many roles and a good wife is

Karyeshu Dasi, Karaneshu Mantri
Bhojyeshu Matha, Shayaneshu Rambha
Rupecha Lakshmi, Kshamaya Dharti
Shaddharma Yuktha Khalu Dharma Patni

A wife is in work, a faithful servant; in rendering advice, a Minister; in food, a Mother; in the bedroom, a Rambha, (the celestial dancer); in figure and grace, Lakshmi; in patience and forgiveness, the Earth. Adept in these six Dharmas (Duties), is veritably your devoted wife.

22

Secretary to Govt of Assam, Industries, Power, Mines & Minerals and Public Enterprises, Guwahati and Chairman Managing Director of Assam Gas Company (Feb 1977 – Oct 1978)

SECRETARY INDUSTRIES, POWER MINES AND MINERALS

The composite state of Assam was vivisected in 1972 after a prolonged agitation of the hill tribes, mainly Khasis, Jaintias, and Garos, for a separate state. Prime Minister Indira Gandhi accepted their demand for a separate Hill State, and the state capital, Shillong, became part of Meghalaya.

Assam had to build its capital in the Plains on an emergency basis. As Guwahati was already the commercial capital of Assam with infrastructure such as an airport, railway terminal, etc., it was considered convenient to shift to Dispur near Guwahati, which became the new capital of Assam.

In February 1977, I was posted as Secretary to the Assam government at Dispur, the new capital of Assam. The hastily built Secretariat buildings at Dispur were ramshackle and looked like a cluster of barracks. Officers were staying in small quarters. Rana KDN Singh, a senior IAS officer with experience in industrial development, was the Chief Secretary. I called on the CS and senior officers like Paramasivan, SML Bhatnagar, the Trivedis, and others. I was allotted a small quarter in Dispur. My neighbours were SD Phene, PN Rao, and Sreedhar who had just returned from a posting in Australia.

My portfolio covered industries, power, and minerals departments, and concurrently, the CMD of Assam Gas Corporation, a PSU of the Assam government. I reviewed the current issues and urgent matters with the officers. Assam did not have an Industrial Policy Statement with defined objectives and a plan of action. Assam, however, had development corporations like the Assam Industrial Development Corporation, the Assam Small Scale Industries Development Corporation, and the Assam Financial Corporation, which served some NE States. There was a severe shortage of qualified professionals and experienced officials who could set the direction, pace, and train the staff of the corporations and guide entrepreneurs.

NEED FOR INDUSTRIAL POLICY STATEMENT

I felt that a clear and well-defined industrial policy with appropriate incentives would encourage local industrialists and entrepreneurs, as well as attract entrepreneurs and industries from outside the state. We had to accord priority to infrastructural development by way of provision of land, power, water, and access to good communications for the transport of raw materials and finished products. Assam had a shortage of entrepreneurship, skills, and investments. It needed more qualified managerial personnel. Assam, being an agrarian economy, industrial development and the initiation of organised promotional efforts were given little thought or importance.

Assam is a corridor state through which goods, services, and people have to move to reach the other NE States. The Indian government did set up industries based on oil and gas resources like Oil India Limited, Indian Oil Corporation, and other installations of ONGC. Yet, even they had to contend with a lack of skilled and trained workforce, high transportation costs, etc. One of the problems of Assam, which is not recognised adequately, is that due to the high rainfall, Assam has a short working season of only six months in a year.

There were some medium-scale timber and plywood industries, tea garden factories, and engineering firms to serve the needs of the tea industry. Strangely, even though tea gardens are spread all over Assam and the state was producing the largest quantity of tea with substantial revenues, there were no facilities to convert the tea into a finished, blended, and value- added product, generating additional revenue. Assam did not even have a Tea Auction Centre, a vital meeting point for sellers, buyers, and exporters. The Assam-grown tea was sent for auction, grading, packaging, and marketing to Kolkata and then exported to the UK, Russia, UAE, and Europe. Big tea companies like Lipton, Brooke Bond, etc., had their offices in Kolkata, and the blended and packaged tea was named after these companies, thereby robbing the product of its Indian character, Assam Origin, and geographical indication.

Assam established its own Tea Auction Centre by the early 1990s, and the credit for it must go to the then Chief Secretary HN Das, who had to battle quite a few vested interests who stood in his way. Though the central government provided transport subsidies for movement into and out of Assam by rail as support for the industry, it was not adequate. For want of an adequate local market, quality production, high costs of transport, and inadequate marketing efforts, quite a few medium and small-scale industries became sick.

Assam's natural resources were its forests, oil and gas reserves, coal (with high sulphur content), tea, and some agricultural products. There was scope to encourage modern medium-scale industries, particularly in the automobile and engineering sectors and some plastics manufacturing. It required the strengthening of industrial development corporations, the encouragement of local entrepreneurship, and a concerted effort to sell Assam as an investment destination for the rest of the country. With the presence of the army, there was a need for fresh rations, milk, fish, and meat on the hoof. The dire need was to attract investment by providing necessary infrastructure and government support through incentives for skills development to generate local employment. Gujarat, Maharashtra, Tamil Nadu, and Andhra Pradesh have taken many pioneering steps for industrial development by setting up skill development facilities and technical institutes.

Prior to the partition of the country, the Northeast was reasonably well connected, through East Bengal with adequate road and rail links. Even the river route was very profitably leveraged for large-scale transportation of tea, jute, cement, and steel; however, with a hostile East Pakistan, this facility was all but destroyed. Gigantic effort was needed to recreate these socio-economic overheads which required sustained attention of the Central government and massive outlays. This was not forthcoming during my tenure and for many years after that.

Assam, and indeed the whole of the Northeast, was severely handicapped due to inadequate transportation facilities, small markets, remoteness and distance from the main markets of the country, non-availability of mineral resources except oil, gas, and coal, and the absence of an entrepreneurial class. Unlike some other states, Assam also lacked a well-organized and sufficiently pervasive banking and credit-generating system. No investment can be expected to flourish if credit is not easily available. No doubt, the then-disturbed political condition was a serious deterrent for any private investor to invest in Assam.

It was only much later, with the setting up of the North-East Council for both economic and strategic reasons, that a truly significant effort for Socio-economic development was initiated, and tangible results were achieved.

The country at that time was not favourably inclined towards private enterprise under the policy of state socialism and a penchant for nationalisation. Nehru wanted to transplant the Soviet model of growth into India. That system enabled the then USSR to implement a vast program of industrialisation, through a dictatorial system, at the cost of and denial or curtailment of human and social rights.

Nehru and Indira Gandhi carried this dogma further. They introduced a regime that nationalised banks, the coal industry, and a full-scale license and permit raj. New enactments such as the MRTP and FERA imposed severe restrictions on the expansion of capacity and establishment of new industries. Populist measures to alleviate poverty drained the exchequer, and there was hardly any growth in revenues. The rate of economic growth, which was no more than 3.5% under Nehru, came down to a mere 3%, hardly enough to compensate for the growth of the population. A long era of what was termed the "Hindu Rate of Growth" followed.

The economic and political framework provided an extraordinary degree of political freedom (except for a short while during the Emergency declared by Indira Gandhi), emphasizing individual rights without a mention of duties, coupled with a near denial of economic freedom. This was in sharp contrast to the path followed by South-Eastern Asian countries, most of whom had attained independence from colonial rule either along with or after India's independence. Their approach exercised political control along with full economic freedom and encouragement of private enterprise. Consequently, all these countries collectively known as the "Asian Tigers" literally roared and sped forward on the path of rapid economic advancement and improvements in all facets of the quality of life. Even communist China leaned towards this path under Deng Xiaoping (*after the demise of Mao Tse Tung),* bringing an end to the system of total political and economic control. These countries were not merely successful in wiping out poverty but posed a serious challenge to the industrialised Western world.

VISIT TO GUJARAT

We thought that a state like Gujarat, which was making credible industrial progress, should be studied, and useful lessons drawn for application in Assam. I undertook a trip to Gujarat to study their efforts at industrialisation. My batch-mate G Sundaram, then Director of Industries, arranged for my visit to Ahmedabad and the Naroda Industrial Estate. I visited some small-scale units and the Reliance Industries Textile Unit, which was, at that time, promoting Vimal fabrics. It was a revelation to me that the number of people employed in the modern factory was much less. In contrast, the people employed in the design centre for sarees, suiting, shirting, and for securing orders for their products were much higher. There was a large exhibition hall displaying a range of textiles. Purchasers could buy goods without any restrictions and place orders for them to be dispatched within 3 to 4 days. Discussions with senior officers suggested that Assam should attract medium-scale industries based on its natural resources and industries, which could meet local needs and strengthen the transport sector. The repair and overhaul of heavy vehicles and the manufacture of trailers and farm equipment moving all over North East India would be a viable proposition.

ASSAM INDUSTRIAL POLICY STATEMENT

We called meetings with industrial associations and prospective industrialists in Assam where government officials could interact, understand, and solve the problems of industrialists who were desirous of investing in Assam. We drafted the Assam Industrial Policy statement for approval by the cabinet. We solicited the support of local as well as entrepreneurs from the rest of the country. We took steps to turn around the sick industry. We sought the support of industry experts and companies who could turn around the industry, expand, or diversify the capacity to make the unit profitable.

EVEREST CYCLES CASE

Everest Cycles, a medium-scale unit that manufactured cycles at Guwahati, was incurring heavy losses due to competition, high cost, limited market, and quality issues. We proposed to TI Cycles, a premier company in Chennai, to revamp or purchase the unit at a negotiated price. Their officials visited, studied the unit, and were willing to take over the company. There was a hue and cry that Assam was selling its only medium engineering industry established by a local industrialist to outsiders. This put an end to this proposal and other similar proposals, particularly forest-based units such as hard-board, plywood, wooden furniture, etc. One of the problems faced was that people wanted all jobs to be reserved for local persons when there was a shortage of skilled workers and managers. In view of the growing unemployment in the state at that time, Assam was also passing through the throes of agitations regarding the immigrant issue, language issue, and the Bodo problem. We had to steer clear of these issues and concentrate on the promotion of Assam as an investment destination. We held a few meetings in Calcutta with Assam tea garden managements to interest them in investing in Assam, utilising agricultural produce and its wastes, and developing the paper industry. We projected that Assam could support jute mills, paper mills, silk production, and cement factories. The Regional Research Laboratory at Jorhat did some studies to utilise local materials and generate employment.

There was a pressing need for roofing materials like CI sheets and pipes of different sizes for transporting oil, gas, water, etc. We realised that one problem was the slow movement of cargo and goods due to slow-moving goods trains into and from Assam. We felt that the electrification of railways would speed up the large-scale movement of goods, reduce transport costs into and out of Assam, and ensure that goods reached the markets in time.

ATTEMPTS TO EXPAND HYDEL GENERATION CAPACITY

With the separation of Meghalaya from Assam, a major part of Hydel power generating capacity went to Meghalaya and Assam became dependent on Meghalaya for power. The potential for hydel form of renewable energy in NE India is high. There was abundant scope to utilise hydel sources in Arunachal Pradesh and to a limited extent in the Karbi Anglong district of Assam. At that time, the Lieutenant Governor of Arunachal Pradesh was Lt. Col. KA Raja. As I had known him earlier, I met him at Itanagar and explained to him the purpose of my visit. During discussions, I suggested that Assam could construct hydel dams in the Kameng division close to the plains to begin with, which would provide a good head and drop to generate around 250 to 300 MW of power. Assam would be responsible for the construction of the infrastructure, roads, and communications. This could grant employment to the local people of Arunachal Pradesh. Assam would impart the requisite skills to them. Assam would be prepared to pay the royalty for the water used. I suggested a royalty payable to Arunachal Pradesh at 1 paise for 1 unit of power generated. A draft MOU was also drawn up. I expected that it would ease the power problem for industry in Assam, help speed up rural electrification and meet the need for electrification of the railways.

At that time, a person from Cachar district was Minister Power, Assam. He threw cold water on the proposal, saying that Assam could not afford the cost of construction of a hydel dam and that too in another state, Arunachal Pradesh, and that there would be no demand for that quantum of power in Assam. I tried to explain to him that the geographical isolation of Assam was accentuated because of the long distance to markets in the rest of India and the relatively slow movement by train. The electrification of trains with the power available from Arunachal would bring Assam closer to the rest of the Indian market and make Assam a part of the pan-Indian market. It would speed up rural electrification and encourage small-scale industries in the Northeast. We could request assistance from the Government of India, the Finance Commission, or the World Bank. The Minister would not change his mind despite my best efforts and advice from the CM as well.

I was bitter and frustrated that Assam was losing a golden opportunity to break the transport bottleneck, integrate Assam's economy with the rest of the country, and make future investments in Assam easier. It could also bring in entrepreneurship, industry skills, and investments. Timely decisions must be taken and followed up effectively to bring about transformation and change for the better. Unfortunately, this did not happen and delayed the industrialisation of Assam. Recent press reports indicate that the government has now decided to set up a hydel plant of 500 MW in the Kameng district of Arunachal Pradesh, a decision which was unfortunately postponed for fifty years! and has retarded the growth of Assam. One hopes that ministers will listen to sound advice and make decisions while keeping in mind the long-term interests of the people and the state.

CLEAN GAS SUPPLY TO TEA GARDENS FROM ASSAM GAS COMPANY

As CMD of Assam Gas Company, I regularly visited Duliajan, the headquarters to review matters, issue instructions, and take new initiatives. The company was making good profits by laying pipelines and pumping gas and oil from OIL and ONGC to the user industries as it had a monopoly. It was a dividend-paying company, and the government was happy with its performance. We had an intelligent and hardworking General Manager, Acharya, working from Duliajan. In the course of the discussions and my previous experience as Deputy Commissioner of Sibsagar district, I thought that it would be a good idea to lay pipelines to supply gas to all tea garden factories, which would reduce the use of sulphurous coal, cut down costs and make for truly clean and green tea! Due to the initiatives taken, we were able to provide gas pipelines to over 250 tea gardens in the upper Assam districts. It was probably one of the early initiatives to keep Assam 'clean and green.' We even developed a monitoring system to follow the flow of oil and gas, clean pipelines, and recover some paraffin as well.

ASSAM STATE ELECTRICITY BOARD

The power situation in Assam was a cause of great concern due to the growing mismatch between demand and supply and the continuous loss incurred by the ASEB. The metering system for regular consumers needed to be better organised and the system capable of ensuring that every consumer pays for the services received. Periodic revision of tariff was not undertaken. Worst of all, political considerations led to too many people being given jobs in the ASEB, which inflated recurring costs.

The State Electricity Board (ASEB) was constructing the Bongaigaon Thermal Power Station to augment installed power generation capacity. This was a thermal generation plant for which coal had to come from West Bengal.

In the implementation of the projects, many problems cropped up, particularly with respect to the transportation of steel and other equipment. There was a dearth of qualified managerial personnel and skilled workers. We did not have experienced senior Project Managers or officers who could effectively monitor the construction of the power plant. We contacted the Central Government officials to find an experienced and senior officer to be appointed as Chairman and MD of ASEB. The search narrowed down to Lt. General SD Gupta, who had recently retired from the Army's EME. With his joining, there was a sea change in the morale of the staff, the monitoring arrangements were streamlined, and regular inspections were conducted. Emphasis was laid on strengthening the transmission and distribution of electricity as we wanted to take up rural electrification all over the state. Gen Gupta was a go-getter. The Secretary of the ASEB was an IAS Officer, while the finance secretary, PH Trivedi, and I were members of the Board. A question arose relating to General Gupta's pay and emoluments as chairman of ASEB. There were court judgments that said that pension is for past services rendered, and hence, the pension amount received should not be factored in while fixing salary. In the Government, the prevailing rule was to consider the pension amount and deduct it from the fixed salary if the job was in the Government. This was not acceptable to General Gupta as he had retired from the Government of India, and the job in ASEB was under a Board and not under the Assam government. I referred it to the Law Secretary for his advice in light of the court rulings and equity. On his advice, we fixed General Gupta's salary as chairman without taking into account the pension he was receiving. General Gupta was satisfied. He worked hard with a soldier's discipline and leadership and brought about a Change in the thinking, methodology, and working of the Board.

OTHER PROJECTS

We initiated action on setting up low gestation gas-based power projects for a quick addition to capacity. The Government of India had taken up the Kopili Hydel project in the Mikir Hills district. The project was executed by North-East Electricity Power Corporation Limited (NEEPCO). They faced many difficulties but were able to produce power in a reasonably short time.

The Assam Road Transport Corporation was operating reasonably well. The Assam Industrial Development Corporation (AIDC) and the Assam State Small Industrial Development Corporation (ASIDC) have yet to make an impact.

The Assam Financial Corporation (AFC) was set up by IDBI with 49% equity from the Assam government. The Managing Director was an ex-State Bank of India officer, KP Barua, who provided the much-needed managerial and organisational skills with his undoubted competence and previous experience.

The Assam Financial Corporation was expected to meet the financial needs of small-scale industries in Assam and some NE States. Despite concerted efforts, due to a lack of local entrepreneurship and qualified managerial personnel, it did not make the expected impact or fulfil its objectives. Much later, in 2004, the MD of AFC visited AP State Financial Corporation Hyderabad when I was its Chairman for some help and assistance, which APSFC gladly rendered.

The Government looked at the possibility of encouraging agricultural and horticultural crops. It was felt that pineapples, oranges, and turmeric could be processed and exported to other parts of the country. The army located in the North-East was a major consumer not only for food items but also for clothing and shoes. In view of the higher cost of production and inadequate marketing effort, this move failed. The possibility of setting up ancillary and upstream and downstream units to cater to the requirements of large industries like ONGC, oil refineries, and railways was pursued.

PAPER PLANTS

Due to the abundance of bamboo and forest produce, it was felt that paper units could do well. However, the proposal of the Ashok Paper mills in North Goalpara did not materialise as finalising arrangements was difficult with paper mills in Bihar, who was only interested in securing paper pulp but not in modernising the finishing lines at Goalpara for higher value addition. We experimented with the idea of making pulp and supplying it to other paper mills as well. We organised moving bamboo from the hilly forest areas by trucks, which also picked up locally produced bamboo brought to the roadside. This worked well but ran into problems with availability, price, and the cost of transport. The Assam government succeeded in persuading the Central Government to set up a newsprint manufacturing unit at Jagiroad in the then Nowgong district and another paper unit in the Mokokchung district of Nagaland. A paper mill was also set up in the Cachar district.

For all these mills, bamboo had to be sourced from the hill districts where separate autonomous district councils were set up as a policy to devolve basic powers to self-governing institutions, which, while preserving their ethnic identities, enabled them to make rapid economic advancement. Such powers included control over natural resources and mining rights. These bodies had elected executive bodies who viewed with suspicion any efforts by even the Government to leverage resources that nature had bestowed upon them. Prolonged and painstaking negotiations were standard practice, followed by unreasonable demands, causing unconscionable delays in all stages of execution and commissioning, as well as running these plants.

As there were many sick public and private industries, so it was decided to set up the Department of Public Enterprise to promote, regulate, develop, and manage state public sector undertakings. As the Government had taken equity in many private units, such as small plywood, paper, and cardboard units, and small engineering industries, government officials were nominated as directors in these industries.

TOURISM

The natural beauty of Assam, with its undulating hills, forests, lakes, rivers, and picturesque places, offered promising prospects for tourism. The sanctuaries at Kaziranga and Manas were already attracting national and international tourists. Better infrastructure could make tourism a money spinner. There was also scope for organising river cruises along the Brahmaputra during the fair-weather season. With better communications and tourist facilities, Majuli Island could attract tourists. Some enterprising tea gardens were able to attract tourists to stay in bungalows there and visit places nearby. There was also scope for developing tourism in other NE states like Nagaland, Manipur, Tripura, and Arunachal Pradesh. Temples, lakes, historical and religious places could also attract tourists. The problem was to provide the infrastructure by way of accommodation, hotels, and tourist guides.

Assam had no doubt good potential for industrial development, but it had to contend with problems and issues that needed professionals, funds, and effort. The outlook of the Government and people was rather insular due to limited exposure to developments in the rest of India and elsewhere. Though an Industrial Development Corporation had been set up, there were many policy and management inadequacies. It became evident that Infrastructural deficiencies would have to be overcome before investment would flow into Assam and the North-East States.

Modern industry requires ready availability of power, good roads, transport, and logistic facilities to be economically viable. One difficulty that is overlooked in the rest of the country is that Assam has a very brief construction season. Work during monsoons is extremely difficult, if not impossible. A year's construction activities must be compressed within six months of fair-weather availability. This, in turn, requires heavy equipment to speed up construction activity. As the cost of building infrastructure is high, Assam has to rely on the Central Government. Value addition for goods produced in Assam was low due to the long leads involved, low shelf life, and the difficulty in securing raw materials or finding the market for finished products. The Central Government subsidised railway transport to the border of Assam to make Assamese products competitive.

An exercise was undertaken to examine the scope of developing industries based on Assam's natural resources. It was clear that oil, gas, forest produce, timber, limestone, and coal were available. With the refineries, it would be possible to develop a viable petrochemical complex and small clusters of the industry for textiles, silk, engineering goods, manufacture of tyres, motor parts, and setting up of rice and flour mills. The biggest challenge was to develop entrepreneurship, secure infrastructural investment, improved technology, managerial and technical skills, and operation of industries.

Assam was beset with problems of language, religion, tribal and ethnic loyalties, as well as issues relating to illegal immigration, pains of rapid demographic changes, and growing unemployment. Unless the Central government supports the state in building a modern infrastructure along with the development of skills and managerial support and encourages entrepreneurship, it would be difficult to make fast progress.

Discussions with all the Industrial Promotion Corporations, big industries operating in Assam, and interested parties took place. It was decided that a campaign must be taken up to promote Assam as an investment destination, providing an array of options starting from its natural resources, oil and gas finds, agricultural produce, scenic beauty, market development, and scope for growth. We had to set up industrial estates and industrial areas and promote clusters for the development of small-scale industries to minimise marketing costs. Even after four decades, the problems persist, which indicates that things are moving, but very slowly, in the area of industry and socio-economic development of the North East. A concerted effort by the Indian and Assam governments, the NE Council, industrial bodies, and entrepreneurs is needed to break the logjams and make matters move as fast as rivers during floods in Assam. It is high time NE India really made the 'Look East Policy' a reality by acting an hour earlier, like Tea Garden Time, to welcome the rising sun in the East and herald a new and vibrant Assam.

I was quite active in cultural activities, particularly the Andhra Cultural Association at Guwahati. We organised music and cultural functions at Guwahati, which the locals appreciated. One of the invitees who gave a violin recital was the famous Chitti Babu, a Telugu violinist. He was so impressed by our activities that he donated the royalty to a special raga he played called Samudra Priya.

I invited marketing experts to assist in popularising products from Assam as we wanted the Assam handicrafts to become popular in the rest of the country. The experts found that the local demand for Assam handicrafts and cane articles is at Calcutta, Delhi, Bombay, Madras, and Hyderabad, where we can expect good sales.

We used to visit Calcutta often in our quest to secure investments in Assam. We contacted the management of tea gardens and big industrial houses like the Tatas, Marwari firms, Unilever, and India Tobacco Company. As I had worked in Hyderabad, I tried to get some engineering industries started in Guwahati. The response was lukewarm as the cost of transporting raw materials and finished products was making it unviable.

LP Singh, the Governor of Assam, was earlier Chief Secretary of Bihar and Home Secretary at the Centre. He was considered an expert in internal security. He wanted to push through the proposal of the NE Council to provide power in all North Eastern states. He convened a meeting in Shillong, which was attended by George Fernandez, who was Minister for Industry at the Centre. In the meeting, I raised the need to enhance power capacity in the Northeast, strengthen distribution and transmission facilities in Assam, the major consumer of power, and regulate the cost of power to promote industrial growth equitably. My arguments were forceful. The Governor tried to deflect the topic, but George Fernandez asked me to complete my arguments. He appreciated the viewpoint of the Assam government and remarked that the Centre would support augmenting power capacity in the northeast states and its equitable distribution, including the expected power from the Kopili project.

23

Joint Secretary to Andhra Pradesh Government, Industries and Commerce Department (Nov 1978 – July 1979)

ON DEPUTATION FROM ASSAM

After the death of my father-in-law, I sought an inter-state deputation and joined as Joint Secretary in the Industries and Commerce department in Andhra Pradesh in November 1978. Sundaresan was the Second Secretary (Principal Secretary) in charge of the department. I was given charge of Industrial policy and state-level Public Sector Enterprises. The department was well-organised, with intelligent, smart, and hard-working officers. CR Kamalanathan, the joint secretary, dealt with industrial policy and public sector undertakings. The Deputy Secretaries were Jainder Singh and R Chandrasekhar. All three of them later became secretaries in the Centre. The filing systems were appropriate, and the Government Orders (GOs) were self-explanatory. GOs would clearly explain the issue and the basis for the order. Government work in AP was guided by manuals, standard procedures, and set systems, which were in sharp contrast to the leisurely "Lahe-Lahe" or slowly-slowly mode of administration in Assam. In AP, we used to discuss issues with all available information and make decisions. As our recommendations were clear, the Secretary did not modify our proposals. Our orders stood the test of judicial scrutiny as well.

NODAL OFFICER FOR INDUSTRIAL CORPORATIONS

Chief Minister Channa Reddy wanted a nodal officer to keep track of industry initiatives and developments and submit reports periodically. I was appointed as the Government's Nominee Director in all industrial corporations as well as companies in which the government had sizeable investments like the AP Industrial Development Corporation (APIDC), AP Industrial Infrastructure Corporation (APIIC), AP Small Scale Industries Development Corporation (APSSDC) as well as Nizam Sugar Factory (NSF), and Singareni Collieries Company Limited (SCCL). The Nizam's Industrial Trust (NIT) had made investments in some Birla companies like Sirsilk, Sirpur Paper Mills, Hyderabad Allwyn, and AP Paper Mills. I was also nominated as a director in those companies. The government had made investments in ACC, which was then the largest cement conglomerate in India. The exposure to both the Government and the private sector was a great learning experience that gave me a ringside view of activities related to industrial development.

VK Dhar, whom I knew, joined as Secretary. He took a keen interest in guiding me about policy issues as well as the public sector. He was friendly, cheerful, accessible, and a good boss. He would jot down all important matters in a small notebook and give clear instructions for action. He helped me in the clearance of the Godavari and Nagarjuna Fertilizers by the Government of India with his contacts and access to higher-ups in Delhi.

VISAKHAPATNAM STEEL PLANT

The Pylon for the Visakhapatnam steel plant was laid in 1971 by Prime Minister Indira Gandhi, but there was a long lull in action. A lot of groundwork was needed to secure technological support, and mobilise investments, and secure firm allocation and funding from the Union Government and external sources. Visakhapatnam did not have adequate water supply and transportation facilities to support a large steel plant. It needed raw material supplies of iron ore, dolomite, limestone, etc. Matters were getting delayed as many ministries and organizations were involved. The Central Government could not commit the required finances in time as its hands were full with the construction of the Bokaro steel plant with American assistance. Moreover, the demand for steel in India was already being met by steel plants at Bhilai, Rourkela, Durgapur, and the Indian Iron and Steel Company. VSP would have to be an export-oriented plant. Though the proposals for the Visakhapatnam steel plant were posed to Germany, Britain, and other countries, the response was not favourable as the infrastructure and raw material tie-ups were lacking and not up to the mark. The Indian government commissioned Dastur and Company to prepare a feasibility report and a detailed project report. Steel Authority of India Limited (SAIL) was asked to process further action in the matter. We held discussions with SAIL and realised that unless it were a competitive Export-oriented plant meeting global standards, it would not be supported. Infrastructure for the steel plant was costly as a railway line had to be laid to bring iron ore from the Bailadila mines in the Chhattisgarh area. Unless water from the river Godavari were conveyed to Visakhapatnam, the minimum conditions for clearance would not be met. If estimations of the infrastructural cost were added, the project would not be viable. With much persuasion, we could include the cost of laying the railway line under the Five-Year plans of the Railway Board and expansion of the raw- material production and supplies like Iron-ore to the respective ministries to make the VSP a viable proposition.

WATER SUPPLY TO VISAKHAPATNAM STEEL PLANT

The State Government agreed to provide water but needed more adequate funds to lift water from the Godavari River near Rajahmundry and build the Yeleswaram canal to convey the water to Visakhapatnam. It involved land acquisition for the canal, a balancing reservoir, and the prevention of pilferage of the water enroute for agricultural purposes. I took up the matter with Kaja Satyanarayana, the Director of SAIL in charge of the Visakhapatnam steel plant and explained the position. I suggested and sought an interest-free loan from SAIL. He agreed to give a loan of Rs.120 crores from SAIL to the A.P Government for the construction of the canal. The AP government would repay the loan through water charges levied and paid by the steel plant and amounts collected from the Visakhapatnam Municipal Corporation, which was facing a severe shortage of water supply for the growing city. Due to SAIL's helpful and timely solution, the Yeleru Canal became a reality.

I was a Life member of the Indian Institute of Public Administration and had also been an honorary secretary in the Assam branch. I started organising lectures by administrators, ministers, and professors from the University and Administrative Staff College of India at the Secretariat for administrators, academicians, and students. The Chief Secretary, Finance Secretary, and Minister A Madan Mohan, who took interest, addressed members, including many officers working in the Secretariat. I joined as a member of the Hyderabad Management Association. I was elected Chairman of the Hyderabad Kabaddi Association and resumed weightlifting activity at the Hanuman Vyayam Shala.

CONDUCT OF NATIONAL GAMES 1979

The AP Government agreed to host the National Games in 1979 in Hyderabad. The Chief Minister was president of the committee formed to conduct the National Games, while G Rajaram, the finance minister, was the working president. I was appointed as Chairman of the Finance

Committee. As the grant received from the GOI and the AP Government was inadequate, we had to raise supplementary promotional finance from corporations for the games. I was also the Chairman of the Steering Committee of officials and sportsmen who were entrusted with the responsibility of providing accommodation, boarding, and conduct of the national games.

The South-Central Railways, the Hyderabad Municipal Corporation, and the AP State Road Transport Corporation had experienced sports administrators. The Osmania University sports department and Athletics Federation were also roped in. A lot of work had to be done as Hyderabad was not equipped to host the games and did not have a large Stadium other than Fateh Maidan. It lacked good stadia, playgrounds, accommodation, and transport for all athletes, coaches, and office bearers. We had to identify playgrounds for different events and accommodations, provide transport, and organise food for all participants. Tracks had to be laid, sporting material collected and, jackets blazers stitched, flags placed, and tracks inspected. Luckily, we had very good and willing sports administrators like Venkat Ram Reddy, Omkar, Arif Ali, and the Hyderabad Municipal Corporation's sports administrator, Rajagopalachari. We received good support from school managements, who agreed to spare their hostels and cooks. We engaged numerous sportsmen and workers to take charge of the playgrounds. The National Games were conducted very efficiently and received positive press coverage.

AP OLYMPIC ASSOCIATION

With meticulous planning and economy in expenditure, we were able to save Rs. 10 lakhs, which formed the corpus for setting up a building for the AP Olympic Association at Hyderabad. The Chief Minister and Finance Minister, in an impressive function at the Fateh Maidan Stadium, congratulated the Steering Committee for the excellent work done.

TL SANKAR, ENERGY EXPERT

TL Sankar, an expert in the field of energy who had worked on a UN assignment in Sri Lanka joined as a Secretary in the Industries and Commerce department. He was a family friend who had coached me for the IAS interview. I learned a lot about the power sector, energy issues, and industrial development from him. He appreciated my writing skills and requested me that I assist him in drafting the Fuel Policy Report, for which he was the Secretary. I gladly accepted the assignment, which enabled me to gain an in-depth grasp of issues relating to fuel policy, energy, and power sector matters, as well as their impact on the process of industrial development. I consider him my mentor and Guru for educating me on energy matters. He had an inimitable way of convincing or influencing people in a position to push forward new policies. Sankar received the Padma Bhushan Award for his distinguished services in the field of Energy and Public Service.

COMPETITION AMONG SOUTHERN STATES

At that time, there was competition among South Indian states regarding industrialisation and generating employment opportunities. News coverage in the press about industrialisation had commented that the decade of the 1950s belonged to Tamil Nadu under the leadership of Venkatraman, then the State's Industries Minister. The 1960s belonged to Karnataka, where the central public sector enterprises and Electronics provided the lead to establish industries and ancillaries. During the 1970s, AP was vying for the position of lead state for industries. It had set up many industrial promotion corporations and prepared a plan for infrastructure development in which irrigation (water), energy (power), and incentives for industry were given primacy. The 'Joint sector' concept was initiated and pioneered in AP to speed up the process of development by involving the private sector, contributing to the share capital, also giving management control to the private sector. We had farsighted officers like Ram K Vepa, MV Ratnam, TL Shankar, CS Shastri, VP Rama Rao, Jai Bharath Reddy, PL Sanjeeva Reddy, and many others who steered the initiatives.

Government took forward and popularised the concept of 'joint sector' in which the government contributed 25% of equity and offered 26% to the private sector entrepreneur with the right to manage the company. Later, the Assisted Sector concept of government reducing its share in equity to 10% was followed.

Based on the natural resources endowments, AP vigorously promoted the cement industry, ferro-alloys, barytes, small NPK fertilizer, paper units, and wood-based industries. Though bauxite was available, it was in the hill areas where environmental and tribal sentiments had to be respected. The Indian Drugs and Pharmaceuticals Ltd (IDPL) in Hyderabad encouraged its employees to become entrepreneurs and became the nucleus of the pharma industry in AP. Hyderabad is now the Pharma and Vaccine Capital of India. The BHEL plant at Hyderabad actively encouraged entrepreneurs and supported ancillary industries set up by former employees.

A number of Industrial estates were set up in different places to support medium and small-scale industries based on local raw materials to meet local and export demand. Priority was accorded to agro-industrial development and, especially, the dairy, poultry, meat, and marine exports sector.

HYDERABAD GAINS PROMINENCE

With sound foundations laid in the 1970s and 80s, AP heralded the growth of industries through investments and entrepreneurship in the Telangana region, which explains the prominence of Hyderabad in industrial growth and development. Hyderabad is now the Pharmaceutical, Software, Defence, and Aero-sciences capital, Educational and Scientific Institutional centre, and, of late, the hub for IT, biotechnology, and related developments. We owe a debt of gratitude to those pioneers who laid the foundation for industrial development, exports, employment creation, and overall techno-economic growth.

I was looking after matters pertaining to the Visakhapatnam Steel Plant. Mr. Bhattam Sriramamurthy, an MLA, would send representations and lead delegations to meet the CM to expedite work on the plant. The slogan in those days was "Visakha Ukku, Andhrula Hakku," meaning "Steel Plant at Visakhapatnam - The Right of Andhras." Channa Reddy was earlier the Minister for Steel in the GOI and was aware of difficulties in securing clearance and finances for the project. He would call me ahead of the meetings and ask me to reply to Bhattam Sriramamurthy. He would, at the end of the meeting, tell Bhattam that he had heard him and that the Joint Secretary had explained the correct position. The government would soon appoint a Special Commissioner for the Visakhapatnam Steel Plant, and we could expect that AP would definitely get the Steel plant at Visakhapatnam. I was promoted as the Secretary to the AP Government and soon after posted as Commissioner of the Visakhapatnam Steel Plant and ex-officio Secretary to the Government for Major Industries. I took charge and visited Visakhapatnam to study the ground realities and held discussions with the Collector, Arjun Rao, a competent go-getter.

CYCLONE AND THE CALL OF DUTY

My uncle, IJ Naidu, was the AP Chief Secretary. His son's marriage was fixed in East Godavari district in 1979. As he was very busy, he asked me to take care of arrangements for the marriage, transport, and accommodation of our relatives at the bride's place. We reserved two railway coaches for the journey from Secunderabad and enjoyed the banter en route. My uncle came to attend the marriage venue in the morning while the function was in the evening. Unfortunately, the weather drastically changed in the afternoon due to a cyclone causing havoc on the east coast with high-speed gales and torrential rain. The CM asked the CS to get back to Hyderabad to gear up the official machinery and supervise relief and rehabilitation efforts. My uncle had to rush back to Hyderabad by car, driving all through the night in foul weather. I had to take care of the formalities and ensure the safe return of our relatives, friends, and the bride's party to Hyderabad. I realised the truth of the adage, "Man proposes, God (destiny) disposes." As Chief Secretary, his priority was first the welfare of the people, the honour of the government, and only then his welfare and that of his family. I felt proud that he promptly responded to the call of duty. It was truly a case of "Duty before Self."

CM Channa Reddy and CS (my uncle) boarded an Indian Airlines flight at Hyderabad in 1980 to attend a meeting in Delhi. The plane had just taken off at Begumpet when it crashed on the runway. Luckily, none of the passengers were injured, but they were severely shaken up. We heaved a sigh of relief.

24

Commissioner Visakhapatnam Steel Plant & Ex-Officio Secretary, Major Industry (July 1979 – July 1980)

I was posted as Commissioner of Visakhapatnam Steel Plant and Ex-Officio Secretary for Major Industries. Government had earlier passed a Land Acquisition Act to acquire lands required for the steel plant to freeze prices of land as on the date of the Act. Due to delays in the clearance of the steel plant and the rising costs of land, the farmers were unhappy about the low price fixed for the lands under acquisition and resented the action of the government. They wanted the land prices to be fixed as on the date of the actual acquisition of the land. I visited the villages where the entire land was to be acquired to meet the requirements of the steel plant. The early estimate of land required was around 3,000 acres. Subsequently, the Central government wanted around 25,000 acres of land to be acquired, including the Gangavaram Port area and nearby land. This meant that we had to acquire entire lands from a few villages. This caused much resentment among farmers. They wanted assurance that land prices would be fixed fairly, the viewpoints of the farmers taken into account, and at least one person from every family would be provided a job in the steel plant. It was clear that the farmers would agitate till they secured an assurance that the government would compensate them adequately, offer an alternative place for their rehabilitation and employment of a family member, and provide relief till they were able to stand on their own feet.

I had a discussion with the collector, Arjun Rao, who was an active officer. He felt that unless proper relief and rehabilitation are provided near the acquired area, it would be difficult to undertake acquisition. After discussion, we searched for a suitable place and land to resettle affected families near the main road from Visakhapatnam to Anakapalle, which provided opportunities for livelihood in the growing city of Visakhapatnam and the business centre, Anakapalle. We were able to zero in on an area near Pedagantyada village.

We decided to provide house sites to all affected families and give them an advance amount to construct their own houses. As an incentive, we offered them a levelled layout, smart models of housing with requisite roads, drainage facilities, and provision of electricity and streetlights. We held a series of meetings with village leaders who agreed to move provided the site was ready. We were able to organise the shifting of the land-loser families from the villages over a fortnight by meeting the cost of transporting the household effects and cattle to Pedagantyada also giving them some monetary support till they could secure employment. We assured them that after due scrutiny, we would endeavour to employ at least one qualified person from each affected family who had lost land. We provided facilities for skills training as well.

The Central Government was debating the need for another steel plant as the existing steel plants were meeting the demand for steel. We could convince the Central government that the demand for steel and power would keep rising in India as it embarked on industrialization and economic development. We quoted to the Ministry of Steel the famous remark of Prime Minister Nehru, who was told that India was already self-sufficient in meeting its steel demand. Nehru seems to have remarked, "If one day, all the farmers in India were to decide to use steel ploughs, instead of wooden ploughs, what could be the demand, and will the present plants meet the needs?" This remark ended the Ministry's thinking that India's steel demand had already been met. The Steel Ministry was concerned about securing the latest technology for any new steel plant in India. The capital cost of a steel plant is very high. Unless external financial support and foreign exchange were available, it would be difficult to support a new steel plant. However, efforts were made to attract British and German assistance. The German team visited Visakhapatnam but said that they were already fully committed to the Rourkela plant and would not be able to give technology or financial assistance at that point in time. The United States said that their hands were full with the work that was taken up for the Bokaro Steel Plant. The British team that visited Visakhapatnam said that the only hope for the steel plant taking off lies in its ability to export steel from Visakhapatnam port at a competitive price, which was probable only with assured availability of adequate quantities of iron ore, dolomite, coke, and other raw materials. They expressed their inability to provide any assistance through technology or finance.

It became clear that suitable infrastructure would have to be built at Visakhapatnam and logistics organised to bring raw materials, particularly iron ore from the Bastar district of Madhya Pradesh, now Chhattisgarh, adequate water supply and re-assess demand for steel and decide on the product mix which could meet both domestic requirements as well as export needs. The AP government was clear that the cost of infrastructure was making the plant unviable. It was decided that we should work to secure the approval of the Central government and Indian Railways to meet the cost of laying the rail line for the transport of iron ore from Bailadila to Visakhapatnam as part of their Five-Year Plan. The port had to be suitably strengthened to handle iron ore and other raw material requirements. The State Government would take care of power and water requirements. The Centre would consider giving clearance to the plant only after a properly detailed project report was made, the likely cost of the project was estimated, and the method of financing was decided.

We had to make a number of trips to Delhi to convince the Railway Board and Steel Ministry to include the railway line from Bailadila to Visakhapatnam as part of the Five Year Plan of the Railways. Since the Centre or the state government took over a large portion of the infrastructure cost, the project cost was reduced with a better internal Rate of Return. Dastur and Company prepared a Feasibility Report and a Detailed Project Report that the Government of India scrutinised. The project was cleared at the cost of about Rs 2500 crores. The preliminary work started in earnest with the posting of engineers, HR personnel, and others, but things got delayed as the Centre was unable to release adequate finances in time. They were finding it difficult to provide funds that had already been committed to the Bokaro steel plant, which was in an advanced stage of construction.

We were worried that the financial cum technology tie-up had not been completed and could lead to delays. In a review meeting, we suggested to CM Chenna Reddy that as he was earlier the Union Steel Minister and had good contacts with Russian political and senior technical experts, we should approach the government of Russia through the Ministry of Steel to solicit both technology and financial assistance. The Russian government deputed Deputy Prime Minister of Russia, Mr Arkhipov, to visit Visakhapatnam to hold discussions at the political and administrative levels.

RUSSIAN DEPUTY PM VISITS VISAKHAPATNAM

The news of the visit galvanized a lot of action in Hyderabad and Visakhapatnam. The CM wanted me to take charge and make all welcome arrangements, which should be spectacular, unprecedented, and memorable. He wanted me to be in Visakhapatnam ten days in advance to prepare for a grand reception, finalize the public reception venue, and present him with a welcome address in the traditional manner of India.

I camped in Visakhapatnam and held discussions with political leaders, elders, and educational institutions. It was decided that seven welcome arches would be erected between the airport and the Park Hotel on the beachfront. Every arch represented a cultural aspect of Visakhapatnam and AP and was artistically and tastefully decorated. Flags of Russia and India were printed and given to citizens and children to wave when the motorcade of the VIP passed through the welcome arches. Welcome address on behalf of the CM and AP Government was approved and printed on ivory silk cloth with rollers and tassels as was the practice in ancient times and given in a silver case. Welcome address was read out and given in an artfully engraved silver case. Such facsimile addresses were also presented to the members of the Russian delegation. Arkhipov expressed his happiness at the grand reception accorded to him.

On the momentous occasion, Arkhipov announced that Russia would support the Visakhapatnam steel plant by providing technology, expertise, and finance for importing equipment and would send a technical team to process matters further. Russia announced that it would be willing to assist in initially setting up a 3 million tons per annum plant with the provision to raise it to 10 million tons. This announcement led to jubilation among the crowds as their dream of a steel plant for AP would materialise.

The CM, secretariat officials, and all of us boarded the reserved compartment on the train bound for Hyderabad late in the evening. The CM was exuberant, excited, and happy that AP would at last get a steel plant. He remarked on the way that Orissa was also working for a steel plant, and hence, the officials of AP must be complimented for stealing a march over Orissa.

On the way, at Tuni railway station, the local MLA and other VIPs entered the compartment with dozens of large steel tiffin carriers, many vegetarian and non-vegetarian dishes, and a variety of fruits and sweets. The CM invited me to his coupe and complimented me for the excellent arrangements and conduct of the meeting. He was so happy that he served some dishes and urged me to eat well and relax. He thanked me for the excellent reception and AP bagging the first integrated steel plant in South India.

In the Secretariat, we were more concerned about arrangements for skill training and employment opportunities for local people. The scope for upstream, downstream, and ancillary industries had to be studied. I was designated as Ex-officio Commissioner for Employment Services related to the steel plant.

25

Managing Director, Nagarjuna Fertilizers and Chemicals Ltd. Secunderabad A.P. (July 1980 – Oct 1981)

In July 1980, I was appointed as Managing Director of Nagarjuna Fertilizers Limited, a company floated by Shaw Wallace and Company, a liquor manufacturer. Shaw Wallace was earlier a marketeer of Coromandel Fertilizers along with EID Parry, but the appointment was terminated. They were on the lookout for another marketing assignment. The chairman of Shaw Wallace, Mr. Hayward, thought that setting up a fertilizer plant in Andhra Pradesh, which was a major consumer of fertilizers, could help them enter the fertilizer business and deploy the existing marketing staff. They secured a Letter of Intent from the Indian government to set up a urea plant at Kakinada based on naphtha as feedstock. The plant was estimated to cost Rs 175 crores for producing about 0.5 million tons of urea.

Shaw Wallace proceeded with the preliminary work of setting up the naphtha-based urea plant called Nagarjuna Fertilizers and entered into an agreement with Foster Wheeler and Company, UK, as a consultant and EIL, PPDIL, and other firms for technical support and as contractors for the construction of the plant. They set up offices in Kakinada and Hyderabad. TC Narayan was appointed as Managing Director to steer the company, KV Antony, a senior technical expert who had retired from Fertilizer Corporation of India as Technical Director, and Venugopal, from Best and Crompton, as Finance Director. Some senior officials were also appointed.

With the Oil crisis in 1974, naphtha became scarce and costly. The government said that it could not supply naphtha and suggested fuel oil as feed stock. The estimated cost of the plant escalated to Rs 400 to 500 crores, much beyond the financial capacity of Shaw Wallace, which realised that it was difficult to mobilise finances of that order and was on the lookout for a co-promoter who could protect their investment and interests in marketing.

MY BROTHER VIJAYAKUMAR DIES IN AN ACCIDENT

My younger brother, Vijaya Kumar, was married to Dr. Lakshmi. He joined IIT Bombay at Powai to do his Ph.D. in Internal Combustion Engines. In September of 1980, he unfortunately died in a train accident in Bombay. My elder brother and I went to Bombay, dealt with police formalities, and brought his body and belongings to Hyderabad. It was a shocking, unbearable loss for the family, friends and relatives. It was very poignant as his wife was pregnant and delivered his second child, a girl named Suneetha, posthumously. My mother was distraught but stoically carried on her duties. She asked me to take care of my brother's wife and two children. Vijay's son is now a software engineer in the US. He has two sons who are at school. Suneetha, also an MS from the US, is working with Wells Fargo in Hyderabad and is in a good position. She has a 12-year-old son studying at Bharatiya Vidya Bhavan Public School in Jubilee Hills, Hyderabad.

Wallace approached the Andhra Pradesh Government, seeking their participation in the project by way of allocation and acquisition of land at Kakinada, participation in the equity of the company, and other support required to push the project through. The Chief Minister of Andhra Pradesh, along with M Sanjeeva Rao, MP from Kakinada, and senior officials of Government, met the Central government along with Shaw Wallace officials to work out a plan of action. They were advised that the project required a lot of technical and external financial support. They suggested that the company should seek support from International financial institutions and the UK government for financial and technical support. They advised that IDBI should be approached for their advice and suggestions in the matter. In the meantime, the project clock was ticking, finances were drying up,

Pressure was building up from consultants and contractors for payment of their dues. Shaw Wallace, realising the gravity of the situation, wanted to withdraw from the project. But they had spent a lot of money, and unless another promoter stepped in to complete the project, all their investment would have to be written off, and payments would have to be made to the contractors. They approached the Andhra Pradesh government, suggesting setting up a public limited company with other partners and organising a public issue to get the requisite equity. Loans could be obtained from financial institutions. In January 1976, the Andhra Pradesh government decided to join as co-promoter and released Rs15 lakhs as equity. Nagarjuna Fertilizers became Nagarjuna Fertilizers and Chemicals Limited (NFCL), a public limited company.

The main consultant, Foster Wheeler, and other contractors started claiming their dues, which had been pending since 1975. Attempts were made to secure equity investment from the International Fertilizer Union and Haldor Topsoe of Denmark, each promising to contribute 6.5 million rupees. There was a great deal of uncertainty about the final feedstock, promoters, and method of financing. It became a problem to secure finances, promoters, technology, and the supply of assured raw materials and to decide on methods of implementation. As the project cost was very high, the financial institutions wanted a turnkey contract to be entered into with a reputed organisation that had executed large fertilizer plants.

The Andhra Pradesh government realised that Shaw Wallace had handed over their baby to the state and now had to pilot the project as their investment in equity was higher than that of the original promotor. Shaw Wallace quickly handed over management of the company to the Government, which appointed CS Shastry as Managing Director in December 1978.

Foster Wheeler, PPSL, Engineers India Limited, and local contractors suspended work and started claiming their dues. The AP government sought advice from the Central government and the Industrial Development Bank of India. The Planning Commission suggested that it would be better to set up an NPK fertilizer plant, which would cost around Rs 50-60 crores and meet the needs of AP for balanced fertilizers. IDBI suggested that ICI, UK, or Zuari Agro Chemicals Limited could be contacted to ascertain their interest and willingness to become promoters. CS Shastry was, in the meantime, transferred.

DISCUSSIONS WITH IFC – WASHINGTON

I was placed in additional charge as MD of NFCL. There were indications from IFC Washington that they would consider financing or assisting the project. A team from NFCL visited Washington for discussions with IFC, which received very good support from M Narasimham, who was India's Executive Director of the World Bank and a former RBI Governor. His special assistant, YV Reddy, who later became the Governor of the Reserve Bank of India, organised a meeting with Moen Qureshi, the Vice President of IFC. We secured an assurance that a competent technical team from IFC (W) would visit Kakinada, study ground conditions, estimate the project cost, and suggest a way forward.

IFC TEAM VISITS KAKINADA

A team of six experts was sent by IFC (W) to Kakinada to examine the infrastructural and other needs of the plant, hold discussions, and estimate project costs and modalities of transfer of technology. They visited Kakinada and, with a tooth-comb approach, reviewed the infrastructure, existing arrangements, availability of technical personnel, and ability of the management to push through the project and to make their own estimate of the cost and the requisite technical arrangements. The team was worried about the availability of water for the project. We took them to the Godavari, a perennial river, at Rajahmundry to assure them of adequate water supply and that we would be constructing a summer storage tank to store and supply water not only to the project but also for Kakinada town and future requirements of industries. The British expert who saw the River Godavari remarked that he was expecting to see a river like the Thames in London. Instead, Godavari River was like 100 Thames, and he realised that abundant water would be available! He felt that one more fertiliser plant could be supported. The team was more than happy with the groundwork done and recommended technical support and financial assistance from IFC with some conditions.

The team estimated that the project cost would be around Rs 400-450 crores and it would be advisable to entrust it to a competent turnkey contractor so that the risks of escalation in cost could be curtailed. In such a case, IFC and other parties could consider participating in both equity and loan sanctions.

In the meantime, as advised by IDBI, KK Birla, chairman of Zuari Agro Chemicals Limited (ZACL), called on the CM and senior officials in a bid to participate in the equity of NFCL as the controlling promoter. They wanted financial, technical, and turnkey arrangements to be in place before they would invest and for the company to bear all pre-operative expenditures. Only after the turnkey contractor was selected and accepted by them and the earlier expenditure incurred regularised would they make any investment. ZACL entered into an MOU with the Andhra Pradesh government in June 1979. Zuari's nominee would be a director on the NFCL board without any investment in equity. Zuari wanted to include an NPK plant as part of the NFL. It became clear that Zuari would bring in their share of equity only after the AP government tied up all matters relating to the project and took risks and be the cat's paw in their game.

In the meantime, there was a change in the Government, and T Anjiah took over as CM. The Second Secretary, B Pratapa Reddy, advised me to brief the CM about Nagarjuna Fertilizers. I met him in the Greenlands guest house where he was staying. He was in the drawing room wearing a lungi and banian. As I had known him as a labour leader when I was a student, he recognised me, greeted and hugged me. He thought that I had come for a request, like a posting as Collector at Hyderabad or some other choice of posting. I told him that I was too senior in service to be a collector and was now MD of Nagarjuna Fertilizers. I had come to brief him about the latest position and that KK Birla of Zuari would probably meet the CM and explain their viewpoint. He heard me patiently.

KK Birla wanted the government to agree to a turnkey contractor of his choice and to get the NPK plant included in the license. Zuari would invest on their terms, and the government should not start another DAP plant. After a couple of meetings with Birlas, the CM insisted that Zuari must first contribute their equity to the company and become a real promoter by sharing costs incurred by the company, and only then would the government consider taking further action. There was a stalemate.

GENESIS OF THE DAP PROJECT

Government was concerned about a lack of progress on Nagarjuna Fertilizers. As a second string to the bow, it started separate exercises for setting up of a DAP project at a much lower cost but higher turnover based on imported raw materials. Such a project could be executed with less finance and with secure, sound, and willing partners to invest in equity. Zuari was unhappy with this development. Finding that the AP government was not willing to agree to their conditions, they withdrew from the project on 15th January 1982. Almost 4 years of hard work put in by the government and expenditure incurred would have to be written off. It was a frustrating and bitter experience. Since the project cost estimates and the way forward were clear, we had to try for a new promoter seriously. The House of Galadaris of UAE made a bid to invest in the plant, but their proposal was not pursued because of the risks involved in dealing with a mercurial middle-east investor and disapproval of their proposal by the Central Government.

26

Managing Director Godavari Fertilizers and Chemicals Ltd, AP (OCT 1981 – Oct 1982) and (Sept 1983 – Aug. 1990)

IDEA AND ADVENT OF GFCL

Since DAP was imported or brought from other states for use in Andhra Pradesh, the government accorded high priority to its manufacture in the state. The genesis of the idea lay in the report of the Ministry of Chemicals and Fertilizers in 1980, recommending a DAP plant in South India.

DAP, a high-analysis fertilizer with 18% nitrogen and 46% phosphorus, is applied to strengthen the root system and improve crop yields. Our soils have a surfeit of nitrogen but a deficit of phosphorus. Used as a basal dressing, DAP is adaptable and suitable for most soils and crops in the country. It gives the best input-output and cost-benefit ratio to farmers and is the most sought-after premium Phosphatic fertilizer.

LETTER OF INTENT

I visited Delhi very often to answer many queries and secure the Letter of Intent from the Centre for a DAP plant at Kakinada.

DG Rao, Technical Advisor in the Ministry felt that DAP would be a better proposition than NPK fertilizers in improving soil health and reducing the number of applications. A plant based on imported raw materials would be cheap and help farmers. He suggested a way forward and provided a lot of literature and references regarding the best operating DAP plants worldwide. The Joint Secretaries, V Rama Subba Rao, Shyamal Ghosh, and later, Mrs Jhala, guided us in processing the proposal for setting up a DAP plant in Andhra Pradesh.

We obtained a Letter of Intent for the manufacture of 3 lakh tonnes of DAP per annum. Godavari Fertilizers and Chemicals was incorporated, inspired by the sacred river Godavari, the "giver of boons." We acquired another 230 acres of land to consolidate our holding of about 720 acres of land for GFCL, opposite the Kakinada Anchorage port. This was to take advantage of a future Regular Port under planning, which would enable both liquid and solid imports of raw materials and export of finished products.

PROVIDENTIAL IDEA ABOUT IFFCO AS CO-PROMOTER

Indian Farmers Fertilizer Cooperative (IFFCO) was then the largest producer of Urea, DAP, and NPK fertilizers in India. M. Srinivasa Reddy, an MP from Chittoor district of AP, was appointed Chairman of IFFCO. He issued a press note that IFFCO was interested in setting up a fertilizer plant in South India. I wrote a letter congratulating him on his appointment. Press reports indicated that he had convened an IFFCO Board meeting at Tirumala. I visualised the opportunity of making IFFCO a co-promoter of GFCL, which would make for a beneficial partnership between the government and India's premier fertiliser cooperative. I persuaded Baga Reddy, Minister Industries, to write to Srinivasa Reddy to consider joining the AP government as a co-promoter for the proposed DAP fertilizer plant. Baga Reddy was reluctant to write and was not sure whether IFFCO would agree. I told the Minister that there was no harm in writing a letter to the Chairman of IFFCO. I drafted a letter, which he signed.

I reached Tirumala, where the Board meeting of IFFCO was being held. The peon insisted that I write my name on a slip, which he would give to the Chairman. I did so. But no call came. I waited patiently for about two hours. I was called after the board meeting was over. I handed my visiting card and the letter from the Minister to the chairman. After reading the letter, the chairman became apologetic for having kept me, an IAS Officer, waiting so long. He had thought that some person seeking a job had sent in the slip!

I told him the purpose of my visit and reminded him about IFFCOs intention to set up a fertilizer plant in the south. He immediately called the Managing Director, RK Talwar. I explained to him the Government's proposal to seek the participation of IFFCO in Godavari Fertilizers so that they could benefit from their experience and technical expertise. After listening to me attentively, Talwar said IFFCO would like to examine our proposal. He said he would request Sebastian, the general manager of the Kandla DAP plant, an expert in phosphatic plants, to hold discussions with me and that the Board would take a decision after receiving Sebastian's comments.

Talwar said that he came from a family of freedom fighters from West Pakistan and was interested in India's self-sufficiency in fertilizer and economic development. IFFCO was interested in setting up a fertilizer plant in the south and would cooperate with the Andhra Pradesh government if a Memorandum of Understanding was entered into for the manufacture of fertilizers.

DARSHAN OF LORD VENKATESWARA

Talwar hesitatingly made a request. Some directors and employees of IFFCO who had come to Tirumala for the first time were keen to have Darshan of Lord Venkateswara that evening as they were to leave for Delhi by flight the next day. I spoke to the Executive Officer, Tirupathi Tirumala Devasthanam (TTD), who arranged a special evening darshan for the IFFCO team with Ved-Aashirwad, prasad, shawls, and photographs of Lord Venkateswara at the Ranganayaka mandap. They were overjoyed and excited that darshan had been such a delightful experience and profusely thanked me.

A BLESSED VISIT AND A VOW TAKEN

I was happy that our proposal and my visit to Tirumala had received a positive response from IFFCO. I felt that the Lord had blessed it! I made a silent prayer and vowed that if the DAP plant came up, I would place the first bag of DAP produced at our plant at the feet of Lord Venkateswara for blessing and for use in their flower garden.

IFFCO AGREES TO JOIN AS CO-PROMOTER

After my visit to Kandla and discussions with IFFCO, they asked us to send a draft MOU for their consideration and approval. The standard MoU for a Joint Sector agreement provided for the appointment of the MD by IFFCO, and the Chairman would be the Chief Secretary as the nominee of the AP government. A series of discussions took place within the government and with IFFCO. Talwar, MD of IFFCO, said that they were satisfied with the pre-project work done by GFCL and the assurance of IDBI's financial support. However, they, as co-promoters with 25% equity, could not spare a senior person as MD since IFFCO was already stretched for senior personnel with work at the Phulpur, Kallol, and Aonla projects. He felt that as I had already held discussions with IDBI and was conversant with project work, IFFCO would have no objection to the government appointing both the Chairman and the MD. They also noted that IDBI wanted the MD to continue till the project was commissioned.

IFFCO would provide technical support as required by the company in areas of project construction, training in DAP plant operations, and, if needed, marketing efforts in AP. After discussions, IFFCO agreed and signed our MOU, including the provision that the AP government could nominate both the Chairman and MD.

This was a unique agreement where the government was placed in full control of the company, though IFFCO, a fertilizer major, contributed 25% of the equity and had the right under the Joint Sector concept to appoint the managing director and run the company. It was a rare case of a government public limited company joining hands with a cooperative body and not a private party. The Memorandum and Articles of Association were registered, and the company was incorporated as Godavari Fertilizers and Chemicals. The Board of Directors was constituted accordingly, and I was appointed as MD.

IFFCO was motivated to become a co-promoter of GFCL to increase its presence in Andhra Pradesh. It released its share of equity quite early along with the government. The tie-up with IFFCO, a national-level cooperative society that was operating many fertilizer plants, was a shot in the arm for Godavari. It helped GFCL in tendering and bid evaluation along with Madras Fertilizers Ltd. IFFCO trained many batches of our locally appointed recruits in plant operations at Kandla. Their technical inputs and advice helped us to operate the DAP plant at 100% capacity during trial runs without any hitches with our own operators!

BOARD OF DIRECTORS

The MoU provided for the appointment of the Chief Secretary of the AP Government as Chairman, the Managing Director, two nominees of the state government, two Directors from IFFCO, and two professional independent directors. The first Board of Directors had Chief Secretary SR Ramamurthy, B. Pratap Reddy, Principal Secretary of Industry, and KM Ahmed, Secretary of Finance (Planning). The first Chairman of the Board was followed by BN Raman, GV Ramakrishna, GR Nair, and VP Rama Rao. The Directors from IFFCO were M Srinivasa Reddy, Chairman, MH Avadhani, MD, and later, Tandon, Executive Director. Among the Independent Directors were KK Pillai from VST, MRB Punja, Ex-Chairman of IDBI, and NB Prasad, former Chairman of ONGC. Subsequently, Satbir Singh Kadian, Chairman of IFFCO, and CP Mathur joined the Board on behalf of IFFCO.

The AP government had the right to appoint the MD for a period of 3 years. However, I was appointed as MD in 1983 for a term of 5 years as IDBI had stipulated that I was to be associated with the project and should continue till the project was completed. I was given an extension for two years till 1990 when PC Parekh took over the charge. It was my long tryst of seven years in the fertilizer sector.

The Board Meetings were held at GFCL or in the conference room of the Chief Secretary at the Secretariat. The directors welcomed this as lunch was served by the government guest house, which is well-known for its delicious Hyderabadi cuisine.

The first Company Secretary was J Krishnamurthy, followed by KV Ranga Rao, who did excellent work for the success of our public issue of Rs.15.75 crore in 1986, the largest in that year. He was followed by VS Rao, an LLM, and a gold medallist. He was meticulous in maintaining the minutes and prided himself that the Chairman had never struck out a single word in the draft minutes submitted by him through MD!

I used to meet the Chairmen personally in their office with the draft minutes. They would simply ask me whether I had gone through the minutes and was satisfied with it. If I said yes, they would glance and sign the minutes. It was probably due to the trust they had in my accurate recording and drafting skills. The only occasion when a minor spelling correction was made was by GR Nair, a fastidious MA in English Literature.

PRE-PROJECT WORK COMMENCES

A lot of pre-project work had to be visualised and completed before construction could commence at the site. As the plant was dependent on imported phosphoric acid and liquid ammonia - both hazardous liquids - we had to select land for the plant near a port. While Visakhapatnam was a suitable location, water availability was a severe problem. Vacant land was available 10 kilometers away, necessitating the laying of costly pipelines from the port to the location and intermediate pumping.

SPLIT LOCATION AND THE SOLUTIONS TRIED

Due to the lack of berthing facilities at Kakinada port, the project was a 'split location,' involving logistics of movement of hazardous raw materials from Visakhapatnam to Kakinada with associated risks and costs. We had to transport both phosphoric acid and liquid ammonia from Visakhapatnam to Kakinada. The Retention Pricing Scheme would not reckon the extra cost due to the split location. The cost of transport by road tankers was prohibitive. We explored the possibility of transporting by rail tank cars, but the rail tank cars would have to be built to conform to the Railway Design and Safety Organization (RDSO) and other international standards.

COASTAL MOVEMENT OPTION

We gave up the idea of transporting the hazardous material through small ships or large coastal barges from Vizag to Kakinada due to high capital costs, and related risks. Due to the high swell of the sea off the Kakinada coast, large ships could not discharge hazardous liquid cargo into smaller barges. I sought the advice of Admiral RD Katari (Retired), the first Indian Chief of Naval Staff - a distant relative of mine. He told me that the transfer of hazardous liquids at sea between big vessels may be possible but not between big tankers and small barges due to high swells in the ocean. He opined that movement by rail was a safer and better option.

PIPELINE MOVEMENT

We explored the option of laying underwater pipelines connected to an embedded fixed anchor hose point at sea near Kakinada. We got a grant from the Netherlands government to undertake a feasibility study for various options including mooring buoys and floating platforms. The report ruled out the option of a fixed anchor point as the sea bed on the east coast was soft and unstable. The sea was turbulent for about 3 to 4 months in a year when cargo could not be handled.

As MD NFCL, I noted that France had a lot of expertise in setting up phosphoric acid plants in Morocco and North Africa. With the French company's assistance, I visited Morocco and Senegal and saw large phosphate mines and phosphoric acid plants. We saw the fixed hose arrangement in the sea off Dakar in Senegal for transporting phosphoric acid and liquid ammonia for a DAP plant. Later, we met the CEO of the company in Germany which had constructed it. He convened a meeting of experts who said that the Bay of Bengal being turbulent with slushy, alluvial bed and prone to cyclones, it would not be advisable to build a fixed-platform for mooring or fixed buoys.

RITES ENGAGED FOR RAIL MOVEMENT STUDY

The feasible option was to move the material by rail from Visakhapatnam to Kakinada. In consultation with the Chairman, Railway Board, and RDSO, we appointed Rail India Technical and Economic Services (RITES) to study and recommend the best method of an economic closed cycle movement of rail tank cars and suggest the best cycle turn-around time.

SPECIAL ARRANGEMENTS FOR RAW MATERIAL MOVEMENT

In India, phosphoric acid was earlier moved in mild steel truck-tanker barrels with rubber lining to prevent corrosion of MS plates. The rubber lining reduced the quantity of phosphoric acid held and discharged from the barrel. We opted for stainless steel tank barrels mounted on rail wagons for phosphoric acid transport, which were manufactured and used for the first time in India.

Liquid ammonia was usually moved in refrigerated road tankers, which had to be further cooled at the destination. As a large quantity of ammonia was to be moved, we opted for refrigerated ammonia rail tank cars. Our tankage at Visakhapatnam used to receive cold liquid ammonia from ships, which was transferred to the ammonia rail tank cars, which had in-built insulation arrangements to minimise the increase in temperature between Visakhapatnam and Kakinada and delivered directly to the ammonia tankage at the DAP plant.

We were able to secure the designs and specifications for the phosphoric acid and refrigerated ammonia rail tank cars. This hastened the project work. The rail tank cars were mounted on rail frames manufactured by SIMCO and Texmaco in Calcutta and barrels by Richardson and Cruddas in Mumbai. Liquid ammonia and phosphoric acid barrels were designed and manufactured in India, and cargo was transported by rail for the first time in the country!

Vizag Port Trust initially allotted a berth at the outer harbour for unloading phosphoric acid and ammonia, but the AP Pollution Control Board did not allow it. We shifted to the inner harbour which cost us an additional Rs. 2 crores. The berth was suitable but close to the point of sewage discharge from Visakhapatnam town. With help from an R & D Engineer in BHEL, Hyderabad Dr U Yugandhar, we used a poly-amide micro-membrane to cover the discharge outlet, which effectively filtered 99% of the sewage, leaving water near the berth clear and clean. We received good support from all the Chairmen of Visakhapatnam Port Trust RKR Gonela, TR Prasad, and PVRK Prasad and Port officials.

RAILWAY SIDING

The nearest Rail point to the plant was the Kakinada Town railway station located 9 Kilometres away. The railway siding had to pass through the Nagarjuna site to reach the GFCL site. With the help of South-Central Railway (SCR), we secured used rails from a dismantled track at highly depreciated prices. This was a big savings in cost. SC Railway also helped us procure a locomotive (engine) and laid the track which connected the DAP plant and the bagging plant. A retired loco driver trained our staff.

SUMMER STORAGE WATER TANK AT SAMARLAKOTA

Godavari Irrigation Canal provided raw water to Kakinada municipality. The canal was closed for maintenance for 2-3 months during summer. IFC Washington and IDBI were concerned about water supply during the summer months, but their fears were allayed. Kakinada Municipality received clearance from the government for building a water storage tank to supply 2 Mgd of water to the municipality. We wanted an additional 3 Mgd of water to meet our present and future requirements. A large summer storage tank was constructed near Samarlakota to meet the requirements of Kakinada municipality, GFCL, and NFCL. We assisted in securing consent from farmers to lay underground pipelines through their lands over 23 kilometers.

As Regional Iron and Steel Controller for AP and MP states, I met N Tata Rao, who was then a Chief Engineer in MPEB and later became the Chairman of APSEB. I met him at Vidyut Soudha in Hyderabad and requested that he visit GFCL and suggest how GFCL could get a 132 KV transmission line to the plant. He took the trouble to visit Kakinada and assured that APSEB would build a 132 KV substation and provide a transmission line to GFCL. A taskmaster, he ensured that the power lines were laid much ahead of time. Kameshwara Rao (ex-SAIL plant), who was our Manager (Electrical), made all local arrangements. The plant had no problems with power availability.

CONSTRUCTION WORKS

We appointed a retired Chief Engineer, Reddy, who had worked as Advisor (Buildings) to the UNDP, as our Civil Works Advisor. We took on Deputation, an engineer from MES and recruited some civil engineers. We constructed the compound wall and, for one season, observed the flow of storm water and drainage from the land before deciding on the layout of roads and locations of the main plant and factory buildings. To save time on construction work, we decided to level the land required for the plant. We identified the location of the main DAP building, storage, bagging plant, silos, railway line, and other off-sites. We spent Rs. 70 lakhs on preliminary work, which later saved us a lot of time and money.

Kakinada is a cyclone-prone area, and buildings had to be constructed taking into account the highest wind and gale speeds. We engaged IIT (Madras) to suggest the layout, piling specifications, and other related matters. VT Raju, a well-known civil engineer who later became Director of IIT (Delhi), along with his team visited Kakinada. They considered records of the last 100 years and concluded that the highest wind speed was 132 miles per hour. Buildings were built to withstand that gale speed. Despite many cyclones at Kakinada, the DAP plant has not suffered damage. We planted saplings of trees along the boundary facing the sea that grow at different heights, like a crescent, to deflect cyclones and dissipate their energy. To avoid heavy structural corrosion in the coastal areas in front of the sea, for the first time, the plant structures, usually made of steel, were totally constructed with reinforced cement concrete (RCC), including field pipe racks. Soil testing indicated the need for piling for heavy structures; IIT recommended platform piling for the main buildings at Kakinada and Visakhapatnam Port. This was done expeditiously by Simplex Engineering.

PLANT CONSTRUCTION STRATEGY

After internal discussions and meetings with potential contractors, we categorized the project work as:

Pre-engineering and construction of off-sites which takes a lot of time and must be ready "just in time" before the main plant commences production

Storages of Ammonia and Phosphoric acid – both hazardous liquids- at Visakhapatnam and Kakinada and transport arrangements to Kakinada Construction of two trains of the DAP Plant.

Our site at Kakinada beside the sea was at a low level. We excavated earth on the northern and western boundary of the site and raised the plant location area of 300 acres by about 1 meter height. The excavated areas became our green belt!

PROCUREMENT DEPARTMENT

Selection of main contractors for the plant and off-site facilities was done by our Contracts and Procurement department headed by Prabhakara Rao, a very capable, upright officer who did not hesitate to call a spade a spade. We had no complaint from any contractor or suppliers about the transparency of our transactions, procedures, and processes or payments on time.

PROJECT MONITORING DEPARTMENT

The project monitoring team was headed by SJ Naidu and ably assisted by V Kutumba Rao, both engineers with years of project experience. They devised a simple but effective monitoring system with the assistance of our consultants, Tata Projects Limited, who devised a special system called PRISM, a precursor to the concept of a Dashboard.

TPL – CONSULTANTS FOR OFF-SITES WORK

Tata Projects Limited (TPL) was appointed as the consultant for designing off-site facilities and supervising the construction work of the main contractors. We insisted, and TPL agreed to set up their home office and detailed engineering facilities at Secunderabad to ensure speedy preparation of drawings, giving effect to changes and their speedy transfer to Kakinada.

Pre-engineering and off-site planning work started on 1st July 1985. We constituted small groups for different work sites to closely schedule and issue weekly work orders and monitor the progress. Steel and cement were procured centrally for issue to civil contractors. If work was likely to be impeded by the contractor for want of finances, we purchased the material from the contractor's account to ensure that work was not hampered.

Tata Projects Ltd did a good job in the timely issue of drawings with assured quality of work. The off-site work progressed on schedule. Among the larger off-sites were a 20,000-tonne Silo for storing fertilizers built by Larsen and Toubro, the bagging plant by McNeill Bharat Ltd. Steam generation plant, a raw-water treatment plant, and other support structures for the large phosphoric acid tank and two ammonia Horton spheres and the canteen. The foundation for two DAP trains and the conveyor system was also part of their work.

MAIN DAP PLANT – BY HDO

The main DAP plant on the slurry process was assigned on a turnkey basis to the reputed engineering firm Hindustan Dorr Oliver, who had constructed as many as 14 DAP plants in India and abroad.

AMMONIA AND PHOSPHORIC ACID STORAGE

We selected Toyo Engineering Limited as our contractor for ammonia and phosphoric acid storage at Visakhapatnam and Kakinada. Hitachi Zosen of Japan gave the drawings, and Toyo Engineering (India) Ltd did detailed engineering. The storage contract was awarded on a turnkey basis. To prevent premature expenditure, we gave the order in June 1986 just after we had gone for public issue. They constructed a 20,000 tons phosphoric acid and two 10,000 tons ammonia storage tanks, which had to be kept at -33°C with double valve wall insulation at the Visakhapatnam Inner Harbour with requisite facilities for movement of ammonia and phosphoric acid by rail tank cars and requisite tankages at Kakinada. We provided water curtains for safety and environmental reasons. Lloyds of UK conducted a risk management study and designed a fail-proof system to prevent any likelihood of leakages, fire, or explosions in the storage and pipelines with the latest safety precautions. We set up small expediting-cum-inspection groups to track work on the construction of phosphoric acid and ammonia wagons and other heavy equipment being fabricated at vendor workshops.

GREEN BELT

A team from the AP Pollution Control Board visited the plant and wanted us to control tail gas pollutants and provide for a 2-km wide green belt around the northern and western boundary of the plant to prevent any gas or dust pollution in the direction of Kakinada, about 4 km away. We arranged tail-gas scrubbers to prevent particulate and gaseous pollutants from recovering useful gases and prevent the escape of particulate gaseous pollutants.

DAP is a zero-effluent plant as it is water-negative. To satisfy the AP Pollution Control Board, we prepared a small water pond for the plant pipe discharges. We raised different varieties of fish in the pond to prove that the gaseous effluent was not harmful to marine or bird life.

Some local activists filed a petition in the Supreme Court to prevent further construction work on Godavari fertilizers. We engaged Kapil Sibbal, a prominent advocate, to argue our case and were allowed to proceed with Construction of the Plant while planting local and native plants in a half-km green belt instead of two kilometers.

The local Divisional Forest Officer Padmanabham requested that we spare some land to raise local tree saplings on our premises for their use. We utilised the opportunity by requesting him to raise saplings for our green belt. We complied with the stipulation of the Supreme Court by setting up a 2-acre nursery within the plant premises to raise saplings for the green belt, also organised Van Mahotsav. This area is now a green forest with a variety of birds, ducks, small animals, and reptiles.

MONITORING ARRANGEMENTS

AC Dora General Manager, a veteran of 30 years of experience in fertilisers, headed the plant. He used to coordinate all activities at the Kakinada plant. He was ably assisted by VRK Rao who took care of Operations. Later, VCS Rao became the company's GM at Kakinada.

KS Pappu was in-charge of all maintenance work. He was good at predictive, preventive, and protective maintenance.

SJ Naidu and V Kutumba Rao, along with Prabhakar Rao at Hyderabad, monitored the progress of project construction with an eye on time and cost control.

The construction group worked out the strategy, plan of action, and monitoring mechanism, as well as a sound Management Information System (MIS) to monitor the progress of construction work with the use of well-designed PERT charts and S curves. A daily meeting at the site was held by the General Manager, AC Dora, with heads of departments like Port-handling, Materials Management, Orders Department, Marketing, HR, and Finance which the MIS group attended. The GM would hold a weekly meeting to review project progress as per the weekly schedule. I used to attend the meetings if I was in Kakinada. The GM would also conduct a monthly meeting to review progress as per schedule, take corrective action, and send the minutes by telex from the plant to the headquarters. I would do a monthly review of the progress with our General Manager of Monitoring, SJ Naidu, which the Procurement & Materials Management, HR, Marketing, and Finance Heads attended. I also held a quarterly meeting at Secunderabad, which was attended by our consultants and CEOs of our main contractors, such as TPL, Toyo, HDO, L&T, and civil contractors. This kept the pressure on and ensured that the work went according to plan.

MARKETING OF DAP - SETTING NEW TRENDS

The construction of a fertilizer plant takes about 3-4 years. In the meantime, we had to educate farmers about DAP and its use and seed the market with Godavari DAP fertilizer obtained from the Central government. This was to prepare our teams to market the entire product of 3 lakh tons of DAP when the plant goes into production. The AP Marketing Cooperative Federation (MARKFED) distributed fertilizers in the state. A senior officer from Markfed, joined GFCL to start the Marketing department. At that time, Coromandel Fertilizers terminated the services of their marketer, Shaw Wallace and Company whose staff were laid off. It was a God-sent opportunity. We appointed the best among them with good contacts with dealers and customers. They quickly enlisted dealers to promote, popularise, and sell our Godavari brand, DAP. Overnight, we had the basic marketing set-up!

The Central government allotted us a ship of 15,000 tonnes of DAP to dock at Kakinada for our seeding program. We recruited C Raghava Rao, then a Manager (Marketing) in Coromandel Fertilizers, who had an MBA from the first batch of Andhra University. He was soft-spoken and good at planning, supervision, and execution. He had a nice way of enlisting dealers and persuading farmers to adopt DAP for its advantages. Several Telugus opted to serve in Godavari to work nearer home. I sat on the interview boards for the selection of candidates based on suitability, temperament, attitudinal and behavioral skills, and ability to converse pleasantly. We soon had the nucleus of eager-beaver marketing staff.

WE GET SET TO GO

We soon realised that marketing was a tough task. Godavari was a **new company**, DAP a **new product** and we had to develop a **new market** with **new staff** and enrol **new dealers!** We brainstormed and worked out our strategy and plan of action. A sound dealer network and farmers' contacts were made, and transport arrangements were tied up. Publicity on the special characteristics of Godavari DAP, a quality product from a government company, was done through AIR, press reports, leaflets, and cinema slides. The AP Agricultural University and Research Institutions in the state like Central Tobacco Research Institute (CTRI) at Rajahmundry, Sugarcane Research Institute (SRI) at Anakapalle, Paddy Research Centre (PRC) at Marateru and Cotton Research Centre (CRC) at Nandyal and Oil Seeds Research Station at Hyderabad were contacted to seek advice on correct usage and application of DAP. Leaflets were distributed to inform, Educate, advise, and convince farmers to adopt corrective measures to restore the fertility of the soil, use balanced fertilizers, and enhance crop yields.

THE BAG – OUR LOGO - PROMISE OF BOUNTY

We finalised the design, size of the bag, colour, weight, and ability to withstand rough haulage and usage. We adopted an HDPE bag in light yellow, which is considered auspicious in rural areas. Our logo was red and green, and there was a closing security thread. The logo was a victory stand with three blocks. The tallest block was marked F for (Fertilizer), the second G for (Government), and the third C for (Cooperatives). Above the fertilizer block was a panacle with nine grains (Nava-dhanya), the symbol of prosperity. F for Fertilizers and Farmers was on the winner's stand while G-Government indicated a Government Company and C the Cooperatives of IFFCO supporting the farmers. All three winners were champions of Farmers, Farm Productivity, and Farmer Prosperity!

A 50 kg DAP bag packing was the norm in usage for an acre, but the suggested dosage of DAP was 40 kg per acre. Though it costs a little more to buy bags, we adopted the 40 kg bag to make it convenient and economical for the farmer. We supplied custom-made 20 kg and 10 kg packs for small farmers and used them in tribal areas. For home and kitchen garden uses, we supplied 5 and 1 kg packs. We imported a weighing machine for correct calibration.

Farmers need a suitable mix of nitrogen (urea), sulphate of potash, muriate of potash, ammonium sulphate, or different combinations of NPK. Selling only DAP is not economical and does not meet all the farm needs. We secured an allocation of both Urea and DAP from the Centre for our seeding program and sold it in AP in a blitzkrieg operation with publicity saturation. We received a positive response and acceptance. Route mapping and appropriate bundling helped us to send requisite packages of fertilizers by truck to small dealers on the way.

Many big fertilizer companies located outside AP had difficulty selling DAP and NPK fertilizers because they wanted a good dealer network and adequate staff in AP. We agreed to market their urea and mixed fertilizers and potash if they were agreeable to sell their product in "Godavari Bags"; we sent them Godavari branded bags and sought commission for meeting the cost of the supplied bags. The bag mentioned the name of the producer and supplier and was packed for sale by GFCL. Several companies did so, which gave free publicity to the Godavari brand, and we earned good marketing commissions as well!

HANDLING OF IMPORTED FERTILIZERS – A PROFITABLE BUSINESS

The Central government was happy with our marketing efforts and enquired if we were interested in handling Urea and DAP ships as their handling agent at Kakinada also selling the products. We agreed to do so and took two ships, Urea and DAP, on a trial basis. Later, we handled many Urea and DAP ships at Kakinada. To streamline ship operations and transportation, we put a team of engineers to work out the optimal method of unloading fertilizer ships at mid-sea, quick transport to shore, with re-packing and bagging arrangements on shore with the correct quantity and ready for fast transport direct to dealers' outlets. They worked out the optimal tonnage and size of barges to bring the bags to shore. We organised machine weighing and bagging on shore with direct dispatch through trucks to dealer points, reducing or eliminating the use of intermediary godowns and saving on time and cost.

The Central Government gave 60 days credit for port handling and sales, during which time we had to unload ships, send material for consumption or sale, collect the amount, and remit it to the government. In case of delays, the handling agent would have to pay 12% as interest. We streamlined our handling operations by aligning bagging, truck availability, and transport, much like an assembly line operation, and dispatched to dealers within 3 to 4 days. The sale used to be completed quickly, and the amount was collected well within a month. The availability of urea and DAP enabled us to popularise the Godavari brand. It was a profitable business. The press lauded our initiative to earn money during the construction stage.

KRISHNAPATNAM PORT FORAY - THE TREND SETTER

Due to the long lead, the cost of transportation of fertilizers to the Rayalaseema districts was high. We examined the possibility of unloading ships at Krishnapatnam port in Nellore district (which was then a minor port) but with a good draft of 15 meters. It was handling small-sized ships due to a sand bar and the absence of a navigable canal, which prevented big ships from berthing alongside and had to be dealt with mid-sea. With the Port Officer Kakinada, Capt. S. Raju, Raghava Rao, and GN Rao, I visited Krishnapatnam port to examine the possibility of unloading 15000 – 25000 ton fertilizer ships. We noted that due to the lack of a dredged canal, large ships had to anchor at sea and unload into small barges. On return to Visakhapatnam, we requested that the Dredging Corporation of India dredge a small canal through the sandbar on a trial basis. This proved that Large ships could berth alongside. We handled the first sample fertilizer ship of 15000 Dwt, which negotiated through the canal and unloaded goods at the berth site. It was successfully accomplished, and we were elated. Our handling contractors, Naidu Dasaratha Rami Reddy of Nellore, efficiently organised handling operations and transport of goods to their godown and thence to our dealer points. The Government later decided to develop a regular port in Krishnapatnam. It is now exporting iron ore from NMDC and importing coal for coal-based power plants.

FROM FARMER-TO-FARMER COUPLE

The fertilizer bags used to traditionally show an Indian farmer with a big moustache and a turban. The fact is that not only the farmer but also his wife takes an active part in spraying fertilizers, planting seedlings, weeding, and harvesting operations. We decided that our bags should portray not only the farmer but his better half as well. Our bags showed a beaming farmer with his wife carrying a heap of golden grain. Later, we showed a farmer with a tractor and the wife wearing a lot of jewellery. The message was clear: the use of DAP leads to prosperity for farmers. ***The wife of the farmer appeared on the Godavari fertilizer bag for the first time in India***

Godavari thanked her and her hubby for our success!

GODAVARI GRANULES FOR CONVENIENCE OF USE

On a field visit to Rayalaseema, women farmers told me that the DAP granules dropped in the seed drill along with the jowar seed got stuck in the seed drill. The granules were not of uniform size and were sometimes damp. Handling granules while spreading them was messy, and women were worried that their delicate palms would be affected. They wanted us to produce hard, uniform-sized, round granules to enable smooth passage through the seed drills. This task was entrusted to our technical team, which, within a month, was able to develop the process for hard and round granules much like pearls. This became a plus point for our Godavari DAP usage in dryland areas. Farmers, our partners in progress, are the ultimate users, patrons, scientists, and judges!

DEALER AND FARMER MEETS

We organised many dealers' and farmers' meetings to explain the correct and timely usage of fertilizers. Agricultural department officials attended the meetings to reinforce our suggestions. A lot of leaflets on the usage of DAP was distributed. We sent our Godavari publicity van to such meetings to educate farmers through films at village markets and bazaars and religious or cultural functions. We used these opportunities to select progressive farmers, prepare demonstration plots to demonstrate and enthuse other farmers to take advantage of the use of DAP.

GODAVARI AT KUMBH MELA

We were very active at the time of the Kumbh Mela in Allahabad and Pushkars on the Godavari and Krishna rivers, at which a large number of farmers and devotees attended. This helped us to popularise our brand in North India. GFCL extended its market to cover Maharashtra, MP, UP, Bihar, Punjab and Rajasthan.

NAARM – REFRESHER COURSES

We used to send marketing executives to the National Academy of Agricultural Research and Management (NAARM) at Hyderabad for a refresher course training to update, upskill, and upgrade them on the latest developments in the agricultural sector. We followed the system of job rotation to provide them with experience in port handling, logistics, accounts, public relations, and reporting systems. The training was intended to groom executives to do the entrusted job with self-confidence. When the plant was getting ready for operations, we gave all our staff basic knowledge about our plant operations, training them in fire drills and emergencies in case of fire or leakage of hazardous material and advising them on precautions and actions to be taken. We stressed the importance of time and cost management.

SITE FACILITIES

At the site, the siren would be sounded for reporting, tea break, lunch, and closure time. A canteen was set up to provide good food at subsidised rates. Classes on management, marketing, ethics and values, good behaviour, and conduct were held. I used to take some classes. Security staff were vigilant, and there was no theft of materials. There were no disciplinary cases during my tenure. The HR department maintained cordial relations with the Kakinada Municipality, Zilla Parishad, Medical College, and Railway Station Masters. We could secure railway reservations at short notice!

BALANCED FERTILIZER USE – DAP (DI AMMONIUM PHOSPHATE)

Farmers were using a lot of urea and NPK fertilisers without realising its adverse effects on soil health and plant nutrition. Urea was used for green growth, but it did not help increase the yield of grains. We set out to educate farmers on the balanced use of fertilizers and the role of DAP in strengthening roots and increasing yield. To publicise the proper use of fertilisers, we took on the deputation of Agronomy Professor A. Lachanna from AP Agricultural University and an agriculture graduate, VS Raju, who had earlier worked in Nigeria. We had a team to advice farmers to talk about the need for soil testing and fix the deficiencies in soil nutrition. Andhra soil was deficient in phosphorus, potash, zinc, sulphate and some micronutrients. We introduced DAP to farmers as a high-analysis fertilizer.

FARM PRODUCTIVITY - FARMER PROSPERITY

We succeeded in conveying the unique message of DAP as a high-analysis fertilizer to the farmers by coining a simple message in Telugu on the use of DAP in contrast to NPK mixtures with the message – ***"Perugu Peruge; Majjiga Majjige,"*** meaning Curd is curd, Buttermilk is buttermilk. Thin buttermilk (NPK) cannot be compared with thick curd (DAP). This clear and direct message to farmers paved the way for DAP, a new product in a new market, to be quickly and widely accepted. Farmers got the message that DAP was a basal dressing for paddy and other crops, which was essential for better yields and was much cheaper per kg of nutrient. Our slogan was ***"Increase Crop productivity for farmer's prosperity."*** In fact, our vision was **"farm productivity for farmer prosperity."**

ONE STOP SHOP - GODAVARI FERTILIZERS

As the farmer needs all three nutrients N, P, and K, depending on soil conditions and crop sown, selling only DAP did not make sense. We had to procure and sell urea along with DAP and, if possible, potash and micro-nutrients. We decided to promote Godavari Fertilizers as a "**One Stop Shop"** for fertilizers by making available Urea, DAP, MOP, and SOP at our outlets.

MARKETING CONCEPTS PUT TO WORK

Marketing comprises the 4 'P's of Product, Packaging, Placement and Price. We added people to it. We linked the Ps correctly and secured good results. It was supported by the media, such as the cinema (slides and documentaries), TV (TV shows), AIR (talks and jingles), and publicity vans and press reports. Posters, wall paintings, pamphlets, and articles in agricultural magazines supplemented this. We produced an in-house magazine called 'Godavari Ripples' for circulation to our employees, dealers, and farmers.

To succeed in our effort to establish the Godavari brand indelibly in the minds of our employees and customers, we used to emphasize the importance of quality, standards, timely delivery, reasonable price, and selfless service. To succeed in our efforts to establish the Godavari brand indelibly in the minds of our employees and customers, we used to quote a Sanskrit sloka: ***"Vasthur Mulyam, Pramanena, Samayena, Mitha Vyayena, Sevena, Amulyam Bhavathi".*** It means mulyam – the Price of an article or service, Pramanena - quality or standard it connotes, Samayena - timely delivery, Mitha vyaena – at low cost or the price differential, Sevena - the service that accompanies makes the product priceless (valuable) ***"amulyam bhavati".*** The Price must become Priceless in the eyes of the Purchaser.

DEALER NETWORK

With a mix of experienced and enthusiastic young employees, Godavari quickly extended its network to over 2,500 dealers. We were emboldened to send a rake load of fertilizers to Marmagoa and Nepal (Raxaul) led by Nukala Sudhakar, one of our young marketing executives who rose to the occasion and handled the job successfully. Dealer meetings, farmer meetings, simple messages, slogans, and media publicity in AP, Maharashtra, UP, and Bihar made Godavari a popular and preferred brand of fertilizers.

We moved fertilisers during the off-season to the areas of usage. With great demand from UP and MP, we organised rake movements of fertilisers and organised sales from the destination platform itself. This saved us storage costs during transit and ensured quick sales and collection. We sent rake loads to MP and UP, where we had warehousing facilities, and in other places, advised our dealers to take delivery of stock at the railway platform or from our warehouse by giving bank drafts. This proved successful, and our collections are trouble-free.

THE GODAVARI FAMILY AND BUSINESS CULTURE

The average age of our marketing staff was around 26 years. They came from various disciplines like arts, science, agriculture, and MBAs. We had outstanding marketers recruited from MNCs and national companies like MK Vishwanatham, N Sudhakar, Gopichand, CR Rao, Satyanarayana Raju, K Satyanarayana, M Gopalakrishna Rao, I Krishnamurthy, S Chandramohan, G Subba Reddy and T Seshagiri Rao who created the market for Godavari in Bihar and UP, Suresh, Sarat Gummadi and many others. They were pioneers who built up the name, fame, and creed of Godavari fertilizers. They collectively created and gave shape to the concept of a "Godavari Family" comprising employees, material suppliers, dealers, farmers, truckers, shareholders, and other stakeholders associated with Godavari fertilizers. The stakeholder concept was put into practice much before it became a creed.

C Muralikrishna, a computer engineer from ECIL, started our computer department. Instead of following the conventional method of setting up a full-fledged centralised division, we opted for the 'bottom- up' customised system by devising a simple operating system for each department like Marketing, Finance, HR, Project monitoring, and Company-Secretariat. It helped us to confidently handle a massive number of transactions with 2500 dealers and regularly monitor our financial and supply chain transactions. As a result, we were able to close our annual accounts for the year ending 31st March by the end of April. It proved very useful for our public issue, as we had to handle over 93,000 shareholders.

GODAVARI FERTILIZERS – STRIKES A BELL

Progressive Andhra farmers had purchased lands in Orissa, MP, Maharashtra, and Karnataka and settled down there. There was a strident demand for Godavari Fertilizers from them! During my tours to their villages, I received a warm welcome from them at Katni in MP, Mauda near Nagpur, and Gangavathi in Karnataka. We forayed into the Bellary district of Karnataka - my native place - with a big bang and splash by setting up a marketing office at Bellary. With enthusiastic local support, we quickly secured large orders. This alarmed Karnataka Markfed and Mangalore Chemicals and Fertilizers (MCFL), who resented Godavari's entry into their territory. They wrote to the Central Government to restrict our area of operations to AP as MCFL could meet the needs of Karnataka. We reluctantly closed our marketing operations in Karnataka. Farmers of Bellary continued to obtain our fertilizers from across the border less than 10 km away.

PUBLIC RELATIONS DEPARTMENT

We set up a Public Relations department to promote the company and its brand and help with our marketing. We took on the deputation of RS Pampana, a senior Deputy Director from the AP Information and Public Relations department. He hailed from Rajahmundry and was an actor and sportsman. He spoke a few dialects of Telugu and had excellent contacts. He was a live-wire PR person, brimming with ideas. He worked closely with the marketing department. Credit should go to him and the employees in the Marketing and PR department for putting Godavari on the fertilizer map and for instant recall of Godavari DAP as the preferred fertilizer of farmers.

A UNIQUE CALENDAR-CUM-PANCHANGAM

We designed a unique annual calendar in English and a local almanac or 'Panchangam' in Telugu. On one side of the calendar, we highlighted the dates and times suitable for agricultural operations like ploughing, harrowing, raising nurseries and planting crops, spraying pesticides, harvesting, etc. The calendar was a big hit with farmers, and multiple reprints were made to meet the demand.

CALENDAR

We printed regular calendars with colour photos of Lord Shiva, Lord Vishnu, Lord Rama, Mahalakshmi, Goddess Durga, and Saraswathi, which were in demand. We got them printed at Tirupur and Sivakasi. Strangely enough, there was a clamour from NRIs for more calendars as they wanted to distribute them to their friends in the UAE. Later, we issued Hindi versions of the Panchangam and calendars for distribution in Maharashtra, MP, UP, and Bihar.

GODAVARI RATHAMS (CHARIOTS)

To carry the message of Godavari Fertilizers to rural areas, we procured a Publicity van and designed it to meet our requirements. It provided space for our posters, leaflets, cassettes, small giveaways, sample agricultural implements, and video films. The subsequent advanced versions of the publicity vans called "Godavari Ratham" were more elaborate and used for exhibiting documentaries on Godavari and film shows. All regional marketing officers were provided with a publicity van. We also deployed vans with Hindi publicity material for use in Maharashtra, MP, UP, and Bihar.

EXHIBITION AT HYDERABAD

We held a 3-day exhibition on Godavari Fertilizers with the latest display boards, commentary, and music in Jubilee Hall of Public Gardens in Hyderabad, inaugurated by the CM Rama Rao and IFFCO Chairman M. Srinivasa Reddy and attended by senior officers of state government and public sector organisations, AIR, DD, the press and public.

FARMER/DEALER MEETS

Annual dealers' meets were held along with our marketing officers to assess demand for fertilizers and make proper logistical arrangements for ensuring timely supply. Dealer meets organised in districts prior to the agricultural season helped us assess the demand for fertilizers and prospects of sales. During dealer meets, we invited senior AP Agricultural University faculty to Advise farmers on sound agricultural practices, the use of fertilizers, and crop protection measures. This provided us with direct contact with dealers to receive their suggestions. Dealers were presented with awards for their highest sales, innovative practices, customer relations, and shop decoration. We decentralised our promotional efforts by sanctioning money to dealers for authorised display and publicity to increase their sales.

IMPROVED AGRICULTURAL IMPLEMENTS

Farmers were not using proper, custom-built agricultural tools and implements, leading to frequent breakages, injuries, and fatigue. Some women farmers in AP complained that the local sickles were not sharp, were heavy, and often used to break. In MP, medium-scale industries were manufacturing agricultural implements like sickles, harrows, ploughshares, iron baskets, crow-bars, pick axes, and spades as per standards at Raipur and Bhopal. Vanadium steel sickles were made in two sizes and shapes and were suited for use in different operations by men and women. We standardised the implements to suit the needs and made bulk purchases. Some local engineering firms at Tenali and Rajahmundry started manufacturing such implements in AP itself. Later, they began manufacturing other agricultural implements and attachments for tractors. We presented such articles as gifts or prizes to farmers who quickly adopted and used them. We made it a practice to give prizes such as implements, tiffin carriers, thermos flasks, torch lights, tool sets, gloves, masks, and decorative items to cattle.

FORAY IN PESTICIDE MARKETING

There was a problem of pest attacks affecting various crops. We encouraged and helped small pesticide manufacturers to produce quality pesticides. We posted Quality Assurance Inspectors to guide, check, and Clear pesticides for sale under the Godavari brand. Under the 'one-stop shop' for fertilizer and other inputs, we thought pesticide supply would help farmers, and got in touch with the RRL - now, Indian Institute of Chemical Technology -at Hyderabad for guidance. Its Director, AV Rama Rao, was very helpful and gave good advice and suggestions. Much later, we set up our own pesticide manufacturing company.

FERTILIZER ASSOCIATION OF INDIA (FAI)

Satyanand, Secretary of FAI at Delhi, used to advise on technology, marketing, and Retention Price Mechanisms to Fertilizer companies. Godavari Fertilizers became a member of FAI, which used to conduct seminars and annual meetings of all fertilizer industry delegates in Delhi. The annual meetings helped us develop good contacts with CEOs of fertilizer companies and senior executives. I was elected as Chairman of the FAI (Southern Region) later.

TRAINING OF PLANT OPERATORS

We selected local bright young ITI and polytechnic students. After their induction training, we sent them to the IFFCO plant at Kandla to work as regular DAP plant operators and bagging supervisors at the Steam Generation plant, as well as phosphoric acid and ammonia storages and general plant operations work! This innovative move helped our Kandla-trained operators to confidently run the two DAP trains on their own at more than 100% capacity in the commissioning and trial runs.

GODAVARI - A TIME-CONSCIOUS AND COST-CONSCIOUS COMPANY

At the plant security entry point, we had a board displaying the number of days left to complete the project. This reminded our staff and contractors' employees about our philosophy that "time is money" and that we were committed to completing the project on time. We prominently placed notice boards at different places to address the need for time and cost consciousness in project management. Our slogans were "Plan the Work - Work the Plan" and "That day's work must be done that day itself." We promised to give a Godavari embossed "wristwatch" to all our permanent employees on the scheduled date of the plant's commissioning. We did so, and the promise was fulfilled!

Selecting excellent contractors with experience and prompt payments ensured that the project was completed on time and in accordance with the highest international standards.

FINANCIAL MANAGEMENT IN GFCL

Fertilizer, an input for farm production, comes under the Essential Commodities Act, which enables the government to provide timely availability at an affordable price. As local production is inadequate, fertilizers are imported to cover the shortfall. The prices of imported fertilizers fluctuate based on worldwide demand, supply, climate, and other factors.

RETENTION PRICE

To encourage indigenous production and rationally fix prices of fertilizers, the government set up the Fertilizer Industries Coordination Committee (FICC), which works out the cost of production of each fertilizer factory in India and provides a 12% post-tax return on capital investment called Retention Price at the operational norm of 80% capacity utilization of installed capacity.

FREIGHT SUBSIDY

Fertilizer has to be dispatched according to seasonal demand to areas of consumption by rail and, after that, by road or only road to the points of sale. The average cost of freight by rail and road for each fertilizer plant is called freight subsidy. The difference between government fixed price and cost of production, including freight charges, is reimbursed. The early fixation of the Retention Price and its payment has a significant impact on the working capital requirement, financial management, and profitability of the company. Due to our split location, the import of phosphoric acid and ammonia at Visakhapatnam and its transportation cost by rail over a distance of 160 km from Visakhapatnam to Kakinada had to be computed and allowed. We engaged an external expert to study the FICC norms on how other fertilizer companies had secured reasonable retention prices, freight subsidies, and timely reimbursement. Though the GFCL plant was at the "threshold of a high fertilizer consumption zone," our task was to take our fertilizer to the "doorsteps of the farmers."

MARKETING COST MANAGEMENT

Management of marketing costs was a crucial element of the project, which determined our profitability. We recruited some bright, young, and intelligent chartered and cost accountants from reputed financial and investment corporations. IFFCO helped us by deputing a cost accountant, Ramchandra Rao, who unfortunately died due to jaundice, leaving behind two young daughters who were employed in our company on compassionate grounds. IFFCO later deputed V Sambasiva Rao, who helped streamline our operations.

During my visits to IDBI, IFCI, and Sicom, I spotted two bright, young, highly qualified financial managers, GRK Prasad and MLN Acharyulu, who were sharp, intelligent, innovative, and industrious and appointed them in GFCL At interviews, we would select persons with an aptitude for learning, job orientation, and the "can-do spirit." In short, get the correct Position – Person fit.

SEED MARKETING OPERATIONS

We secured separate working capital limits for our seed marketing operations and stock holding. We secured imports on Letters of Credit while sales were on a cash basis. We handled 14 fertilizer ships and were complimented by the Fertilizer Ministry and FICC. Our dealer network and supply chain arrangements enabled us to sell a good quantity of imported fertilizers. Hence, we had no difficulty in selling our entire DAP production when our plant was commissioned. Though there was a large silo in the plant, it was made clear to our executives that the production of our factory must go directly to the dealers' sale point and not through our large silo, which was to be utilised only for imported fertilizers and that too, during the off-season!

ADDITIONAL WORKING CAPITAL- NOVELCONTRIBUTION

With the increase in funding needed for handling, seeding, and regular marketing, IDBI reassessed additional working capital needs as Rs. 5.35 crores and was willing to sanction Rs 4 crores. But they wanted Rs.1.35 crore to be brought in by the promoters. IFFCO said they could not transfer cash but could provide urea worth Rs.66 lakhs to Godavari for the sale proceeds, which could be utilised as their cash contribution. The AP government gave us a "sales tax concession" of Rs.66 lakhs, by which we fulfilled the stipulation of IDBI.

WE EARN ON SALES OF UREA AND OTHER NUTRIENTS

We agreed to market the urea of other companies on a commission basis, provided the material was packed in "Godavari Urea" bags. This became a regular additional source of income and spread the perception that Godavari sold both DAP and Urea and that dealers could conveniently obtain supplies of many nutrients from the same source.

Suppliers of urea, NPK, and other nutrients like MOP - SOP, as well as micronutrients, offered us a cash discount of 24% on prompt payment. At our borrowing cost of 14%, we were making a clean 10% margin of profit on our purchases!

The seed market operations, sales of urea of other companies, and other fertilizers like MOP, SOP, and NPK mixtures during the first year resulted in a profit of Rs.80 lakhs! The press lauded our efforts to earn money even before going into production!

RETENTION PRICE AND FREIGHT SUBSIDY FIXATION

We vigorously followed up with FICC and secured a Retention Price within three months of going into production. The freight subsidy was quickly determined, which helped our cash flow management. In the very first year of production, from September 1987 to March 1988 (7 months), we operated at 67% of our installed capacity.

VISAKHAPATNAM PORT OPERATIONS

The import of raw materials at Visakhapatnam port was handled by Two very competent and efficient officers, Tatalu and Mutyalu Naidu.

Suppliers of shipments of phosphorous acid and ammonia provided us with a fairly long credit period at low international interest rates with reasonable terms, which provided good margins.

PROJECT COST

The estimated project cost of Godavari Fertilizer was Rs.108 crores comprising equity of Rs.32 crores and a loan of Rs.76 crores with a debt-equity ratio of 2.4:1. The financial institutions that appraised the project rated it as a technically feasible, economically viable and financially sound project. They sanctioned term loans to the extent of Rs.60 crores, including foreign currency loans of Rs.9 crores. This was the largest loan advanced to an industry in Andhra Pradesh at that time. A consortium of seven nationalised banks financed the remaining 16 crores.

Of the equity component of Rs.32 crores, Rs.8.28 crore (26%) was subscribed by the state government, Rs.7.97 crores (25%) by IFFCO, and the balance of Rs.15.75 crores (49%) by the investing public during May 1986.

PUBLIC ISSUE

The approved financial plan of IDBI included a public issue of Rs.15.75 crores. We appointed SBI (Capital Markets) as our advisors, Ms. Pressman as advertising agent, and CISCO as our merchant bankers. With wide press coverage on the progress of construction, the seeding program, and the growing popularity of Godavari DAP, our Merchant Bankers advised us to go in for an early public issue in 1986 as an economic recession was forecast for 1987-88. It was almost 18 months before the scheduled commissioning of the plant! Our Board decided to go in for a public issue in May 1986. We met leading investors and brokers in Mumbai, Delhi, and Calcutta to brief them about Godavari Fertilizers and its progress and seek their support for the public issue. GRK Prasad, Executive Assistant to MD, and Company Secretary K. Ranga Rao assisted me in successfully piloting the public issue. The public issue provided for the reservation of shares to farmers, cooperatives, Non-Resident Indians, business associates, and the public. We had to instill a corporate culture in a public sector company by educating our own executives and going for the public issue. Andhra Pradesh did not have an investment culture at that time, unlike Gujarat, Maharashtra, Rajasthan, and Delhi. We wanted a widely-held share holding.

PUBLIC ISSUE POSTER

We designed a poster in Telugu showing a proud farmer putting one hand over a fertilizer factory and the other twirling his mustache with the slogan "Godavari Sharu, Labhaniki Maro Peru," meaning Godavari share is the other name for profit! We contacted banks and dealers to exhibit our posters, distribute leaflets to their customers, and educate them on the utility of holding Godavari shares, which they gladly did. We enthused farmers and cooperatives to purchase Godavari shares. We explained that a share was akin to the land, which appreciates in value, also provides returns by way of one or two crops (Dividends) as income. Just as the land value would appreciate over time by improvements made, share prices would also appreciate.

Many bank managers in AP were aware of shares but had never handled shares of a public issue. We convened meetings with branch managers of State Bank of India and Andhra Bank to brief them about the public issue, share applications, receipt of share amount, etc. They gladly exhibited Godavari Share Issue posters on the bank premises and supplied share application forms. This helped us promote the public issue to bank customers all over AP.

PUBLICITY

We started a field campaign in all districts of AP and important market Towns to publicise our public issue and distribute propaganda materials. We extensively used radio, TV, and press. We received wholehearted support from Mohan Kanda, then Registrar of Cooperative Societies, S Ramakanth Reddy, then Director, Agriculture, and in particular, K Chandramouli, who was Deputy Registrar of Cooperative Societies in East Godavari District. Our marketing staff and GN Rao, the Administrative Officer, played a stellar role. The public issue was oversubscribed thanks to the efforts of all concerned, particularly our merchant bankers and advisors. The quick receipt of the share amount strengthened our financial position and saved us considerable bank interest.

NRI CAMPAIGN

A team of officers, advisers, and merchant bankers led by me visited Mumbai, Baroda, Ahmedabad, Rajkot, Jaipur, Delhi, and Calcutta to explain to investors the merits of Godavari fertilizers and investing in its shares. We toured the Middle East as we had reserved a quota of shares for NRIs. We visited Dubai, Abu Dhabi, Ras-al-Khaimah, and Sharjah in UAE, held meetings with NRIs and local banks, and explained the progress of Godavari with a short film. We visited Oman, Doha, Kuwait, Bahrein, and Muscat. The banks in the UAE and the Middle East agreed to accept applications and money for the share applications. Chairman Sravan Kumar, our merchant bankers, and I then proceeded to the UK, where we held meetings in London, Manchester, and Liverpool with bankers, financial firms, and investors. We received a good response from Indian residents.

The public issue of Rs.15.75 crore in May 1986 was the largest public issue in 1986 and, despite the looming recession, was oversubscribed. Over 18,000 farmers and 2000 cooperatives took shares in the company. In addition, every employee in the company became a shareholder. The company registered over 93,600 shareholders. The early inflow of share money reduced the drawdown of bank loans and helped us to commission the project within the estimated cost.

FINANCIAL MANAGEMENT

We built up a professional finance department, which did an excellent job ensuring both cost and time controls for project execution, marketing operations, and management of working capital. The focus of the finance team was on costing, internal controls, prompt accounting, and data at the fingertips. We set benchmarks and financial ratios, which our internal auditors checked, and statutory chartered accountants for compliance. Production and trading accounts were kept separate by decentralising port Handling operations, sales of urea, etc. We developed a Costing Manual, which proved useful for cost control and data submission for fixing retention prices and freight subsidies.

The focus of financial management was on team building and developing innovative financial and management techniques suited to the needs of the company. Internal financial systems were streamlined, an internal audit cell was created, risk analysis was done, and insurance arrangements were tied up with all four insurance companies. We wanted each activity to be profitable and the *finance department a Profit Centre*. We obtained separate limits for trading operations and imported materials and developed some expertise in Foreign Exchange management. We made cash profits of Rs 80 lakhs in the first year of operations and saved a similar amount through trading and FE management.

GFCL - PROJECT MANAGEMENT CASE STUDY AT IIM (A)

Prof. Tripathi of IIM Ahmedabad contacted me to visit Ahmedabad to deliver a lecture on Project Management in GFCL, as it was selected as a case study for MBA students. I addressed a gathering of faculty and students and shared the published material and steps taken to complete the project in time within the estimated cost. It was lauded as a rare instance of good project management among public sector enterprises and in state public sector undertakings. Prof. Tripathi invited me occasionally to give lectures on other subjects as well.

It was the combined and coordinated efforts of all concerned that made the Godavari story a model case study in Project Management.

The steady progress soon became a cynosure of the fertilizer industry. Those associated with the project considered Godavari Fertilizers their “Karma Bhoomi” and the company yet another parent and a second home. This ‘bonding’ ensured a family-like environment where everyone cooperated with one another. The clarity of the concept, context, content, connectivity, communication, and cooperation led to Godavari’s success in all its endeavours.

Godavari received many awards and plaudits from the press, learned farm journals, magazines, and experts, including the CMs and the Secretary of the Ministry of Fertilizers. Our employees celebrated every commendation and award. I humbly dedicated all awards to employees and their families. I realised that *"Vina-Sahakar Nahi Uddhar," without cooperation, there is no progress*. Also, "all hands must heave when the task is heavy." The Godavari bonding, commitment, and cooperation made the heavy task easy, light, and joyful.

MODEL ROOM – A GIFT FROM TOYO ENGINEERING LTD

Japanese top brass of Toyo and Hitachi Zosen commenced work at Godavari with their traditional Shinto prayer for success. They completed the construction work a little ahead of time at Kakinada and Visakhapatnam. To express their gratitude to GFCL, they constructed a model room near the main gate with a beautiful table model of the Godavari plant in a glass-covered display box. They provided charts and photos showing various stages of construction. The model room was a boon. It enabled us to explain details to our visitors before showing them around the plant. We made a small video-cum-audio which was played for the visitors. We built an upper story in the model room as an open pavilion with a fixed rotatable telescope and binocular stand. VIPs used to witness games and sports events held on the campus. Visitors to the plant included schools, polytechnic, and college students. We used to give them Godavari badges, sweets, chocolates, pencils, erasers, and leaflets about Godavari and show them around the plant.

VIP VISITS TO PLANT

Many VIPs visited the plant. Among them were the Governor of AP, Kumudben Joshi, CMs NT Rama Rao and M Chenna Reddy, Ministers from the Central Government, Secretary Fertilizers KD Vasudeva, TL Sankar, and groups of farmers.

R Prabhu, Union Minister for Fertilizers, and CM Rama Rao visited our plant on 11-4-1987 to see its progress. He complimented the company on the good layout and progress achieved and hoped that the plant would go into production as scheduled.

PUBLIC RELATIONS

The PR department covered VIP visits and held local press meets to cover events. They highlighted that the long-awaited fertilizer plant would go into production shortly. They took an active interest in organizing dramas, sports, and games for the executives, staff, and their families. Competitions for bagging plant employees were held, and prizes like Tiffin carriers, Flasks, and torch lights were given to foster bonding. Soon, word spread among their wives that hard-working employees got prizes. Wives of husbands who did not get prizes took the message to heart and probably berated their husbands. Very soon, our bagging operations improved beyond our expectations. The bagging plant workers, at the time of my farewell, graciously invited my wife and me to have lunch with them, along with our GFCL plant staff and executives.

Many radio jingles and songs on Godavari were set to music in Vani Studios, located in our office building at Secunderabad. Some of the budding artists, including CS Ramachar, a famous music composer, set the music, which helped in our publicity activities.

GUEST HOUSE AT DELHI – A HOME AWAY FROM HOME

We had a guest house-cum-liaison office in Safdarjung Colony in Delhi. A retired manager from the Food Corporation of India, RK Seth was our Chief Administrative Officer who had excellent public relations and contacts with the government, the Fertilizer Association of India, and other Fertilizer companies in Delhi. We had an Omni vehicle with driver Sebastian and cook Rajan. The office was used for holding meetings or discussions with experts. Many of our project cost estimates for clearance by IDBI were done there. G.M. Rama Rao, then GM, and NK Jain of Kribhco (who became Chairman NTPC later on) were regular visitors to the guest house and helped me prepare cost estimates.

SERIOUS CAR ACCIDENT

At Delhi around noon, while I was on my way to Shastri Bhavan in our Omni vehicle, a car hit us from behind and sped away. Our vehicle turned turtle and was upside down. This was a serious accident which could have led to death. Luckily, some vehicle drivers and passers-by lifted the vehicle and set us free. We survived with minor scratches and no fractures.

GUEST HOUSE AT SECUNDERABAD

At Secunderabad, we purchased a three-bedroom flat as a guest house opposite our main office. This enabled us to accommodate our marketing and other technical staff from Kakinada when they visited the headquarters for work. We subsequently hired another 3-bedroom flat on the same premises to meet the growing need for guest house accommodation. This proved to be economical and convenient.

GUEST HOUSE AT KAKINADA EARNS US GOODWILL

Government accommodation and hotel facilities at Kakinada were inadequate. We set up a Guest house for company guests and VIPs. Our hospitality was greatly appreciated. It became our unofficial public relations department! It paid us dividends by generating goodwill.

PRESS MEETS

The local press correspondents were invited once a month to the plant to report on its progress. When the plant was getting ready for trial runs, we organised a meeting of editors of Telugu press, national press representatives, and editors of Chemicals and Fertilizer magazines in India. This led to a spate of reports about Godavari Fertilizers and its unique efforts to put AP on the fertilizer map of India. Press reports gave us free publicity. Some misguided activists raised issues of likely pollution. Their fears were soon dispelled.

WITHIN THE ESTIMATED COST AND TIME

IDBI expected the project to be completed in 33 months from Date Zero. During the mid-term review, the time for commissioning was cut down to 28 months. We commissioned the first DAP train on 17th December 1987 and the second train on 11th January 1988 against the schedule of March 1988, a clear two months ahead of schedule and lower than the estimated cost!

A PROMISE REDEEMED

Godavari Fertilizers went into production in 1987. We carefully collected the first bag of DAP from the first lot of fertilizer produced in the factory. I placed it at the feet of the Lord at Tirumala temple along with a lorry-load of DAP bags for its flower garden. I fulfilled my vow and redeemed my promise.

We appointed GN Rao, Deputy Collector, as Administrative Officer to manage land acquisition and land records. A highly work-oriented executive, he would bulldoze and quickly get work done. With the increase in ship unloading and transport logistics work, P Janardhan Rao, a Senior Grade Deputy Collector, joined. He streamlined port operations and the transport of fertilizers. We took on board a Senior Grade Deputy Collector, C Uma Malleswara Rao, a Ph.D. in agriculture, to help in popularising DAP as a preferred fertilizer. He had to leave as he was promoted to the IAS. S Balasubramanyam, a meticulous, upright, and honest officer of the Registration department, took over. He ensured good governance in port handling and logistics work. He was later promoted to Joint Executive Officer of Tirumala Tirupathi Devasthanam and retired from that post. He used to provide accommodation, darshan, and prasad for GFCL employees without any hassles. Subsequently, S. Venkateswar Rao, another Senior Grade Deputy Collector worked with us. They concurrently looked after the Human Resources department. Incidentally, all senior grade deputy collectors who worked in GFCL were promoted to the IAS.

HUMAN RESOURCES (HR) DEPARTMENT

Bhaneshwar Rao of Nagarjuna Fertilizers was our Personnel Manager for some time and was later taken over by P Vimala Prasad and BS Prasad, who managed all the recruitments in the company. Prabhakar Raju also worked as Chief Personnel Officer. We took on deputation S Krishna Rao, a Superintendent from AP Secretariat who handled liaison and worked in our Transport division.

Mahajan, HR Chief in IFFCO, helped us prepare a manual for the HR department. All policy issues were decided after discussions ably assisted by officers from sister public sector organisations. Vimala Prasad and BS Prasad did yeoman service in recruitment, training, and maintenance of records. As a result, we had no complaints, strikes, or thefts of material from our plant. They took an active interest in the welfare of our employees, including contract labour in the bagging plant and canteen staff.

GAMES AND SPORTS – NATIONAL KABADDI CHAMPION- SHIP

We encouraged our staff to take an active interest in games and sports, enact dramas, and participate in literary activities. We instituted prizes for these activities. We encourage multi-skilling of our employees – our drivers could drive vans, jeeps, locos, fire tenders, tippers, and excavators or ambulances. Security staff could drive trucks and vehicles. Our operators could switch from one plant to the other easily. This enabled us to run the plant with 460 employees against the sanctioned strength of 785.

We conducted the 35th National Kabaddi Championship in Hyderabad at LB Stadium in 1987. Our CM NT Rama Rao and Renuka Chowdary, then MP, attended the tournament and gave away prizes. At Kakinada, we conducted the Kabaddi championship, weightlifting, and volleyball tournaments. We sponsored awards for the East Godavari Weightlifting championships. Chief Guests for these meetings were MS Sanjeevi Rao, then Minister for Electronics, and Amitabha Bhattacharya, then Joint Collector of East Godavari district.

Many of our young marketing and other managers were getting married. We made it a policy to give a marriage gift of Rs.1, 000 and depute our publicity van with audio-visual facilities to entertain guests during late-night marriages, which is common in AP. This created good fellowship and Bonding, ultimately leading all the employees to consider themselves as belonging to the larger "Godavari Family".

In the recruitment of security staff, we gave priority to strong and well-built people. We found that people engaged in loading trucks in Srikakulam district, like Hamalis, were suitable for both security and bagging plant requirements. Priority was given to weightlifters. They won many prizes at the district and state level. We honoured weightlifters from West Godavari Weight Lifters Association and, in particular, national weightlifters from Visakhapatnam Port Trust.

Some employees formed a cooperative society to purchase land and construct residential houses. They requested that I permit the naming of the housing colony "Gopalakrishna Nagar." I forbade them from doing so and advised them to pick some local name.

GOVERNMENT COMMENDATION

The Board of Directors placed on record its appreciation of my services in commissioning the plant ahead of schedule and within the estimated cost. The AP government also commended my services for the successful conduct of the public issue.

MANAGER OF THE YEAR AWARD BY H.M.A

On 24-7-1988, the Hyderabad Management Association (HMA) selected me for the prestigious **"Manager of the Year Award"**. Shiv Shankar, Union Minister for Fertilizer, Coal and Power, presented the award at Jubilee Hall, Hyderabad.

INAUGURATION OF THE GODAVARI FERTILIZER PLANT

After trial runs and commissioning of the plant were completed, we decided to formally get it inaugurated in December 1987 by CM NT Rama Rao. We held a large public meeting in our fertilizer silo. IFFCO Chairman Srinivasa Reddy, the then Zilla Parishad Chairman, M BalaYogi (who later became Speaker of the Lok Sabha), our Chairman Shravan Kumar, B Satyanarayana, and I were on the dais.

Shravan Kumar gave the welcome address while BalaYogi and other speakers complimented the CM, MD, and executives of Godavari Fertilizers for putting Kakinada on the fertilizer map of India and giving a push to Development of Kakinada Port.

I GET ANOTHER NAME

The Chief Minister NT Rama Rao, in his euphoric, cinematic manner of delivery in chaste, flowery Telugu, said that "he was throwing open the Temple of Prosperity in AP for the benefit of farmers and hoped that AP would become Annapoorna for the whole country and export rice from Kakinada." He said that he had shifted Gopalakrishna (me) from the post of Commissioner of Commercial Taxes to GFCL as its MD, and the inauguration of the plant ahead of schedule showed that his choice and decision were correct. With a flourish, he said that "he was bestowing a new title for the MD as "Godavari Karmagara Vishwakarma, Roopakalpana Shilpi Godavari Gopalakrishna, Mana Siddha Hastam" meaning, the creator, designer, sculptor, and builder of this factory is our own Gopalakrishna, a hands-on achiever, Continuing, he said, "he was proud to dedicate the factory to the farmers, the people of AP and India". Tears blanked my eyes. This became the headlines in the local and national press.

I felt elated that my seven years of work were recognised and lauded. I gave the vote of thanks and declared a day's holiday for all employees who had put in hard work for the success of Godavari fertilizers. As promised, a few top officials were called to the dais and presented specially designed HMT wristwatches as a token of gratitude for their dedicated services. Later, all employees were given the watches.

After the hustle and bustle of the function was over, I recollected the advice my mother had given to me to work not for self-interest, but for the public interest. I shed tears of joy as I imagined how happy she would have been, if alive, to see that her son had made the then invisible dream, a visible factory and seemingly impossible task an accomplished fact. After a long time, the dream was fulfilled, and I had a sound sleep!

APPLICATION FOR UREA PLANT

We applied to the Central Government to set up a urea plant with a five lakh tons capacity per annum to secure our own supply of urea along with DAP.

We located a large extent of government land at Balabhadrapuram, about 30 km from Kakinada, adjacent to the main railway line and natural gas pipeline from Tatipaka to Kakinada and quite close to the Rajahmundry–Kakinada state highway. We wanted to manufacture urea, NPK fertilizers, calcium ammonium nitrate, and pesticides at that site. The proposal was not followed up after I left GFCL.

I used to tour a lot to enthuse dealers, farmers, and our marketing staff. I keenly observed the conditions of crops, met farmers, our marketing staff, and dealer-shop customers, and gave suggestions. Farmers and dealers started to refer to me as Godavari Gopalakrishna instead of M Gopalakrishna!

Long before the Government and the Corporate Sector formally recognised Corporate Social Responsibility (CSR), GFCL voluntarily undertook many socio-economic and culture-oriented activities.

KAKINADA PORT BYPASS ROAD

GFCL provided 12 acres of its land on the northern boundary for the construction of a new road bypassing Kakinada town to avoid the movement of heavy trucks and dust pollution. This road is now the highway for the transport of goods from Nagarjuna Fertilizers, Godavari Fertilizers (now Coromandel), and Kakinada Port.

NEMAM VILLAGE

Nemam, a village near the plant, was adopted and supported with fertilizers and guidance to boost agricultural production and dairy activities. The villagers were encouraged to grow vegetables and greens. They supplied both vegetables and milk to our canteen. Twenty years after I had relinquished charge, the villagers requested me to open a new temple constructed in the village. I did so, participated in bhajans, and received prasad.

KAKINADA TOWN BEAUTIFICATION

Traffic islands at Kakinada were beautified, and bus shelters were provided in the town. We assisted in repairs of the Theosophical Lodge in the city. At Hyderabad, we beautified the Telugu Thalli Island near the Secretariat, which was then called Godavari Circle; it was later shifted nearby due to the fly-over work.

CYCLONES AND FLOOD RELIEF

The east coast was subjected to frequent cyclones and inundation. We assisted in providing food and water to the flood-affected farmers and, later, fertilizers as well. The CM NT Rama Rao and the then collector MVPC Sastry handed over the relief materials, including fertilizers for re-sowing crops.

PRISONERS PARTICIPATE IN RELIEF WORK

We received emergency calls from both the collectors of East and West Godavari districts during the cyclones for the supply of food to people in the relief camps. One of my boyhood teachers, K Krishnamurthy, was the Chief Jailor of the Rajahmundry Central Jail. With his assistance and motivation of the prisoners and local support, we were able to get food cooked, packed, and supplied to the flood-affected villages from the jail by helicopter, including some large lankas (River Islands). Wives of our officers took an active part in the relief operations. Press reports lauded our efforts.

My tenure in Godavari was a great learning experience in project management and industrial development. It taught me the importance of teamwork and networking. It called for discipline, determination, and dedication. I learned the need for empathetic treatment of employees. I received several awards, which I humbly dedicated to officers and staff who helped make Kakinada a Port and Fertilizer city, heralding industrial growth and development in Andhra Pradesh. A Civil Service officer had turned into a Planner-Project Manager.

SERVANT LEADERSHIP - THE HALLMARK OF A CEO

When Godavari Fertilizers and Chemicals was set up ahead of schedule and within estimated cost, it was discussed in corporate circles! I was quite proud and elated but also worried. My elder brother advised me to call on the former Matadhipati (seer or pontiff) of Kanchipuram. Paramacharya, aged over 80 years, was camping during Chaturmas (rainy season) near Hyderabad. I did so and paid obeisance to the pontiff. Strangely enough, even before I could speak, he said, "I can read your thoughts and feelings and doubts that brought you here. Though you have done a good job, it has not given you complete satisfaction. I know your dilemma. You think that you are the creator, owner, or malik of a beautiful garden with several varieties of plants and flowers. It would be best if you instead looked at your job as that of a Mali or gardener of the company. In a garden, the Mali must study the terrain, observe the monsoon, and, depending on the nature or 'svabhava' of the plant, earmark land and encourage its growth. The garden will have some areas that are dry and rocky, some wet and have water, some that are fertile and suitable for raising crops, and some areas that are shaded. It is Mali's duty to select the area suitable for the plant. Plants like Crotons grow well in shady conditions. Plants like Bougainvillea grow well in dry and rocky places. Different varieties of plants and flowers need different conditions for their Growth. In wet areas, you can grow food crops in abundance. Your duty as Mali is not one of supervising others but one of understanding their needs and requirements and helping people who are like saplings so that they grow to their fullest potential and promise. You will be happier and more satisfied if you consider yourself not the *Malik* chief executive but the chief gardener Mali developing the company garden. You must be *Mali- cum-Malik*. The sooner the chief executive changes his role and route, the better it is for the company. You can take advantage of every employee's potential and capacity and enable each one of them to grow to their fullest endowment and development". This changed my perspective, eroded my ego, humbled me, and enabled me to see reality objectively. Humility is indeed a silent power but not adequately recognised.

27

Recalled during President's Rule as Commissioner, Home & Political Passport and Public Relations Department, Government of Assam (Oct 1982 – March 1983)

I secured a posting in the Andhra Pradesh government on Inter-State deputation and was posted in the Secretariat in AP and later as Managing Director of Godavari Fertilisers, which was at a crucial stage.

I unexpectedly received a call from the AP Chief Secretary, who told me that the Assam government required my services urgently and wanted to recall me for a short period during President's Rule to handle the prolonged agitation by the people and students in Assam.

BACKGROUND

The entry of illegal immigrants from Bangladesh and the probability of their voting as Assamese citizens were agitating the minds of the local people. This was not merely altering the population composition; it was adversely impacting the political landscape. Unless the situation was tackled immediately and effectively, Assamese apprehended that political power would slip into the hands of the immigrants, and the local interests and prospects could be permanently jeopardised. The students, backed by the intelligentsia, demanded a revision of electoral rolls to weed out ineligible non-citizens from electoral lists before any elections are held in the State of Assam.

Despite the ongoing agitation with the involvement of the public and the non-cooperation of government servants, the Indian government wanted first to hold elections for the State Assembly and then find a political solution. Assam was under President's rule. However, the agitators did not want elections to be held without the electoral rolls being revised after weeding out all illegal immigrants.

Earlier in 1979, the Parliamentary elections were held under very difficult conditions. Despite the completion of legal and Constitutional requirements for holding elections, the agitating students ensured that not a single nomination was filed anywhere in the entire Brahmaputra valley. Students all over the state organised human barriers in front of the offices of returning officers and physically prevented potential candidates from filing nominations. The only exception was Barpeta, but even there, the Returning officer rejected the nomination on technical but valid grounds.

Elections were held in Surma or Cachar valley, a predominantly Bengali-speaking area where the students' agitation did not have any impact; two MPs were elected, and they were the sole representatives of Assam in the new Lok Sabha. My successor, Assistant Commissioner in Guwahati, Sridhar, was the then CEO (Chief Electoral Officer). Despite manifold difficulties and even threats to his life, Sridhar bravely soldiered on and ensured that the Constitutional and legal responsibilities were fulfilled. He could not do much if no one filed nominations. The CEC conveyed his appreciation to Sridhar for conducting elections "at grave personal risk and danger".

Despite intensified agitation and even violence in Assam, the Central government surprisingly wanted elections to be held to the State Assembly. The State government had to comply with this fiat in whatever manner possible.

It was against such a background and circumstances that I was recalled to my parent cadre as Home Commissioner. I expressed my inability to join Assam due to official work, some domestic problems, and personal medical needs. The Union Home Ministry wanted me to join Assam urgently, as according to them, there was no other officer available in Assam who could effectively deal with the prevailing situation and conduct elections. The Advisor to the Assam Governor RV Subramanian, IAS (Retd), an Assam cadre officer, insisted that my services were essential.

The AP government was unwilling to release me as the Godavari Fertilizer Project was at a crucial stage. In the meantime, on the advice of the Assam government, Prime Minister Indira Gandhi spoke to the AP Chief Minister, requesting him to spare my services for a short period till Elections are conducted. I got the impression that the GOI was of the view that the student movement could be suppressed using force and elections conducted as it was a Constitutional mandate.

The Chief Minister of AP called me and advised me to join as Home Commissioner in Assam for a short period. He assured me that I could come back after the elections were conducted. In deference to the PM's and CM's advice, I met the CS and proceeded to Assam, where I was given an assurance that I would be repatriated to AP as soon as elections were conducted.

I joined as Commissioner for the Home, Political, and Public Relations departments in Assam at Dispur in October 1982. I called on the Chief Secretary, Ramesh Chandra, for instructions. He was a man of few words and just said, "You are an Assam cadre officer. I need not brief you, and you can take action as required and only keep me informed in important matters". I met the two Advisors to the government, RV Subramanian and R Natarajan, a retired IAS officer from Orissa, who advised me to call on Governor M Mehrotra. They briefed me about the nature of the movement of the All Assam Students Union (AASU) and the non-cooperation of employees of the Assam government who were actively participating in the agitation.

THE ASSAM AGITATION – GENESIS

The detection, deletion from the electoral rolls, and deportation of foreigners and illegal immigrants was a long-standing demand of the people of Assam spearheaded by the All Assam Students Union and All Assam Gana Sangram Parishad. In 1979, the agitation had assumed a virulent form. Civil disobedience affected all sections of the population. Government servants went on wild-cat and pen-down strikes, state-wide bandhs, and Rasta-Roko programs. Schools and colleges were all closed, many of them forcibly, and the education system in the State nearly collapsed. Except for essential services, work in the government offices came to a standstill. It appeared that Assam was under a state of siege. The agitators demanded to use the voters' list of 1961 and 1971 as reference points and deport all those whose names did not figure in the lists. Subsequently, detailed verification could be done to ensure that the remaining illegal immigrants are deported from Assam.

The AASU and All Assam Gana Sangram Parishad (AASGP) spearheaded the agitation for the deportation of all illegal immigrants from Assam. They roped in women to participate in the Rasta Roko and hold torchlight marches at night to postpone the elections.

I understood the sentiments of the leaders of the All Assam Students Union and Assam Gana Sangram Parishad, who were fighting to protect the interests of the Assamese people who were overwhelmed by the immigrant problem. They were finding fault with the indecision of the

Union government and the unwillingness of the State Government to take strong action as warranted to deport the illegal immigrants.

The demand of students to reflect the opinions of almost all sections appeared justified on more than one ground. Compared to undivided Bengal and East Pakistan, Assam was sparsely populated, with plenty of fertile land and abundant water. Before the creation of Pakistan, when Sir Sadullah was the CM of Assam, he had initiated a scheme named the "Grow more Food" campaign. This, according to him, required the import of workforce from East Bengal due to insufficient workforce available in Assam. It opened the doors for the immigration of Bengali Muslims, especially from Mymensingh District. The then Viceroy Lord Wavell reportedly remarked that Sadullah's objective was not so much "grow more food but grow more Musalmans".

After Independence, Assam closed this door and initiated strong measures to stop further immigration. It intensified efforts to detect and deport illegal immigrants with strict border controls, preparing village-level NRC (National Register of Citizens) and deploying special police squads in border areas. Those who did not find their names in the NRC or could not prove that they were descendants of a person whose name is in the NRC were to be automatically deported under the provisions of the Foreigners Act. Funds for the creation of Tribunals and Special Forces meant exclusively for this task were provided by the GOI. No doubt, there was quite a lot of resistance from some of the Ministers and Muslim MLAs arguing that some genuine Indian Muslims were being forcefully deported.

After the creation of Bangladesh, there was a sea change in the policies of both the Indian and Assam Governments. Electoral considerations assumed prominence, and the existing Muslim population and the immigrants, even if illegal entrants, began to be viewed as a captive vote bank for the Congress party. The strict border control mechanisms were diluted, the National Registration of Citizens (NRC) remained without any updating, and the staff employed for this particular purpose was dismantled and diverted to other tasks.

The percentage of the Muslim population in Assam, which was only 14% at the time of independence, rose to 27% and has further shot up to about 34% now. Six districts in Assam are now Muslim majority with large-scale mushrooming of mosques and madrasas along with radicalization of young minds by preachers from Bangladesh. These developments pose a threat to national security, especially in the Siliguri corridor, aptly called the "Chicken's Neck," which can be strangled and the Northeast isolated by insurgencies or hostile enemy action.

Assam intelligentia, witness to the fragmentation and dismemberment of the state, wanted to safeguard the Assamese language, its unique cultural heritage, and peaceful co-existence with ethnic tribes. The uncontrolled entry of illegal immigrants from Bangladesh and the occupation of tribal lands upset the demographic and electoral equations in Assam. The tensions led to a prolonged agitation to Detect, Delete (from electoral rolls), and Deport, all illegal Immigrants. The Tribunals were set up for that purpose, but officials were unequal in terms of their tasks. People's anger rose to the level of a civil disobedience movement with near universal support of the people.

This unchecked influx of migrants affected lower Assam districts and even the tribal inhabited areas. The Assam government constituted ***"tribal blocks"*** to protect tribals and their livelihood as they were dependent on land and agriculture, and the tribals' land rights were fully protected. In these clearly demarcated areas, no non-tribal could purchase land, and even tribals could sell their land only to other tribes. The tribe had heritable land titles but restricted transferable titles. The land revenue administration was to ensure that if any non-tribal either bought or occupied these tribal lands, such a transaction was not registered, and the ineligible purchaser or occupant was to be evicted.

Despite such a provision, due to connivance and lack of integrity, over time, quite a lot of land belonging to the Tribals was taken away from them. It came into the hands of the illegal immigrants, causing considerable anxiety, anger, and even unrest among many tribal groups.

A number of student leaders of AGSP and AASU were detained under the Preventive Detention Act. The mother of one of the senior leaders of the AASU who was detained died. His family members approached me for his release on parole to attend his mother's obsequies as he was the eldest son. I understood the family's anguish and dilemma. I enquired whether the family members would stand surety and guarantee his return to detention after performing the obsequies within three days of parole time. The family agreed, and I took the responsibility, much to the chagrin of our advisors. The said leader kept his word and reported to the police, who took him to detention. The story ended smoothly, like *"All's well that ends well"*.

The students' agitation resonated among almost all tribal groups as their lands and reserves were in jeopardy of encroachment by Muslim immigrants. There were often clashes between Tribals and immigrants and, in many cases, considerable violence and setting of homes and huts on fire. Police had to intervene and use force to bring about a semblance of Normalcy. The tribals were not appeased, and anger was simmering.

The functioning of government offices was seriously affected as the students formed local Election Resistance Committees. Even government employees willing to perform their duties were intimidated by warnings and gheraos in the offices.

The agitation intensified, creating an environment of uncertainty and fear. The army had to be called out in January and May 1980 in aid of civil administration to restore law and order.

The declared original objective of the agitation was to ensure the cleaning up of electoral rolls by eliminating post-1971 illegal immigrants. Unfortunately, the movement took an ugly turn when Hindu refugees who had to flee East Pakistan to save themselves from violence directed against them were also targeted. The movement, hence, lost quite a bit of its legitimacy. It also led to open hostility towards all Indians from the rest of India due to fears that the Assamese would become a minority in their own state. This led to muted or vocal demands for secession from India and the formation of groups who believed that an armed struggle was needed. This resulted in a complete loss of moral underpinnings of the agitation. The movement's legitimacy was also eroded along with the sympathy it had earned in some quarters outside Assam.

Such an unfortunate, misguided, and ill-thought-out change in the objectives of the movement brought about an escalation in direct attacks on so-called "outsiders," which included a whole lot of people from Bihar, Nepal, etc.,

Sadly, even government officials were targeted. In April 1981, the Commissioner of Upper Assam, located at Jorhat, ES Parthasarathy, was killed in a bomb explosion in his office by a pressure IED placed under his seat. This created panic among officers and staff in the Government, and an acute sense of insecurity descended upon the official machinery.

The agitation was continuing unabated when I reached Dispur and took charge. The Secretariat at Dispur was well guarded. The Deputy Commissioner's offices and the Superintendent of Police's offices in the state were functioning almost normally. I decided to visit all districts to see at first hand the prevailing situation, talk to DCs, and make my own assessment of priorities and requirements in different parts of the state. I visited Goalpara, where I was SDO, and Jorhat, where I was DC, and picked up my personal staff, such as an armed guard, cook, etc., all of them Assamese. I was provided a Pilot and Escort vehicle by Assam police personnel. I believe my appointment was welcomed in government circles as I was a cadre officer, quite fluent in Assamese, and well-known in some parts of the state.

I called for the CRs of suitable persons for the appointment of an intelligent, trustworthy, and dependable Joint Secretary in the Home Department to ensure officer-oriented, quick decision-making with utmost secrecy in the decisions and communications. I picked up S Manoharan, a bright young officer who had done a special defence course at Wellington. We strengthened the department with specially screened and selected officials and stenographers. We used to move files by hand to ensure the secrecy of decisions. Due to uncertainty and long office hours, we made boarding arrangements with a good canteen in the secretariat to ensure that work is done promptly in a time-bound manner; we strengthened the communication facilities and, particularly, the telephones. We had direct RAX (Restricted Access) and PBX telephones connected to the DCs, SDOs, and top police officials.

I called on the DGP PC Das, the senior IGP (Special Branch), MIS Iyer, and IGP KPS Gill, who gave me their assessment of the situation and action being taken to conduct elections. PC Das, who headed the police force, was the senior most IGP. He said that KPS Gill, IGP would coordinate all actions connected with the conduct of the Assam elections. MIS Iyer, another senior IGP, would assist me in the deployment of armed forces and provide intelligence reports. I had to mainly deal with KPS Gill (IPS-1957), a tall, well-built Sikh who was known as a straightforward officer with good command over the force, a motivator, and a good planner.

I called on the Senior Advisor R.V Subramanian, who was a war recruit to the IAS from the army and knew my uncle. The advisor appeared to be a man in a hurry and gave the impression that he alone was running the government and that his decision should be construed as the indisputable decision of the government. He was hard-working, meticulous, and kept copious notes. He would collect information directly from the Deputy Commissioner of Kamrup district at Guwahati, Shri Agnihotri, and many others to collate and decide on the course of action. He would call me half a dozen times in the course of the day to cross-check facts and to know if I had any additional information not available to him. I told him that I needed time to study and attend to many matters and work out a strategy after a discussion with the CEO and senior police and civil service officers. I requested that he call me only once in the morning to give instructions and that I meet him at his convenience in the evening to brief him on the action taken. He agreed, and I could attend to my already onerous responsibilities without any undue interruption. I told him that I would take an hour for my lunch, during which time I would listen to soothing songs and music to relax and relieve the tension of the job. My wife would ring me up at that time and update me on matters at home. I had a gruelling 10-12 hours a day schedule with very little guidance and support. I tried to finish each day's job on the same day. At night, I would note down the main events and points for action the next day.

The Advisor used to hold Special Coordination Committee meetings daily in the evening with officers of the army, railways, banks, and the central government offices to collate information and decide on coordination arrangements. This mechanism proved useful as all the senior officials could exchange information and know the Government's approach and their role in assisting the government. We could get useful feedback on the impact of government moves and actions, as well as local press reports and comments in addition to the IB and SB reports.

Whenever necessary, I used to call on Governor Mehrotra -whose father, Justice Mehrotra, was known to me as Assistant Commissioner at Guwahati-. Who was very sober, affable, and had the ear of the PM. He used to call me occasionally to get my views and brief me about what was happening on the political front in Delhi.

The Congress Party used to send their own observers from New Delhi to understand the reasons for an environment of mistrust and continuing agitation, which, at times, was turned virulent by the student bodies. Rajesh Pilot and senior press editors and reporters like Shourie, Bhattacharya, and Prasad would meet us for information on the government's viewpoint and proposed actions and give us their assessment of the developing situation. They were trying to obtain inside information regarding the conduct of elections, the date of polling, and or extension of President's Rule in Assam. We kept government moves and actions under wraps, particularly the dates for elections and law and order arrangements to ensure peaceful polls.

The Chief Electoral Officer, S L Khosla had worked out a tentative 3-day schedule for conducting elections for the 126 Assembly constituencies and 12 Parliamentary constituencies. We had to find willing personnel as Presiding Officers, Polling Officers, and adequate police or home guards to man about 12000 polling stations to facilitate 96 lakh voters to cast their votes.

The President's Rule, which was imposed in Assam, was scheduled to end by the 28th of March, 1983. The consensus that emerged amongst officials was that we should conduct a 3-day election with no indication of the dates of elections and issue the election schedule only at the mandatory time. The constituencies were classified as a) Safe constituencies, b) Partly safe constituencies, c) Difficult constituencies, and d) Extremely difficult constituencies where violence could be expected.

Police estimated that we required about 40 police battalions or 270 companies. They wanted the government to give effect to the National Security Act, the Armed Forces Special Powers Act, and other enabling acts to conduct elections. In case of mass agitation and arrests, we would Need jail accommodation in Assam or nearby states. We thought that school buildings could be commandeered and a barbed wire fence around it could, as a last resort, serve as a jail in Assam.

We had to secretly mobilise numerous buses and trucks to carry the poll material and polling staff to all the polling stations. In view of the non- cooperation of government employees in election duties, we were faced with the major difficulty of finding willing polling and presiding officers to man the polling stations. While we could find local personnel for the safe and partly safe constituencies, we required about 2500 - 3000 officials for the difficult polling stations. In view of the difficulty in mobilising locals to conduct elections, we would have to rely on personnel from other states.

As Bengali-speaking personnel were viewed with suspicion and hostility by local people, obtaining assistance from West Bengal was ruled out.

BIHAR GOVERNMENT SUPPORTS US

The other nearby big state that could provide personnel, transport, and polling officials was Bihar. A team comprising the Chief Electoral Officer, IGP KPS Gill, and myself went to Patna in December 1982 and held discussions with the Chief Secretary, Home Secretary, and senior officials regarding assistance for deputing polling personnel, providing accommodation and transport and secretly moving the personnel by rail and road to the polling stations. Issues like providing insurance coverage, allowances, remuneration to staff, repair facilities for their transport, etc., were discussed.

Considering the possibility that we may have to detain many agitators to ensure the smooth conduct of elections, we made enquiries if the arrested could be sent to jails in Bihar. We found, to our horror, that jails in Bihar were already overcrowded, and any additions would be courting trouble and risk re-creating the long-forgotten Black Hole of Calcutta. This idea, therefore, was given up.

After prolonged discussions, the Bihar government agreed to spare the services of Block Development Officers along with their roadworthy jeeps to enable teams of four persons to travel along with their jeeps from Bihar to Assam. We decided that 500 officers from Bihar should be transported by rail to important rail junctions like Maligaon, Rangapara, Mariani, Tinsukia, and North Lakhimpur. These activities were carried out in secrecy.

Government was also majorly concerned about the safety of road movements through Assam, the corridor state connecting all other states in the North-East, and of the oil and gas pipelines from Assam, which was supplying crude oil to the Barauni refinery in Bihar. Disruption of the slender transportation links with the rest of India could result in the closure of the Indian Oil Corporation refinery at Guwahati. Assam was dependent on rail to import most essential commodities, particularly sugar, lentils, and edible oils. The exports from Assam were tea, timber, and plywood.

The worsening agitation was causing deep concern regarding the safety and security of the entire rail and road network, the functioning of refineries, oil fields, etc. Assam started witnessing subversive activities as several small militant groups emerged. We received information about arms purchases and forming guerrilla groups with the support of China, Burma, and hostile Nagas. Crucial portions of roads were dug up to prevent vehicular movement. They placed logs with nails on roads to puncture vehicles. There were fears of crucial bridges being blasted. There was complete civil disobedience, and work in government offices and banks came to a standstill. Despite all this, we had to perform our duty to conduct elections.

Meanwhile, tension was brewing among the personnel of the Assam Armed Police, who did not like the deployment of Armed Battalions from outside Assam. On one occasion, the Assam Police Battalion at Goalpara opened fire on the CRPF post. We rushed to the post by helicopter and landed nearby. I spoke on the microphone in Assamese to the Assam Police to stop firing on CRPF, and I was the Home Commissioner who had earlier been SDO of Goalpara. Luckily, firing from Assam police stopped. We met the Assam police and CRPF and advised them to maintain good relations with the CRPF, who had been called for duty by the Assam government to supplement local armed police strength and not replace them.

Prime Minister Indira Gandhi visited to review the situation, which was causing more strain on the already heavily overworked administrative machinery.

The staff of Food Corporation of India (FCI) Godowns and many nationalised banks went on sympathetic strike, creating problems for the supply of food grains to ration shops and disbursing cash to customers. We had to break open some FCI Godowns and distribute food grains to ration shops. Anticipating the bank's strike and the problem of ready cash availability, we drew Rs.3 crores cash as a precautionary measure to tackle immediate requirements.

We received several reports from districts about the inability of police to control incidents of sporadic violence and the breakdown of law and order due to inadequate forces. The situation in parts of Goalpara, Kamrup,

Darrang, Nowgong, Sibsagar, North Lakhimpur, and Dibrugarh was quite alarming.

VS Jafa was the Commissioner at Jorhat. He was a colourful personality who considered himself a scion of a Rajput warrior. He stayed in the Assam Tea Company bungalow and would ride on a horse at Jorhat. During local disturbances, he led police parties while seated on a police jeep with his personal weapon to impress the lay public that he was a fearless person and would not hesitate to open fire if necessary. I had to mildly admonish and advise him not to expose himself, as a senior officer, to personal danger like his predecessor, Parthasarathy.

COMPLAINTS AGAINST POLICE OFFICIALS

Supported by the local press and intelligentsia, including the legal fraternity and academia, complaints were filed against police officers who were sometimes interrogating persons in their bungalows instead of police stations to avoid embarrassment to them. Agitators encouraged such persons to file court cases accusing police officers in plain clothes of calling them to their residences and not police stations, threatening them with court cases if they did not cooperate with police. Their real intention was to deprive police officers of the protection of the law under section 197 of the CRPC while discharging their official duties. The allegations were that police were not on official duty, and hence, criminal cases could be filed against the concerned in their capacity and not as police officers.

In consultation with the Law Secretary, we sought the services of KTS Tulsi, an eminent legal counsel practicing at the Supreme Court, to defend our police officers. In some cases, we took the help of a former Advocate General of Kerala. In important cases against senior police officers, we appointed Siddhartha Shankar Ray (CM of West Bengal) as our senior advocate for the Assam government. We had to visit Delhi frequently to brief Ray at his residence at 5.00 am so that he could be armed with the latest information when appearing in the Supreme Court for mention. Luckily, the Supreme Court heard our pleas and understood the situation. We won all our cases!

Due to the fact that my actions to defend police officers resulted in personal antagonism from the so-called leaders of the movement, KPS Gill advised me to carry a revolver to protect myself in an emergency when my personal bodyguard was not available. Accepting this advice, the government issued me a non-prohibited .38 Calibre service revolver and license.

We were asked to meet some VIPs at Bagdogra airport, and a military aircraft was arranged. There, we met the Prime Minister, Mrs. Indira

Gandhi, the Cabinet Secretary, Rao Saheb Krishnaswamy, and other GOI officials. We explained to them the severity of the agitation due to civil disobedience, anti-election agitation, and non-cooperation from public and government employees. We spelled out our needs and sought police reinforcements, financial assistance, etc. In fact, we were in dire need of polling personnel, in addition to what we had arranged from Bihar. We projected this to the Cabinet Secretary, and he assured us of his full support. Mrs Gandhi listened to us patiently and said that she was aware of the difficult situation in Assam and that we would get all the support needed. She wished us success in conducting elections despite difficult conditions, which was a constitutional need and duty.

In consultation with the CEO, we worked out the details of the deployment of election staff and the related logistics. We requisitioned trucks, buses, and cars to ferry polling staff and officers to polling stations. We had to mobilize mechanics for repairs of requisitioned vehicles and alert the State Health Transport Organisation (SHTO) and Assam Road Transport Corporation to stand by for assistance. In some cases, we had to requisition elephants to carry poll personnel through jungle and swampy tracks.

DISCUSSIONS WITH THE UNION GOVERNMENT

Back in Guwahati, we reviewed the situation and decided that we must get the approval of the Ministry of Home Affairs for necessary clearances and sanctions to meet the expenditure and seek other required support. We wanted to add a second string to our bow. We requested to spare around 400 young probationary officers of the IAS, IPS, and other services undergoing training in the Foundation course at Musoorie for deployment as presiding officers. With complete secrecy, probationers were flown in along with ample dry rations like fruits, bread, biscuits, wafers, and dry fruits to last for about a week in remote polling stations.

In the first week of February 1983, the staff from Bihar started arriving by train and road. After the briefing, we arranged for their movement to the polling stations. The All India Services probationers from Mussoorie arrived. Many of them had yet to receive their pay and asked for some money to defray their local expenditure. We paid them some ad-hoc advance. A couple of them visited Fancy Bazaar and Police Bazar at Guwahati for sightseeing. Unwittingly, with a sense of bravado, they said that they had come to conduct elections in Assam. Both were roughed up. We held a meeting with the probationers and advised them about the need for secrecy and courteous behaviour. While instructing the probationers,

I noticed among the probationers Pradeep Chandra, an IAS officer whose father, Chandra, was a respected Civil Service officer whom I knew well.

The poll elicited good public support and participation in the entire Cachar district. In the Brahmaputra valley, there was minimal participation, While voting was confined to just a few pockets. In fact, a call had been issued by the movement leaders for a total boycott of elections. While all polling stations were fully manned - we had ensured this - there was negligible voting, but some votes were cast as the Congress Party and minority communities in some areas supported the election.

It was constitutionally imperative to conduct elections, and the Presidential Order was due to elapse. The people of Assam disapproved of the conduct of the polls, which was voiced through the press, and the low percentage of voting due to the boycott of elections by the people of Assam. Some of the press headlines said that "Police were silent witnesses of crime but did little to prevent it" and "it was the most disastrous election held in recent times." The entire press in Assam highlighted that "it was a sham election".

Our immediate task was to ensure the safety of polling personnel and their repatriation, which was done.

TENSION IN THE NELLIE AREA

We received reports that there was considerable unrest among the tribals, mainly plains tribes called Lallungs in the Nowgong district, due to an influx of immigrants who had grabbed vacant tribal and government land like village grazing reserves or general reserves meant exclusively for the tribals. The simmering strife and tension between locals and immigrants exploded just after the completion of the elections, as some immigrants were suspected of voting despite the people's fiat. This resulted in the Lallungs descending en-masse at Nellie on the immigrants in the dead of night and indiscriminately massacring some of them and setting their homes on fire. The police forces that had been deployed for the conduct of elections were dog-tired and had scanty information on the possibility of clashes. By the time the forces could be deployed, huge damage had already been done. Tewari was the DC of Nowgong, and PC Sharma was the DIG. Both officers toiled for a whole week and restored order. While the situation was brought under control as quickly as possible, a lot of work had to be done to find alternative homes for the displaced, and relief was provided for a considerable period. Many children became orphans and had to be sent to orphanages.

The Congress party alone was able to poll some votes, which amounted to less than 5% of the electorate in the Brahmaputra valley. It no doubt won all the seats in the Cachar valley.

It is on this tenuous and undemocratic basis that the Congress party projected its claim to form a government and elected Hiteshwar Saikia as the party's leader. While the legitimacy of this government and the process by which the Congress laid its claim is questionable, nevertheless, Saikia was sworn in as Chief Minister of Assam by the Governor on 12th March 1983.

The Governor called the two Advisors, the Chief Secretary and myself, to the Raj Bhavan. He thanked us all for responding to the call of duty and conducting the elections. He said that I would be released immediately. I heaved a sigh of relief. The Governor graciously presented to me a Shawl and Rhino memento, the symbol of Assam, as a token of appreciation from Assam Government for my services in conducting elections amidst turmoil and problematic circumstances.

As DC at Jorhat, I knew CM H Saikia as a Panchayat Samithi President. I wished him success and took his leave. I flew to Hyderabad the next day for a well-deserved rest from hectic activities and the 12-hour-long work schedule for six months. I relaxed at home before I joined duty in AP, where I was posted as Commissioner of Commercial Taxes.

During my stint in Assam, I had indeed gone through an ordeal by fire and witnessed first-hand how easily violence can be instigated. The massacre by the Lallungs in the Nellie area, described earlier in detail, is a stark reminder for the administration to keep its ears close to the ground, anticipate developments, and take preventive action well in time. The law and order administration was remorseful and felt sad that a little more vigilance and advance intelligence could have saved many innocent lives.

In an environment of tension and non-cooperation from government employees, all the DCs and SDOs in Assam rose to the occasion, performed well amidst hardships, and conducted the elections. It proved that the Civil Services, the police, and employees, if trusted, can deliver despite difficult conditions. The Sub-divisional officers, though young, did much better than some of the DCs due to their good anticipatory skills and desire to prove themselves by making intelligent advance preparations. They ably tackled both foreseen and unforeseen events.

In retrospect and reflection, I recollected what the Bhagavad Gita exhorts that "One has to do his duty regardless of the results" and that "Equanimity in the discharge of one's duty is real Yoga" – I was also reminded of the IAS motto of "Yoga Karmasu Kaushalam" – Efficiency in work is the real Yoga and one must be a Karma Yogi. I realised that proficiency (Praveenya) is an individual attribute and efficiency (Kaushalyam) is a team effort, and both must converge and culminate in effectiveness (Saphalyam) – Something for Civil servants, leaders, and readers to ponder upon. We had conducted an election where the purpose was not democratic, the process was flawed, and people were unhappy – we had merely done our ordained duty.

28

Commissioner of Commercial Taxes, Government of Andhra Pradesh, Hyderabad (April 1983 – September 1983)

On return to AP in April 1983, I was posted as Commissioner of Commercial Taxes. It was a large department responsible for the implementation of the AP General Sales Tax Act, Entertainment Tax, Profession Tax, Horse Racing and Betting Act, and other minor trade and commerce-related taxes. The department accounted for 60 percent of the state's Revenues! It was earlier in the Board of Revenue that forwarded tax proposals or amendments to Acts to the government in the Revenue or Finance department. A Sales Tax Appellate Tribunal heard petitions from taxpayers and advocates. It was headed by a District Judge and two senior officers with experience in commercial taxes and revenue matters as Members.

S Krishnamurthy, Joint Commissioner was on deputation to the Sales Taxes Appellate Tribunal. S Ganapati Shastri, Joint Commissioner (legal), briefed me about departmental functions and stressed the importance of sound legal drafting of acts and notifications. The department had mobile 'Flying Squads' headed by a senior officer of Deputy Commissioner's rank to keep vigil and prevent evasion of tax.

Hyderabad and Visakhapatnam, followed by Guntur, Vijayawada, and Rajahmundry, contributed the bulk of the commercial taxes. The biggest taxpayers were the Oil companies. There was a good system of assessing taxes and monitoring collections to ensure proper payment of revenues to the Government.

TAXES COLLECTED FROM TIMES IMMEMORIAL

Taxes are inevitable. The Manu Smriti, an ancient Indian code, says, "Just like the leech, calf, and bee which draw only very small quantities from their respective feeds (i.e., blood, milk, and honey), similarly, a King should, by his orders, take from his subjects, very small amounts of taxes" [7.129-Manu Smriti].

Kautilya says that "the king, like a honeybee, must draw only a wee bit of honey from a blossom without hurting it." In the modern welfare state, due to large-scale commitments to people, taking small amounts of taxes may not suffice. Hence, the *'bhramara-pushpa nyayam' or 'the Bee and Flower justice system'* may not work.

In ancient India, Vyasa, Manu, Kautilya, and Sukra set elaborate procedures for taxation. Kara (Tax) Siddhanta theories in ancient texts stipulated that taxation should be reasonable and equitable. Vyasa and others emphasised that the king should always bear in mind that oppressive taxation results in hatred and wrath of the subjects. "If the calf is permitted to suck, it grows stronger. The king, therefore, should collect taxes from the subjects, bearing in mind the fact that excessive milking weakens the calf itself and resultantly harms it. (Mahabharata XII.87.20-21)". While keeping the golden mean, tax should be just, fair, and equitable. It is the responsibility of the tax officer to seek a delicate balance and reach the revenue targets.

The department wanted to estimate the gross production of commodities and manufacturing in AP and the inflow of goods for consumption in the state other than transit goods to arrive at the volume and value of goods sold in AP. The department strengthened check posts on borders and main roads and railways to monitor the volume and value of goods transported by road and rail. The state was exporting agricultural goods like rice, food grains, tobacco, chilies, and ghee, among other manufactured consumer goods. The gross quantity of taxable goods was estimated to arrive at an estimate of the collectible taxes. We used the data as a barometer to fix targets for the collection of commercial, purchase, and other related taxes. We noted the rate of economic growth of India and the state to monitor whether our tax collections were in tune with the general trend of the economy. We found that the rate of growth of commercial taxes collected was higher than the rate of growth of the National and State economy.

VAT ON LIQUOR INTRODUCED FOR THE FIRST TIME IN AP

The UK and France collected taxes based on a Value Added Tax system. The manufacturer supplies the commodity to the consumer through various stages of the supply chain, with value added at every stage of its forward movement till it is sold. It would be unfair to levy tax on the tax already paid and fair to tax only the value added at every stage of the movement or manufacture in the value chain.

Field investigations revealed that dealers in the liquor trade were resorting to large-scale tax evasion. They did not include the state Excise Duty component paid on liquor in the sale bill. Packing materials such as bottles, labels, and cartons were separately billed at the lower rates of tax and not at the rate of tax applicable to liquor. Liquor was subject to a single-point tax. The liquor companies took advantage of this and made a lot of money by avoiding tax on several stages of the sale. Manufacturers supplied stock to their own company-run distributors, who, in turn, sold it to a wholesaler, who, in turn, sold it to a retailer before it reached the consumer. The sales tax paid at the manufacturer's end on a liquor bottle was Rs.30, while the end consumer had to pay the market price of Rs.1000 – 1200. The government was obviously losing a lot of revenue. Value addition along the supply chain escaped tax. To plug such large-scale leakage of revenue, after several rounds of confidential discussions, Ordinance No.19/83 was promulgated by the government duly amending the Andhra Pradesh General Sales Tax Act, 1957.

Thus, the **VAT** system of tax was introduced in Andhra Pradesh in 1983 on the sale of liquor for the first time in the country. Turnover of liquor that had suffered tax at the previous point of sale was deducted for arriving at the taxable turnover of the subsequent dealer. We did not come across any fraudulent claims of deduction or fake invoices.

MERIT OF VAT

When goods are liable to tax at the point of first purchase and at every point of purchase or sale, the levy has a cascading effect. The main merit of the Value Added Tax (VAT) is that it eliminates the cascading effect. It is, in reality, a tax on the last sale with the provision of a 'set-off 'or 'credit' of tax paid at the earlier stage. VAT is thus truly a tax only on the value added at each stage of the transfer of goods.

Simultaneously, Section 6-C was inserted in the Act from 8.7.1983, providing a separate tax levy on packing materials. Under the new provision, the rate of tax on packing materials would be the rate of tax applicable to the goods packed. Thus, regarding the value of bottles and cartons, the tax had to be paid at the rate applicable to liquor as they formed part of the commodity. The steps taken fully protected the revenue interests of the state, and the sales tax revenues surged.

Liquor consumers were happy as it lowered the final cost, and the government collected higher taxes. The liquor manufacturers were sore since their source of unaccounted money and windfall profits was severely curtailed. The big liquor companies filed an appeal in the AP High Court, which dismissed their petitions on the grounds that the tax had been made a multi-point tax and that only the value-added portion was being taxed. Aggrieved by the decision, the liquor manufacturers filed a petition in the Supreme Court, which upheld the decision of the AP High Court. The department officials were elated by the verdict, which upheld the decision. I was complimented for introducing the concept of VAT on liquor as a test case, which succeeded and paved the way for the future. I realised that my law degree had helped me. Civil service officers should be taught the law to help them understand, implement, and interpret laws.

HOTELS – BARS AND RESTAURANTS

It is difficult to estimate amounts payable by hotels, bars, and restaurants as their earnings vary. We estimated their revenues by taking into account peak hours and slack hours of business, input value, and sales value to determine reasonable taxes. By trial and error, we were able to fix some broad norms, and after discussions with leading hotels, we fixed the criteria and tax liability. The Hoteliers accepted this. It helped us to improve collections.

ENTERTAINMENT TAX

We received several complaints about large-scale avoidance and evasion of taxes by Cinema halls. In coastal Andhra, people were crazy about cinema, especially women. In the Telangana region, men were major patrons. Cinema halls sprouted in Hyderabad and district headquarters, big towns, and commercial places. Telugus have a fascination for cinemas, and AP then accounted for almost a third of the cinema halls in the country!

Commercial tax officials used to visit cinema halls just before shows to stamp tickets and keep tabs on collections. Cinema owners would, in addition to our stamped tickets, issue informal, unaccounted tickets and make money on the sly. We felt that it was a waste of the workforce to tie down our staff for the meagre collections and wanted to arrive at a rational basis of levy on tickets and collection, which was both simple, reduced evasion, and ensured higher revenues.

A small team of bright young officers were asked to study the issue. They took into account several factors like how old the cinema hall was, its capacity, number of shows, number of categories -- whether it had balconies, private cabins, and other facilities - whether it was an ordinary, air-cooled or air-conditioned hall, provision for parking space, toilets, refreshment stalls, canteens, etc. The type of pictures exhibited, i.e., new pictures, old pictures, and the number of shows held, like matinee shows, first shows, and second shows. It also factored in the language of the film, Hindi, Telugu, and other languages. There were no multiplexes at that time. Modern cinema halls were exhibiting 35 mm and 70 mm films with stereophonic sound. Some new ultra-modern cinema halls - the precursor to the latest trends of comfort and convenience - had come up, like Ramakrishna, Tarakarama, Maheswari, Parameswari, Meera, and Sangeeth Talkies at Hyderabad, which exhibited the latest films with a full house for all shows on the first one to two weeks. To simplify the commercial tax levy on cinema halls, we worked out the average occupancy of cinema halls and average ticket revenue for most cinema halls and fixed the tax amount, which was acceptable to the cinema industry. However, we had difficulty in convincing the ultra-luxurious cinema hall owners who were highly placed politicians or businessmen. Some of them approached us for downward revision of the normative decisions in their case and bring them on par with the ordinary cinema halls. We explained the logic of our criteria to them and tried to convince them. After initial reluctance, they fell in line and paid the taxes.

ENHANCEMENT OF POWERS OF CT OFFICERS

With the growth of the economy, income levels rose, which warranted a review of the powers of commercial tax officials and their empowerment to handle bigger cases. This was welcomed and accepted by officers at the CTO level and above, although it involved complicated assessments. Surprisingly enough, officials at the level of Inspectors and Assistant Commercial Tax Officers did not want enhancement of their powers. Apparently, they were happy to deal with lesser income cases like small shops, kirana shops, pan shops, petty traders, and hawkers. They probably felt that assesees having higher education and income would take the help of chartered accountants to prepare their returns, leaving less scope for Mamools, i.e., bribes.

When I was Commissioner of Commercial Taxes (CCT), I got a call to meet the CM the next morning when he expressed concern that both Nagarjuna Fertilizers and Godavari Fertilizers were not making progress after I was recalled to Assam. The Principal Secretary of Industry, TL Sankar, had advised him that I should be re-posted as Managing Director of Godavari Fertilizers and Nagarjuna Fertilizers to give a push to both projects. CM wanted my consent to post me as Managing Director of Godavari Fertilizers. I had just settled down as Commissioner of Commercial Taxes and was enjoying my work. I was taken aback and quite disturbed at being shifted so soon after my return from Guwahati. I requested the CM to give me three days to think over the matter and give my answer.

I SEEK MY MOTHER'S ADVICE

Back home, I told my mother about the discussion with the CM and his proposal. I told her that the post of CCT was a coveted one with offices all over the state and accounted for 60 percent of government revenues. In my earlier posting, I had slogged a lot to get promoters, tie-up technologies, and revive the Nagarjuna project, but it had not taken off. I told her that I would tell the CM that I was not interested and did not want to join the NFCL or GFCL again.

My mother instinctively sensed my disappointment. She calmly asked me whether IAS officers had earlier worked as CCTs and whether other IAS officers would be posted as CCTs. I said that was the practice. She said, "I guess you will be one of many such Commissioners. In the post, you might feel important and comfortable. To me, at best, you may earn some more revenue for the government. On the other hand, the CM is worried about meeting the needs and welfare of the farmers. He has personally called and requested you to take up a difficult task, which is to help provide plenty of fertilizers to farmers. If I were in your position, I would accept the challenge of setting up a fertilizer factory, which no IAS officer in AP has done till now, rather than work in a mundane job with no challenge. If you succeed, the fertilizers produced in the factory would help a million farmers and make our state Annapoorna. All would bless you for the abundant crops they will reap by using fertilizer. The company will employ many workers, appoint dealers, and create a chain of employment opportunities. If I were given such a chance, I would gladly take up the challenge to help farmers produce more food rather than seek to continue in a challenge-less, cushy routine job. I know that if you apply your mind to the task, you can do it. I am confident that my son will think and make the correct decision".

I pondered over her rational, national, and service-oriented views and advice. I realised that my mother's thinking and outlook were selfless, far more objective and logical than mine, which was selfish. It made me feel petty and narrow-minded before her broad-mindedness. It reminded me of my first duty to the nation as an Indian and an All India Service Officer who should be Indian in outlook, expert in Administration, and practice the creed of Service to the nation and its interests. I realised that my mother had trust and belief in my commitment to my job, duty consciousness, and ability to do well.

My mother had placed public and social interests higher than her son's interests. I felt proud to have a mother like her. I recollected what the epics say - "Man in his quest for fulfilment must move from Selfishness (Swartha) to Unselfishness (Niswartha) to Selflessness (Aswartha). My mother had become my Guru to transform me. I told her that I would go by her advice and accept the challenge.

The next day, I met TL Shankar, Principal Secretary, Industries, and the CM and conveyed my consent.

A meeting of Commissioners of CT of the four southern states of Tamil Nadu, Karnataka, Kerala, and Andhra Pradesh used to be held by rotation. At the conference held at Cochin in Kerala, the CCT of Tamil Nadu, Karnataka, Secretary Revenue A.P, BN Jaisimha, and I attended. We discussed the need for uniformity of tax rates and procedures. An attempt was made to ensure near uniformity of taxes, free flow and movement of goods and services in South India to function like a common market. It was a 3-day conference.

MY MOTHER PASSES AWAY

Late in the evening, on the second day, I received a bolt from the blue and soul-wrenching news from my elder brother that my loving, caring, revered mother had passed away due to a heart attack before she could be taken to the hospital. I was devastated, numb with shock. I regretted not being at her bedside. I cursed myself for attending the meeting at Cochin. BN Jayasimha, our Revenue Secretary, consoled me. I could not sleep that night as memories kept me awake. I reached Hyderabad just before noon and went straight to our house. There was a large crowd of our relatives and her admirers. My sisters, sisters-in-law and my wife were weeping inconsolably. My doctor brother was calm and told me that her cremation was fixed the next day.

It was a poignant scene when my uncle, elder to my mother, kissed her on the forehead and said that he had lost his sister and foster mother. Her younger brother, an IAS officer and former Chief Secretary of AP, cried that his sister and guide had passed away and he would have no mentor in his life. At the cremation ground, my two uncles wanted me to recite some Shlokas from the Bhagavad Gita before she was consigned to the flames. I did so and prayed for her Sadgati. I felt a void in my life with no one to whom I could turn to or from whom I could seek advice and guidance. When the flames engulfed her body, I thought her breath had become one with the air. Her eyes had returned to the sun, her body to the earth, and her soul seeking its further journey and destiny. My distraught mind found solace in reminiscing about her abundant compassion and love towards all those who came into contact with her. A sudden calm descended on me, and I remembered her words that, "Life must go on even when a dear one has gone." These words, which she had said when my younger sister had passed away at Warangal, re-echoed in my ears. Our home was no longer the same cheerful place - where no guests ever returned without taking food and feeling happy for the visit, for my mother would cheer the most despondent people and light up the house with her bright smile, welcoming words, inquiries about their welfare and mention of some happy incident or the other. Our family and friends bid farewell to a great lady and a pious soul. Her advice was dispassionate but action-compassionate, braced with love and infusion of courage to face life as it unfolded.

As news of her death spread, the crowd of relatives from our native place and visitors swelled at the funeral despite Sec.144 CRPC orders in force due to some local disturbances. As a tribute to her life, memory, and a humble homage, I instituted three awards in her memory, two at Hyderabad, one to be given to an "Ideal Mother" by the Kapu Sangham and another for "Best Woman Achiever" by the Hyderabad Management Association: the third award to be given to the Best girl student from St. Philomena's High School, Bellary.

REDUCTION IN SALES TAX ON GOLD

A classmate who came from a family of gold merchants and grain dealers told me that the high sales tax on gold, which was already costly, was affecting the gold business. The sales tax on gold and gold ornaments was 4%. The President of the Gold Merchants Association at Hyderabad, who was also the President of the Federation of Andhra Pradesh Chambers of Commerce and Industry (FAPCCI), met us with a delegation of gold merchants and gave a representation for a reduction in sales tax on gold and gold ornaments. They assured me that if the sales tax were reduced, the department would get more revenue as sales would increase. I listened patiently and asked them whether they would guarantee that sales would increase. They assured me that with lower taxes, trade would pick up, and tax collections would improve. I cautioned that if our collections did not increase, we might increase the tax in the next budget. They accepted the challenge. We moved a proposal to the government to reduce the sales tax from 4% to 2%. Women were elated, and tax collections improved.

PROMOTION OF COMMERCIAL TAX OFFICERS

Litigation in the department was at its peak on the finalization of the seniority list of Deputy Commercial Tax Officers as several direct recruits and promotion seekers approached the Administrative Tribunal and High

Court. There was a prolonged delay in effecting promotions. All the issues were sorted out quickly to promote many DCTOs as Commercial Tax Officers. As all the vacant posts of CTOs were filled up, the morale of CTOs was up, and this helped the department to function effectively.

The CT department had intelligent and competent officers who delivered on targets and were forward-looking in their attitude and application. We introduced computerization in a small way at border check posts and for computational purposes in the office.

During my tenure in Commercial Taxes, I realised that the levy of taxes and its collection was a constant battle of wits between the government and the taxpayer. Consultation with and education of the public on new levies and the linkage between tax payment and economic development can soften and smoothen the process of levies and collection of taxes. The levy should be affordable, reasonable, fair, and equitable, and the taxpayer must pay the tax willingly.

Good Governance in tax administration requires debate, dialogue, discussions, deliberations, and decisions to arrive at fair and equitable taxes. We also need the informed consent and approval of the legislature, the government, and the taxpayer. My tenure as CCT was short, but it was a great learning experience in taxation and administration.

POSTSCRIPT

While input tax credit was allowed on intra-state sales, there was no credit provided for CST, which is levied on inter-state sales, which became a bone of contention between states. It was agreed that CST at 4% would be phased out along with reducing rates of tax by 2008, and the Central government would compensate states for losses incurred by the introduction of VAT. Existing sales tax exemptions, largely a legacy of incentives to attract industry like deferment or waiver of sales tax for a certain period, stand withdrawn and converted to deferments with suitable adjustments.

After seven years of discussions between states and the Central government, Commercial Taxes were replaced in 2017 by the uniform Central General Sales Tax (CGST). It comprises taxes imposed by the Centre and the State governments and Taxes in the course of inter-state transactions. GST has now become a unified tax all over India, except on articles in which the state continues to exercise jurisdiction, like liquor, petrol, diesel, etc. GST was expected to show a higher rate of growth in the future. This has indeed been proved correct.

29

Managing Director of Nagarjuna Fertilizers & Chemicals Ltd. (Sept 1983 – Sept 1984)

In 1983, I was posted as MD of Godavari Fertilizers and also placed in additional charge as MD of Nagarjuna Fertilizers.

Despite several efforts by the Government to induct a good promoter to take over and implement the Nagarjuna Fertilizers, it proved difficult to get a willing promoter because of the high cost of the project. The IDBI suggested that we should issue an advertisement soliciting enquiries from good parties capable of implementing the project. IDBI indicated that we should give preference to local promoters. In response to the advertisement, two parties, namely, Nagarjuna Group, headed by KVK Raju, and Andhra Sugars, indicated their interest in setting up the Fertilizer plant.

After detailed discussions by a High-Power Committee and consultations with Financial Institutions, Nagarjuna Group was selected as the Co-promoter. I was relieved of my charge as MD of Nagarjuna Fertilizers. Nagarjuna Group had the backing of IDBI to finance the project. There was some delay in setting up the project, but the Nagarjuna Group was able to construct and commission the plant in Kakinada. The plant was doing well, but due to adverse market conditions, delay in the finalisation of the retention price, and high cost of borrowing, Nagarjuna Fertilizers and Chemicals Limited had to face and overcome many problems. The company was doing well but is reported to have run into financial problems.

30

Additional Secretary to the Government of India, Ministry of Mines, New Delhi (Aug 1990 – Aug 1994)

MINISTRY OF MINES

I was empanelled by the Government of India and posted as an Additional Secretary in the Ministry of Mines. I handed over charge as Managing Director of Godavari Fertilizers and joined duty in Delhi in August 1990.

PK Lahiri, Secretary in the Ministry, welcomed and asked me to meet Usha Vohra, Additional Secretary, who was anxious to hand over charge and take over as Secretary in another department. She briefed me and handed over the charge. I called on Minister A K Goswami, who was from Assam. He welcomed me and wanted the Ministry to attain self- sufficiency in important non-ferrous metals and non-atomic minerals. Unfortunately, Goswami died in a car accident in Assam.

The Secretary asked me to attend a Review Meeting of Secretaries called by the Cabinet Secretary the next day as he had to attend another meeting. I did so. Cabinet Secretary Naresh Chandra, whom I had not met earlier, asked me which ministry I was representing. I told him that I was an additional secretary in the Ministry of Mines and had joined just a day ago. He asked my name, cadre, and year of allotment and told me to carefully listen and report the gist of the discussions to the Secretary.

The next day, we had to attend a meeting in the Planning Commission regarding Plan allocations for the Mines ministry. The Joint Secretary, M L Majumdar, and I attended the meeting held by MC Gupta, who was the advisor of the Planning Commission. When I reported the gist of the discussions to Lahiri, he said that the joint secretary had already briefed him that I had effectively put across views of the ministry. He said that I would have to look after the Geological Survey of India (GSI) which required both toning and tuning to make it more effective. In view of my corporate experience, I was asked to look after all the public sector undertakings under the ministry.

The Mines Ministry was very compact and relatively small. The two joint secretaries, PC Mishra and ML Majumdar, briefed me on the functions of the ministry and their own duties. I met the Directors S Krishnan, Chandra Mohan, and DK Tyagi, all bright young IAS officers. Bajwa, the Director, was looking after GSI. Later on, S Deo joined as Joint Secretary in place of PC Mishra. The discussions enabled me to get a bird's eye view of the work and priorities of the ministry, which was responsible for assessing the requirements of non-ferrous metals like Aluminium, Zinc, Copper, and Lead in India and deciding on the quantities to be imported.

PSUs OF THE MINISTRY

The CMDs of National Aluminium Company (NALCO), Bharat Aluminium Company (BALCO), Bharat Gold Mines Limited (BGML), Hindustan Zinc Limited (HZL), and Hindustan Copper Limited (HCL) of the ministry met and briefed me about their organizational issues and the support and assistance required from the Ministry. The Director General of GSI, the DG of Indian Bureau of Mines, and the Controller of Mining Leases briefed me on their work. The Director of the Indian School of Mines paid a courtesy call. I got an overview of the work of the ministry, its attached and subordinate offices, and priorities.

Quarterly Allocation meetings used to be held with representatives of the Ministry of Commerce, Industry, Minerals and Metals Trading Corporation (MMTC) and other major users to determine the requirements and to decide on the quantum of imports and allocation of metals to users. With the liberalization of the economy and financial reforms in 1991, there was no need for the Government to continue the quarterly meetings for the imports and were discontinued.

NATIONAL MINERAL POLICY

India produces 89 minerals, 4 fuel minerals, 52 non-metallic, 11 metallic, and 22 minor minerals. Minerals are finite, non-renewable, and exhaustible resources. Mineral deposits are unevenly distributed worldwide and often covered by overburden. Interdependence among nations is inevitable. The Ministry of Mines is responsible for the optimal and economic development of non-fuel and non-atomic minerals and all non-ferrous minerals.

The National Mineral Policy on non-fuel and non-atomic minerals was approved by the government in August 1990. In the wake of the 1991 economic reforms and Industrial policy changes, the Mineral Policy had to be reviewed. It was revised in 1993, which indicated the direction of the reforms and made changes to the existing laws and rules governing mineral development. The policy stressed the need for modernizing the industry with an emphasis on science and technology. It noted the need for the conservation of mineral wealth in harmony with ecology. It stressed the principles of reducing, reusing, recycling, and refining minerals along with beneficiation, reduction of waste, and production of high-purity minerals and metals. The recycling of Aluminium and recovery of Lead from used batteries was encouraged.

The Mines and Minerals Regulation and Development Act (MMRD), as well as its Rules, were amended in the light of the New Industrial Policy and ground realities. Major minerals were under the Union Government, while minor minerals were under the State governments, which started levying Cess on major minerals in addition to royalties to bolster their revenues. Aggrieved parties approached the Supreme Court of India, which in September 1991 held that the levy of Cess by the state governments was null and void under the provisions of the Act. A Validation Act was quickly passed in March 1992, which regularized the Cess collected by the states. Oil-producing states like Gujarat, Assam, and later on, AP wanted a provision for review of Royalties on oil and gas and its equitable sharing between the Union Government and State Governments.

The Ministry had entered into a number of collaboration Agreements with the United Nations Development Program (UNDP) and BRGM of France for technical cooperation and training in surveys, exploration, and utilization of minerals. We held meetings with the governments of Australia, Hungary, and China for imports and technical assistance in the development of non-fuel and non-atomic minerals.

The Ministry of Coal was located on the same floor as the Ministry of Mines in Shastri Bhavan. My batch-mate BK Singh was the additional secretary in the coal ministry. At the same time, Kosal Ram of AP was the Financial Advisor, and Sachdeva was an advisor on coal mining, safety, and other technical aspects. There was good interaction with the Mines, Coal Ministry, and Power Ministry. This enabled us to take an integrated view of the mining sector and coordinate action with concerned authorities.

FEDERATION OF MINING INDUSTRIES (FIMI)

The Federation of Mining Industries (FIMI), composed of private sector mining Companies, was very cooperative, and its Secretariat Head,

R K Sarma, was a very knowledgeable person with good contacts and a pleasant conversationalist. He ably represented the common interests of the Mining Sector. We learned a lot about the problems and issues of the private-sector mining industries.

I was deputed to undergo a short course on National Remote Sensing conducted by the NRSA at Dehradun, which was an eye-opener to the possibilities of using NRSA not only for mineral exploration but also for other services and ground mapping, which would be useful to the public.

Getting accommodation in Delhi is a herculean task. My good friend V K Srinivasan from the Ministry of Works and Housing helped, and I got Government accommodation in Tilak Lane. It was close to Shastri Bhavan, where the Ministry of Mines was located. The AP Bhavan, India Gate Lawns, and the Bengali market were close by. As it was near the National Stadium, it suited the morning walk of officers at the India Gate. There were a large number of Telugu and South Indian officers residing in the government quarters at Tilak Lane, which was jocularly called 'Telugu' lane, instead of Tilak Lane' Pragathi Maidan, where exhibitions are held, was within walking distance.

A large number of relatives and friends who visited Delhi used to stay with us. Our weekends were spent showing them around Agra, Bharatpur, Fatehpur- Sikri and Dayalbagh, popularly known as the Taj Mahal Circuit. Some of our relatives used to visit Mathura and Brindavan, which had a grand south Indian temple. The priests of the temple, who hailed from Srirangam, were known to my wife's family. Some relatives wanted to visit Rajasthan, particularly Jaipur, Ajmer, and Udaipur. Enterprising relatives wanted to visit Himachal Pradesh and Shimla, while religiously inclined took tourist coaches from Delhi to Kedarnath, Badrinath, and Gaurikund.

SUNEETHA AND THE CABLE CAR

My niece Suneetha, a convent student, wanted to visit Himachal Pradesh. My wife and I visited Shimla with her. She was thrilled to find snowfall and to ride a horse at the Mall in Shimla. We visited Chail to give her the thrill of travelling high in a cable car between two hills. Suddenly, the cable car stopped mid-way due to an interruption in the power supply. Suneetha was scared and started crying and clinging to my wife. We assured her that as soon as power was restored, we would be safely back on land. Power was quickly restored, and the episode ended happily. Suneetha even now remembers the incident and recalls the thrill of the cable car as well as its scary moments.

While in AP in 1988, I was selected for a one-year fellowship programme at Queen Elizabeth House in the UK, but the CM did not agree to relieve me again on the grounds of public interest! I was belatedly selected and deputed for an Advanced Management Program at Banff School of Management in Canada in January 1992. It was bitingly cold at Banff, located in the Rocky Mountains in Alberta province of Canada. It was an International Course attended by many senior officers from governments and private sector companies.

I visited Calgary, Edmonton, and Vancouver. There were a large number of Indians working in industries in Edmonton. I visited the East-West Laboratory, which was like a miniature United Nations with people from all over the world working there. In India, we were finding it difficult to get an accurate analysis and composition of sea-bed nodules collected from our marine surveys to enable scale-up extraction and production parameters and to set up a pilot plant on economic lines in India. I discussed the matter with the senior executives in the laboratory, who demonstrated their competence and capability of analysing different samples from 'grams to tons quickly and simultaneously working out the separation, beneficiation, and best processes for the Pilot Plant for extraction of pure metals. On return to India, we sent some samples to the laboratory, which did an excellent job and quickly gave us a clear idea of how to proceed economically.

In 1993, I was deputed for a training course at the Administrative Staff College of India at Hyderabad on the financial crisis of 1990 and the 1991 Reforms. Y V Reddy, the then Joint Secretary in the Ministry of Finance, explained the dire situation in which India was placed and how, with advice and deft action under the guidance of Manmohan Singh, Finance Minister, and P V Narasimha Rao, the Prime Minister, the country was able to get over the crisis.

SURVIVED AN AIR CRASH AT DELHI AIRPORT

At that time, there was a prolonged strike by pilots of Indian Airlines. The Government hired foreign pilots with planes to tackle the strike. I was scheduled to take a flight from Hyderabad to Delhi upon completion of our course on 8th January 1993. We were to take a flight on an Uzbek Russian TU-154 aircraft piloted by a Ukrainian. The flight, which was scheduled to take off at 5.00 pm, was delayed and rescheduled to take off at 11:30 pm. I had dinner at our home in Secunderabad and reported at the airport in due time. To ensure stability, the front portion of the plane had to be first filled up by passengers before the rear portion was filled. The plane took off. I was seated in the front portion and buckled up in my seat. The aircraft took off after midnight. I was reading a book when the hostess announced around 2.00 AM (midnight) that the plane would be landing at Delhi airport shortly. I could see the landing lights at the airport and on the runway.

The pilot touched the runway at great speed to land. There was a loud thud, and the plane, instead of slowing down and cruising on the runway, rose again with the high speed of the impact, landed violently for the second time on the runway, and overturned. The plane landed topsy-turvy before stopping, and passengers who had their seat belts on were dangling upside down. The severe jolts woke up the passengers, many of whom were sleeping. Luggage in the lofts was strewn helter-skelter. Passengers who were awake realized that the plane had crashed and quickly unbuckled, helped others, and got ready to exit the plane before it caught fire. Passengers searched for their luggage, personal articles, glasses, and other essentials like medicines and said their prayers. I lost my hand baggage and my spectacles. Some passengers were hysterical, crying and saying their prayers like Hare Ram, My God Jesus, etc. I recollected my training at the Civil Defence Research Institute in Nagpur. Along with a couple of passengers, we unbuckled straps and lowered the passengers. I opened the Emergency Exit Door of the plane over the wing to provide a safe exit for the passengers. The opening was on the top of the wing of the plane, which was 6 to 8 feet high from the ground. I helped some lady passengers. We got onto the wing portion and jumped down, followed by some other passengers, including foreigners. We noticed that some parts of the plane were on fire.

Luckily, the plane broke into three parts, a safety feature designed to provide scope for passengers in each section to jump down to safety on the ground. The heavy engines were thrown apart; fire erupted, and sounds of explosions intensified with the tearing of the fuselage and burning of the seats and luggage in the plane hold area.

The Air Control Tower at Delhi, which had given instructions to the Plane to land, did not follow up till the parking of the plane. Luckily, the pilot of a Thai Airlines plane, which was due to take off, saw the crashing of the plane and some flames erupting and reported to the air traffic control, who promptly sent rescue vehicles to transport the passengers to the First Aid Dispensary and then to the Terminal. Passengers who had jumped out of the plane, some with minor fractures and injuries, got into the Airlines bus and were taken to the First Aid Centre. The staff there, who did not anticipate patients at that time, fumed and scolded the passengers for transgressing the airport rules and coming through the airfield instead of from the road beside the compound wall of the airport! Not aware that we had just escaped with our lives in an air crash! We had to inform them that it was not our intention or voluntary action to violate any law or order, but it was done in an emergency as our plane had crashed! This assured them. They promptly attended to passengers who were injured in the course of their jumping down with empathy, care, and concern.

After First Aid, we were taken to the terminal at about 3.30 AM. The Indian Airlines staff offered us some tea and told us to come back later in the morning to see if any personal articles in the damaged and burnt plane could be salvaged, identified, recognized, and allowed to be taken away after due clearance. Passengers who have lost their luggage will be entitled to some compensation (inadequate and meagre) as per rules based on the registered weight of the baggage, as shown in the manifest. No compensation was provided for the passengers who were carrying valuable items in the booked luggage and/or handbags. I was carrying some Jewelry and a pair of diamond earrings my wife had left at home in Hyderabad in a suitcase that had been checked in and loaded as baggage. Unfortunately, I found that my suitcase, clothes, etc., were totally burnt and not traceable in the smoke-out rubble. I could, however, recognize and retrieve remnants of two gold bangles of my wife, which were in a case and not burnt. The earrings were not traceable.

I thanked God for saving the lives of all the passengers. Probably, God had other plans for the passengers to fulfil their destinies. My office driver, Ghan Shyam, was waiting with the vehicle outside the airport. I made my way out and went straight to my house in Tilak Lane, Delhi. After I reached home and had a cup of tea, I broke the news to my wife. She thanked the stars, performed a special Pooja in the house, and asked me to forget the loss of the Jewelry and my clothes. I started using my spare set of spectacles.

As usual, I went to the office and informed Secretary V Krishnan about the crash. He was a batch-mate of N Kanungo, the then Civil Aviation Secretary. He volunteered to take me to his office so that I could narrate the experience of the plane crash and explore the possibility of speedily securing compensation for the loss incurred. We did so.

While I was in office that day, S K Bagchi, Resident Commissioner of the Orissa Government, came to see me in connection with some aerial, geological, and radiometric surveys under progress in Orissa. He casually broached the subject of the air crash which had been splashed in the newspapers of that day. I told him that I was one of the passengers on the plane and had been lucky enough to survive the accident. He was shocked and astounded that I had just that morning returned home after surviving the air crash but was attending office as if the Air crash was not unusual! He spread the news among his colleagues that I had casually taken the air crash incident and was attending office as usual! This led to a number of phone calls from colleagues and friends in Delhi and elsewhere congratulating me for the miraculous escape, as many of them had seen the photographs of the crashed Aeroplane in that day's newspapers. I was reminded of what Bhagavad Gita says: "Man is entitled to his duty but not to the results of his duty," which is in God's hands. Yoga is Samatvam, or equanimity of the mind in thought and action. Such yoga leads to effectiveness at work. I was just discharging my duty and facing life as ordained.

I thought that I was destined to live and should thank God for His mercy and compassion He has showered on me.

GEOLOGICAL SURVEY OF INDIA (GSI)

The Geological Survey of India, with headquarters in Kolkata, was established in the year 1851. It has a glorious record of 173 years and has surveyed over 90 percent of India and mapped its geological features. It has estimated and established the potential reserves of various minerals in the country. In this large multi-disciplinary organization with relevant skills, the officers spend six months during the fair weather in the field for Survey, Mapping, and Exploration work and return to the office to complete the paperwork and publish the results of the exploration.

GSI covered most of the land area but did not make much headway in hilly and forest areas, which covered 22 percent of the land area due to Forest Regulations and Tribal laws. We encountered much difficulty in securing permissions from the state governments, forest departments, and organizations working to protect the ecology of the region. We wanted the GSI to study the Himalayan Region and its stability, explore prospects for geothermal energy, and intensify the search for bauxite, diamonds, gold, nickel, and other scarce minerals in other areas.

RESTRUCTURING OF GSI

With the development of Science and Technology, the need for specialization in the areas of geophysics, geochemistry, and Ariel, as well as Marine Surveys, became important. Priority was given to the Continental Shelf and Extended Economic Zone surveys and the prospects of seabed mining for important, scarce, and useful minerals not found on the land. GSI was operating three ocean exploration ships under the 'Sagarika' name series and had met with some success. The ships picked up Seabed nodules for further analysis.

With the setting up of the GSI Regional offices and manning them with the relevant professional skills, we were able to intensify the search for minerals and build up specialized knowledge of each region and its overall prospects. The Regional offices took a lot of initiative to popularize geology through Geological Parks and their importance. It established Geological Parks to educate the public on the geological formation and evolution of India. The Parks caught the imagination of the public. Children were thrilled to see realistic fibre figures of dinosaurs, mammoths, some extinct animals, and fossils.

There was a demand from the Specialist officers of the GSI for due recognition and eligibility for higher positions in the GSI. The geologists pressed for the restructuring of GSI to provide better scales, promotion prospects, and other benefits. We had to balance the demands of the Pure and Applied geological personnel before restructuring the GSI. I frequently visited the GSI headquarters at Calcutta and the Regional offices and the camps where fieldwork was in progress to understand in-depth, the work of the GSI and examine the reorganization proposals in the context of the Economic Reforms, changed circumstances and aspirations of various disciplines within the organization. With cooperation, we were able to restructure and provide better pay scales and opportunities for promotion and motivate the officers to accord greater importance to fieldwork and quick analytical work to get the best results and publish the findings.

We faced the problem of ensuring good tenure for the Director General of the GSI. Many of them were competent officers but had brief tenures to make an impact. We tried to devise a pipeline of succession despite the problems of seniority in government organizations to give them two to three-year tenure.

NATIONAL MINERAL AWARDS

As part of the restructuring and a measure of recognition of officers and scientists who were pushing the frontiers of geological sciences and technologies, National Mineral Awards were instituted to reward outstanding geologists and allied geoscientists. The awards carried a lot of prestige and have become highly prized and recognized. The Minister, Secretary, and Additional Secretary would conduct the Awards function. I used to read the citations. The Secretary would comment that it was for a good reason as I had a loud voice, which could be heard even if the microphones failed!

LATUR EARTHQUAKE

In October 1993, there was a severe earthquake in Latur in Maharashtra. To allay the fears of the people and to locate the epicenter of the earthquake, a team from GSI and NGRI visited Latur and made a detailed study of the fissures underground. The team ruled out the possibility that the weight of Koyna Dam water was responsible for the Latur earthquake.

The dormant volcano on the Barren Island of Andaman Nicobar became active and spewed a lot of lava. A team from GSI visited Barren Island to study the causes and effects of the volcano and analyse the lava.

FOREIGN COLLABORATIONS

The Ministry collaborated with BRGM of France and signed three agreements to secure aid and assistance for the technical training of our officers in modern surveys, analysis, and utilization of the data to promote and support scientific mining and mineral-based industries. BRGM did a very good job in regard to training our officers in searching for Copper, Lead, Zinc, and Gold. They assisted us in multi-metal exploration in greenstone schists and for Manganese. We entered into an agreement with China to explore minerals.

We had a collaboration agreement with Australia, which is a mineral-rich continent that supplied minerals, particularly coal, to India. The Australian Government, through Austrade, their industrial and commercial wing, extended an invitation to me to visit Australia and hold discussions with the Australian Geological Survey at Canberra, mining companies in Perth, Melbourne, Sydney, and other mining sites to attract investments for developing the mining sector in India. Australia is a continent with a small population near the coastal areas and was extensively using aerial surveys to map not only the visible surface geology but also aerial radiometric and aeromagnetic surveys to intensify the search for iron ore, water, and diamond in remote and inaccessible locations. I had the opportunity to have an in-depth discussion with Geological Survey of Australia, international mining companies in Melbourne about the potential for collaboration, technology exchange, and the exploration and exploitation of mineral resources. This led to interesting developments that helped the Indian Mining Industry to benefit from the new technologies.

VISIT TO VIETNAM

I led a team of officers from the MMTC, HZL, MECL, etc. to Vietnam to examine the scope for exploration for Rubies, other gemstones, gold, and also the scope for imparting diamond-cutting skills to Vietnamese. It was a thrilling and exciting visit to know first-hand from the Vietnamese Generals how Vietnam withstood the might of the US and France and pressures from China by sheer grit and emerged victorious. We travelled through the length and breadth of the country and noticed the similarities between the way of life in India and Vietnam. The scenarios reminded me of Assam. We stayed in Hanoi, the capital, and visited the Ho-Chi-Minh Memorial Museum, which was a thrilling experience. We saw statues and sculptures of Indian Gods and Goddesses like Saraswathi, Ganesha, and Durga. Devi showing the sway and cultural influence of India in Southeast Asia. We stopped at Singapore, Bangkok, and Hong Kong on the way. We saw the impact of Indian civilization and culture on the people of those places.

AERIAL SURVEYS

We engaged a company from Australia to conduct an aerial survey for diamonds and mineral prospecting in the Bastar district of Madhya Pradesh and parts of Orissa. The small planes used to fly at a height of a hundred meters with powerful resolution cameras. They flew over the land with a grid spacing of about 5 meters to capture relevant data. The data not only covered the surface areas but also minerals and water up to a depth of 300 meters. This methodology has now become commonplace and used extensively by the private sector to reconnoitre, prospect, and apply for mining licenses. Such aeromagnetic surveys were done for Oil India Limited for Petroleum Reserves and diamond prospecting.

TEHRI HYDRO ELECTRIC DAM STUDY

The Central Government wanted to construct a Hydro- electric dam on the river Tehri in Uttar Pradesh, which the local people stoutly resisted. There were many doubts about the Geotechnical soundness of the proposal as well as its adverse impact on the ecology of the region and the livelihoods of the people. The Ministry of Power wanted the Mines Ministry to set up a team to study the Geotechnical and related aspects of the construction of the dam. A committee was set up under my Chairmanship to study the issue in-depth along with Harsh Gupta, Director of the National Geophysical Research Institute at Hyderabad. With the GSI team, we analysed all the Geotechnical data, visited the site, met the local people, and submitted our report to the Government, which decided to construct the dam under the aegis of the Tehri Hydro Development Power Corporation (THPDC) with geotechnical analysis and suitable safeguards.

GRANITE EXPORTS

Export of granite of various hues picked up in a big way to the European Union, China, and the United States, primarily for tombstones, facades of buildings, and elevators. Some of the granite stones were highly valued and priced because of their rarity. One of them was black granite with gold star-like spots called Galaxy from Andhra Pradesh. Granite Exports touched Rs.900 crores in 1994 with good prospects and has continuously grown since then, providing employment and export earnings.

IMPACT OF ECONOMIC REFORMS

The Economic reforms brought about a profound change in the attitude and priorities of the Ministry. The new Industrial policy on foreign investments, which raised the equity of foreign investors from 40% to 51% in Indian companies, brought about a sea change. The National Mineral Policy of 1990 was revamped in 1993 to enable new initiatives and attract investments in the mining sector with an emphasis on simplifying procedures for the issue of prospecting and mining leases and the facility for the transfer of such leases to other parties. Priority in exploration was accorded to scarce minerals, and speeding up the pace of acquiring self-sufficiency in critical minerals and reducing imports of minerals and metals. Detailed aerial surveys and marine services were accorded priority.

A review was conducted to re-fix the priorities and focus on the most important needs. The services of Indian scientific organizations like CSIR, the Indian Institute of Science, Universities, and leading industries were utilized. The focus was to update, upskill, upscale, and speed up work on important matters. The emphasis was on exports of iron ore, pig iron, some steel products, granite, and Barytes.

UNDP AND SEMINARS

I used to attend the meetings of the UNDP on Lead and Zinc, which constituted a Study Group of the UNDP on lead and zinc. I was elected as Vice President of the said group. This helped me to understand global trends and issues and to project the scope for the development of the mineral industry in India and many mining nations. It helped secure the visits and cooperation of mining companies from all over the world to India. We held many International Conferences and Seminars on the Mining Industry, which attracted a lot of interest from the mining companies. I presented papers at International Conferences on the prospects of the mineral industry in India and the scope of its development in Montreal, Perth, Melbourne, Marrakesh, Edmonton, and many other International Conferences in India.

NATIONAL ALUMINIUM COMPANY LIMITED (NALCO)

Economic changes led to a review of the functioning of the public sector undertakings under the Ministry. National Aluminium Company Limited (NALCO) was our showpiece and mascot. We had agreements with France and Canada for technical support. Nalco had its refinery for Alumina at Damanjodi in Orissa while the Smelter was in Angul. Alumina from Damanjodi was transported to Angul. We had a lot of problems in the road transport of Bauxite and Alumina to Angul and the finished products from Angul or Damanjodi to Visakhapatnam port in A.P for exports. This was quickly overcome. Aluminium is a big guzzler of power, and Nalco's expansion proposals require a large and continuous supply of power. With the constant increase in power capacity and capabilities, we quickly acquired self-sufficiency in Aluminium. Its export intensified with the setting up of more power plants and streamlining of the rail logistics for coal movement from the pithead to the Power plants and the Smelter. We noted the scope for the downstream industry as aluminium usage increased all over India and streamlined product movements.

The **Special Review Group on Mining** chaired by me brought about changes in the Mineral Policy of the Union Government. The **Committee on long-term requirements of Bauxite for Aluminium** identified the extent of bauxite reserves available in the country and the scope to produce aluminum with due regard to the ecology, and social concerns of the affected region, and the aspirations of the people.

POLITICAL PRESSURES

The MD of Nalco was a competent professional who had worked earlier at the Visakhapatnam Steel plant. The Minister was putting a lot of pressure on the CMD to give lucrative contracts and selling rights on its products to chosen persons by overlooking or overriding the principles of good governance and commercial logic. His Special Assistant threatened the CMD that false allegations would be made, and cases would be filed against him if he did not fall in line. He would be suspended if he did not act according to the bidding of the Minister and himself. The CMD would meet me, express his fears, and ask for advice. I got the details and accompanied him to the Secretary to brief him. I separately discussed with the Secretary to work out a strategy to checkmate the threats held out to the CMDs. It was also brought to the notice of the PMO and Cabinet Secretary. But Pantulu got scared and resigned. As fate would decide, the Minister, later on, reportedly committed suicide due to family and political pressures, including corruption charges, while his special assistant was prosecuted.

BALCO (BHARAT ALUMINIUM COMPANY LTD)

We had another Aluminium plant at Korba in Madhya Pradesh run by Bharat Aluminium Company Ltd (BALCO). The company had received technology from Hungary. I visited the plant and discussed the problems with the CMD. I visited a place where the Vedantha Guru Shankaracharya had meditated on the future of the Matts established at Jyotirmath, Puri, Dwaraka, and Sringeri. His intuition told him that in the future (now), teachers would be young and students old (unlike the times he lived in). The Guru would be silent, and students in silence would be able to think for themselves and find their solutions in solitude and constant inquiry. How truly he had visualized the future. A real Acharya whose institutions have survived for nearly a thousand years to date.

Bauxite was transported from Orissa to Bilaspur and Korba, posing a lot of logistical problems. The power plant at Korba was not operating at an optimum level, and it was securing additional power from the Madhya Pradesh State Electricity Board. Due to inadequate and erratic supplies, the company had to set up its own power plant, which did not work well. The Power plant was entrusted to the National Thermal Power Corporation for maintenance, which improved its performance. There was a lot of demand from the private sector for the sale of Balco. It was finally taken over by Vedanta Group, which has increased its capacity, improved its performance, and is making good profits.

HINDUSTAN COPPER LIMITED

India is perennially short of copper. Hindustan Copper Limited (HCL), with headquarters in Calcutta, had its mines at Ghatshila in Bihar, where the ore was fast getting exhausted. Some copper deposits were found in Malanjkhand in Madhya Pradesh, which had to be developed with better leaching arrangement and microbial action. It had another plant in Khetri, Rajasthan, that manufactured copper. It also had a wire drawing unit at Taloja in Maharashtra. As it was a profit-making company, it was made a Schedule-A (PSU), which provided greater financial powers and decision-making authority to the Board of Directors.

SIKKIM MINING CORPORATION (SMC)

The Government had a controlling share in the Sikkim Mining Corporation (SMC), which was recovering tungsten and other minerals from the river Teesta, which flows from Sikkim to West Bengal. The Teesta River is now the point of dispute between the Bangladesh Government, the state of West Bengal, and the Indian Government due to the dam constructed on the river Teesta. Bangladesh wants a greater share of the water flows.

BHARAT GOLD MINES LIMITED (BGML)

Bharat Gold Mines Limited (BGML) was set up in the Kolar district of Karnataka by John Taylor and Sons of the UK to prospect and develop goldmines and has been operating for over 100 years. Gold occurs as veins with varying content of gold amidst other rocks. They had some of the world's deepest underground mines going down to depths of 6000 feet, which necessitated the use of oxygen masks and Miner's headlamps to dig for gold. They have to operate underground tunnels following the gold vein under hazardous conditions. Miners have to go down the shift in elevators to the required levels and work on the various tunnels and passages to retrieve the gold ore and send it to the central place on small trolleys and then lift the ore to the surface for further processing to reclaim and refine the gold. As KGF had the deepest mines in India, the Tata Institute of Fundamental Research (TIFR) set up a laboratory in the mines to study the impact of Cosmic Rays at lower depths.

Scheduled caste labour from Tamil Nadu was recruited for the tough and hazardous mining operations. Such families now constitute the fourth generation of miners. Due to the exhaustion of gold veins, mining has become uneconomic. The company was producing less than a ton of gold every year and attempts to improve the position did not succeed. The production of gold started decreasing, and the cost of extraction increased, leading to heavy losses.

The company was declared sick and referred to the Board of Industrial and Financial Reconstruction (BIFR). International companies, and in particular, Australian companies that had a lot of worldwide experience, examined the scope for recovery of gold from the tailings and low-depth opencast mining and recovery but found it uneconomic. Many of the miners were suffering from health problems due to inadequate nutrition and polluted air and were afflicted by Silicosis and lung problems. Tuberculosis was quite common. To alleviate their distress, the government set up the National Institute of Miners Health (NIMH) to work out methods for the health of the lives of miners and the treatment to restore them to normal health. The National Institute of Rock Mechanics (NIRM) was set up to study the behaviour of rocks, mechanics of the movement of rocks, earth tremors, rock slippages, and other related studies. Mining activity ceased, and the mines were shut down, leading to widespread poverty and crime. Two films called KGF I and II have been produced recently to portray the difficulties of the former miners, some of whom have been taken to crime.

HINDUSTAN ZINC LIMITED (HZL)

Hindustan Zinc Limited (HZL), with its headquarters at Udaipur in Rajasthan, was set up to explore and exploit the Rampura Agucha mines for zinc and lead. The CMD was A. Wadhawan, a distinguished professional with good commercial skills and human relationships. Under his leadership, the Lead Zinc factory at Visakhapatnam was doing well. His signal contribution was the development of lead-zinc mines and the building of the zinc-lead smelter at Chanderiya. It was a modern State of the Art smelter completed in time and enhanced the profitability of the company. The workers were well trained with a number of dedicated professionals and experts whose services were sought by other companies. HZL encouraged local arts and crafts as well as singers and dancers. Wadhawan took a great deal of interest in mineral development in India and organized several national and international mineral meets. The country reduced the imports of lead and zinc and moved towards self-sufficiency in zinc. It extracted a lot of lead, silver, and gold as by products from the processes. HZL had a good team of executives like Paliwal, Parvateesam, and Seshavataram, who, later on, headed large organizations. I was involved in the company's activities in matters of technology, tie-ups, and product marketing.

Wadhawan was Chairman of the Standing Conference of Public Enterprises (SCOPE) in Delhi, which is the apex body for all Central Public Sector enterprises under the Union Government, and later on, became Chairman of the Public Enterprises Selection Board (PESB).

FLEETING TENURES

I noticed that the tenure of senior officers at the Secretary level in GOI was short and tenuous. This became quite clear in the case of the Ministry of Mines. I worked for four years in the Ministry of Mines. During this period, I saw four Ministers – Goswami, A K Sen, N K Salve, and Balram Singh Yadav. I also saw four Secretaries during my tenure – P.K. Lahiri, R.K. Dang, V. Krishnan, and Jhingran. This highlights the fact that the tenure of senior officers in the Indian Government is short and tenuous. Journalists may like to call it fleeting and uncertain. This is probably one of the professional hazards faced by civil servants at higher levels!

As no orders were received from GOI or the A.P. Government about my posting, on completion of my tenure of deputation to the Ministry of Mines, I decided to take four months of earned leave pending a posting.

I have had a lot of experience at the state and central levels in the development of varied industries and related policy matters for about half of my service career. I learned that the canvas at the national and international levels was, however, large and needed objective analysis and consultation with various agencies before making a decision. This causes delay. This process takes a lot of time and subjects the Government to a lot of criticism. My stint in the Ministry was a good learning experience for understanding the importance of minerals in life and of men and matters and men who matter.

31

Special Chief Secretary to Government of Andhra Pradesh and Commissioner for Industrial Promotion, Hyderabad (Jan 1995 – May 1995)

AS SPECIAL CHIEF SECRETARY IN ANDHRA PRADESH

After my tenure in the Ministry of Mines, I was awaiting posting orders from the Central Government or the State government. Indications were that the Central Govt. would take some time for the promotion of Additional Secretaries as Secretaries. My colleagues in Andhra Pradesh informed me that NT Rama Rao, who had won the elections and became the Chief Minister, wanted me to join A.P. with the rank of Chief Secretary. They advised me to call on the CM at Hyderabad. I did so.

Rama Rao's health had noticeably deteriorated, and relations with family members were strained. Age was telling on his health, and he was worried about who would look after him, as he had distributed his properties by then. He married Lakshmi Siva Parvathi, a Harikatha exponent and a divorcee with whom he was living in a bungalow in Banjara Hills. His family disapproved of his marriage.

N Jaya Prakash, an upright IAS Officer – who later on set up the NGO Lok Satta, was working as Special Secretary to the CM. I knew him as a collector in E.Godavari District when I was M.D of Godavari Fertilizers. I met him to call on the CM to ascertain details about my posting. He took me to meet the CM, who did not appear to be in good health. His wife Parvathi was with him. He introduced me to his wife and said that he fondly remembered my services as MD of Godavari Fertilizers and my expertise in Industries and public speaking. He said that he had plans to separate the normal functions of law and order and coordination, vest them in the CS, and appoint another CS exclusively for industrial development and related matters. He said that I would be posted as Chief Secretary for Industries and coordinate all departments concerned with industrial development. I felt that the proposal would erode the unified authority of the CS as the head of the civil services and adviser to the cabinet, with overall responsibility for good governance and administration of the state. Such a proposal would break the unity of command in the secretariat and the field and may not work in practice.

I returned to Delhi to ascertain about the Government of India's plans. I learned that the GOI orders would take some time. My family members wanted me to come back to Hyderabad as I would be retiring in a couple of years. Meanwhile, I received orders from the AP Government appointing me as Special Chief Secretary and Commissioner for Industrial Promotion, a new post for coordinating activities of departments like Power, Environment, Mining and APSEB, AP Pollution Control Board, and all industrial corporations involved in industrial development. B V Rama Rao was then acting as the Chief Secretary. Later, MS Rajaji, another batchmate, was appointed as Chief Secretary, who assured me of support for piloting proposals requiring clearance by the Cabinet.

As I had worked earlier in the Industries and Commerce Department, I was familiar with the officers, staff, and work. Sheila Bhide was the Secretary of Industries. She was a competent and intelligent officer with good knowledge of industrial development. KV Rao was the Secretary for Mines. We had an intelligent officer, Vinod Agarwal, who handled industrial estates and court cases.

CM would come to the Secretariat quite early in the mornings when he would be calm and active, though he was not in good health and appeared to be on steroids. But by afternoon, the effect of the steroids probably faded, and he appeared to be drowsy and not attentive. Observing his health condition, I requested the CM to allow me to brief him early in the morning as soon as he came to the secretariat. He agreed to do so, and I would meet with him to inform him about the latest developments and seek instructions when needed.

THE SIGNING OF MEMORANDUM OF UNDERSTANDING (MoU's) FOR POWER PLANTS IN A.P

The Central Government was worried about the deteriorating power supply position in India. It advised state governments to invite applications From parties who wished to set up power plants without seeking government incentives. It fixed a short date for the state governments to sign a Memorandum of Understanding with such parties. As gas and oil were found in the Krishna-Godavari Basin, it was expected that many gas-based power plant applications would be forthcoming. The state government sought applications for setting up power plants by the midnight of 31st March 1995, giving very little time for the parties to submit detailed proposals or for the government to examine and evaluate the proposals. There was a rush and pressure from parties to sign MOUs. Not all of them had good financial or past credentials and the capacity to set up such plants. In the normal course, the Secretary, Power had to vet and sign the MOUs on behalf of the government. EAS Sarma, then Secretary, Power declined on norms of good governance and morals to be a party to the decision or sign the MOUs without following due process. In view of this development, the CM called and asked me to sign the MOUs on behalf of the government as Special CS and Commissioner for Industrial Promotion. Under the circumstances, I was expected to receive, scrutinise and sign the standard MOUs on behalf of the Government. I consulted the Chairman of APSEB and others involved. The press wrote about the pitfalls of hastily signing MOUs with private parties without due process. In the industries department, officers were also not happy. I brought this to the notice of the CS, CM, and Minister Chandra Babu Naidu, but they insisted that the MOUs be signed as the deadline is approaching. I pointed out the pitfalls of the proposal and signing of the MOUs without due scrutiny.

Chandrababu Naidu insisted that the MOUs be signed as the Government had called for applications and should not back off from signing the MOUs especially when A.P. was having chronic power shortages. He appeared keen to speed up industrial and economic growth. I expressed my fears and views, but both the CM and NCB Naidu insisted that MOUs should be signed by midnight of the appointed date. I reluctantly agreed to do so on condition that the full Cabinet would authorise me to sign the MOUs and approve the action taken to sign the MOUs on behalf of the government. The Cabinet ratified the action taken by me as Special CS for industrial development. MS Rajaji, CS ensured that the cabinet approval and ratification of my action came within three days of the signing of the MOUs.

Though MOUs were signed by some local and external parties, only one MOU fructified. Spectrum Industries set up a 220 MW power plant based on natural gas from KG Basin at Kakinada, utilising Rolls- Royce technology. The project ran successfully and vindicated the signing of the MOU. Subsequently, some more gas-based power plants came up later.

But some plants had to close down operations due to inadequate availability or the high cost of gas.

CM's BID TO ATTRACT INDUSTRIES

The Chief Minister was keen to attract investments to speed up the industrialisation of A.P. He wanted to address captains of industry at the meetings of the FICCI, CII, All India Manufacturers Association, and other industry bodies at Delhi, etc., We used to prepare draft speeches, brief and accompany him to such meetings which evoked a great deal of interest about the infrastructure facilities, incentives, prospects, and opportunities in AP Several enquiries were received and some investments made in different sectors of the economy and particularly in the pharmaceutical, IT and services sector.

A local group, Rain Calcining Company's MD was from Hyderabad and educated in the US. He set up a CPC (Calcined Petroleum Coke) Plant at Visakhapatnam. The CM was scheduled to inaugurate the Rain Calcining plant and the iron ore Slurry pipeline from Bailadila to Visakhapatnam. Rain management hired a Boeing plane from Hyderabad to Visakhapatnam and back to carry the CM's party, officials, and guests. The CM inaugurated both projects and made a fervent appeal to set up plants in AP and utilise the Visakhapatnam Port facilities to start export- oriented and port-based industries.

Due to the drive to attract industries to A.P., several proposals were received. To scrutinise proposals at the Secretariat, I requested the Chief Secretary to forward names of bright young IIT and IIM passed officers to help me in the formulation of policies and scrutiny of proposals. Neerabh Kumar Prasad, who was an IIT-IIM graduate, and Harpreet Singh, another IIT-IIM graduate, joined the Industries Department. They were enthusiastic, eager to learn, and willing to work hard. We used to have intensive discussions on industrial policy, incentive schemes, and the pros and cons of proposals. We wanted to break the deadlock on the issue of multiple clearances and sanctions by the departments and organisations, leading to delayed decisions. We tried to make it easy to do business with the Government.

STATE INVESTMENT PROMOTION BOARD (SIPB)

After a series of discussions, we identified the need for a "Single-Window" for receipt and quick clearance of applications and issue of Government permissions and orders. We introduced the concept of "Ease of doing Business" with the Government by aiding and assisting aspiring entrepreneurs by providing them Escort Officers.

Our brain-storming sessions led to the conceptualisation and suggestion of setting up a **"Special Investment Promotion Board" (SIPB),** headed by the CM with the Chief Secretary or Special Chief Secretary as Secretary and concerned departmental secretaries from Industry, Energy, Forest, etc. and the Industrial Development Corporations involved and the Director of Industries as coordinating officer. The intention was to introduce a Single application, copies of which would be sent to the concerned departments to give their recommendations after preliminary examination within a period of 15 days. A consolidated note with issues raised by all concerned departments would be discussed in the State Investment Promotion Board. The government accepted this proposal, and the SIPB was set up. The process was further streamlined. Industrialists appreciated the initiative taken by the industries secretariat. NK Prasad and HP Singh did an excellent job operationalizing the SIPB system.

With the growing number of applications to set up industries, it became clear that Hyderabad was already attracting or likely to attract IT, pharma, chemical, engineering, medium, and small-scale industries in and around Hyderabad in view of its central location, availability of cheap land, good communications and proximity to important Centres like Chennai, Bengaluru, Pune, Mumbai, Vizag and Bhubaneswar, all within an hour's range by air and with good rail communications.

PORT DEVELOPMENT AND INDUSTRIAL CORRIDOR IN COASTAL ANDHRA

A.P had started exporting marine products, such as food grains, pig iron, fruits and vegetables, tobacco, meat, and beef. Fishing trawlers were operating in the Bay of Bengal. Prawns were raised in water ponds all along the shore for export.

Gujarat State had set up a "Maritime Board," which helped develop many small ports along the West Coast, leading to the location of large port-based factories for fertilizers, power plants, and Petrochemical industries. Many of them are export-oriented which led to a fast pace of industrialisation, employment, and economic development. The concept of port-led export development took a lot of time to materialise in A.P.

We mooted the idea that the Government should take the initiative to develop Ports – large, medium, and small – all along the coast at Bhavanapadu, Kalingapatnam, Bheemunipatnam, Gangavaram, Kakinada, Machilipatnam, Nizampatnam, and Krishnapatnam to facilitate both Coastal and Ocean shipping. Godavari Fertilizers had earlier proven the scope for the development of Krishnapatnam Port.

A.P. BECKONS INDUSTRY AS AN INDUSTRIAL DESTINATION

Coastal Andhra, with a high proportion of irrigated land, was the granary of paddy, crops, horticultural products, and marine exports. AP was a surplus area for grain, fruits, vegetables, fish, and milk. Chennai and Calcutta were the main consuming centres.

It was at the forefront of the Green (Agriculture-vegetables), White (milk), Blue (fish), Pink (meat), and Yellow (oil seeds). Revolutions. A lot more had to be done to improve Value Addition and earn export revenues.

INDUSTRIAL CORRIDOR PROPOSAL

The Grand Trunk Road from Chennai to Calcutta is the communication and connectivity spine of coastal Andhra. The Railway line and the Electricity grid run parallel to the Highway. The Yeleru Canal from Rajahmundry to Visakhapatnam could provide water and meet the basic requirements of industry like land, power, water, and communications by road and rail. Industries could be located all along the communication cum spine corridor - with easy access to water and a nearby port or future port. We prepared a concept note. The government appreciated the idea but did not take the initiative to set up the Maritime Board or give impetus to the Industrial Corridor idea. Much later, the idea crystallized, and the Chennai– Kolkata Industrial Corridor took shape. It teaches us that delayed action is progress postponed if not denied!

OIL AND NATURAL GAS

With the discovery of natural gas and oil in the KG Basin of the Bay of Bengal, the scope for developing gas-based Petrochemical industries near a suitable port was discussed. The Government set up a Committee under the Chairmanship of N B Prasad, TL Sankar, and me. We examined the scope and the prospects for the utilization of natural gas, laying of pipelines, and gas-based industrialization through the development of Refineries and the Plastics and Petrochemicals industry.

A.P. BECKONS AS AN INDUSTRIAL DESTINATION

In the race to attract industries, we visited Bengaluru, which was the hub for IT industries. Harinarayan, MD of APIDC, S.Subba rao, Chief Public Relations officer, and I went to Bengaluru to project to industrialists, scope and prospects for industries at Hyderabad and other places in A.P and our tailor-made incentives. We highlighted the fact of the central location of Hyderabad with a number of Universities, Research and Scientific organisations and National Institutes, including DRDO. Qualified and skilled engineers are available, and government support is assured. Our team visited Texas Instruments, which had set up an R&D Centre in Bengaluru for Software Technology Research Innovation and promotion. We gave presentations to Infosys, Wipro, and leading industries in the Software Technology Park of India (STPI) complex in Bengaluru. We called on N R Narayana Murthy of Infosys, who showed us around the Infosys plant in Bengaluru and agreed to consider setting up an office in Hyderabad if suitable land at a reasonable price is provided. We were happy with his assurance. He took us around the installation and explained the genesis of the company. He remarked that it has very little capital investment but a lot of human investment in his company. He jocularly mentioned that in the mornings, the value of his company was high, but late in the evening, after the IT engineers left for home, the value of the company would go down very sharply. We understood that it is the intellectual capital that was highly priced. In addition, we required organizational, marketing, and social capital to be successful.

INDUSTRIAL SICKNESS

A.P. was beset with the problems of growing sickness among medium- and small-scale industries, signs of deterioration in the maintenance of industrial estates, and the perfunctory functioning of some industrial development corporations. We noticed that the APSFC, which was a star performer, had started slipping with political interference and growing NPAs.

INDUSTRIAL ESTATES IN A.P.

We reviewed the position of Industrial Estates to improve their facilities and maintenance. We helped set up new industrial estates and took up the expansion of industrial estates like Nacharam and Kothur Industrial Estate. BS Pasricha, who was an M.D. of APIIC, provided invaluable assistance. Some initiatives for the development of renewable energy and restructuring of state-level undertakings were taken. A Committee was set up for this purpose. We encouraged CII, FAPPCI, FICCI, and AIMO to hold seminars and conferences to promote Industries. The CM and Minister for Industry played a leading role. We organized meetings with industrialists like Anand Mahindra, Murugappa Group, TVS, and Shriram Group. In one Meeting, the former P.M. of Israel, Ben Gurion, gave an inspiring speech about Israel's industrial development. As a result of one such meeting, Mahindra and Mahindra set up their vehicle factory at Zaheerabad, and some new industries came up. We had the satisfaction that Hyderabad was slowly getting recognized as an investment destination with an investor-friendly Government.

On the political front, troubles were brewing between the CM and his son-in-law, Chandrababu Naidu. Government officials were feeling uneasy and reluctant to take action, except in routine matters. The environment was surcharged, and political developments were uncertain. In the meantime, the Government of India promoted me to the rank of Secretary to the Government of India and posted me as CMD of Rural Electrification Corporation Limited, which was financing the State Electricity Boards for Rural Electrification schemes. I met the C.S. and CM and requested them to relieve me to join in Delhi. The CM reluctantly agreed to release me.

Though my tenure as Special Chief Secretary was very short, I had a lot of job satisfaction as it involved industrial planning and development and making A.P., a preferred destination for investment and economic growth, something close to my heart.

32

CMD, Rural Electrification Corporation and Chairman of SCOPE (Standing Conference of Public Enterprises) (June 1995 – July 1997)

I joined as Chairman and Managing Director of Rural Electrification Corporation (REC) in May 1995. MA Aziz, Technical Director, and Finance Director briefed me about the activities and issues in REC.

REC was established in 1969 as a fully-owned Government company. It was based on recommendations of the Rural Credit Survey Report headed by Dr. B Venkatappaiah, ICS, to finance State Electricity Boards, undertake rural electrification for pump-set energization to bring more area under irrigation and increase food production. Its main sources were funds from the government and plan schemes to promote Rural Electric Cooperatives. REC provided area-based planning and technical support to the SEBs for network design, distribution systems planning, and erection of distribution substations. It worked on standardizing equipment and construction practices' material specifications. It had 17 Project Offices in the states for providing technical support for and in coordination with SEBs.

RURAL ELECTRIC COOPERATIVES

It set up Rural Electric Cooperatives with the support of panchayats, rural institutions, and the involvement of local people to implement rural electrification schemes in limited areas with power supply from the SEBs. The Cooperatives helped bring down the cost of local schemes by providing voluntary labour and local help in the casting of cement poles and stringing of cables to the pump sets.

Central Institute for Rural Electrification (CIRE) was set up by REC at Hyderabad to provide training facilities for personnel of SEBs, RE Cooperatives, concerned departments, and banks. CIRE organized many training programs on rural electrification, technical developments, and standards for Indian and international participants from Africa, the Middle East, Indonesia, and South Asian countries. REC developed norms of cost, standardized the equipment, and advocated best practices and procedures. The vast rural electricity distribution network in India stands testimony to REC s' capability in planning, supervision and implementation.

REC had financed nearly 30,000 projects and provided electricity for pump-set energization to over 6 million pump-sets in 3, 20 ,000 villages. As REC loans were on relatively soft terms, they helped SEBs to implement projects in the States speedily and on a sound technical basis. Almost 80% of the RE works in the country were financed by REC. RE Cooperatives in 11 States of India had completed 100% pump-set energization and village electrification with local support in a limited area of operation. It appeared that, in some cases, its service was better than that of the regular SEB serviced areas.

LOAN REPAYMENTS LAGGING

Though REC was disbursing funds to the SEBs, the repayments were lagging, and arrears mounted. This constrained the REC from increasing the quantum of loans to speed up rural electrification. We realized that a financial review was necessary. We appointed two firms of Chartered Accountants to analyse the balance sheets of SEBs to ascertain their creditworthiness and ability to repay loans. The SEBs were graded to determine the extra allocation of funds to the better-run SEBs. We informed the SEBs that REC would note and reckon the quantum of dues paid by the SEBs and, as a bonus, increase, allocate, and release funds to them.

An internal study of the sources and mode of securing finances by Project Finance Corporation (PFC) and Indian Renewable Development Agency (IREDA) revealed that they had, in addition to government fund releases, tied up with World Bank and International financial organizations for long-term low-cost funds. They were also financing private sector parties for their development needs.

FINANCIAL TURN AROUND

We decided to speed up the evaluation of REC by the Overseas Economic Cooperation Fund (OECF) of Japan, which was willing to extend loans. After intense negotiations with them, we were able to secure a long-term Loan at low-interest cost, to be repaid over a period of 30 years. This helped us improve REC's financial position. The annual profit of the corporation, which was hovering in the range of Rs.17 to 19 crores, jumped up to Re 60 crores, wiping out accumulated losses. With the finances improving, we had temporary or short-term surpluses of money, which we deployed on overnight lending and other short-term lending. We did not wish to lose any interest as the amounts were large but for short periods. In the absence of digital transfer of money at that time, we had no alternative but to send an officer from REC headquarters to Mumbai with cheques by plane and place them as deposits with borrowers cleared by the RBI. We were later permitted to issue Bonds to which banks, LIC, and other institutions subscribed. We were also allowed to issue Taxable and Tax-free bonds, which helped us raise finances at a relatively low cost to meet growing demand.

REC- LENDING INCLUDED UNDER RIDF

The commercial banks were finding it difficult to get loan applications to fulfil their target of giving 30% of small loans to agriculture and rural development under stipulated norms. Working on the idea of getting REC loans included under the Rural Industrial Development Fund concept, we met the CMD of NABARD, P Kotaiah, who gave us good suggestions. We then discussed with C Rangarajan, then Governor of RBI, and his Executive Assistant YV Reddy. RBI included loans to REC by banks as part of RIDF disbursement. As a result, we received funding not only from the government but also from international agencies and banks. This paved the way for our financial turn-around. We also tried to help some SEBs who had physical assets by offering them Sale and Leaseback deal arrangements. MPEB made this available and opened up another financing channel to help SEBs.

RENEWABLE ENERGY INITIATIVES

Rural electrification through Renewable Energy sources in remote, inaccessible hill areas and river islands attracted our attention. The Ministry of New Energy Sources (MNES) was offering many incentives. IREDA had surplus funds and was willing to fund REC to finance renewable energy sources, subject to their standards of appraisal and evaluation of the profitability of the projects and suitability of the applicants. We agreed to follow their standards and took on deputation some officials from IREDA to set up a strong Appraisal division in REC. We also got in touch with the new Cooperative Renewable Energy Supplies Technical Association of the United States.

I had visited Australia earlier in connection with mineral development and had seen the development of renewable energy and its utilization. Australia has done a lot of work on solar and wind energy as well as hybrid systems supplemented by diesel sets to supply power in remote mining areas and resorts and to lift water from streams at low depths. They had also started putting rotating parabolic solar panels on vehicles to catch the sun as it moved from east to west, much like the sunflower always facing the sun. The Australian government, in its bid to popularize renewable energy sources, extended an invitation to me to present a paper on India's initiatives and that of REC at Sydney in Australia. This gave me an opportunity to learn about the latest developments taking place in Australia and in other countries that participated in the seminar. I had to meet many Indian professors working at Australian universities. I visited New Zealand and saw highly automated geothermal-based power plants.

This opened my eyes to the scope of development of renewable energy sources, be it water, solar, wind, or hybrid combination. REC wanted to take up experimental projects in Rajasthan, HP, Gujarat, and Tamil Nadu. We contacted General Electric, who expressed their interest in setting up a large 250 MW solar plant in Rajasthan, provided the land was allotted to them on a fairly long lease. They, however, expressed fears that dust and sand could pose problems in keeping solar cells clean. Tamil Nadu took the lead in setting up wind power mills with the assistance of Holland and Germany, which proved successful and met a substantial portion of their power needs. We also experimented with energy generation from irrigation canals by utilizing the low-speed flow of water without a good head by floating a centrifugal fiberglass contraption that could lift the water to a height of 30 feet. We tried some experiments to lift water to overhead filter tanks to provide drinkable water and the scope for generating power from lakes having sluice gate arrangements at varying heights.

To demonstrate the utility of tapping small hydel projects on a trial basis, we requested a company manufacturing small turbines to set up a 2 MW hydroelectric plant on the "Ita" river in Arunachal Pradesh close to Itanagar, its capital. This unit functioned well and provided power to Itanagar. This set the direction for HP and Sikkim to set up hydel projects on small rivers and perennial streams, which provided good head and scope for power generation for a long period every year.

STRENGTHENING THE BOARD OF DIRECTORS

P. Abraham, Secretary of the Ministry of Power, was helpful in pushing through the ideas of REC to bring about a change in the thinking, direction, and speed of adopting the latest world-class practices and methods.

We wanted to strengthen the Board of Directors to prepare a Vision and Mission Statement and to assess, evaluate, and support worthwhile projects. We enlisted the services of professors from IIT, IIM, concerned public sector undertakings, Central Electricity Authority, and Ms. Gayatri,

Joint Secretary, as the nominee of the Power Ministry. The Board proved invaluable and fully supported our initiatives.

CIRE UPGRADED

With many new proposals and technical improvements in the electricity domain, we decided to strengthen the Central Institute of Rural Electrification (CIRE) at Hyderabad to disseminate the latest knowledge and technical developments to personnel from SEBs, REC, and many developing countries. We enhanced the level of CIRE by bringing on deputation the Technical Director of APSEB Sugunakar Rao and a Professor of the Jawaharlal Nehru Technological University (JNTU), Radhakrishna. We recruited engineering, management, and science-oriented young officers in REC and sent the first batch to CIRE for a year's induction training. CIRE attracted participants from all SEBs, Power Sector undertakings, and foreign countries. We extended the lodging and boarding facilities to the participants. CIRE set up a Model Energy Park, which was inaugurated by Minister for Power Venugopalachari, who also participated in a Commonwealth Seminar on Rural Electrification.

The Central Board of Irrigation and Power (CBIP), which coordinates action between power and irrigation departments, extended assistance to SAARC countries like Nepal, Sri Lanka, Burma, and Bhutan for common benefits. India was interested in utilizing the hydel resources of Bhutan and Nepal, also extending technical assistance for power generation and buying surplus power. CBIP organized an International seminar at Kathmandu where I was requested to present a paper on the prospects of power development in the foothills of the Himalayas. It gave me an opportunity to visit Pashupatinath temple and call on King Mahendra and his wife. I felt that the joint development of hydroelectric sources all along the Himalayas would ensure the availability of surplus power and break bottlenecks of rail and road transport to the North-East.

MOUs WITH GOVT OF INDIA – FROM MINI RATNA TO MAHARATNA

The Central government introduced the system of Memorandum of Understanding (MOU) between the Government and Central Public Sector Undertakings in regard to mutually agreed targets of performance and Financial results. REC signed an MOU with the Power Ministry. For two years, the performance of REC was declared as "Excellent." In 1996, REC was made a "Mini Ratna" while larger profitable PSUs became Navaratnas. The disbursement of finances by REC, which was in the range of Rs. 500

crores crossed Rs.1000 crores, and profitability improved. REC is now a Maharatna Company!

Internal discussions in REC and CIRE indicated that rural electrifi cation had quickly picked up in Southern states and some Northern States like Punjab, Haryana, HP, Maharashtra, and Gujarat. But rural electrification was poor in UP, Bihar, MP, Orissa, West Bengal, and Assam. The BIMARU State's phenomenon was noticeable and had an impact on rural electrification.

REVIEW OF DEFINITIONS OF RE

The earlier definition of village electrification was based on the energization of at least one pump set in the village's revenue area. This was a misnomer as a village should be considered electrified only if the village had streetlights and at least a certain proportion of houses had electricity. Electrification was initially confined to the provision of power to some Harijan Bastis (HBs) and Girijanwadas, primarily for street lighting. The government introduced a scheme called Kutir Jyoti to provide at least one bulb in each Dalit house. Rural Electrification slowly moved its focus from pump-set energization to village electrification and household electrification.

Electricity had to be carried to remote, hilltop, and river island villages where the cost of transmission was very high, and demand was low. There was a need to develop localized electrification for such places. REC encouraged local entrepreneurs to set up Local Area Renewable Power arrangements through solar or wind power by providing technical and financial support.

UNBUNDLING OF GENERATION – TRANSMISSION AND DISTRIBUTION ARRANGEMENTS

The economic and financial reforms led to "the unbundling" of generation, transmission, and distribution arrangements, which were under the SEBs, to encourage private sector entry. The Orissa government was the first to unbundle and privatize some aspects of distribution. UP also tried to do so but without much success.

TECHNICAL DEVELOPMENTS

REC had developed expertise in planning for RE and helping SEBs in using appropriate equipment and transformers. The SEBs were beset with problems of high transmission and distribution losses due to voltage fluctuations, limited use of capacitors, and poor quality of cables and transformers, compounded by inadequate maintenance, repairs, and supervision. Small improvements in capacitors, transformers, and related equipment did not bring about noticeable or expected improvements. There was a lot of energy loss due to long distances and theft. All losses were conveniently ascribed to the free supply of power for agriculture and a lack of metering arrangements and norms. This had a deleterious effect on the quality of the electric supply and finances of SEBs. State governments fell in arrears to SEBs, compounding the problems.

SYSTEM IMPROVEMENT SCHEMES

SEBs wanted funding for System Improvement Schemes (SI), particularly for distribution and transmission. We realized that the costly power produced was disproportionately getting dissipated before it reached the consumer. Transmission losses were in the range of 30 to 40%. We wanted to rectify the situation by taking up a program for System Improvement, both in transmission and distribution. Many old systems had to be replaced by better systems and equipment. OECF agreed to fund specific proposals after appraisal if the latest diagnostics and technologies are used. As several transformers had to be replaced and new substations for 11KV and 33 KV set up, we realized that the cost would be high. They were willing to support a few special projects but wanted REC to fund the remaining work. We called a meeting of all the leading nationalized and private banks to seek their support by way of low-cost funding and, wherever possible, under the RIDF scheme to help us finance SI schemes of the SEBs. Luckily, since standards had been fixed and technical development had advanced, the banks agreed to finance REC. They also agreed to finance small hydel projects and small renewable energy projects. This changed the portfolio of the REC, which had now become a regular financier for small projects of non-SEB customers as well as many customers involved in unbundling of generation, transmission, and distribution. REC has extended its portfolio of assistance by financial-cum-technical appraisal of projects and is on the way to becoming a Development Agency and a Maharatna.

REC MOVES TO SCOPE COMPLEX IN DELHI

REC had sought and paid for accommodation in the SCOPE (Standing Conference of Public Enterprises) Complex building on Lodhi Road, which housed all central public sector undertakings and was allotted office space in Sector-Core-4. The SCOPE management had taken an extra interest in providing the office with good furniture and fixtures as I was Chairman of SCOPE. It was a stupendous task to carefully shift all files, records, and books from Nehru Place to the SCOPE building. The Chief Administrative Officer, Gp Capt. Capt. HG Dasari, with strong support from SS Nanda, PS Manchanda, and others, completed the task on schedule.

TRANSFORMER COMMITTEE

The Indian Transformer Manufacturers Association (ITMA) was pressing the Power Ministry to constitute a committee for transformer production and development. I was appointed as Chairman of the Transformer Committee, whose report was well received. It led to the development of amorphous metal core transformers and single-phase high-voltage distribution systems. The "fail-safe" transformers developed received good response from SEBs and users. Some of the progressive manufacturers produced high-quality amorphous metal core transformers and started exporting them to Bangladesh, Sri Lanka, and other countries. ITMA organized a large exhibition in Mumbai showcasing its latest electrical equipment and a spectacular display of transformers.

The **Planning Commission Group on Rural Electrification,** chaired by me, laid out plans for village and household electrification and expanded the scope for renewable energy development to supplement power from other sources. It helped provide power to difficult mountainous and remote areas.

INTERACTION WITH SEBs AND STATE GOVERNMENTS

I visited SEBs at Bengaluru, Chennai, Bombay, Jaipur, Lucknow, Calcutta, Bhubaneswar, and Chandigarh and Secretariat officials to ascertain requirements and understand their technical and administrative problems and to improve the collection of arrears.

BIHAR STATE ELECTRICITY BOARD

Bihar SEB had not paid REC dues for quite some time, and arrears were mounting. We received several complaints of misuse of REC funds, illegal draw of power from 11 KV feeders along the distribution lines and in towns and crowded places. Bihar wanted REC to continue funding even though they were most irregular in paying accumulated dues. REC sharply reduced funding to BSEB. The Chief Project Manager of REC at Patna requested me to visit Patna and take up the matter of payment of dues with the Bihar Power Secretary and Chairman of BSEB, as well as meet the Minister for Power and the CM to find a solution. The Secretary to CM Lallu Prasad spoke to me on the phone and requested me to visit Patna and call on the CM to find a solution to the impasse. I went to Patna, where our

CPM and Chief Engineer, BSEB, advised me to visit Vaishali and see the work done to carry power through a new distribution line. On the way, I found rampant and open theft of power by shopkeepers and house owners. Many households in small towns on the way had no meters. As the CE of BSEB was traveling in the same vehicle, I asked him why the BSEB was unable to stop such flagrant illegal tapping of power. I was told that subordinate staff of BSEB were assaulted when they tried to stop the theft of power. I understood their difficulties and the prevalent law and order situation.

BIHAR SECRETARIAT MEETING

I attended the meeting called at the Secretariat in Patna by the Chief Minister to discuss Rural Electrification funding in which the Power Minister, Power Secretary, and the Secretary to the CM were present. The CM began by accusing the government of India and REC of not giving funds to BSEB as they requested. I patiently heard his tirade and politely told him that the BSEB's large and mounting arrears of loans was a cause for concern. However, REC was still giving loans for schemes that were in progress and had released the requisite funds. REC had received disturbing news that funding provided to BSEB was diverted for other purposes. The CM took objection to my remarks and asked the Chairman BSEB about my remarks, and he asked his Chief Engineer to reply. The Chief Engineer said that some funds sanctioned by REC had been diverted for the purchase of 40 jeeps for use by other departments of the government. With this remark, the CM, the Power Minister, and the officers went silent.

CM then changed his tone and wanted me to sanction more funds as BSEB was in a dire situation. I offered to review the matter again, provided that some substantial amount of arrears had been paid. At this point, the secretary to the CM intervened to conclude the meeting, citing some other CM engagements. I requested that he send the minutes of the meeting for our records. The minutes did not come!

MEGHALAYA STATE ELECTRICITY BOARD (MSEB)

The Meghalaya State Electricity Board (MSEB) was supplying power to Assam SEB which was not paying dues because of a dispute about the quantum of the power provided. MSEB was in financial distress, and the officials' DA was frozen. The operational losses mounted while revenues declined. REC, a big lender to the Board for implementation of RE schemes was concerned. The Chairman of MSEB, V Jafa wanted the Assam state government to take over the responsibility of repayment. The Principal

Secretary to Government Ranjan Dutt, a tough officer, felt that repayment of loans was the responsibility of MSEB, which was receiving an annual grant-in-aid from the government, though it was a commercial organization. Due to the stalemate, it was REC that was not getting any loan repayments with the risk of the loans turning bad. This matter could spill over to the public domain, and press reports would cause avoidable embarrassment. I went to Shillong to resolve the impasse. As I was earlier in the Assam cadre, I knew both the Chairman and the Secretary. I met them separately and, later on, held a joint meeting and mediated, which softened their rigid stands, the issue was amicably sorted out, and repayments began.

KN Kumar, then Secretary of MSEB, in a later note, said, "I recalled with admiration how Gopalakrishna resolved the matter, first by meeting the two officers separately and later making them sit together; and arbitrated a solution that addressed everyone's concerns without ever lowering anyone's dignity or position. Hailing from the Assam cadre, Gopalakrishna knew both the officers as his junior colleagues in the IAS and they respected him so much that they had no option but to soften their rigid stands. I was an eyewitness to the subtle persuasion and the sense of humour with which he sorted out not just the issue but the large egos of people in high positions. "A matter that simmered for almost six months and was threatening to become a public controversy was fixed amicably because of the sheer strength of Gopalakrishna's personality. It was a textbook lesson for a young IAS officer, and I realised that I was watching the Master in action. It was an art that people like me can only watch in awe and admiration and try to learn but probably can never master".

MINISTER'S VISIT TO ANDHRA PRADESH

The Minister of State for Power, Mrs. Urmila C. Patel, wanted to visit a Rural Electric Cooperative to understand people's participation in development work and how people's support for rural electrification could be mobilized. I accompanied her from Hyderabad to visit the Cooperative Electric Supply Society (CESS) at Sircilla in the Karimnagar District. Mrs. Chitra Ramachandran, IAS, accompanied us on behalf of the AP government. The Minister inaugurated and switched on the connection to a newly installed pump and power connection to a residence at Sircilla. At the request of the public in Sircilla for additional funds, we commissioned a study on RE Cooperatives by the Administrative Staff College of India (ASCI), which submitted its report giving useful suggestions. We sanctioned a special grant of Rs 5 crores to the Sircilla CESS cooperative.

We visited the Vemulawada Raja Rajeshwara Swamy temple for Darshan. J Chokka Rao, the former Minister, was the Chairman of the Temple Trust Board. Mrs. Urmila Patel was received with temple honours and was presented with Prasad, a shawl, and a saree. I was given temple honour. As my wife did not accompany me, I requested Chitra Ramachandran to receive the saree they had arranged for my wife. Chitra told me that it proved advantageous to be in the entourage of a senior Officer as she had received a saree with God's blessings!

MEETING OF PRIME MINISTER WITH CMs – POWER SUPPLY TO AGRICULTURE

The Power Ministry and Planning Commission were concerned that free power without metering was being given for agricultural purposes which would, in the long run, dent the finances of the State governments and SEBs. The Prime Minister, Mr. Deva Gowda, presided over a high-power committee meeting attended by Chief Ministers who were asked to give their views. Except for a couple of CMs who wanted to meter electricity to prevent misuse, ensure conservation, and ensure efficiency, all other CMs wanted free electricity for agricultural purposes. If leakages in distribution and transmission are plugged, the provision of free electricity for agriculture will become manageable. In the case of financially weak states, the Finance Commission could make special allocations. The PM appeared to be dozing when the CMs were speaking, but he was very alert as he responded appropriately and correctly to the questions posed. However, there was no consensus, and no decision was taken; the meeting served as an alibi that the matter was under consideration. Lots of talk and activity but no action!

INTERNATIONAL CONFERENCES

REC organized many international seminars on rural electrification, Renewable energy resources, energy conservation, and efficiency in Hyderabad, Bangalore, Chandigarh, and Mumbai. REC was invited for presenting papers in Australia, Sydney, and Perth. The United Nations Development Program (UNDP) and World Bank held seminars and invited REC to participate in a seminar at Marrakesh in Morocco. UNDP advised developing nations in Africa to seek advice and assistance from India to develop renewable energy resources and speedily lay transmission and distribution lines.

PUBLIC RELATIONS

To improve public relations and spread the message of REC under the "Electricity for All" campaign, we issued many leaflets in different languages with relevant information on rural electrification. The annual reports got a new look with lucid text and photographs. A documentary film was made on the activities of REC and its role in bringing light (Ujwal) to millions of homes. Computerization was introduced, and the staff was trained to speed up decisions and computation for evaluation purposes.

CYCLONE IN AP – SCOPE PROVIDES ASSISTANCE

A severe cyclone on the East Coast in November 1996 caused unprecedented damage and havoc in coastal Andhra Pradesh with heavy flooding. Venugopalachari, Minister of State in the Power Ministry, wanted Central PSEs to contribute their mite for the relief and rehabilitation of cyclone victims, restoration of communications, and provision of food. Some companies in the power sector had already donated a day's pay to the employees for cyclone relief. The Executive Committee of SCOPE requested all Central PEs to donate a day's wage towards the cause. There was a spontaneous and good response. A large amount was collected and handed over to N. Chandrababu Naidu, CM of AP at Delhi.

RECOGNITION AND AWARDS

Due to the collective efforts of all REC employees, our efforts in the turnaround of REC were recognized. I received the CITD Award for Excellence from Prime Minister Manmohan Singh. I received an Award from the Central Board of Irrigation and Power from Shankersinh Vaghela, the then CM of Gujarat, and the Best Finance Manager Award from the National Federation of Engineers (NAFEN) in Delhi.

33

As Chairman of SCOPE – Spokesman of the Public Sector

The Standing Conference of Public Enterprises (SCOPE) is the apex body of 246 Central public sector undertakings under the Government of India. It sorts out Inter-Public sector issues and brings problems and issues of the public sector to the notice of the Bureau of Public Enterprises and concerned Ministries for support and redressal of grievances. It is funded by membership contributions from the CPSEs. MA Hakim, a senior retired officer from the Food Corporation of India, was the Secretary General of SCOPE, who was competent and had good contacts.

AS VICE CHAIRMAN

AC Wadhavan, CMD of Hindustan Zinc Limited, was the Chairman of SCOPE. He met me when I was CMD of REC in 1995 and told me the post of Vice-Chairman in SCOPE was vacant and elections would be held soon. The Executive Committee of SCOPE was of the view that as I had been MD and CMD of State Level Public Enterprises in Assam and Andhra Pradesh and now as CMD in Central Public Sector Enterprises, I would be a suitable choice as Vice-Chairman, Wadhawan requested me to accept the post. I was formally elected as Vice-Chairman of SCOPE.

The term of Wadhawan as Chairman of SCOPE was expiring, and elections had to be held. There was consensus among the Public Enterprises (PEs) that the election of a CMD IAS officer as Chairman would help SCOPE at a time when dis-investment of PSEs was on the anvil. I was elected unanimously as Chairman and received congratulatory messages from the PSEs of Assam and AP as the first Telugu person to hold the post.

The SCOPE office and REC office were in the SCOPE complex. I used to walk across from REC to the SCOPE office and attend to the myriad problems of PSEs. We also had requests from state-level PEs for help and assistance. PEs had many vacancies at the CMD, Functional Directors, and senior executive levels. Financial allocations were inadequate, and the Damocles sword of closure was hanging on PEs. Press reported that the government would close loss-making PSEs or resort to heavy retrenchment of staff through voluntary retirement schemes. There was an air of fear and despondency among the sick and loss-making units. The Memoranda of Understanding of PEs with the government on performance parameters and targets was pitched high and did not consider relevant factors and difficulties.

THE FEARSOME FOUR 'C'S

The profitable PEs did not have requisite autonomy and were unable to take quick decisions and respond to market needs. PEs were apprehensive and hesitant to take action due to the four fearsome Cs - Comptroller and Auditor General (CAG), Central Vigilance Commissioner (CVC), Committee on Public Sector Undertakings (COPU), and Central Bureau of Investigation (CBI). To allay their fears, we called a meeting of all PEs in SCOPE, which was addressed by VK Shunglu (my batch mate), then the Comptroller and Auditor General of India. He addressed the PEs about the functions of the CAG. In the context of globalization, he said PSEs would have to integrate Indian accounting standards with international standards. He assured CEOs that he would review hard audit cases brought to his notice and see that time is given for corrective action and justice is done.

VIGILANCE CONFERENCE

We organized a 3-day conference on vigilance, which N Vittal, then Vigilance Commissioner addressed. Vigilance officers from State and Central PSEs and banks frankly expressed their views and fears about taking decisions, hence the practice of remitting decisions to committees. KV Natarajan, then Vigilance Commissioner of AP, gave the valedictory address. The Secretary General of Lok Sabha addressed SCOPE officials about COPU (Committee on Public Undertakings) and broad linkages between PEs and Parliament. CBI officials spoke about their investigative and prosecution work and that without evidence, they would not file cases or make undue arrests.

SPRINGBOARD INITIATIVE

Women's representation in PSEs was gradually increasing, but adequate facilities for them were not provided. No programs have been developed to understand women's problems, quickly solve them, and motivate them to perform well. They complained of inadequate maternity leave, chances of promotion, and career advancement. They encountered the 'glass ceiling' in opportunities, promotions, and career advancement.

SCOPE's worldwide search for the best Women's Development Program zeroed in on the UK's program called **'Springboard'**. It was pioneered by Liz Willis and Jenny Daisley, two highly-rated trainers who had conceptualized and implemented the program with resounding results. SCOPE selected eight women from different sectors of PSEs and deputed them for two months of training in the UK. In return, they shared their experiences in their own PE and other PEs. They also trained 220 women executives in a two-month program. The program's objective was to raise confidence levels, camaraderie with fellow women, time management, social interaction, work-life balance, and competence building. Requisite course material like a workbook for 3 months was supplied, and their reactions were recorded. It yielded very good results. We received many requests to extend the program. We held a seminar on the Springboard Women's' Development Program, which Mrs. Sarala Gopalan addressed, then Secretary of Women and Child Welfare Development. Smt. Najma Heptullah, Vice-Chairman of Rajya Sabha, graced one Springboard Women's Program. This program proved useful and was later extended to State-level PEs, thanks to the efforts of Central Public Enterprises and the Public Enterprises in the States.

WIPS (WOMEN IN PUBLIC SECTOR)

The Springboard Women's Program enthused women employees to set up an Association called Women in Public Service (WIPS). Some women CMDs like Dr Reena Ramachandran, supported by lady officers Anjali Hazarika and others, enrolled many women employees and extended their sway. We organised a conference at SCOPE, which was inaugurated by Minister for Women and Child Welfare, Mrs. Margret Alva, who gave the valedictory address.

REPORT ON GOOD GOVERNANCE

SCOPE wanted to promote good governance in the public sector and commissioned a study by Dr YRK Reddy, then Professor at the Administrative Staff College of India. We published a booklet providing the current status of Governance in PEs, which recognized that providing good governance was an essential tool for securing public cooperation and better performance. In fact, this was the pioneering effort at governance in the public sector, which, at that point in time, was ahead of the corporate sector.

SCOPE AND ILO (INTERNATIONAL LABOUR ORGANISATION)

The public sector in India was the **'largest employer'**. The International Labour Organisation recognized SCOPE as a prime representative of employers in India. Labour standards were issued by ILO, which, if accepted by nations, become national labour standards. Labour organizations like INTUC, AITUC, HMS, represented the labour component. The Chairman of SCOPE, who represented the employer component, attended annual meetings of the International Labour Organisation in Geneva.

I attended the International Labour Organization Conferences in Geneva, where views on labour-related legislation in India and measures taken to improve conditions of labour and work were discussed. Due to varying levels of literacy and the nature of employment, countries were allowed leeway to follow national standards and raise them to international standards. Attempts were made to improve living wage, hours of work, health facilities, and retirement benefits. The practice of child labour other than in agriculture, cottage industries, and family occupations peculiar to India was discouraged and penalized. All issues were discussed, and decisions were made based on consensus. It was an eye-opener on the conditions of labour in different parts of the world and the process of decision-making on a universal basis. My stay in Geneva enabled me to visit the World Health Organisation and its museum, which effectively portrayed developments in the health sector.

SCOPE organized a seminar on international labour standards in New Delhi and Bengaluru, while ILO held a seminar at Shimla.

SCOPE held the 18th Industrial Relations Conference at Bengaluru, which representatives from all state and central public sector undertakings in South India attended. Representatives from ILO and the Labour Ministry addressed the gathering. Union Labour Minister M Arunachalam inaugurated the conference while I gave the keynote address.

STATE OF PES

The Government was considering a major revamp of the public sector. It wanted to close many loss-making PEs and privatize some of the profit-making PEs. This created concern among the PEs. SCOPE sought their views on the proposed changes. The SCOPE team visited Calcutta and held a full-day discussion. Their difficulties primarily arose from the supply-demand gap, outdated machinery, a large aging workforce, low productivity, and decreasing marketability. Market preferences also changed.

We visited Chennai, where the major complaint was regarding the closure of the Indian Surgicals plant, which could open the floodgates of surgical implements imports. This was compounded using Russian technology, whose standards and equipment sizes differed from those of the US and other international standards. In Bengaluru, many of the industries were in the defence, power, or electronics sectors. They appeared confident with good orders and were doing well. However, Bharat Gold Mines was sick, and Hindustan Machine Tools (HMT) and Indian Telephone Industries (ITI) were also ill. We visited Bombay, Ahmedabad, Bhopal, and Jaipur and ascertained their problems and issues.

HELP TO INDIAN TELEPHONE INDUSTRIES (ITI)

ITI was not doing well, and the Government was considering its closure or sale to the private sector. The CM, an Air Force officer, requested SCOPE to bail them out of their difficulties. The Planning Commission and Arjun Sengupta, Member, were sympathetic to the cause of public sector units. I called on Arjun Sengupta and explained the situation. He agreed to visit Bengaluru with me to understand the problems faced by I.T.I. and suggest suitable action. We showed him around the factory and discussed its problems. Sengupta understood the issues and, in return, allocated additional funds to I.T.I., which turned around and, after that, performed well.

DISINVESTMENT COMMISSION (DIC)

The Government, in a bid to reduce losses and sell off some P.E.s, set up the Dis-investment Commission (D.C.) with G.V. Ramakrishna, a highly regarded Secretary and former Member of the Planning Commission, as its Chairman. He was Chief Secretary of A.P. and also Chairman of Godavari Fertilizers and Chemicals Ltd when I was the Managing Director. We held many internal meetings in SCOPE with leading C.M.D.s like Raghavan of BHEL, Pandey of SAIL, and CMD of NTPC, R.E.C., NALCO, R.C.F., SCOPE representatives besides brain-storming sessions to formulate the views of SCOPE, to be presented to the D.I.C. I drafted the SCOPE report for the Disinvestment Commission. We also presented the SCOPE's views on disinvestment to the D.C. in November 1996. Our report was appreciated for its clarity, presentation, and suggestions. The Report identified the problems faced by P.E.s by quoting extensively from other reports.

An analysis of the performance of P.E.s indicated that 130 PEs, which constituted about 50% of P.E.s, had earned a profit of Rs. 72,000 crores, while 109 enterprises had incurred a loss of Rs.49, 000 crores. Article 12 of the Constitution of India considers P.S.E.s as the State, which proves a constraint for making decisions on a commercial basis and is subject to Writ jurisdiction. Our memorandum quoted the views of the Committee on Public Undertakings of Lok Sabha, which said, "P.S.E.s suffer from over-direction and over-control by the government choking creativity of management at all levels". We highlighted that autonomy helps decision-making and builds work culture, competitiveness, productivity, and profitability.

HOLDING COMPANY FOR CPSEs

We suggested setting up a Holding Company or sector-wise holding companies to keep the government at arm's length but enforce accountability. In the case of the sick industry, the scope for performance contracting could be considered in addition to top-level changes. We suggested grading of sick industries on objective criteria to determine whether there was scope for their turn-around and revival before selling. The idea of selling profitable units or shares was criticized by a section of the press saying that the Government, which had nationalized private banks, was now resorting to selling its house silver.

SCOPE CALLS ON PRIME MINISTER

I led the SCOPE team to call on Prime Minister Deva Gowda and presented the memorandum on behalf of the P.E.s to him. He patiently listened to us and said that the government would await the views of the Disinvestment Commission before taking a decision. He said that the government would meanwhile institute "Excellence Awards" for P.S.E.s doing outstanding work.

PERFECT HEALTH MELA

PEs working in the pharmaceutical and drug sector wanted to hold a Perfect Health Mela with a SCOPE pavilion. IDPL displayed the drugs they manufactured and the support they gave to budding entrepreneurs for setting up units based on active ingredients and basic molecules they produced. This highlighted the need and led to the development of the Pharma industry in India. Hindustan Latex India displayed a range of goods, including condoms, pessaries, etc. Justice AM Ahmadi, Chief Justice of India, and the actor Raj Babbar inaugurated the Mela.

A conference on "Public Relations in the Public Sector - Changing Paradigms" was held in June 1996 to project a positive image of the public sector and motivate P.R. personnel and P.E.s to use and utilize the services of Door Darshan and All India Radio to good effect.

KALEIDOSCOPE – A PEEK VIEW OF THE PUBLIC ENTERPRISES

SCOPE was publishing a monthly magazine, "Kaleidoscope," which covered information on developments in the public sector and events conducted by PSEs. It carried articles and information about industrial trends all over the world and became the medium for fostering contacts between and among the Central and State level P.S.E.s. It published a Special issue on the public sector in July 1996, which is a prized copy.

34

What I Learned in the IAS

The Constitution of India provides for All India Services like the Indian Administrative Service (IAS), Indian Police Service (IPS), and Indian Forest Service (IFS), to advise the political executive and provide good governance and administration in the country. They help bring about uniform systems of management and governance throughout the country and serve people by raising their socio-economic standards and cultural growth.

The All India Services officers are recruited after a tough All India Civil Services Examination conducted by UPSC. It tests their intellectual abilities, personality, attitudinal and behavioural traits, and suitability. The civil services of India are considered among the best in the world. Though recruited centrally, officers are allotted to state cadres and serve in states in which they are borne and belong. They also serve in the Government of India whenever called upon to do so. This arrangement links and brings their field knowledge and expertise to both governments, the Centre and State, in policy-making, implementation, review, and evaluation processes. It helps provide good governance throughout the country.

MOTIVATION TO JOIN THE IAS

My maternal uncle, IJ Naidu, was an II World War recruit army officer and was selected to IAS in 1944. My mother would constantly hold him up as a role model and motivate me to study well and join the IAS. I appeared for the IAS examination in 1961 and was selected for the 1962 batch at the age of 22 years.

I served in the IAS in the Government of Assam for 12 years, AP Government, and in the Central Government for 12 years, a total period of 36 years, before retiring at the age of 58 years in 1997.

I had earlier served for one and half years in the Andhra Pradesh Government as Probationary Deputy Collector and Revenue Divisional Officer at Guntur. Almost four decades of my life were spent serving the nation and the people of India in various places, posts, and fields of activity.

From "CAN I DO" to "I CAN DO"

Service engenders a positive feeling of capability to understand and work in any entrusted job. Officers begin with many doubts about themselves and their tasks. The most important among them is the question, "Can I Do It"? This often puts one away from doing something important. One has to steel oneself and move towards a positive attitude of "I Can Do It." This switch over from "*Can I Do*" to "*I Can Do*" calls for a great deal of determination, self-confidence, planning, and concentration. It also calls for a good deal of cooperation and coordination of several persons involved in accomplishing a task.

THUMB AS THE LEADER OF TEAM WORK

The best example of leadership that one can think of is your hand and the fingers of your palm. In India, we believe that each finger represents one of the five elements or *Pancha Bhutas* - different elements and personalities. The Little finger represents water '*Jal*' and has a clinging tendency. It feels like the smallest finger and solicits the support of other fingers. The next is the Ring finger, representing Earth. All wealth comes from the earth *'Prithvi.'* This finger, no wonder, likes an adornment, like a ring. The next finger, which is the Middle finger, is the tallest. It represents '*Akash*' or sky. It expects all others to respect it. The index finger, '*Vayu*' or air, has the habit of pointing out other persons' mistakes. The Thumb is not handsome; it is short and stout, and no ring adorns it. It represents fire, '*Agni*,' the fire in your belly, your passion. This helps sustain your energy at your job and achieve your objectives. It has the great advantage of being able to touch, coordinate, and get all fingers to cooperate. It is also the strongest finger and is used for thumb impressions. When all fingers cooperate with the thumb, it becomes a strong fist and shows great determination and strength. When the thumb is up, it conveys success; when it is down, it means that you have not done your best. The palm and the fingers together represent cooperation and coordination. In *'Abhaya'* mudra, the palm can protect you. In '*Varada*' mudra, it can bestow benefits. Throughout service, you have to remember the importance of teamwork, in which the Thumb is the leader who brings about teamwork. One has to work like the thumb to become the leader.

A GOOD CAREER

The IAS examination is considered very tough as it is a test in many subjects of confidence, competence, and, more importantly, personality. It provides for a meaningful, satisfying and good career with many opportunities to serve people and for personal growth. It is a wholesome, life-long learning experience. I had the good fortune to serve in two states, Assam and Andhra Pradesh, and the Union government, which provided me with the opportunity to serve in the districts, to tour all over India and abroad to negotiate technology transfer, seek foreign investments, prepare policy papers and formulate or assist in the preparation of the Mineral and Energy policies of the Union Government.

ETHICS AND VALUES- PILLARS OF THE SERVICE

The purpose of any 'service' is to serve – the poor and the needy. Service is called SEVA – I interpret and liken S – for Selfless Service, E - for Empathy, V - for Voluntariness, and A - for Attentiveness in the service of people and nation. I tried to adhere to this philosophy in service and life.

The IAS for me is to be ***"Indian"*** in outlook and delivery of services, provide ***"Administration"*** with good governance, ethics and eternal values of India, and render **Service** as a means to selflessly serve and try to wipe as many tears as possible.

I held many jobs in my career -- in the government, regular assignments after retirement, consultancy, chairmanships of committees, and President of many NGOs. I can tell you that there was never a dull day, nay, or even a dull moment in my career, service, and life. I experienced immense joy in small successes in tasks done and the help given to people. It was an unending lifelong saga of learning. It bestowed and imparted saleable management skills. Those skills proved invaluable and gave me post-retirement jobs in the public sector and later in other public limited corporate directorships.

The man management skills that an IAS officer gains in service stand by him all through life. They provide a 360° perspective of events and prioritisation of issues and solutions.

In the eyes of the public, an IAS officer is looked upon as a person who can be entrusted with difficult jobs and can be counted on to find practical solutions. It is up to the officers to live up to the reputation and expectations of the common man – the Aam Aadmi. As one faces various situations, one learns stoic calmness and the ability to respond appropriately.

It is the classic example of "*Nityam Adhiyanah*", or continuous learning. The expectations of people instils self-confidence, a sense of purpose and Duty- consciousness. It changes one's mind set – from a doubtful **"Can I Do"** to a confident **"I Can Do".** Three powerful words or the mantra, *I CAN DO*, are self-motivational. With deep thinking, discussions, debate, and dialogue, coupled with determination, discipline, dedication, and delegation, any difficult task can be easily performed.

One realises that yoga is excellence at work. Yoga is equivalent to linking thought with action, resulting in excellence, efficiency, and effectiveness. It encourages *Praveenyam* or proficiency, *Kausalyam* or efficacy, and leads to *Saphalyam* or accomplishment. The Bhagavad Gita says, *"YOGA KARMASU KAUSHALAM*", which is the motto of the IAS. However, for an IAS officer, being a *Karma Yogi* is not adequate. He has to be a *Bhakti Yogi* or *Jnana Yogi*, as the situation demands. He has to be *a Raja Yogi* or King Philosopher and rule like King Janaka by combining the correct proportion of *Gnana* (knowledge), *Bhakti* (faith and devotion) and *Karma* (purposeful action) to gain public approval. A *Karma Yogi* is selfless, honest, accountable, objective, and open-minded, with integrity besides leadership qualities. In addition, he is truthful, trustworthy, transparent, tolerant, and, above all, tactful. He must have such tact that he stays out of trouble, but if he gets into trouble, he knows how to get out of it quickly!

Appropriate training, guidance and mentorship as a probationer under a competent collector (master) and district-level exposure make one confident and resilient. It builds 'coordinative' skills, the hallmark of a generalist who can decipher the needs and priorities and take the best possible action with available resources. In the past, an IAS officer was considered mature if he had held the post of a district collector or head of a department and had some Secretariat exposure. The positions cover the essentials of administration, coordination, specialisation, policy formulation, and evaluation. There is, however, criticism that an IAS officer is a "jack of all trades but master of none". Managing "men and matters and men who matter" is probably mastering all trades and the masters!

IAS bring "clarity" in priorities to set goals, define people's roles, prescribe paths to be taken, mobilise resources, and achieve results. IAS officers, because of their past experience, man-management skills, and coordinating ability, excel in crisis and disaster management. Maintaining good relationships is a necessary skill, but his word must be as good as his act. IAS officers should always remember what the Chandogya Upanishad says,

"Yadeva Vidyaya Karoti,
Shraddhaya, Upanishada
Tadeva Viryavattaram Bhavati"

That which is done with "full knowledge" like *Do why, Do what, Do when, Do where*, with Faith in the cause and one's ability and taking into Consideration, attendant circumstances within and outside, leads to excellence of the highest degree.

In the course of my long career and association with professional organisations and NGOs, I received many commendations, awards, and rewards. However, I consider that the best reward in my long career and service was that I did not get any adverse remarks (love letters) or memos from the Government about any lapses in my performance of duties! Some of the jobs to which I was posted were difficult, dangerous, and fraught with risk to life and limb and had to be achieved with inadequate resources, guidance, and support. As a conscientious officer, I did my best and never expected recognition or reward. My work probably spoke for itself. Hence, no adverse remarks were communicated!

It is for the discerning readers to judge whether I was competent, upright, and conscientious in performing my duty.

The charms, challenges, trials, and tribulations in service, its status, and the esteem in which it is held are what attract young civil service aspirants from different disciplines for varied careers and memorable experiences. When I was young, I was outspoken and called a spade a spade – With experience, I have mellowed. Better known as a good speaker, I have now evolved into a listener and a life-long learner.

The service enabled me to handle difficult assignments in the national interest, which built my reputation as a man for all seasons. I gained expertise in law and order management and in the promotion, regulation, and development of industries with "hands-on" experience in steel, fertiliser, finance, energy, minerals, and metals sectors. That experience helped me gain the reputation of a capable CMD, Director and a **"turn- around"** expert. This opened up independent Directorships in listed companies and the corporate sector. And not least, many friends, well- wishers, and senior officers moulded me by smoothening my rough edges. I express my gratitude to Chief Secretaries of Assam and Andhra Pradesh, Secretaries to the Union Government and the many colleagues and staff with whom I worked and learned the skills of administration and man-management. Duty and Service were my fellow travellers in life's journey, and all my family members, particularly my mother and wife, played a central role. My mother was my "GURU", infusing courage and a "never say die" attitude. My wife, with patience and fortitude, has stood by me in all our tribulations.

My only regret is that I could not pursue my Ph.D. But some organisations in Hyderabad persist in addressing or referring to me as "Dr", presumably because of my speeches and erudition. Public recognition exists, though the law and universities do not acknowledge it. I hope to do my Ph.D, God willing.

In the course of my service, I acquired many epithets. Some of my batch mates in the service would address me as 'Gopal' or 'Muddusetty'. In Assam, I was known as Naidu or Nayudu. In Mizo Hills, MG Naidu meant "Machine-Gun" Naidu. In AP, I was Godavari Gopalakrishna. In my hometown, Bellary, friends and relatives know me as Gokul. As I grew old, the honorific "garu" was added to my name.

I am considered a good speaker, capable of speaking on a variety of subjects and can hold the attention of the audience. Due to the goodwill of many friends, I was invited to give lectures for students, colleges, management institutions, and public and private sector companies, as well as at convocations and memorial lectures. I have given over 1200 lectures, of which 60 lectures have been earmarked for publication, consisting mainly of talks on ethics and values, management, fertilisers, energy, minerals, etc. I hope to publish them shortly.

Names are given to identify persons, encourage them to cultivate their good qualities, remember their ancestors or pedigree or delineate their oddities or uniqueness. It is sometimes their nickname or assumed name, as in the case of several cinema actors and film stars. The names are sometimes confused when more than one person in the extended family or locality has the same or nearly the same name. In my case, in my hometown, there were 3 boys named Gokul – one was Cowl Bazaar Gokul, one was Kodagal Gokul, and I was Bungalow Gokul.

Similarly, Gopalakrishna is a common name - There was an M. Gopalakrishnan who was Chairman of Bharatiya Vidya Bhavan School in Hyderabad. Since admission to prestigious schools like Bharatiya Vidya Bhavan (BVB) in Hyderabad was regulated, there was a big rush to contact the chairman of BVB, M Gopalakrishnan IAAS, whose calls would come to me. I could assess the pressure for admissions in the school from the number of calls received.

Another Gopalakrishnan was an IAS officer (1954) of the AP cadre. He worked as Deputy Director at Lal Bahadur Shastri National Academy of Administration and in the AP Secretariat. On some occasions, his salary would be credited to my bank account, making me wonder whether I had received a raise or a promotion! Within a couple of days, I would get a call from the bank manager of my service namesake about the wrong credit and that I need not daydream about windfall credit or accelerated DA payment. In rural areas – persons were identified by name like fair Ramappa's son, dark Thimmappa or Thin Rangappa's son, stout Veerappa and the like or such and such mothers' son - This simple, graphic and easy method to remember names and persons has now become impersonal Aadhar Number Difficult to remember or reproduce! Has the purpose of the name been Forgotten? Or that names do not count, and only numbers count now.

35

Thoughts on Retirement

I retired on 31st January 1997, at the age of 58, after serving Government for 37 years. Retirement is a time for reflection on what life gave and taught me. My family rejoiced that I had returned home for a well-earned rest. In life, there are moments of elation, joy, happiness, as well as hopelessness due to the inability to rectify wrongs as swiftly as one would like. Government and public sector service provided ample opportunities to tour within the country and abroad. It opened my eyes to the need for India to rapidly gain economic strength. The global impact that the Indian diaspora is making throughout the world is a matter of pride. Active, relatively young, and in good health, I pondered, "What next?" I did not have to wait long as I received unsolicited offers of employment. I chose to join the Institute of Public Enterprise (IPE) as Director.

I am fortunate to have a loving, sharing, and caring family, personal staff, and domestic help. Their motto is "one for all and all for one." In the family, "Ek is Anek" and "Anek is Ek". There were times of deep despair when I lost my mother, foster mother, brothers, and sister, and moments of joy when children did well and received awards or approbation. From self-improvement and development (Swahita) one moves to (Sarva Jana Hitha) or Universal welfare. Individualism must become universalism.

There was never a dull moment as I tried to update, upgrade, and uphold ethics and values. Maintaining a diary, time management, and a lifestyle with yoga and exercise has kept me healthy and active. I had four near-death experiences akin to escaping from the jaws of death. There's probably still work for me to do.

Government pays scales and pensions have been periodically revised upwards. Old age is now given due credit with age-related increases in pension. Many pensioners now receive more pay than when they were in service!

The political bug bit me; I contested as an independent candidate for the MLC Graduates Constituency of Hyderabad–Mahbubnagar and lost. I drafted manifestos for a political party.

My tenure in the Government and Corporate sector strengthened my belief in truth, trust, transparency, teamwork, and good governance. I was associated with several professional, sporting, and social Service organisations. It was like transitioning from receiving awards to judging and presenting Awards. Thanks to my speaking and motivational skills, my past networks revived, became diverse, and expanded. Aspirants for UPSC examinations flocked to seek guidance, motivation, and mentoring. I realised that 'listening' is essential to understand and resolve the problems of students seeking a career in Civil Service. I love teaching, coaching, and mentoring students and candidates for UPSC, APSSC, and TGPSC Class-I examinations, and conducting Mock interviews. Coaching institutions and candidates sought my guidance. To do so, I update myself on current events and trends, requiring me to study like a candidate.

Friends have advised me to write my autobiography-cum-memoir covering seven decades of my life.

36

What Life has taught me?

Born in the 20th century, I have welcomed the 21st century as a witness to tumultuous changes in political, economic and social fields. I participated in India's first Independence Day at a simple ceremony at school, saw the lowering of the British flag and raising of the Indian Tricolour amidst claps of students, singing of the national anthem and a chorus of Jai Hind. I saw the ceremony but understood its significance much later. I played a small part in conveying its import, message and impact on the hopes and lives of its people.

REORGANISATION OF STATES

Nearer home, the States Reorganization Commission under Fazl Ali and Justice Mishra Committee reports bifurcated Bellary district. The three taluks of Adoni, Aler, and Rayadurgam formed part of Kurnool and Anantapur districts in the newly created Andhra state on 1st October 1953. The remaining taluks, including Bellary city, became part of Mysore state. Sporadic agitation by the Telugu population of Bellary city for the merger of Bellary taluk with Andhra state fizzled out due to the large number of Kannada-speaking population in the rest of the District.

CONSEQUENT CHOICES

Many relatives who were army, police or government officials and their families faced the dilemma of choosing where to go based on job and economic prospects in the future. There were four options – (1) Remain in Bellary in Mysore state, (2) Seek opportunities at Chennai in Madras state, (3) Seek a future in Andhra state, and (4) Migrate to Hyderabad After the merger of Andhra state with Telugu speaking Telangana region of Hyderabad state to form Andhra Pradesh was on the cards. It was clear that opportunities would be more in a larger, linguistic state of Telugus called Andhra Pradesh. Many families of Bellary, including ours, chose to migrate to Hyderabad to secure better educational facilities and job opportunities.

LINGUISTIC REORGANISATION OF STATES

India which had won freedom, was settling down to usher in an era of economic and social progress when it got caught in the throes of linguistic turmoil.

The agitation for the first linguistic state of Andhra, with the death of Potti Sriramulu after a marathon 53-day fast, led to widespread disturbances and the formation of Andhra state on 1st October 1953. Soon after that, on 1st November 1956, Telugu-speaking areas of Hyderabad state and Andhra were merged with Hyderabad as its capital.

The bifurcation of Hyderabad state and the merger of Kannada-speaking areas with the old Mysore state led to the formation of Karnataka state. The Marathi-speaking areas of Hyderabad were merged with Maharashtra state. The bifurcation of large states and the constitution of new states became a continuing process aided by the economic logic of decentralised smaller states and their identification with language and ethnicity. This speeded up development in new states.

In Assam, I was witness to the creation of Nagaland, Meghalaya, and later Mizoram states due to clamour for self-rule based on ethno-tribal needs and to protect their cultural traditions and way of life. With the emergence of Meghalaya, the desirability of a separate or a common cadre for All India Services in Assam and Meghalaya was deliberated. A joint cadre for Assam-Meghalaya was agreed to and constituted. Elsewhere, Punjab was trifurcated into Himachal Pradesh, Haryana, and Punjab. Bihar was bifurcated to create Jharkhand. UP was bifurcated to provide for the State of Uttarakhand while there are demands for its further re-organisation. Maharashtra state was split to provide for the new State of Gujarat. The unwieldy and large Madhya Pradesh was bifurcated, and a new state, Chhattisgarh, was born.

There were many issues, debates and some discord about the need and logic for the creation of new States. The issues were sorted out fairly amicably with a large measure of accord among the states. The creation of smaller states spurred faster development despite some teething problems and justified their creation.

BIFURCATION OF ANDHRA PRADESH

The state of Andhra Pradesh was formed on 1st November 1956 with the merger of Telugu-speaking areas of Hyderabad state with Andhra state. There was an agitation in the Telangana region in 1969 for a separate state, which subsided with the 6-Point formula and informal agreements on the sharing of political power, but it was a short-lived truce. The agitation for a separate state became virulent in 2000 with the entry of students and the fast of K Chandrasekhar Rao. High-level committees were set up but did not receive acceptance, and unrest spread. The Government of India announced a bifurcation of the State but withdrew it due to a strong reaction from the State legislature. As the agitation continued, the Government of India finally announced that the formation of Andhra Pradesh and Telangana states would take effect in June 2014.

Ten districts of erstwhile Hyderabad state became part of Telangana, and the remaining 13 districts of Andhra went to AP. The Andhras were the first to agitate and secure a large linguistic state for Telugu speakers. They now have two Telugu-speaking states! It appears that local culture, outlook, way of life, dialects within linguistic groups, and economic viability played an important role apart from politics of finances, power, vested interests, and influence. An objective view is that "change" is a continuous phenomenon as conditions and circumstances keep evolving. We should accept change as a constant in life. It is not the change or the rapidity of change that should bother us but the slowness of our recognition and response to changes in what should concern us.

Civil service as a career has largely influenced and delineated my life and destiny. In this journey, there were many twists and turns. What appeared to be the end was only a bend in the road! One must weigh options carefully and at every stage, consult seniors, and make decisions that are in tune with one's natural thinking and duty. On occasions, one feels that some twists in the journey are quirks of fate and conveniently assigned to one's past karma or unfulfilled desires. Service teaches you to objectively analyse issues and events and make decisions in tune with ground realities and beliefs. Failure is a good teacher, while success is, in some cases, merely window dressing like respect begetting respect.

One's family and friends play a decisive role in moulding one's life and personality. Life is enlivened by participation in cultural activities, games, sports, reading, and getting support or encouragement at every stage of life. Some classmates from school are life-long friends, while some friendships are ephemeral. I have one non-complaining friend - Books. During college, I had the habit of searching for cheap editions and old books sold on footpaths to quench my thirst for knowledge and help spend time during leisure in my long bachelorhood days. Reading is my Solace – the wish and pleasure of having a good day!

In need and deed, my family stood by me. My mother, aunts and foster mother, brothers, sisters, and loyal servants were companions, advisors, and friends. After I got married, my wife joined them. Friendship in the course of service and among close relatives has been a stabilising feature in my life. I have learned from them that service must be selfless and benefit not one but many. Ek must become Anek! The family, by sharing your problems, lessens the sorrows and increases the joys of life. It is a refuge during moments of despair and inconsolable times. It also teaches you to give back -with empathy for people who need not merely monetary assistance but sympathetic commiseration. It makes one believe in giving rather than in earning - which may be the key to the philosophy of philanthropy.

Amongst peers, if I am considered good or competent, it is probably due to their good nature and large-heartedness, besides the blessings of elders. With age, your desire for approbation or benefits decreases. It leads to *Nishkama Karma*, performing a duty for duty's sake. Instead, one starts thinking about whether he had done his best and led a useful and purposeful life.

In times of distress, one needs family's support and mentors or 'gurus' or spiritual persons to guide one. In that category are Swamiji of RK Mutt, Hyderabad the late ParamarthanandaJi, my grandfather, late Govindarajulu Naidu, my uncles and aunts, my mother, late Bramaramba, my foster mother, late Kanthamma, and my elder brother, late Sundararajulu, and last but not the least my wife, Sujatha. Some friends have given me courage and encouragement. Their influence has been quite pervasive, and in their absence, I often think of the objective advice they would have given me on current issues and problems. God's mysterious and miraculous ways of guiding one's life develops a sense of fate and its ordainment. My autobiography tries to reminisce and recollect small anecdotal events like beads strung on a necklace and a mala (Rosary) for life, reminding one that events will pass by. It enables you to develop dispassion and compassion. That is the equanimity of the mind that Bhagavad Gita advises us to cultivate.

Some parts of my book may be relevant and appeal to some readers, some portions may be irrelevant or may elicit different views and opinions. I leave it to the readers to judge and form their opinion on whether I had lived a worthwhile life or not.

During my career, I had pleasant, informal, and good relationships with many Chief Ministers like Sarvashri BP Chaliha, Golap Barbora, Sarat Chandra Sinha, and M.M Chowdhury in Assam and Ministers like KPTripathi, CSTeron, DK Baruah, Jagannath Singh, and Gajen Tanti.

In Andhra Pradesh, I got on famously with CMs D. Sanjivaiah, M Channa Reddy, J Vengal Rao, T Anjaiah, NT Rama Rao, Nadendla Bhaskar Rao, N Chandrababu Naidu, N Janardhan Reddy, K Vijaya Bhaskar Reddy,

YS Rajasekhar Reddy and K Rosaiah and Industries Ministers M Baga Reddy, Vidhyadhar Rao, G Brahmaiah, N Amarnath Reddy and G Sanjeeva Reddy, President, Indian National Trade Union Congress.

In the Union government, work was transacted through internal discussions, inter-ministry consultations, and consensus building. Ministers were either highly educated or politically oriented. Ministers generally allowed the bureaucracy to make or suggest decisions. Some ministers were interested in making money through large contracts or award of unmerited concessions. Honest officials were often side-lined or put into trouble by such ministers. The trust and confidence between ministers and secretaries, as seen in Assam and AP states, is often missing these days.

Many efficient officers were put in trouble due to recalcitrant ministers. One hopes that the Prime Minister and the Cabinet would rectify the situation, reward good conduct, work and behaviour and provide an environment for truth, trust, and good relations, which are essential for reviews, new initiatives and innovations for good governance for the present and the future.

PART-2

POST RETIREMENT-SEWA WITH BHAVA

PART - 2
POST RETIREMENT- SEVA WITH BHAVA

1

Director, Institute of Public Enterprises (IPE)

On retirement from service as CMD of REC in 1977, while winding up my establishment in New Delhi, I heard an announcement on TV that the AP Government had notified me as Vice-Chancellor of Dravidian University (DU) being set up to give a fillip to the development of Dravidian languages like Tamil, Telugu, Kannada and Malayalam. I was surprised as I was not consulted, nor was my consent taken. The next day, Kasi Pandian, IAS (1963) told me that he had discussed the matter with the CM, who was keen to set up the University at Kuppam in Chittoor district and appoint me as the first VC. The appointment created a dilemma.

I was neither a Ph.D. nor an academic and did not have the qualifications for the post. My only credentials were that I knew Sanskrit and Telugu, was fluent in Kannada, and had working knowledge of Tamil and Malayalam. The Dravidian University was expected to foster linguistic and related studies of Dravidian languages.

I felt that the concept of the DU indicated that the Southern languages were distinct and had no connection or linkages with Aryan languages. It could create a chasm between Sanskrit-linked languages and South Indian Languages. Many southern languages, except Tamil, had freely incorporated alphabets, words, and roots from Sanskrit, Pali, Prakrit, and Tamil. I was in a dilemma and was pondering over the matter.

CALL TO JOIN AS DIRECTOR OF IPE

Meanwhile, I got a call from Justice P Jagan Mohan Reddy, former Chief Justice of AP High Court and Judge of the Supreme Court, that Institute of Public Enterprise (IPE), Hyderabad, devoted to Research and Studies of Central and State Public Enterprises was in need of an able and competent director. TL Sankar, IAS, had worked for more than a decade earlier as Director of IPE. The Governing Body of IPE was considering me for that post. He wanted me to accept the post in view of my experience and background. He said that Dr NB Prasad, who was Chairman Board of Governors of IPE, would get in touch with me. I told Justice Reddy that I was winding up my affairs in Delhi and on return to Hyderabad, I would discuss the matter with him and decide. The IPE was in the Osmania University campus. It had obtained affiliation from Osmania University for a part-time evening 3-year MBA course called MBA (PE) intended for executives working in the public sector or persons interested in joining the public sector apart from studies on Central and State Public Enterprises.

At Hyderabad, my family felt that I should relax after retirement and not take up any assignments, and the Kuppam job would keep me away from home.

Prof. Ramakishnayya was the Vice-Chancellor of Osmania University (OU). He was an old friend whom I had known as a Professor of Management at OU. I met him, posed my dilemma, and sought his advice. He pointed out that DU was still in the conceptual stage, physical facilities would have to be built, and teachers would have to be recruited before classes could begin. While the VC post was prestigious, it was not a bed of roses with many teething problems, including funding. He said that IPE was not doing well because of financial issues and a lack of good faculty. It needed a strong administrator with a public sector background. As I was CMD of PSEs at the Central and State level and Chairman of SCOPE, he felt that my contacts with the public sector could help turn around IPE. He left the final decision to me. I met TL Sankar, who advised me to join IPE as Director.

I called on Justice JaganMohan Reddy and Dr NB Prasad and conveyed to them my willingness to join after receiving permission from the Union government. As the job was in the field of education in a recognized institution, permission was given. I joined IPE in August 1997.

INSTITUTE OF PUBLIC ENTERPRISE (IPE)

A large number of public sector undertakings in the core sectors were set up to capture the commanding heights of the economy. The then VC of OU, DS Reddy and Prof VV Ramanadham took the initiative to set up IPE in May 1964 as a registered society under the Societies Registration Act. SS Khera, ICS, who was Cabinet Secretary, helped the institute, which was involved in research, education, and training for civil servants. In 1976, it was recognized as an Institution of Eminence by the Indian Council of Social Science Research (ICSSR) and received small grants from it and the

AP government. It admitted research scholars for the award of Ph. D by OU. Later, other universities affiliated IPE for the award of Ph.D.

TL Sankar, an expert in energy studies, was part-time Director for about 11 years and full-time for 2 years. During his tenure, networking with various government departments and academic institutions was strengthened. IPE concentrated on research on public enterprises, training of IAS officers, and management education by offering an MBA (PE), an evening course of 3 years duration for employees of public sector enterprises, and a newly started daytime Post Graduate Diploma in Business Management (PGDBM).

IPE had a very good library but poor infrastructure for the conduct of classes and inadequate facilities for the faculty. There was a shortage of faculty who were hitherto guiding research work and taking classes in the evening MBA (PE) course. In the morning PGDBM course, there was an acute shortage of accommodation, canteen, sports, and other facilities. Part-time lecturers supplemented the limited senior faculty. IPE had good credentials as a research institution but was yet to make a mark in management education and consultancy work as the faculty did not have experience in consultancy work.

MANAGEMENT CONSULTANCY

While in Delhi, I was engaged in consultancy work for Asian Development Bank (ADB), KFW, DFID, UNDP, and other organizations in the domains of Minerals, Public Sector and Energy. One of the consultancies entrusted was the study on "Restructuring of Public Sector Undertakings in Madhya Pradesh State", which included a detailed study on the M.P. State Road Transport Corporation. To provide consultancy experience to IPE faculty, I wrote to the ADB to transfer the consultancy awarded to me to IPE as I was now its Director. ADB agreed to do so. Dr RK Mishra and officers in the AP government and APSRTC were engaged in the study under my guidance, which ADB appreciated. This proved a morale booster for the faculty and a harbinger of consultancies.

TRUCKERS PROJECT

HIV AIDS was causing concern worldwide, and regional monitoring units were to be set up to monitor the movement of trucks and truck drivers in view of the relatively high prevalence of HIV AIDS among truck drivers. We bagged the *Truckers Project* to monitor the habits of truck drivers and conducted periodical check-ups to suggest measures to control HIV AIDS.

SOCIAL SAFETY NET

We secured a project from DFID UK for a study on *Social Safety Net for* people who were laid off, voluntarily retired, and or pensioned off due to sickness in industry and other reasons. The bulk of them were employees retrenched from the public sector or government. It was a pioneering move, and our faculty did a wonderful job. Dr V Sitha was in charge.

BIOTECHNOLOGY UNIT (BTU)

IPE set up a Biotechnology Unit (BTU) supported by the Netherlands Government to explore its applications in agriculture and forestry. It experimented with the propagation of tissue culture and modern methods of crop protection, reduced usage of pesticides and increase the shelf-life of fruits and vegetables. The Unit was headed by Chairman Dr MV Rao, an eminent agricultural scientist, former Deputy Director General of ICAR and Ex-VC of AP Agricultural University, a Padma Shri awardee for his outstanding services in propagating modern methods of wheat cultivation. As Director of IPE, I was on the Steering Committee. My wide contacts with institutions like the IICT, ICAR, and Panchayat Raj, Agriculture, Horticulture, and Veterinary departments helped me transfer the latest technologies for field application. It was a simple 'Lab to Land' process. Though the BTU unit was small, it made a big impact since it actively interacted with farmers and *Krishi Vignan Kendras* and changed farmers' mind sets to embrace and adopt the latest methods for increasing production and productivity. BTU had some diligent scientists and researchers. Unit head, G. Pakki Reddy, was the driving spirit and totally dedicated to his job. The Netherlands Government, which had sponsored the BTU, was happy with its performance, extended the project, and gave an additional sum of Rupees 30 crore with additional work features. The AP Agricultural University later took over the unit.

NATIONAL INSTITUTE OF TOURISM & HOSPITALITY MANAGEMENT (NITHM)

The AP government wanted to set up an Institute for Tourism and Hotel management. The state co-opted me as Chairman of a Sub-group for working on AP Vision 2020. We invited Sri Madan Bezbaruah, Union Secretary of Tourism, who was known to me, to visit IPE and advise us on the matter. He responded positively and suggested that IPE could prepare a project report for setting up a National Institute of Tourism and Hospitality Management (NITHM) in Hyderabad. IPE's Project Report was approved, and the Tourism Ministry gave approval and funds to set up the NITHM

Hyderabad. A faculty member of IPE, Dr GS Rao, was appointed as Director General of the Institute.

REPORT ON ELIMINATION OF RURAL POVERTY

IPE was assigned a project to eliminate rural poverty by the AP Department of Rural Development. We recruited faculty with field experience and enumerators and submitted the draft report to the government. Satisfied with the report, the government wanted us to suggest setting up an agency to implement the recommendations. We recommended the setting up of "The Society for Elimination of Rural Poverty (SERP)", which is continuing its activities creditably all over AP and has done remarkable work.

We did some assignments for the Municipal Administration, Veterinary and Animal Husbandry departments. They accepted our recommendation to provide 'Mobile veterinary dispensaries' to treat animals in villages instead of making them come to the veterinary dispensaries when sick, for treatment. With improvements, they became multi-purpose vans that enabled artificial insemination activity, helped propagate modern methods of feeding animals, cultivation of fodder, provision of inoculation and vaccination for prevention of diseases in animals.

MANAGEMENT COURSES – ENTRY BASED ON CAT

A review of the syllabus and academic work of management courses highlighted the need to upgrade the syllabus for the PGDBM course and options at IPE. To raise standards of teaching and enrolment, we sought affiliation from IIM Ahmedabad by revising our course of study based on a Common Admission Test (CAT) administered to all IIMs. We secured clearance from IIM (A) to participate in selection through CAT examinations supplemented by interviews. This ensured better quality of students from all over India. We provided flexible specialization options in the course, like Personnel Management, Marketing Management, Business Analytics, etc. We supplemented faculty lectures with guest faculty and lectures by CEOs of companies.

SANSKRITI – A MEGA STUDENTS EVENT

To attract better quality students and highlight our courses, we started a mega student event called "Sanskriti" at IPE in 1998. It attracted participants from 50 MBA colleges. A Mela was also organized with the help and assistance of a number of industrial units who contributed a large amount of money as prizes for a variety of programs such as quiz competitions, elocution, analytics, etc. This boosted IPE's image, and we were able to get a large number of applications for admission to our PGDM course from all over India.

SAMITHI

We introduced another event, 'Samithi', where CEOs of companies in different sectors were made judges at seminars in IPE conducted by our students. A boy and a girl from the first year and the second year would participate and speak for and against a topic of current interest. Our idea was to exhibit the knowledge, speaking, debating, and elocution skills of our students to the CEOs. This helped in securing good placements.

PLACEMENTS

My contacts as SCOPE Chairman with ONGC, NTPC, REC, NMDC, NALCO and large CPSEs helped in the placement of our students in different companies besides summer assignments. In a couple of years, we were able to secure 100% placement for our students with attractive pay packets in prestigious companies in various sectors of the economy.

To build confidence and provide help to students, we recruited Lt. Col. GR Rao, who was an Engineer and an MBA, as a Placement Officer. He and his assistant, LS Murthy of the Air Force, guided the students. In a short time, the students themselves formed groups for visits to Bangalore, Pune, Delhi, and Mumbai to personally contact big companies, give presentations, and persuade them to visit IPE for interviews and placements.

MENTORING

I took classes occasionally for the PGDM and MBA (PE) students and noted the level of discipline in the class and the questions asked by students. I kept an open house and interacted with students to help them develop confidence, speaking and conversational skills. We held separate classes for those who came from Telugu medium and struggled to converse in English. We also introduced special classes to teach a foreign language to enable students to bag jobs abroad. French, Spanish, and Arabic were taught. We introduced the concept of mentorship to students. Each faculty member was assigned six students to be mentored and guided, allay their fears and problems and be in touch with their parents to inform them of the progress of the students. ML Saikumar and Jyothi, psychology lecturers, did an excellent job as mentors.

INDUCTION PROGRAM

To allay the fears of parents about the nature of the course and the safety of female students, we started an induction programme for students and parents. It was a 3-day program. The Chief Guest for the opening day was a revered monk from Ramakrishna Mutt, Swami Paramarthanandaji, who was a good and witty speaker. On the first day, students and parents were introduced to the faculty, who briefly talked about the subject they would teach, the duration of the course and the scope for placement. The Institute staff showed parents around with visits to the library and classrooms and answered their questions. Lunch would be provided to all students, parents, and faculty. On the second day, students would be told about the institute's expectations of discipline, conduct, and behaviour, as well as the use of the library, canteen, method of study, etc. On the third day, they would be advised regarding the options that students had and the use of sports and other institute facilities. The Induction Programme broke the ice and built good bonds between faculty, parents and students.

We used the help of SCOPE to address all concerns of central public sector undertakings regarding the syllabus for PGDBM and provide a birds-eye view of the public sector and its importance. SCOPE helped us by providing relevant linkages. It instituted a Rolling Shield for an Annual Debate on the public sector to be conducted by IPE which was made a member of the Executive Committee of SCOPE.

AWARD FOR 100% ATTENDANCE

IPE instituted an award for a student with 100% attendance in class. I had expected a girl student to bag the award. Lo and behold, a boy student got the award! I was surprised and asked the boy to meet me. I asked him how he managed to get 100% attendance, despite so many distractions, other engagements, games, sports, etc. To my surprise, the boy said, "Sir, you don't understand such simple things. I wonder how the government made you an IAS Officer". I thought he was impudent. I angrily demanded that he explain the remark. He said, "Sir, please listen patiently. My Lecturer would have read 10 to 15 books, which would have taken him a month or 45 days of study. He summarizes his learning and addresses the class for about 45 minutes. If I listen attentively and carefully for 45 minutes, Sir, it saves me 45 days of study. That is why I never miss a class. Before attending the class, I read the portion. My listening in class is like my revision of the lesson". I realized that the chap was super intelligent and had found an easier method of study. This echoes what our ancients believed in. 'Sravanam', i.e. listening, leads to

'Mananam' (remembering), which leads to 'Dharanam' or thinking and understanding; this, in turn, leads to 'Dhyanam' (concentration). The student had become my teacher!

Ph.D SCHOLARS

As OU and some other universities had given us affiliation, we had Ph.D. scholars who were registered with the institute. The OU used to invite me to participate in the thesis presentation by scholars and comment on it. During my tenure, nine research scholars from IPE got their Ph.D. from OU. The Research scholars would also take some classes for the students.

SOME NEW INITIATIVES

We strengthened the infrastructure, administration, and faculty to take up management consultancy and computer training programs and conduct Management Development programs. We also constructed a new block for MBA courses, enlarged the library and subscribed to research publications. We recruited lecturers and introduced special classes on ethics and values. We improved the canteen and accommodation facilities and provided playgrounds with volleyball and basketball courts. Dr RK Mishra was appointed as Dean of Research. He conducted academic council meetings to review the syllabus and course content. He identified weak points in our pedagogy and course content and made it comparable with IIMs. He later became Director of IPE, and made it a premier management Institution. We started emphasizing 'case studies' and the participation of students in both internal and external competitions to evoke a competitive spirit and to project IPE as the Best MBA College in Hyderabad. It is a matter of pride that IPE continues its lead.

With the new and vibrant image of IPE, we secured munificent donations from large central public sector undertakings and increased grants from ICSSR and the AP Government.

COMPUTER COURSES AND TRAINING OF PSE EMPLOYEES

IPE had an early start in the introduction of computer training for public sector enterprises in AP and India. TL Sankar had persuaded Dr Guruswamy from Tamil Nadu to join as Head of the Computer division. We provided a computer room with 30 computers for conducting courses for officials from central and state public sector undertakings and our MBA students. Guruswamy later became VC of the Madras University and was succeeded by ML Saikumar who put our computer training on the map of

PSEs and India. IPE can claim that training in computers and MS Office triggered the use of computers in AP.

IPE started a 1-year PG Diploma course in software and its applications. The course was so good that Satyam Computers, AP Electronics Development Corporation and Wipro sent their newly recruited employees for training.

The Computer division held an international conference on "Software Engineering and its Applications" and a national conference on "Enterprise Resources Planning" which was conducted by Prof. S Sadagopan and Prof Chandrasekhar from IIM Bengaluru. Two conferences on "Medical Informatics" were held, and proceedings were published. A national conference on "E-commerce" was also held.

MANAGEMENT DEVELOPMENT PROGRAMS

IPE was conducting training programs for IAS Officers to give them exposure to modern trends in management and introduction to computers. The Department of Personnel and Training in Delhi used to send officers for courses ranging from 3 days to 15 days. As accommodation was not available, we had to put them up in hotels while classes were conducted in IPE. I used to give lectures to the participants in those courses. We conducted nine programs to meet the requirements of Central and State level public enterprises. We sent out circulars about our training programs, which attracted participation from not only public sector undertakings but also from private industry. This programme became a money-spinner for the IPE. Some of the new programs we introduced were on Good Governance, Corporate Governance, Project Management, Personnel Management, Marketing Management, etc. These programs attracted the attention of large public sector undertakings. Our appeals for support led to donations from central public sector undertakings and improved the financial position of IPE.

SPRINGBOARD PROGRAMME

Enthused by the success of the Springboard Program for women conducted by SCOPE, IPE started a 3-day program for women employees to raise their morale, improve self-confidence and cooperate with other women employees to help sort out their problems. This attracted a good number of participants, and the word spread. We had participants from organizations in Tamil Nadu, Kerala, Karnataka, West Bengal, Maharashtra, Rajasthan, Delhi, and U.P.

COMMITTEE ON ECIL

Electronics Corporation of India Limited, a unit under the Atomic Energy Commission (AEC) located in Hyderabad, was a pioneer in introducing computers in India. They began by importing computers, dismantling them to study the design and manufacture them at a lower cost to meet India's growing demands. They also supplied specialized equipment for the Defence and Atomic Energy departments. They took many apprentices for training who later sought jobs in ECIL itself. Soon, there was a surfeit of apprentices, who were all absorbed into the organization. The structure became unwieldy, and it distorted the organizational structure and hierarchy. AEC was worried. IPE had conducted a course for ECIL, which their HR Head, R Natarajan, attended. He wrote to AEC to engage IPE to undertake a diagnostic study and suggest a way for restructuring ECIL.

AEC constituted a committee with Director IPE as Chairman, Professor BR Virmani of Administrative Staff College of India, and Gupta, CMD of Uranium Corporation of India, to study the problems of the Electronics Corporation of India (ECIL) and the restructuring. IPE conducted the study and submitted its report to Chidambaram, Chairman of AEC. He invited the committee to Mumbai, heard its views, hosted a lunch and thanked us for the excellent report we had submitted. AEC implemented our suggestions on restructuring with accountability for results and a lean and mean organization apart from voluntary retirement schemes. The measures introduced resulted in a turnaround of the company. ECIL has ever since been making profits!

A recent publication of the IPE in 2022 entitled "Creating, Building and Sustaining an Institution" has traced the history of IPE and the contributions and efforts made by Directors and faculty. A reference has been made to my tenure in IPE. Extracts from the book are reproduced below:

"Mr Gopalakrishna, a career bureaucrat, took over as the Director of IPE in 1997 and remained in the office till 2000. With his entry, strong leadership was provided, and the management development programs were resurrected, which made the institution much stronger in terms of activities and revenue generation.

During his tenure, he took up activities for campus development. He was responsible for forging new alliances and brought in many prestigious projects. Mr Gopalakrishna brought in fresh thinking and initiated work on broader issues plaguing the governance and public systems. It was during his tenure that the Institute took up assignments on some very critical issues of health and human development. A comprehensive review of

IPE activities was taken up from (1996-2000). IPE emerged as a highly specialized Centre for research, consultancy, and training and carved out a niche in the areas of Public Sector Management and Public Policy.

There was a big step-up in the activities of IPE, particularly in training and consultancy work, leading to a net surplus in all four years. **A Truckers Project** was taken up to study health management issues. This was a Targeted Intervention project on HIV/AIDS and a very critical component of the Health and Family Welfare Department. For this purpose, a **Regional Monitoring Unit (RMU)** was set up at IPE. The other important program that Mr Gopalakrishna initiated was the DFID-sponsored project on Reskilling and Retraining of employees under the **Social Safety Net of Govt. of India**. He continued with great vigour and strength, IPE's tradition of training for civil servants. These programs were sponsored by the Ministry of Personnel, Government of India. During this period, the position of Dean of Research was created, and Prof R.K. Mishra became the first Dean of Research at IPE.

During the mid-1990s, a very important project assigned by the Asian Development Bank to him to study the Restructuring of Public Enterprises in Madhya Pradesh was transferred to IPE, which invested a lot of time and resources in research related to public enterprises and the public sector in general. Its findings were widely utilized by various institutions like the Committee on Public Undertakings (COPU), several ministries of the Government of India, the Planning Commission, the Finance Commission, the Standing Conference on Public Enterprises, the Department of Public Enterprises, the Comptroller and Auditor General of India and pay revision committees set up by Government of India from time to time.

Gopalakrishna, as the Director of the institute, took many measures to strengthen IPE linkages with public sector enterprises. IPE became a member of the Executive Committee of the Standing Conference on Public Enterprises. IPE cooperated closely with SCOPE in research, training, and consultancy. Vigorous efforts by the Institute resulted in securing some interesting research and consultancy studies. SCOPE instituted a rolling shield for an annual debate to be conducted at IPE on a topic concerning the public sector in India for business school students".

During Gopalakrishna's tenure, nine PH.D were awarded to IPE scholars. Gopalakrishna organized a lecture on the topic of Enterprise Revenue Management, delivered by S Venkataraman, Former Governor of RBI, in 1999.

There was a sharp increase in the ICSSR grants during Mr. Gopalakrishna's tenure. The income of IPE from various sources showed an increasing trend during his IPE days. From Rs.119.06 lakhs in 1996-97,

Rs.143.61 lakhs in 1997-98, Rs.250.58 lakhs in 1998-99 and Rs.244.38 lakhs in 1999-2000."

I worked for three years and was satisfied with delineating the growth path to make IPE a premier management institution. It has built up a good reputation for teaching, research, and extension work and is considered a premium Management College. It has moved to its own campus in Shamirpet and is continuing its good work.

2

Chairman of APSFC

In 2001, PK Saha, CGM from the Small Industries Development Bank of India (SIDBI), Hyderabad, called and told me that the SFCs Act (State Financial Corporation) was amended in 2000. SIDBI, as a promoter of APSFC, wanted to nominate me as Non-executive Chairman of Andhra Pradesh State Financial Corporation (APSFC) and wanted my consent. Soon after that, the AP CM called me and asked about my plan of action and the time required to turn around the sick Corporation. I told him that I would have to study the position and guessed that it might take about 2 years to put it back on the rails. With government support, it could be turned around even earlier. The CM assured government support. Dr JC Mohanty, Managing Director of APSFC, met and briefed me about the issues and problems that APSFC faces. I was appointed as Chairman and took charge on 5th February 2002.

APSFC was set up under the State Financial Corporations Act, with equity from SIDBI and the AP government for supporting and financing small and Medium-scale industrial units. It was a professionally run corporation but had fallen on bad days due to political pressures to sanction loans and slack supervision in collections, leading to high levels of non-performing assets (NPAs). SFC was incurring losses. It was on the brink of bankruptcy. SFCs had to function in a very competitive environment, with banks financing the SME sector and providing working capital. The Subramanian Committee on State Public Sector Enterprises had recommended its privatization, while the consultancy firm Adam Smith suggested either privatization or closure of APSFC. The morale of officers and staff was low, and there was uncertainty about the Corporation's fate and its future. Discussions with the GMs who had grown with the organization made me feel that though the task was difficult, it could be turned around as it was a professional outfit with experienced executives.

I held discussions that indicated that there was capital inadequacy while loans and arrears were mounting. SFC had contracted high-cost SLR Bonds and loans, which left very little interest margin. With a poor collection of dues, non-performing assets (NPAs) had increased. It was clear that low-cost loans had to be obtained to repay the high-cost loans. I met Venugopal Reddy, Governor, RBI for support in the turnaround efforts of the SFC, who put me on to the Dy. Governor V Kamesam. He, in turn, put me in contact with the Chairmen of SBI, Canara Bank, and PNB, all of whom I had earlier known as REC Chairman. As interest rates slid due to the economic downturn, SFC was able to secure low-cost loans from banks, and we repaid the high-cost loans. This triggered the turnaround of the Corporation. We introduced a one-time settlement (OTS) scheme, which helped us collect our impaired debts and a little more as land values and demand for assets had risen.

THE SITUATIONAL ANALYSIS

A quick SWOT and Gap Analysis study revealed that it was possible to improve the bottom and top lines with the support of the Board and the cooperation of employees. Capital adequacy had to be improved, but the government was not willing to bite the bullet and infuse the requisite capital as they had slated APSFC for sale or closure. There was only one line of credit from SIDBI. New credit channels would have to be opened. Deposit mobilization was low-key. High-risk SLR Bonds were crippling the organization. The cost of funds was high. Interest spreads were low. Customer relations were poor. There was an immediate need to increase sanctions and disbursements to build a good loan portfolio of fresh loans. For better realizations and to reduce NPAs, a One-Time Settlement scheme was introduced and vigorously pursued. In short, the Corporation geared itself in double quick time.

SFC had a professional Board of Directors. We strengthened it by inducting K Kannan, former CMD of Bank of Baroda, as a Director to improve our appraisal skills, implement the OTS, and introduce good governance practices on par with Banks. His mature advice and suggestions helped SFC find solutions to many issues.

THE PLAN OF ACTION – ONE STOP SHOP

A plan of action was drawn up to project a new image of the Corporation and build trust with customers. We started providing a package of all facilities like loans, tying up of working capital from banks, advice, guidance, and help to entrepreneurs, making the Corporation a

"One Stop Shop." Non-fund income had to supplement our earnings with new avenues and increase employee productivity. A bigger market share had to be achieved in the term finance market by attracting repeat, new, and larger customers from upcoming industries. We positioned SFC as a **'friendly financier'** and partner of SME units in the growing sectors of industry and economy. We secured the willing and enthusiastic support of the staff by organizing internal meetings to explain our strategy and motivate them. Employees were encouraged to give their suggestions for a quick turnaround. We exhorted branch managers to think and "work like local MDs" and come up with ideas and guide budding entrepreneurs. Time limits were introduced for clearance of loan applications based on the amount sought as a loan.

CUSTOMER CENTRIC GROWTH AND EMPLOYEE CENTRIC CHANGE

Restructuring, process re-engineering, and projection of the new organizational ethos and values of customer centricity became our focus for gaining customer confidence and support for the turnaround of SFC.

We drew inspiration from the hidden strengths of APSFC, which were its qualified and experienced manpower and their professionalism. They only had to update their skills, become self-motivated, and improve customer relationships. We clarified their goal, role, route, and focus to regain their past elan and build a new image by teamwork and focus on results. Gaps in knowledge, talent, strategy, performance, credibility, and leadership were noted and filled. We stressed employee productivity and turnover per person.

TRAINING

To improve the knowledge of Branch managers and staff, we organized in-house lectures. We created a training wing with all modern facilities to conduct internal classes and brain-storming sessions with our employees. We engaged a retired GM of IDBI, Surender Reddy, and a young IIM MBA to take regular classes for our staff to update them, impart appraisal skills, and assist us at these meetings. It was supplemented with guest lectures. Our officials were also sent for training at Jawaharlal Nehru Industrial Development Bank Centre and Institute of Insurance Risk Management at the Osmania University campus, as well as other training institutions like the National Institute of Bank Management, SBI Training College, etc.

IDEAS – SEMINARS

We started the 1-Day Entrepreneur Awareness Seminars (1DEAS) Campaign at headquarters and branches about industrial opportunities and SFC schemes and support. Instead of customers coming to the Corporation, the Corporation went to customers! It created goodwill and resulted in a positive perception of the customers about SFC.

LOCAL LOAN SANCTION MEETS – FRIENDLY FINANCIER

We decided to hold ***"On the Spot"*** loan sanction meets with adequate notice to our branch managers at important places all over the state. The MD and Chairman, along with concerned appraisal and loan sanction officers from the head office along with staff, visited various places like Visakhapatnam, Vizianagaram, Rajahmundry, Vijayawada, Tirupathi, Kurnool, Warangal, Nizamabad, and Karimnagar, heard applicants and gave on the spot sanctions. This gave us an opportunity to visit and interact with our customers. The extensive press coverage resulted in a spate of new applications. At these meets, successful entrepreneurs were invited to give advice and guidance to new applicants. The whole strategy was built on customer-centric growth and employee-centric change. The results were beyond our imagination. The Corporation had become an incredible "Friendly financier."

DYNAMIC MANAGING DIRECTORS

Dr. J.C Mohanty, a Harvard University Doctorate, was the MD when I joined APSFC. A diligent officer who believed in systems and methods, he identified the problems of SFC, introduced a voluntary retirement scheme, and organized refresher courses for employees. He limited the recruitment of professionals to fill the gaps. He pioneered the computerization of the Corporation by engaging Ken Soft, a software company that did a fairly good job. The software had some glitches, but these were overcome. The improved software was good. It was adopted by Rajasthan and Karnataka SFCs, which paid some royalty to the Corporation! Mohanty believed in quick action and gave deadlines for the completion of tasks. He used to discuss Board matters with me and seek advice on difficult issues.

Ratan PWatal, who joined as MD in December 2002, had earlier worked in the Prime Minister's office. He had good contacts and was focused on policy issues. He was versatile and improved his appraisal skills and the quality of the Board notes. As Secretary of the AP IAS Association, he upgraded its facilities and organized VIP lectures. A good sportsman, he was Part-time Director of Tourism and Youth Advancement. Hyderabad was selected to conduct the Afro-Asian Games. He was made in-charge of conduct of the games. He took the initiative with our in-house support and expertise to develop custom-built software for the Afro-Asian Games of 2003, along with Project Accounting and related support services. This earned the SFC a handsome sum of 50 lakh rupees as consultancy fee. He was a man of the moment. Ratan was later posted as Chairman of the Sports Authority of India in Delhi, where he groomed Indian sportsmen to participate in world competitions. He was also a Secretary in the Finance Ministry.

Ajeya Kallam joined as Managing Director in March 2005. He was of amiable disposition, and was a man of few words. He kept an open house and encouraged employees to meet him and discuss matters. He was helpful and very courteous. He encouraged the executives to make decisions and approach him when they faced difficulties. He had very good contacts with the State Government and was responsible for securing the presence of the CM, Industries Minister, and Industry Secretaries for our meetings. During his time, we secured substantial equity from the state government and grants of land in the financial district. SFC constructed a building that was rented out and became another non-fund source of income for the APSFC.

I was lucky to have three dynamic and intelligent MDs as colleagues who collectively helped turn the SFC around. It proved that IAS officers, given autonomy and freedom of operation, can deliver results in difficult situations. What they need is the support and trust of the political executive. The success of the turnaround in SFC can be ascribed to good *"political will, managerial skill, and customer goodwill"*.

At the office, I kept an open house to enable our employees, loanees, and loan applicants to meet me and air their grievances and suggestions. This helped me to know the ground realities. I would gauge the views and reactions of the loanees about measures being taken by the corporation to collect its dues and deficiencies in policy and execution matters.

MoU with SIDBI

N Balasubramanian, CMD of SIDBI, invited me to join SIDBI's Board as Director. This helped me understand SIDBI and develop contacts with its other directors. This led to the signing of the Tripartite Memorandum of Understanding - by the AP government, SIDBI, and the SFC, which provided liberal concessions and benefits. N Balasubramanian was happy with the performance of APSFC and reduced the interest payable to 7.5%.

SIDBI agreed to my request to consider offering APSFC the benefit of 2% lower interest, provided APSFC and the State government agreed to sign a Tripartite Memorandum of Understanding. Ratan Watal assiduously followed up on the matter with the State Government and secured their approval to sign the MOU. This was the turning point in the fortunes of the corporation. With a 2% lower interest benefit, we decided to pass on 1% to our customers and availed only a 1% benefit towards our interest margin.

FASTER BOARD DECISIONS

The reconstitution of the Board with experienced persons from banking, accounting, industries, and management backgrounds helped us in taking mature decisions. We increased the number of Board Meetings from an average of one per month to 2 or 3 per month as needed. This speeded up the sanctions. With computerization, the Board proposals followed a process and proper mode of presentation. We encouraged managers who prepared the Board note and GMs who cleared it to be present at the Board to understand the rationale and the issues that are taken into consideration by the Board before reaching its decision. This was welcomed by our officers, who found it a training session on drafting Board notes and the points for decision.

ONE-TIME SETTLEMENT OF DUES

Sec. 29 of the SFCs Act gives immense powers to auction assets and recover loans due to the corporation. India introduced the Securitization and Reconstruction of Financial Assets and Enforcement of Security Interest (SARFAESI) Act to help banks recover dues. SFC used Sec. 29 only in intransigent cases. It prefers to offer a one-time settlement of dues to entrepreneur loanees by offering fair and reasonable terms. To ensure transparency and fairness, we studied the OTS schemes being operated by other banks and attuned our OTS scheme to meet our needs. As the prices of land and assets increased, many loanees came forward to settle their loans. In some cases, we had no alternative but to sell the assets, land, and buildings, which helped clear the loans. This improved the cash position of the corporation. There were no complaints of harassment or corruption regarding the OTS scheme, which enhanced the image of APSFC as a fair lender.

When I joined the SFC, the cost of borrowing was 12.25%, which was brought down to 10%. Due to an increase in the disbursement of loans, up from Rs.300 crore to Rs.460 crore, the gross NPAs, which were around 60%, came down. The Net NPAs were brought down from 27% to 22%. The Capital Adequacy Ratio improved.

SFC was incurring losses for eighteen years in a row. It incurred a loss of (-) Rs.1.13 crore in 2001-02 and made a profit for the first time in 2002-03 after I joined. The SFC had started turning around!

SFC SECURES ISO STANDARDS

In 2001, APSFC became the first SFC to secure ISO-9002-1994, and in the following years, it secured ISO-9001-2000 for all its activities, products, and processes. The officers and staff understood the importance of quality in every aspect of work. It became the standard bearer for quality movement among the Small and Medium Scale industries in AP.

CITIZEN'S CHARTER

APSFC issued a Citizen's Charter in 2002, prescribing time limits for clearance of applications based on amounts applied for and also for redressal of grievances, as envisaged in the Right to Information Act. Regular meetings were held with entrepreneurs to seek their suggestions for improving our services and products and to publicize our financial assistance packages for different industrial proposals.

To give SMEs a fillip, we conducted SME Day, which was graced by the CM and the Industries Minister. We distributed illustrated brochures on loan limits and the range of our services. With the support of SIDBI, our loan limits, which were Rs.5 crore, were raised to Rs.20 crore. We highlighted this fact in all our publicity materials.

Having achieved low-cost finances, we set our sights on improving income from non-fund sources. With improved performance, we were able to secure "Eligible Institution" status from both SIDBI and the State government to accept public deposits. In a short time, we raised a sum of Rs.70 crores. We secured a Non-life Insurance Agency from IFFCO-Tokio to insure the assets of our clients/customers. Subsequently, with an agency from LIC, we introduced life insurance facilities for employees of our own corporation and our loanee executives and employees. We secured an agency from the Stock Holding Corporation of India (SHCIL) to sell GoI bonds. We got empanelled as a Portfolio Resolution Agency by Asset Reconstruction Corporation of India Limited (ARCIL). Our employees soon gained competence in handling these non-fund activities.

WORKING CAPITAL – TIE UP

To bring in better standards of financial governance, Bank Chairmen or MDs were inducted as Directors of SFC. The past MD of SBH, past Chairman of Andhra Bank and Canara Bank, besides the past Chairman of Bank of Baroda, served as Directors, which helped SFC in tying up working capital for our loanees. The banks agreed to train our officers in working capital assessment and accept our appraisal processes. Eventually, the banks used to sanction working capital based on SFC appraisal. This removed a long-standing problem of the loanees.

RAJASTHANI ENTREPRENEURS MEET

Many of our entrepreneurs were from Rajasthan. They requested the CM to address and encourage them to set up industries in AP. The CM and Industries Minister addressed them in the Federation of AP Chambers of Commerce and Industry (FAPCCI), which elicited a lot of responses and applications for setting up industries. The remark made by me about Rajasthanis who followed the tradition of *"Neeche Dukaan, Uppar Makaan,"* i.e., shop on the ground floor and house on the upper floor and *"Saamne Dukaan, Neeche Makaan"* was applauded and became the headline in the newspapers. The entire family is involved in running the shop/industry and serving the customers. This equally applies to our Gujarati Patels, who have contributed to industrial growth in India and piloted the development of hotels and motels in the USA.

AUDIT PROCESS

To improve governance standards and strengthen financial controls, we formed an Audit Committee composed of SSR Koteshwara Rao, a prominent Chartered Accountant and Director, K Harishchandra Prasad, Chairman of a Finance Company, and A Shyam Mohan, an entrepreneur. They did a good job, and we had hardly any audit objections or complaints.

PARISRAMIKA VIJETHA AWARDS

Parisramika Vijetha or Industrial Awards were instituted to honour successful loanee entrepreneurs.166 entrepreneurs received the awards. The awards boosted good entrepreneurs and raised hopes among new applicants.

GOLDEN JUBILEE CELEBRATIONS

APSFC was set up on 1-11-1956, the day when Andhra Pradesh State was formed. Our Golden Jubilee Celebrations started on such an auspicious day. APSFC, which was set up with golden hopes, had come a long way and was celebrating its own Golden Jubilee! All the past Chairmen and Managing Directors who had served and helped build the institution were honoured. On the inaugural day, we honoured the surviving Chairmen and MDs. Among them were Swaminatha Reddy - one of the architects of the corporation - who later became the Chairman of Andhra Bank, and Ramesh Gelli, who became Chairman of Global Trust Bank, Sankara Guruswamy, an IAS, former MD of APSFC who later became the first CMD of Power Finance Corporation. Several MDs had distinguished themselves. CS Sastry received the Padmashri Award; TR Prasad became Cabinet Secretary to the Government of India; D Subbarao became Governor of the RBI; PK Rastogi became Secretary of Steel; and Ratan P Watal became Finance Secretary. They have made us and SFC proud.

UNION FINANCE MINISTER ADDRESSES CAPTAINS OF INDUSTRIES

There was a long-standing request from industries and entrepreneurs to invite P Chidambaram, Union Finance Minister, to share insights about the new industrial policy and financial support for Small and Medium enterprises. I had an earlier acquaintance with Chidambaram and requested him to address officers and staff of APSFC and other entrepreneurs who were keen to listen to him on the occasion of our Golden Jubilee. As a large number of industrialists and the national and local press were keen to attend the meeting, we organized the lecture at JNTU Auditorium on 15th November 2005. K Rosaiah, Finance Minister, and I received P Chidambaram, CM YS Rajasekhar Reddy, and Finance Minister of AP, K Rosiah, CMD of SIDBI N Bala Subramanian, and I were on the dais.

P. Chidambaram addressed the large gathering of entrepreneurs, officers, and staff of SFC, which was attended by MDs of Andhra Bank and State Bank of Hyderabad. He congratulated the APSFC for an excellent performance, its turnaround, and assured support for the State Financial Corporations, provided they were able to face competition from the banking sector and showed good results. It was the first time that a Union Finance Minister had addressed a meeting in Hyderabad at the invitation of the APSFC. This augured well for the Golden Jubilee Celebrations and was a shot in the arm for APSFC.

GOLDEN JUBILEE CELEBRATIONS

During the month-long celebrations, we held Entrepreneurs Day, Customers' Day, and SME Day and organized guest lectures, games, competitions, and a dinner for our officers and staff. We also took them to a local resort to enjoy time with their families. Some of our staff, who were artists, cartoonists, social workers, dramatists, and authors were honoured. The Minister for Revenue was Chief Guest at a drama enacted by APSFC. The celebrations strengthened the bonhomie among the officers and the SFC beneficiaries.

SFC FLEXES ITS MUSCLES – BECOMES NUMERO - UNO

Due to the concerted efforts of employees and the steps taken, SFC turned the corner. It started wiping out its losses and became ***"Numero Uno"*** in the country, a position it regained after eighteen years. This was the result of hard work, smart work, teamwork, network, and efforts of MDs, officers, and staff. Their commitment had made the seemingly impossible possible and visible. APSFC continues to be a profitable SFC.

REMINISCENCES OF APSFC

While relinquishing my post, I felt happy that APSFC, which had a loss of Rs.13.13 crore when I joined as Chairman, had turned around and recorded profits in all four years of my tenure and made a profit of Rs.13.15 crore in the year I left. In retrospect, my role was that of a bridge between the government, the customer, and the SFC, ably supported by SIDBI and other banks. My role was to formulate a strategy and seek and secure support for a turnaround. It involved streamlining Board procedures, proposals, and actions. My real contribution was morale building, guidance, motivation, maintenance of good relationships, and ensuring good Person-Position fit, which elicited positive responses. All through, I emphasized the importance of continuous training, updating and upgrading the skills of our staff, and upholding the ethics and values of a financial institution. We introduced simple key performance indices and success parameters and made the increase in employee productivity an important feature of our work ethic. My tenure in APSFC was a humbling and great learning experience in the service and art of turning around corporations and companies.

3

Andhra Pradesh Gas Power Corporation Limited

In 1987-88, there was an economic recession all over the world, including in India. Andhra Pradesh reeled under severe power shortages. TL Sankar, Chairman of the Andhra Pradesh State Electricity Board (APSEB), had a brilliant idea. Gas was discovered in the KG Basin off the coast of Andhra Pradesh. He wanted to set up a gas-based, short-gestation power project to overcome the power shortage. Japanese companies had "off-the-shelf" gas-based power plants for sale and installation. APSEB drove a hard bargain and was able to get a 100 MW gas power plant on a turnkey basis at an incredibly low cost. It envisaged a public-private partnership power plant.

UNIQUE PUBLIC-PRIVATE PARTNERSHIP

The Indian government was in the process of amending the Indian Electricity Act to introduce "public-private partnerships" to build up power capacity. APSEB took the lead in persuading some large private HT industrial consumers in Andhra Pradesh to join as shareholders with APSEB in a joint-sector venture where the shareholders would themselves be consumers and sell surplus power, if any. It puts into practice the "Prosumer" concept, where the "Producer is the Consumer" and consumers are the producers. A Tripartite Memorandum of Understanding was signed in October 1988 between APSEB, the private Investors-cum-Consumers, and the newly registered AP Gas Power Corporation Limited (APGPCL) as the implementing agency. This became the pioneer of the "Collective Captive Power Plants" under the amended Electricity Act,

AP GAS POWER CORPORATION - STAGE I PLANT

APGPCL's Stage I-100 MW power plant was set up by APSEB as the Lead promoter with a 26% share and private sector companies as co-promoters, contributing a 25% share. In return, they got an allocation of power in proportion to their share at minimal or near actual cost. The remaining 49% shares were contributed by industries seeking captive power according to the extent of their shareholding. The surplus power, if any, was sold at market cost to APSEB or other consumers.

The Gas Authority of India Limited (GAIL) agreed to supply gas from Tatipaka in the AP coast by pipeline to the plant set up at Vijjeswaram near Kovvur on the right bank of Godavari River in West Godavari district. The turnkey plant was built quickly and formally dedicated to the nation on 16th September 1990 by Dr M Chenna Reddy, then AP CM. The power station was operated and maintained by APSEB on a contract basis. The power generated was wheeled through the APSEB grid and consumed by shareholders and consumers at their premises. The turnkey project had an incredibly low per MW capital cost of Rs.1.43 crores, a big cost advantage to shareholders cum consumers.

STAGE II – 172 MW POWER PLANT

There was no firm commitment about additional gas allocation. But buoyed by the success of the Stage I plant, APGPCL and its promoters decided to expand the plant capacity by setting up a dual-feed combined cycle power plant of 172 MW capacity based on naphtha as feedstock with the facility to switch over to gas. The Stage II project was completed and inaugurated by N Chandra Babu Naidu, AP CM, in April 1998.

APGPCL–FORERUNNER OF PUBLIC PRIVATE PARTNERSHIP

APGPCL was the first gas power plant in AP and South India to have the lowest tariff in the country. It was the forerunner of the concept of the combined cycle power plant, which is now part of the Indian Electricity Act 2003. It recorded a high Power Load Factor (PLF) of 90% in 2003-04. It demonstrated that public-private partnerships can be a good business model for the future.

APSEB AS THE O&M CONTRACTOR

APSEB was the maintenance contractor for running the plant. Hence, APGPCL sometimes had a regular full-time Managing Director. The Power Secretary was the Chairman. There was a part-time MD or

Director in charge. The Secretary, Power, and two private promoters of APGPCL met and requested me to join as full-time Director in charge of APGPCL in March 2006.

A retired superintending engineer of APSEB was working in the APGPCL head office, and another senior executive engineer carried out the plant's operation and maintenance work. I visited the plant at Vijjeswaram and acquainted myself with the O&M contractor's staff of APSEB.

I met the office bearers of the Employees Union, who expected that APGPCL would benefit from my stewardship and experience as a former Managing Director of Godavari Fertilizers and Chemicals Limited. They wanted facilities for sports and games and a grant to celebrate the Company Formation Day. I assured them that I would not only provide games facilities but also conduct games at Vijjeswaram for other power-generating companies.

Being familiar with the operations of Namrup Gas power and Lakwa Gas power plants in Assam as Secretary Industries and having laid gas pipelines as CMD of Assam Gas Company to the Tea factories, I quickly gauged the work at the APGPCL plant.

I met officials of GAIL and ONGC to ascertain gas availability. Cairn, an associate of ONGC, had discovered gas in the KG basin, and had set up a gas gathering station onshore, and was supplying gas to GAIL. Reliance had found gas in the KG D-6 area, while Gujarat State Petroleum Corporation had also struck some gas. But they were still to assess the size of the find. I went to Baroda and Ahmedabad to discuss matters and understand the time frame and likely quantity of gas available from Gujarat Corporation and Reliance authorities.

The local head of GAIL briefed me about the work being done to extend the pipelines. There were some isolated instances of gas leakages and local flares-cum-fires which were being promptly attended to. The head of ONGC at Rajahmundry said that they had discovered a large quantity of gas in the KG basin, but it would take some time to set up mid-sea floating platforms and lay pipelines to pipe gas to the shore. One of the ONGC officers who had attended management courses at IPE was the head of HR at Kakinada. He was very helpful in our interactions with ONGC officials and their involvement in CSR activities. I met the local Reliance and Gujarat Oil and Gas Corporation officials and learnt about their plans.

I was visiting the East Godavari district after a long time and was pleasantly surprised to note that a number of new industries had come up in and around Rajahmundry, Kakinada, Samarlakota, Kovvur, and Tanuku. Several engineering colleges had been set up. A distinct industrial culture was noticeable. Marine exports were booming, and there were prawn and fishponds all along the coast.

I used to visit the Vijjeswaram plant once a fortnight and spend a couple of days going around the plant, meeting employees, and sorting out small issues. This has been my management style, focusing on grassroots-level engagement. I was invited by engineering colleges and Rotary or Lions Clubs for lectures, which provided me scope to interact with local people and the press.

We had drawn some technical officers from APSEB to work for our company, oversee and monitor the functioning of the O&M contractor. The small complement of officers monitored and ensured high productivity with due regard to the economy. The company not only operated efficiently but also had zero accident record.

The Stage I- 100 MW plant was running on gas while the Stage II combined cycle plant was running on naphtha supplied through road tankers by HPCL to a naphtha storage tank built by them at our premises in Vijjeswaram.

The Stage II plant broke down and needed a complete overhaul. It was sent for repairs and replacements between May and December 2007. The repairs were carried out by BHEL GE Gas Turbines Services (BGGTS), a joint venture of BHEL and GE. The 30 MW steam turbine was also sent for repairs between January and May 2008. The repairs were carried out successfully, and the plant resumed normal operations.

GAS PRICES AND CONDITIONS OF SUPPLY

Private Companies that entered the oil and gas sector demanded an increase in the price of gas in line with international prices. The output of gas in India was lower than the demand. There was a shortage of 22% against the assured supply of gas. Our plants had to operate on gas or naphtha as per availability for optimal output. GAIL had imposed stringent conditions for the supply of gas to customers like Minimum Guaranteed Off-Take and Take or Pay Clauses, which compelled us to give a minimum guaranteed regular off-take or otherwise pay the penalty even if it did not draw gas for causes beyond our control. The company had to give GAIL at least 15 days prior notice in case gas is not required. This imposed charges without a supply of gas! There were delays in receiving

Insurance amounts for the replacement of equipment, repairs and maintenance works, and loss of profits for the shutdown period. We patiently sorted out the issues.

HPCL CONTRACT FOR NAPHTHA SUPPLY

We had entered into a 20-year fuel supply agreement with HPCL for naphtha supply through HPCL tankers. We learnt that the cost of transporting naphtha delivered to our plant was much higher than the charges for naphtha delivered at nearby authorized supply points. We discovered that the usage of private tankers for naphtha from HPCL Visakhapatnam or outlets could reduce transport costs. Moreover, with more gas becoming available, the need to use naphtha had been reduced. HPCL wanted us to pay for tankages constructed in our plant area by them, as they would no longer be useful for them. We paid off HPCL and used contract tankers whenever necessary with considerable savings. The tankages proved useful during a shortage of gas as we could use naphtha as feedstock.

WATER USAGE CHARGES

We installed large pumps to draw water from Godavari to the plant for internal use and cooling purposes. The Irrigation department was charging us 10 paise cess per kilo litre for water usage, whereas we were agreeable to pay only 5 paise. After a great deal of haggling, we were able to get the concurrence of the department to reduce accumulated water cess from Rs.3.3 crore to Rs.57 lakhs!

The plant was drawing a large quantity of water from the Godavari River for cooling and recycling it and discharging it in the river or the canal nearby, as advised by the Irrigation department. It was really not the consumption of water but the "pass-through" of water, albeit with an increase in temperature that required pumping it back to the river.

The Irrigation department suddenly issued a notice charging an exorbitant rate for water given to us for cooling purposes. We contested the charges, and after discussions, the bill for cooling water charges was reduced from Rs.90 crore to Rs.1.31 crore!

CHANGE OF O&M CONTRACTOR

APSEB has been the Operations and Maintenance contractor since the plant commenced operations. The cost they charged was higher than what qualified private contractors charged. We floated tenders and got good responses from contractors with experience at a much lower cost than

APSEB. We terminated the O&M contract with APSEB, though it led to some hard feelings. We explained to them that commercial decisions need to be taken on sound considerations and not sentiments.

During a severe shortage of power, APSEB requested us to generate more power and agreed to pay the variable cost of naphtha and gas used and a small margin for standing charges. We obliged the APSEB, which paid us Rs. 4.25 crore for the power supplied to them.

CCI ARBITRATION CASE

The Cement Corporation of India (CCI) Tandur, one of our promoter shareholders, had run into losses and was unable to pay dues, and it was referred to the Board for Industrial and Financial Reconstruction (BIFR). APGPCL, which held shares of CCI as collateral security, sold shares to collect the arrears. CCI went for arbitration, which dragged on. Justice B Jeevan Reddy, former Judge of the Supreme Court, was appointed as arbitrator. His order was accepted, and the matter was settled.

GAS SUPPLIES AND PRICES

We faced challenges in the supply and pricing of gas. The steady, reliable source of gas was GAIL, who made good metering arrangements at our plant site and maintained cordial relations. Later, some gas was supplied by Cairn (ONGC) and Reliance. They utilized GAIL metering arrangements at our site to calibrate the gas supplied and the amounts payable. Under the Administered Price Mechanism (APM), GAIL, which was supplying gas at $1.85 per Million Standard Metric Cubic Meters (MSCMD) per day, raised it to $4.20. The government again increased the price of gas from $4.20 to $5.73 per MSCMD.

The cost of power generation at the plant increased. Power from the 100 MW Stage I plant cost Rs.1.53 per Kwh, while the cost for Stage II 172 MW was Rs.1.27 per Kwh. The relative cost for Reliance gas was higher at Rs.2.15 per Kwh for Stage I and Rs.2.05 per Kwh for Stage II. The cost of gas determined our cost of generation. While the APSEB tariff was around Rs.4 to 5 per Kwh hour, our rate was much lower in the range of Rs.2 to Rs.2.15 per Kwh hour.

The Central Government suddenly sprang a surprise that only government or public sector power plants would get the benefit of allocation of gas and that our group captive power plant was not eligible. This was a grave danger signal. Along with TL Sankar, Secretary of Industries & Power, I called on the Director General of PNGRB (Power and Natural Gas Regulatory Board) at Delhi and the Ministry of Petroleum and Chemicals.

Based on our representation of the background in which APGPCL had been established and the stake of APSEB, the Government of India agreed to the allocation of gas at 75% of plant capacity and not 100% to which we were earlier entitled.

PRIVATE GAS BASED POWER PLANTS

Buoyed by press reports of the high quantity of gas found in the KG basin and the growing demand for power, local entrepreneurs rushed to set up gas-based power plants. Among them were Reliance Industries, GVK, GMR, Spectrum and Gowthami. We prepared a feasibility report for setting up a 400 MW power plant under the IPP route (Indian Private Power Producer route) in land adjoining our plant. We applied to the Ministry of Petroleum with the recommendation and concurrence of the AP Government for a firm linkage for gas supplies. We approached farmers for the acquisition of land around the plant and were able to convince them about our need; and persuade them to part with their land when required. One of the senior promoters of the company, M Harischandra Prasad, CMD of Andhra Sugars, had a lot of influence in the Vijjeswaram area and was able to convince farmers to hand over land when required voluntarily. However, due to difficulties in securing an assured adequate supply of gas, pricing issues, and escalating costs, we shelved the project. A lot of effort was wasted.

THE BOARD OF DIRECTORS

The Chairman of the Board and a Director were from the government, while the remaining directors were big and medium-scale industrialists who held shares in the company. Among the big shareholders were Andhra Sugars, India Cements Limited, Amara Raja Batteries Ltd, Maha Cements, and Penna Cements. The discussions were mostly on the supply of gas, generation of power, increase of or additional allocation of power, if available, and price of power, court or arbitration cases.

During my tenure, there were as many as 12 Chairmen and Directors from the government on the Board of APGPCL. All of them contributed by making timely policy decisions to upskill, upgrade, and uphold the reputation of APGPCL as India's low-cost power-generating company and novel model of private-public partnership. We ensured professionalism and did not allow interference in the company's work. As the cost of APGPCL power was low, a lot of pressure was exercised by the Industrial Member Directors to increase the availability of power and additional allocation of

Power supply to them whenever some consumers were unable to draw power due to maintenance, unforeseen break-downs, strikes, or the like. The Annual General Meetings were attended by representatives of APSEB, AP Genco, and other major shareholders and their company secretaries or finance executives. We had a competent Company Secretary, Dr Rajmogli, and a Vice-President (FA), D Venkateswara Reddy.

CORPORATE SOCIAL RESPONSIBILITY ACTIVITIES

There were many requests from villages surrounding the plant for various amenities. As part of our Corporate Social Responsibility, we conducted several activities in consultation with local people. We constructed a small community hall in one village, conducted "Eye Camps" to test school children, adults, and elderly persons, and gave free spectacles. Some riverside villages faced problems of cremating bodies in crematoria due to flooding during the rainy season. We raised the cremation ground level and provided covered platforms and dry fuel wood for cremation. We converted a disused jeep trailer into a hearse trailer, which could be attached to a tractor for conveying bodies during rains through slushy roads to the cremation ground. Villagers and the press widely appreciated this.

We conducted a big Games and Sports Meet for all public sector undertakings in AP, which saw good participation and a large crowd.

4

My Foray in MLC Elections

After thoroughly streamlining the operations of APGPCL, I realized that I had very little to do at the office now. Some friends mooted the idea that as a retired officer with extensive administrative experience, I should seek nomination as a member of the Legislative Council in AP or contest from the Graduates Constituency of Hyderabad and Mahbubnagar. I would be able to contribute to discussions in the Legislative Council and suggest measures for good legislation and improvement of administration in the state. They said that as an administrator, well-known in the public sector, popular in Hyderabad, and a good speaker, I would get support. Moreover, many social service and software industry associations knew me quite well. I was reluctant but was egged on by my friends. My attempts to get nominated in the government quota failed as political considerations prevailed. A retired bureaucrat would not meet the political needs.

I had discussed this with a few friends, many of whom were retired. They felt that I had a good chance to win the election and offered to help me in running my office, thus freeing me from electioneering. The Board agreed to grant me leave as I had arranged for the smooth running of APGPCL during my absence. Some directors also supported the move.

My classmate, P. Janardhan Reddy, an Ex MLA from Huzurabad in Karimnagar district and a socialist leader, accompanied me to meet P Satyanarayana Reddy, former governor of UP and socialist leader from Mahbubnagar, and to seek other leaders' support. They promised their full support and offered to mobilize people to support me. I called on several MLAs from Mahbubnagar, who assured me of their support.

The Telugu Desam party, Congress, and Communists were not interested in contesting from the Graduates Constituency. I received assurance of support from some retired employees of Godavari Fertilizers & Chemicals Limited and dealers of GFCL. I toured the district and campaigned among bank officers, APSRTC staff, Rotary & Lions Clubs, and lecturers in local colleges and schoolteachers.

I was fairly sure of support from the graduates of Hyderabad, given my well-established reputation. However, it so happened that another IAS officer, the President of the Telangana NGOs Association, a few local educated persons, and some educationists were also contesting the elections, effectively reducing my vote share. The only political party that contested and which had a good number of volunteers was the BJP. Students supported their professor, who was the ultimate winner in the fray. Many candidates vigorously canvassed with decorated vans, banners, posters, and personal contacts in a big way to contact teachers and graduates. I was constrained by the lack of finance, volunteers, publicity material, preparatory work, and inadequate canvassing and polling booth agents. Yet another constraint was the cost of the elections and the mobilization of finances. Voters and Teacher's organisations were demanding sizable cash for votes, which I could not afford.

My own resources and that of my family were supplemented by my friends and well-wishers who provided me with vehicles and electoral support. We had to do detailed preliminary work by designing publicity materials, banners, and posters, as well as mobilizing vehicles for canvassing in Mahbubnagar, which is a very large district (now split into three districts). The polling agents wanted regular payments and a vehicle to assist their movements with publicity materials. Luckily, some of my friends spared their vehicles and drivers, and I only had to spend money on petrol, oil, and lubricants. I had to maintain an office in Hyderabad, offices in Mahbubnagar, and other important places.

I addressed quite a large number of meetings with retired teachers, school teachers' associations, and social service groups in Mahabubnagar district. Many of them expected that I would hand over handsome amounts for canvassing or securing the votes of graduates. Telangana sentiments were quite strong. Though I was educated at Mahbub College, Secunderabad, and Osmania University, much before the formation of AP, I was viewed as an Andhra, not born in Telangana. The Telangana sentiment was quite strong. I was not able to match the mobilization of funds and votes like other candidates in Mahbubnagar.

In Hyderabad, I received excellent responses, and I was better known. Despite the number of contestants, I secured the largest number of votes from the twin cities of Secunderabad and Hyderabad but secured fewer votes in Mahbubnagar. However, when the results were announced, I found that an independent candidate, Prof. Nageshwar Rao, whom students and Electorate of Mahbubnagar supported, received the largest number of votes, followed by the BJP candidate, who had well-oiled election machinery to support him. I stood third among 11 candidates.

I realized that voters expected cash disbursements and freebies, which was neither acceptable nor affordable. Independent candidates are at a disadvantage. Voting by graduates was determined by decisions of teachers' unions, political parties, and powerful interests.

Many of the Teachers' unions would approach me for big sums of money for their votes to ensure block voting was in my favour. Some groups claimed that they could mobilize a definite number of votes but wanted money to do so. I frankly told them that I did not have money or inclination to pay for votes. More surprising was the fact that educated voters expected to be paid for transport and exercising their franchise. I used to believe that only uneducated, less educated, and poor voters expected to be paid, but even educated voters expected to be paid.

I fought and won many elections in college and university or other professional organizations where merit and qualifications counted. However, the General and MLC elections are altogether different and difficult game to play. It is a tantalizing steaming cup of tea that leaves a bitter experience and scalds your tongue. That tea had to be made with more sugar and milk, either light or strong, based on the preferences of those enjoying the tea.

After the election results were published, I re-joined APGPCL, where I received a warm welcome back.

5

EMRI – Emergency Medical Research Institute as Public Private Partnership

EMRI: Emergency Medical Research Institute was set up on 15th August 2005 with 14 ambulances and 70 employees at Hyderabad by Ramalinga Raju, Chairman of Satyam Computers with the first CEO and Sudhakar Varanasi on the advice of Dr. Ranga Rao, formerly of A P Medical Service who had worked for 10 years in the National Health Service of the UK. Raju liked the idea of setting up a similar organisation like the National Emergency Number Association (911) in the US and was the driving force. In 2005, Ramalinga Raju invited Venkat Changavalli to expand the Emergency Medical Services Organisation in India.

In 2007, I got a call from Ramalinga Raju, Chairman of Satyam Computers, requesting me to discuss a matter concerning health, society, and government. He felt that India should have an exclusive Emergency phone number similar to 911 in the United States to respond to emergency calls. He was setting up a similar arrangement in India, to begin with, in AP state with a dedicated emergency number **108** to provide immediate free ambulance service for emergency medical attention at hospitals with the support of police and fire services. He proposed a Public Private Partnership (PPP) model with the Government since the support of government departments was necessary for its operations. He requested that I join as an advisor.

A Call centre was set up to receive emergency telephone calls. The first task was to sensitize the ambulance personnel to the emergency, pass on information to police or fire service personnel in the vicinity of the emergency, and train ambulance personnel as needed. Victims had to be taken to hospital in less than 60 minutes, called the 'golden hour' to help improve chances of survival. The ambulance staff had to proceed to the place from where an emergency call was received, assess the needs of Victims on the spot, and provide emergency first aid care while taking them to the hospital or dispensary. This involved training emergency medical technicians and pilots, sensitising them to the importance of their work, and the time factor which determines the chances of survival and recovery of the patient.

For examining the patient, the medical emergency technicians in the ambulance use the "Triad" method to determine whether the case is (a) critical, needs immediate medical care, (b) is a patient of chronic disease, and (c) minor cases which need only home care. Serious cases that require immediate critical care, like severe accidents, burn victims, drowning cases, childbirth, etc., must be given on-the-spot attention and taken to the hospital quickly.

SELECTION OF AMBULANCE

I was involved in the process of selecting an appropriate ambulance vehicle based on medical facilities like bed(s), monitoring arrangements, oxygen supply, essential medicines, bandages, and space for a doctor or health assistant. The van prominently featured the number 108, along with a local name and colours designed to draw attention. It was provided a roof-top light and a distinctive siren to secure fast passage in traffic. I gave many suggestions to improve the van's design and its equipment. CM YS Raja Sekhar Reddy saw the ambulance and gave it his approval.

PUBLIC-PRIVATE PARTNERSHIP

The State Government adopted the project under the Public Private Partnership (PPP) framework. The government met the capital expenditure of ambulances and equipment for the call centres, salaries of front-line staff, and the cost and maintenance of vehicles and medicines.

The private party had to provide for the cost of the office building, land for parking vans, proprietary software, updates for emergency response applications, and the salary of managerial staff. Technology was regularly updated and leveraged by way of call centre software. Geographical maps showing landmarks for easy location of accident sites helped in accuracy and speed of response. It had GPS backing, medical protocol, and back-end support operations. When Satyam Computers got into trouble around 2009-2010 and could not meet the expenses, GVK stepped in as the private sector partner.

The success of the project encouraged other states like Gujarat, UP, MP, Karnataka, Tamil Nadu, Uttarakhand, HP, Chattisgarh, Assam, and other Northeastern states to adopt the same.

The proof of concept of 108 and its acceptance is evident in its adoption all over India. Its successful operation has saved many lives, rendered maternity services, and helped rural and tribal women in safe hospital deliveries. A lot more work still needs to be done to make it a National Health Service.

HMRI – HEALTH MANAGEMENT AND RESEARCH INSTITUTE

A Public-Private Partnership (PPP) was entered into by Satyam Computers and AP Government in 2007 called Health Management and Research Institute (HMRI) to provide a helpline for all types of health-related queries to lessen the burden on the public health system with a dedicated phone number 104. Later, it started sending Mobile Medical Units (MMUs) to villages with regular supplies of medicines for distribution through the 'Asha' institutional setup along with a doctor on scheduled visits, which were intimated in advance to Asha set up in villages. The programs were aimed at helping the rural poor by supplying medicines. A training programme for Registered Medical Practitioners (RMPs) was also conducted.

A small group under Dr. U Balaji of Satyam, who was heading Satyam Foundation, was set up to give shape to the idea of a Health Medical Research Institute (HMRI) at Hyderabad with a dedicated telephone No 104, setting up a call centre to train persons to maintain the call centre and be able to 'sense' and respond promptly and correctly. 'Mckinsey, a consultancy firm, was engaged to assist in the matter. Mckinsey did a good job in identifying problem-likely areas, its scheme of training, and provided training manuals to emergencies. Dr. Balaji was a resilient, knowledgeable person with in-depth experience in social activities. He wanted me to observe the activities, provide suggestions and guidance closely.

HMRI was housed in a rented building at Musheerabad. Satyam Computers deputed their managers to work on finalising the software to be used at the call centre and training new recruits as call operators. The Government Institute of Public Health at Vengalrao Nagar, under Dr. Ram Mohan Rao, assisted by providing advice on public health issues and training health assistants.

The rural areas were mapped, and suitable locations for Mobile Medical Units were identified for providing Fixed Day Health Services (FDHS). I used to address (Town Hall meetings) all employees at the headquarters.

New ideas like distance medical attention and treatment, telemedicine, helicopter services, etc., were pursued by a team of experts to advise and guide primary health centre doctors in the field.

6

On Chairmanship of Committees

Committees are constituted to collectively tackle problems and difficult issues by taking a well-considered and integrated view on the subject and suggesting the way forward by recommending acceptable courses of action or solutions. Committees usually take a long time to complete enquiries and submit their reports. The Constitution of committees helps douse passions and creates an environment in which decisions can be taken objectively. It can be a mechanism to delay and postpone decisions! The judiciary constitutes benches to examine complicated issues to arrive at just, fair, and reasoned decisions.

IAS officers are often made chairmen of committees that involve in-depth examination of issues, hearing parties to a dispute, field visits, securing consensus, examining options, and suggesting or recommending courses of action.

I chaired Government committees where my background and experience were considered appropriate. I would reflect on the committee's purpose, the processes to be followed, and the individuals impacted by or responsible for implementing the recommendations. They covered a wide range of subjects. **The Committee on Performance, Management, and Evaluation System (PMES)** was set up by the AP government to examine the system of reporting and reviewing performance management and evaluation. We made recommendations to simplify the process of reporting and evaluation. The appropriate Performance Indices and Key Result Areas were identified, and the process was simplified. It emphasized the **'outcome'** and **'impacts on society'** rather than the input-output matrix. The periodicity of reporting was rationalized with a focus on performance.

MEMBER, COMMITTEES ON UTILIZATION OF NATURAL GAS ON THE EAST COAST

I was a member of two committees set up by the AP government in the wake of the discovery of natural gas to trigger industrial development and prepare the ground for the petrochemical industry and various uses.

I was the Chairman of the Committee on Pharma Research and Development Fund set up by the AP Government. Our report was accepted by the Central Government, which sanctioned the setting up of the National Institute of Pharmaceutical Education and Research (NIPER) in Hyderabad. It utilised the unused infrastructure of IDPL, which had shut down. NIPER, Hyderabad is doing well and is making significant contributions.

The Committee on Industrial Area Local Authorities in AP (IALA), which I chaired, resulted in improving governance and administration of Industrial estates with townships.

POWER SECTOR

The National Level Committee on Transformers, set up by the Government of India, made far-reaching recommendations leading to the development of amorphous core distribution transformers manufacture and exports. Its recommendations led to many initiatives by the transformer industry and improved the performance and longevity of transformers. India started exporting Amorphous Core Transformers to several countries. The Planning Commission Group on Rural Electrification laid out the plans for village and household electrification and expanded the scope for renewable energy development to supplement power from other sources. It also helped provide power to difficult and remote areas.

MINERALS AND MINING SECTOR

The Special Review Group on Mining brought changes to the Government's mineral policy. The committee on the Long-term Requirement of Bauxite for aluminium identified the extent of bauxite reserves available in the country and the scope for the production of aluminium with due regard to ecology, social concerns of affected regions, and aspirations of the people.

THE INTERNATIONAL LEAD-ZINC STUDY GROUP OF THE UNITED NATIONS ORGANIZATION

I was Vice-President of this Study Group to examine the scope for Mining, and usage of lead and zinc in harmony with the environment, ecology, and society.

NATIONAL MINERAL DEVELOPMENT CORPORATION COMMITTEE

This committee was formed to set up a steel plant in Chhattisgarh and examined issues relating to the use of new technology, manufacturing and logistical issues, and demand-supply matrix. The plant was recently commissioned and inaugurated by PM Narendra Modi.

REPORT OF COMMITTEE ON UTILIZATION OF UGC GRANT BY NISWASS, BHUBANESWAR

The Union Ministry of Human Resources Development, Government of India, constituted a committee under my chairmanship in November 2013 with Prof HA Ranganath, former director of NAAC (National Assessment and Accreditation Committee), and Prof.SP Thyagarajan, former Vice-Chancellor of Madras University, as members. Its objective was to inspect the National Institute of Social Work and Social Sciences (NISWASS), Bhubaneshwar, regarding the utilization of infrastructure grant in aid of Rs. 20 crores and an annual recurring grant of Rs.4.91 crores from the University Grants Commission (UGC) during 2010-2012.

Our committee visited Bhubaneshwar, held discussions with concerned officials, and noted that UGC had not followed the rules in sanctioning both a non-recurring and a recurring grant to NISWASS, which had not adhered to norms of UGC and the Orissa Government for building plan approvals from competent authorities. Moreover, UGC did not approve the change of location of buildings.

Committee noticed several procedural lapses in the utilization of grants released by UGC. We recommended that a panel of Financial and Audit Experts conduct an in-depth financial audit. Until this audit is completed, no further grants under Non-recurring or Recurring head should be released to NISWASS. We also suggested that the UGC should streamline monitoring and supervisory arrangements to ensure adherence to UGC norms of sanctions.

RESTRUCTURING OF ECIL

The Committee for Re-structuring of Electronics Corporation of India Limited (ECIL) studied the inverted hierarchical pyramids caused by over-employment, absorption of apprentices by ECIL, and its adverse impact to the organization and related issues. The Atomic Energy Commission accepted its recommendations, and the restructuring of ECIL led to the introduction of a voluntary retirement scheme, taking up new activities, and higher turnover of the company. The profitability of ECIL increased.

IPE STUDY ON TOURISM

The study of the Institute of Public Enterprise (IPE) on Tourism and Hospitality resulted in the setting up of the National Institute of Tourism and Hospitality at Hyderabad.

Another report of IPE on "Social Safety Net" and the alleviation of poverty led to the setting up of the Society for Elimination of Rural Poverty (SERP).

I took great satisfaction in knowing that the authorities embraced and implemented the recommendations put forth by the Committees.

7

The Changing Scenario: Role of Independent Directors

The role of directors in a company has evolved over time. The Stock Exchange Board of India (SEBI) regulations have clarified many issues, making the roles and duties of directors clearer. Directors are now custodians of all *shareholders'interests*, including minority shareholders. They must also look after the Stakeholders' interests. Directors must be aware of the uncertainties of the business and attendant risks of markets and secure the profitability of the business. The composition of the Board, with directors who have relevant experience in various fields and can identify issues and priorities, helps secure consensual decision-making. The Board is now the custodian of not only the performance and interest of the company but also of public interest.

Companies are choosing people of integrity, expertise, and relevant experience as directors. They have to exercise due diligence in analysing issues and suggest appropriate courses of action. With globalisation, strategic risk management has become as important as operational excellence. Internal and external risks are financial and market risks, but for directors, 'reputational risk' is more important. They must ensure statutory compliance, streamline internal financial controls, and work as a watchdog. They should ensure legal, economic, social, and ethical compliance and maintain amicable relations with trade unions and employees. The directors should take both an 'outsider- and insider' view before deciding on issues.

INDEPENDENT DIRECTORS (IDs)

The Independent Directors are expected to objectively discuss matters affecting the company and, by their collegiate and collective wisdom, analyse issues and bring about consensual decisions. They bring objectivity, Integrity, openness, and fairness to the deliberations of the Board. They are custodians of public interest and, in particular, safeguard the interests of minority shareholders. IDs are increasingly being recognised as Guardians of Corporate Good Governance. With the integration of the Indian economy with the global economy, good governance is important. Global companies emphasise the concept of trusteeship and economic growth with a social conscience.

It is said that there is "More" to business than just business. The "more" denotes morals, ethics, and values in the conduct of business. The independent directors must 'steer' the company boat and not 'row' it. They must help tide over crises and help in conflict resolution.

Independent Directors must adhere to the 6 "T" s of good governance, namely *Truth, Trust, Transparency, Tolerance, Technology, and Tact*. The real task of independent directors is to 'tone and tune' the company's performance and help in talent management and succession planning. They are internal "Whistleblowers" who prevent major or long-term damage to the company's interests and reputation.

The Independent Directors must set the agenda for the Board in consultation with the Chief Executive and monitor the progress of action taken. This includes budgeting, monitoring, and review of action and achievement of targets. SEBI has prescribed the number of independent directors on the Board based on whether the company has a CMD or a Non-executive chairman and an Executive managing director. Disclosures and overall compliances, as required, have to be reported jointly by the CEO, Company Secretary, and CFO to ensure proper checks and balances.

The mandated annual independent directors meeting must be held, and views must be expressed frankly and act as a watchdog against misuse of power. Among the important tasks of the Board is to prepare the *Vision and Mission* statement of the company, build a pipeline of succession to meet local and international competition and be ahead of events and competition. Enhancing the company's competitiveness through total quality management is imperative in the context of Make in India, Made in India, and Make for the World.

Independent Directors are tasked to evaluate the performance of the Board and the chairperson, promoters, directors, chief executives, and non-independent and independent directors. To facilitate this need, a lead director from the independent directors is elected or selected for an objective assessment where necessary, indicating changes required to strengthen the Board further. Independent directors have, therefore, to be guardians of the company's interest as well as that of shareholders.

COMMITTEES — NRC

Companies operate through committees like the Nomination and Remuneration Committee (NRC), which interviews and selects directors, executive directors, and senior executives. It plays an important role in fixing remuneration and performance-linked bonuses. It also reviews the performance of executives for higher responsibility and provides for the pipeline of a succession of crucial key managerial personnel.

AUDIT COMMITTEE

The committee reviews budgets, quarterly financial results, and internal financial control systems to prevent major frauds, misappropriation, etc. It examines all related party transactions and approves quarterly and annual reports besides the appointment of auditors — both internal and statutory -- apart from the assessment of their work.

RISK MANAGEMENT

Companies face many risks — both internal and external — like a flight of talent, foreign exchange fluctuations, supply chain disruptions, working capital problems, supply-demand equations, market conditions, and increased competition. Companies are now constituting Risk Management Committees to visualise and take pre-emptive action. In the context of globalisation, digitisation, frequent occurrence of disruptive events, and supply chain problems, companies are well-advised to do some ring-fencing to protect the company and themselves.

There are grave legal and reputational risks in the acceptance of independent directorship, as has happened in many cases. Directors are well advised to study the balance sheets of the company, make enquiries, and gather data before accepting an offer. They should seek and secure liability insurance coverage. Particular care should be taken to prevent malfeasance and avoid insolvency and bankruptcy of the company.

AS INDEPENDENT DIRECTOR

My reputation as a successful Managing Director and a "turn-around" expert led to several listed public limited and private companies inviting me to join them as an Independent Director. I used to ask for and study their company's latest annual reports, interact with the CEO to ascertain relevant facts, ask them to hand me a detailed note on their current position and difficulties, and then propose a course of action. Only if satisfied, would I agree to serve as a director in the company.

Mother India has to pick up a fast pace if She wishes to become the Third largest economy in the world. In this endeavour, Indian companies and their directors have an important role to play -- in setting direction and agenda for a technologically resurgent and enterprising country, contributing to the needs of the economy, society, environment, progress, and welfare of all living beings on our planet.

8

Directorships – Tool for Industrial Development

An IAS officer must be multi-skilled, versatile, focused, and agile. During his career, he has been posted to 15 or 20 different departments and jobs. His posting as collector presents him with an overview of the functions of government as they converge at the district level. Good governance must eradicate poverty, provide social justice, and ensure the welfare of people. His career is one of constant learning, planning, implementing, guiding, and evaluating, as well as course correction and review of results to secure the best cost-benefits. He soon realises that it is not the input-output ratio but the outcomes and impacts of action taken that are more important.

As I had a fairly long training in district administration both in AP and Assam where I managed various emergency situations and law-and-order challenges, I believed the Government would likely offer me a career related to law and order. However, my postings were primarily concerned with industrial planning, development, and regulation of industries at the State and Central levels.

IRON AND STEEL INDUSTRY

As Regional Iron and Steel Controller at Hyderabad for AP and MP for four and half years, I had a close view of the iron and steel industry and related ancillaries at the large, medium, and small-scale levels. I dealt with pig iron, cast iron, and processes of steel making from the small-scale to the large-scale level. In short, I learned the making, shaping, and treatment of iron and steel materials. I wrote a report on the profile of steel industries in the two states, a paper in 1976 on steel demand and prospects of the steel industry, and estimates of the likely installed capacity in the year 2000. I visited all integrated iron and steel plants in India, Bhilai, Rourkela, Durgapur, Burnpur, Bhadravathi, Tisco, and Bokaro, as well as steel clusters at Ludhiana, Howrah, Raipur, Indore, and Jabalpur. This experience helped me when I was posted as Commissioner of the Visakhapatnam Steel Plant. This experience probably contributed to my appointment as Secretary of Industry, Power, and Minerals by the Assam Government.

ASSAM EXPERIENCE

Assam and the Northeast states have major locational disadvantages due to distance, hilly terrain, and poor rail and road connectivity. This is accentuated by a relentless monsoon, which necessitates the compression of construction time by six months. It is a sensitive area with several ethnic groups and tribal areas surrounded by other countries. Communications by road and rail are poor, which extends the time taken for the transit of goods and materials, as well as the transport of tea and other natural products from Assam to the rest of the country.

Investments in the industry were not forthcoming to the Northeast region due to problems of logistics, lack of infrastructure, and poor demand (except for some food articles, cement, steel materials, and corrugated iron sheets for roofing) due to relatively lower incomes and a near vacuum of relevant industrial skills. The power supply was just about adequate to meet the small requirements of towns and industry. Except for some hydel power projects in Meghalaya and Neepco's Kopili power plant under construction in Assam, there were hardly any large power plants in the plains. Though crude oil and gas were available, very few gas-based power plants came up as it was felt gas should be used for the manufacture of value-added petrochemicals and crude supplied to the Barauni refinery located in Bihar.

This was cause for resentment in Assam, and except for the small capacity Indian Oil Company refinery at Guwahati, there was no attempt on the part of the government of India or the State government to utilise natural resources for its industrial development and progress. This was the seed for the agitation for the second refinery and later for advanced versions of petrochemicals to be manufactured in Assam. The Government of India announced a Transport Subsidy scheme to provide some relief and a competitive advantage to industries located in Assam and goods coming into Assam. This did not help much, as very few industries took advantage.

POWER(ING) ASSAM – SPEEDING SUPPLY CHAINS

The absence of a policy to speed up logistics through the electrification of rail movement was a major handicap for the faster economic and industrial development of Assam. The irony of the situation was that, although the Northeast region and Assam had considerable scope for power generation, this opportunity was not given the adequate and serious attention it deserved from Assam, the most advanced industrial state in the region. I tried my best to impress on the Power Minister and Chief Minister that the industrial development of Assam and the Northeast region would depend on improving power availability for agriculture and industry, communications, securing large investments, training the workforce with adequate skills, taking up large, medium and small-scale industries and encouraging ancillaries. Many industrial estates based on local natural resources and raw materials, catering to local demand, had to be set up. As I mentioned earlier, efforts to harness hydel sources in the Kameng division of NEFA for Assam through the construction of a power station were torpedoed on the ground that the Assam Government should not invest its funds in and for another State. We have to think about the logic of why we now seek Foreign Investments, Technology, and Markets. It is a classic case of pennywise pound-foolish decisions. Political will and managerial skills were probably not adequate to tackle the situation.

The Government of India set up a Small Industries Service Institute at Guwahati to encourage small industries, but entrepreneurs were not available or forthcoming. At that time, there was a near vacuum of entrepreneurship. The Government was more concerned about its regulations, authority, and revenues than its role as a facilitator of industrial development or enlarging the market for local products both inside and outside Assam and the NE region.

DEARTH OF SKILLS AND ENTREPRENEURSHIP

There was a dearth of qualified professionals like engineers, chartered accountants, cost accountants, company secretaries, and technocrats. Many industries needed financial professionals. We faced difficulties in finding qualified professionals.

We had a lot of difficulty in setting up the 220 MW Bongaigaon power plant and Bongaigaon Refinery-cum-Petrochemicals. The Assam State Electricity Board was reorganised, and distribution and transmission lines were laid for rural electrification. Things have, however, changed for the better, and Assam has created the requisite infrastructure and has invited both investment and technical expertise. It is realising its own potential for high value-added products and catering to the rest of India through its agro-horticultural products with value-addition, industrial products, gas-based industries, petrochemicals, specialty chemicals, and handicrafts.

EXPOSURE TO INDUSTRIES IN AP AND GOVERNMENT OF INDIA

On deputation to Andhra Pradesh, I was posted in the Industries department and worked as MD of both Nagarjuna Fertilizers and Godavari Fertilizers and as Commissioner of Visakhapatnam Steel Plant. I was a nominee Director at AP Industrial Development Corporation, and I had to safeguard investments made by the Nizam's Investment Trust and the AP State Government. This helped me understand all aspects of industrial management in a variety of industries ranging from small- and medium-sized to large-scale and sophisticated technology.

As the MD of Godavari Fertilizers, I had hands-on experience in setting up a large fertilizer plant from concept to commissioning. Subsequent postings in the Ministry of Mines and Ministry of Power in the Government of India, as Special Chief Secretary for Industrial Development, and as CMD of REC gave me more profound experience in industries such as power, fertilizers, and chemical industries. I was unanimously elected as Chairman of SCOPE, the apex body of 246 central public sector undertakings. I was the first Telugu officer to hold this office, and I was given a warm welcome by the Delhi Telugu Academy and Andhra Cultural Association. This was a singular achievement as the entire public sector in the country had reposed confidence in me to steer the country's growth and development.

LONG EXPERIENCE AS AN INDEPENDENT DIRECTOR

I probably have the unique distinction of having served as an independent director in many large, medium, and small-scale sector industries as well as industrial development and promotion corporations. After retirement, I had requests to join as a director in many companies. In my long career of 36 years in government and 24 years after retirement, i.e., (60 years), I have served as a director in as many as 50 companies.

My postings in AP, Assam, and the Government of India made me a Nominee director in Central and State public sector, joint-sector, and private sector companies. This gave me a broad idea of the focus and varying management styles in different companies. The private sector was focused on enhancing share value and profit but did not pay adequate attention to new technology, value addition, developing their personnel, and planning for the long-term future. In the joint sector, where the government had either a 26% share or varying degrees of stake, there was some element of corporate strategy, monitoring arrangements, and review of different aspects of management and statutory compliances. In some cases, private promoters were only interested in making a quick buck. This was reflected in the action of entrepreneur-promoters, who, on receiving loan amounts from a financial institution, would purchase a big building and large cars, displaying their newfound prosperity and starting ostentatious living even before the project went into production. The public financial institutions would remark that entrepreneurs were more interested in their personal wealth- growth rather than the successful production and profitability of the companies. There were, however, some very capable entrepreneurs who laid sound foundations for successful companies and the industrial progress of States.

The lack of qualified professionals to guide industrial development and corporations promoted or supported industries slowed down the anticipated fast growth of industries.

The Central Public Sector was quite professional and manned by experienced managers. Their problem was a lack of focus on profits and diffused attention to multiple objectives of economic and social development. As they were mostly monopolies, they did earn good profits. However, companies had a problem of large over-run costs due to delays in the construction of projects. They were not cost-competitive against global prices unless the Government supported them through licensing and import/export policies. The major failure of the public sector was the slow upgradation of technical expertise, marketing, and management, and the lack of focus on securing long-term competitive advantage. However, the overall profit of public sector companies is positive, and they still hold commanding heights in some sectors and aspects of the economy.

GAP ANALYSIS AS TURNAROUND STRATEGY

After my retirement, the government and companies in the private sector requested me to be a director in large and medium industries. In the private sector, the focus was on profits by minimising expenditure, outsourcing, and maximising income. Successful companies concentrate on their brand image, market share, quality of products, growth of share value by way of earnings per share, and comparison of competitor data on profitability to throw up suggestions for improvement. Public companies concentrate on securing competitive advantage through technology, qualified and skilled personnel, marketing, and innovative practices, as well as building core competence. They would do a 'cost and gap analysis' to chalk the way forward. This consisted of analysing gaps in Knowledge,

Technology, Strategy, Scale, Skills, Productivity, Competence, Credibility, and Leadership.

"Change management" was an ongoing process in well-run companies. They involved key personnel and top management in brainstorming exercises and annual meets to fix parameters of corporate planning, rate of growth, and key performance indices. They looked at critical success factors, key indices, and productivity per person and fine-tuned the Purpose, Process, and People involved. Companies were either resource- driven, market-driven, quality-driven, productivity-driven, technology- driven or people-driven.

Despite my age, I continue to receive requests to join as an independent director due to my track record in corporate management and as a turn-around expert and motivational speaker. My exhortation to employees is to become Experts, Excel themselves, exceed expectations, and expand their vision and outlook.

THE KEY TO LONGEVITY OF COMPANIES

At a time when companies are finding it difficult to survive even for a decade, some companies have survived for a long time. Such longevity is due to their ethics and values of service and adherence to good governance with passion and understanding. Companies, to be successful, must move with the times and yet remain grounded in their core competence, ethics, and values of trust, truth, and transparency.

Adi Sankaracharya, the great seer, teacher, and guru of India, after setting up mutts in four cardinal points of India, Badrinath in the North, Puri in the East, Dwaraka in the West, and Sringeri in the south, was worried about their future. Would these mutts survive after him, and if so, for how long? He meditated to find an answer to the problem of their relevance, continuity, and longevity.

He meditated to peer into their future and perceived that the continuity of any institution depends on building the chain of succession of competent, committed teachers-cum managers. There was a need for a senior pontiff or guru to advise and guide the ruling Madathipathi or the CEO to run the institution and a young brahmachari successor under training to take over the mutt in due course. This effectively links the past (seer), the present (math adhipathi), and the future (brahmachari) – three generations at once and all the time!

His intuition also led to the shloka:

"Chitram Vata Tharoor mulay, Sishyaha Vriddah- Gurur Yuva, Gurosthu Maunam, Vyakhyanam, Sishya Stu Chinna Samsaya"

The shloka says that he saw a strange spectacle beneath the Banyan tree (where students were taught). The students were old while the teacher was young! The teacher was silent, but the meditating students appeared to have solved their problems. He thus envisaged the changing role of teaching and learning in the future in the mutt. In the future, the teacher will be young, while his students will be relatively older, as is happening today with the advancement of technology. Young technocrats now teach older CEOs who are students doing their refresher or contemporary courses. The teachers' pedagogy and methodology have also changed. He does not give a lecture but poses questions and encourages students to find solutions. This methodology of teaching and the pipeline of succession in the mutt has probably ensured the continuity and longevity of mutts for over 1000 years! It is a matter for CEOs to ponder over.

SOLUTIONS – NOT MANUALS

The mutts, unlike companies, do not have any manuals, codes, or elaborate rules, procedures, or protocols; they follow certain conventions, practices, and rituals. They specifically provide for periods of silence and meditation to enable each individual to find their own solutions to their problems. If they are of universal validity, they must pass it on to others for universal welfare (Jana Kalyan).

UNSOLICITED OFFERS

A Director should be a 'bridge' between management and shareholders. He should be selected for his expertise, experience, and, above all, objectivity and integrity. The 'independence' in the decision-making of a director is a prerequisite for effective coordinated action. He should ensure good corporate governance as per the acronym SMART, which is Simple, Moral, Accountable, Responsible-Responsive, and Transparent. The Director should assist the company in preparing a vision and mission statement and chalk out an actionable agenda.

Indian companies are now going global, and import-export business is a regular component of their business. Companies have to be technologically oriented, productivity conscious, market and customer-oriented, and safeguard their extended worldwide supply chain. They have to be globally competitive, which calls for a review of the scale, scope, speed, skill, and soundness of operations.

Companies operate through their committees and executives. The audit committee, nomination and remuneration committee, shareholders relationship committee, and Corporate Social responsibility committee plays a vital role in ensuring Truth, Trust, Transparency, and Tolerance limits. The shareholders nowadays hardly have physical or face-to-face meetings and rely on technology to attend Board and Annual general meetings.

In many companies, I was the Lead Director, conducting meetings with independent directors and giving advice and suggestions. I prematurely resigned from a company that was not following our advice and the statute and had run into problems with banks, customers, and income-tax authorities.

Currently I serve as a Director of one listed and two limited companies. I look forward to completing my tenure and devote time to other pursuits, like reading, advising Civil Service aspirants, spending time with friends, and engaging in spiritual activities.

I was associated with several Non-Government Organisations, mostly in professional, educational, and cultural areas. I helped them in an honorary capacity by way of advice, guidance, and support. A lot of work has to be done, and help must come from the Government, corporate sector, enlightened public, and philanthropic individuals.

9

Social Service Activities – National Human Resources Development Network (NHRD)

A former Professor at IIM Ahmedabad TVRao, set up the National Human Resources Development Academy at Ahmedabad and the National Human Resources Development **(NHRD),** an NGO in Hyderabad. He was assisted by K. Satyanarayana, a reputed HR Manager, who shouldered the responsibility of running the Hyderabad Chapter. A dedicated Gandhian and selfless person, a good speaker, and by nature humble, he ran the organisation on a shoestring budget. It enrolled members and published a newsletter that included articles from leading HR personnel and received a good response. I used to contribute to the newsletter.

The NHRD conducted national seminars on relevant subjects for HR professionals. Several CEOs helped the chapter grow and accumulate surplus funds. It operated from its own small 2-bedroom flat in Ameerpet. It conducted lectures in various colleges on HRD matters, with the help of ICBM, Hyderabad, a management college, and organised lectures for students from various colleges in Hyderabad. I was invited to one such lecture when I was a Director of the Institute of Public Enterprise (IPE), which enrolled as an Institutional Member of the NHRD, Hyderabad chapter. Later, I became a Life Member and joined as Chapter President at Hyderabad in 2000. I was re-elected for another term of two years. I was also elected as Regional President of the Southern Region of NHRD.

At that time, both Bangalore and Hyderabad chapters were vying to become the National headquarters of NHRD based on membership, while senior professionals in Delhi advocated for the headquarters to be located in New Delhi. A team from NHRD Hyderabad was able to talk with the Bangalore chapter to withdraw and support Hyderabad as the national headquarters. The National Executive Committee of HRD elected Santrupt Mishra of the Aditya Birla group as President of NHRD. He visited Hyderabad to secure land for the location and construction of the National headquarters. Hyderabad chapter promised to secure a suitable plot in Banjara Hills, a posh locality, from the Government on a 30-year renewable long lease.

I took up the matter with Chief Minister N Chandrababu Naidu, who agreed to allocate a premium plot of land on Road No.12 of Banjara Hills provided it housed the national headquarters. A team of NHRD headed by Santrupt Mishra and local office bearers called on the CM and thanked him for his gesture. We organised a foundation laying ceremony on 11th February 2007 attended by Akhil Busrai, President of NHRD at the national level.

NHRD Hyderabad took the initiative to prepare a Code of Conduct for NHRD professionals and a Pledge to be taken by members to adhere to the Code of Conduct. The National HRD network, with its office in Gurgaon, has now become a global centre for grooming leaders and Professionals for promoting human relations development and leadership to enhance the capability of human resource professionals to compete globally and create value for society. It does so through education, training, research, extension, and experience-sharing.

As the network of professionals has spread throughout the country, it was decided to call it the National HRD Network. A logo was also designed and adopted.

It has over 16,000 members representing multi-national, public, and private organisations including government departments and public sector undertakings and NGOs spread across 33 chapters in India and one in Singapore. SV Nathan, a senior executive of Deloitte working in Hyderabad, succeeded me and later became the President of NHRDN headquarters in Delhi.

To ensure proper succession of presidents of the Hyderabad chapter, all former presidents constituted the Committee of Past Presidents. I was elected as Chairman of the Past Presidents Committee (PPC).

NHRDN Hyderabad set up chapters at Visakhapatnam, Vijayawada, and Warangal. Ravi Dasari, a young HR professional was involved in setting up of the Warangal chapter. K. Satyanarayana and I were invited to Warangal for the inaugural function. I gave a lecture at the Government Arts College at Warangal, which proved inadequate for the large gathering that attended. The lecture received good press coverage and was highlighted by the local press.

On 2nd October 2009, K Satyanarayana, the first President of the Hyderabad chapter, was honoured with an award along with a prestigious title of "***Bapu***." I had the honour of presenting that award as well as delivering a speech on Mahatma Gandhi.

I attended several meetings held in different cities. The President, Abdul Kalam, addressed a gathering in Kolkata and complimented me on my speech. I received *the **"Lifetime Achievement Award"** of* the NHRD from the Vice President of India at Hyderabad.

10

National Board of Accreditation (NBA)

The Indian higher education system is the third largest in the world, with students from India attending institutions all over the globe. The Union Government set up the National Board of Accreditation (NBA) in October 2010 to assess standards of educational facilities and courses in India and accredited colleges, institutions, and courses.

NBA accredited courses in engineering, pharmacy, computer applications, and management based on parameters of physical infrastructure, facilities, contents, duration of the course and degree or diploma awarded, relevant physical and intellectual standards, and student-faculty ratio. Qualified teams of professors and educationists do the assessments by way of a) preliminary and b) final evaluation and are outcome-based. Self-evaluation, site visits, physical infrastructure, qualifications of teachers, laboratories and equipment-research outputs, teacher-student ratio, library facilities, course duration, admission procedures, etc., are taken into account.

ACCREDITATION AFTER INSPECTIONS

The accreditation is done on universally accepted technological and educational norms prescribed by the Washington Accord, signed by 26 US and European countries, and the Seoul Accord, signed by 50 countries in Asia. This establishes the equivalence of courses and degrees awarded by countries all over the world. The recommendations of the site visit teams are scrutinised by the advisory and executive committees of the NBA before giving accreditation.

MEMBER OF THE NBA

I was appointed as a member of the General Council and the Executive Committee of the NBA in 2013. In June 2015, I was a member of the Indian NBA team to Istanbul, Turkey, where a meeting of the International

Board of Accreditation was held to consider India's admission under the Washington and Seoul Accords, where 17 countries attended the meeting. Subsequently, some meetings were held in India to secure accreditation as a member. India is now an accredited member. The equivalence of Indian courses of study and degrees with their counterparts in other countries is a significant contribution of the NBA, apart from improving standards of education.

11

Federation of Telangana Chambers of Commerce and Industry (FICCI)

The Federation of Telangana Chambers of Commerce and Industry (FTCCI), established in 1917, is an apex Chamber of Commerce, Industry, and Trade for the state of Telangana. It was earlier known in Andhra Pradesh as the Federation of Andhra Pradesh Chambers of Commerce and Industry (FAPCCI). It is actively engaged in protecting the interests of industries, trade, and commerce and played a constructive role in policy formulation and articulation of support for rapid industrial progress in Telangana for the last 105 years.

MEMBERSHIP

After the formation of Telangana state, it was renamed FTCCI to represent large, medium, and small-scale industries besides wholesale, retail, and small traders, along with professionals like chartered accountants, advocates, and consultants. FTCCI conducts studies on various subjects related to trade and industries and acts as a knowledge chamber. It prepares concept papers and maintains liaisons with State and Central Governments. FTCCI has more than 2500 members apart from 100 Associations or Chambers. The indirect membership is over 25000. It supports the in-house Institute of Economics in collating and analysing trends in the economy and advising chambers and the Government.

ROLE OF FTCCI

FTCCI plays a supportive role in protecting the interests of trade, commerce, and industry while developing and maintaining good rapport with the state and Central government. It hosts many trade delegations from various countries visiting Telangana. Such interactions and visits play a vital role in increasing business contracts with counterparts. It holds conferences, seminars, and meetings on the latest developments in the fields of exports and imports, economy, industry, marketing trends, investments, taxation, etc. It thus upgrades the knowledge and assistance of its members. It helps organise meetings with tax officials to clarify issues and bring member problems to the Government's notice. It publishes a monthly magazine and prepares background papers on current issues. Though not a member, I have been made an Honorary Member. I continue to be the Honorary Editor of the FTCCI magazine for two decades and am presently on the Jury for selection for excellence awards.

FTCCI presents Excellence Awards to Industries, Associations, Entrepreneurs, and people who contribute to the social, industrial, and commercial progress of the country.

12

All India Services Pensioners Association, Hyderabad

Retired officers of IAS, IPS, and IFS in AP state set up the All India Services Pensioners Association (AISPA) in 1985 in Hyderabad. The bylaws were revised and approved in 2008. Elections were regularly held for office-bearers and members of the Executive Committee, who were drawn from all three All India Services.

The Association dealt with service issues like fixation of pensions, rectification of anomalies, and provision of better health services. The 6th Pay Commission Report of 2006 created many anomalies, which the Association sorted out by contacting officials in the Secretariat, AGs office, and Pension Payment office.

ELECTED AS PRESIDENT OF THE ASSOCIATION

In 2008, the then President of the Association, G Narayana Rao, and Secretaries V Raman Rao and JM Girgilani requested me to join as the President, steer the Association, and sort out pressing issues. The recommendations of the 7th Pay Commission were expected to be announced, and my presence and contacts with both the State and Central Government would help pensioners. I was elected unanimously as President of the Association.

7TH PAY COMMISSION RECOMMENDATIONS

The Association submitted its representation on matters concerning pensioners to the 7th Pay Commission and the Department of Personnel and Pensions in the Union government. The real issues that came up during the implementation of the Pay Commission recommendations were the fixation on seniority, revised salary and pension, and determining entitlements of officers. These issues became the primary focus and were patiently pursued and resolved satisfactorily. As the Pay Commission had given a big boost to pay scales and pensions, the pensioners were quite happy except in some hard cases.

Old Age Health issues are a major cause of concern to the aging pensioners and their family members. Most pensioners were covered by the Central Government Health Scheme (CGHS), while some had opted for the All-India Medical Services Act and Rules implemented by State governments. While facilities under both schemes were fairly similar, the CGHS was considered a better option by pensioners as it provided for a regular supply of medicines from their dispensaries and wellness centres all over India. CGHS has enrolled corporate hospitals to provide inpatient care, surgeries, and hospitalisation with ceilings on expenditure for different surgeries and treatments. It also paid for diagnostic reports. As there was an expenditure limit for various treatments, many reputed hospitals did not enrol. All major government hospitals were recognised by CGHS, and treatment costs were reimbursed to them directly. Pensioners covered by CGHS could admit themselves to approved corporate hospitals, while expenditures over and above the fixed cost would have to be paid by the patient. This caused inconvenience as reimbursement of the extra amount as approved by CGHS took time.

Many officers preferred treatment in corporate hospitals rather than government hospitals due to better equipment, highly qualified doctors' care, treatment, and attention. Though pensioners had to pay costs charged over and above the CGHS ceilings of cost, they did so as many had taken insurance cover.

CGHS IDENTITY CARDS

CGHS used to issue paper family identity cards that needed frequent replacement. It was replaced by specially designed digital plastic cards that are usable in CGHS wellness centres all over India. Medicines that were normally issued for a month were increased to three months' supply at a time. The association members were nominated to sit on advisory committees of CGHS Wellness centres to tackle matters relating to payments and local issues.

The Association helps spouses of deceased Pensioners to secure family pensions, open bank accounts, and assist them in securing dues. The association issued guidelines to pensioners in 2016, updated them, and issued Revised Guidelines in March 2021. The spouses of pensioners appreciated the services rendered by the association to get family pensions and related bank dues.

Pensioners were provided with Health ID cards through good offices of Greater Hyderabad Municipal Corporation (GHMC) and identity cards for entry to the Secretariat.

LECTURES ON HEALTH CARE OF PENSIONERS

The Association organised lectures on health-related matters for the benefit of pensioners on emergency and trauma care, geriatrics, diabetes, orthopaedics, anaesthesia, cancer, hypertension, pulmonary diseases, etc. It did yeoman service during the 2019 Covid pandemic. The association helped pensioners avail vaccination facilities in Government hospitals, which was highly appreciated. Vacations for pensioners along with their families were organised. The association members donated Rs.5 lakhs to CM's Relief Fund besides individually contributing to the Prime Minister's Relief Fund. A small corpus was built up from donations from members for its activities.

GOVERNMENT ACCOMMODATION SOUGHT FOR AISPA OFFICE

The association does not have permanent accommodation for its office. It is utilising premises in Vasavi Seva Kendram, Hyderabad (thanks to Late Narayana Rao) for holding meetings of the Executive Committee. Several representations made to AP and TS Governments regarding the allocation of rent-free accommodation near the Secretariat and an annual recurring grant for the maintenance of staff and records have not yet yielded any results. Now that the new Secretariat building has opened, we hope that the government will allot rent-free space to AISPA and also sanction an annual grant for its upkeep to better serve the pensioners.

SERVICES ACKNOWLEDGED

Late Dr G Narayana Rao was the Vice President of the association and one of the prime movers. Dr. V Raman Rao, as Secretary, has rendered dedicated service for over two decades and is the brains-trust of the association. Late Narayanaswamy IFS and Venkat Rao IPS have codified rules applicable to pensioners. Office staff have kept meticulous records and conducted meetings and AGMs. Accounts have been audited in time.

The members of the E.C., who are drawn from different services, have helped the association maintain close contact with the Secretariat, Finance department, AG's office and Pension Payment office to sort out problems.

CENTENARIANS

The association felicitated G Narayana Chetty (IAS), who lived up to 104 years, and VK Rao, ICS (former CS), the two centenarians. We also assisted families in conducting obsequies and sorting out their problems.

The Association honoured me for receiving the Dean Paul H. Appleby Award for distinguished services to Public Administration by the Indian Institute of Public Administration, a recognition I cherish.

The association regularly conducted EC meetings and the AGM, which were largely attended by members and their spouses, government officials, and CGHS doctors, which helped sort out many small problems. It provided an opportunity for informally meeting colleagues, exchanging notes in a pleasant environment, and rehashing old memories.

With the reorganization of AP state in 2014, the association unanimously decided to continue to cater to both AP and Telangana state pensioners, as many of them have settled down in Hyderabad.

During my tenure, I tried to strengthen finances and improve liaison with the governments of India, AP, and Telangana and sorted out many issues. The problems of pensioners residing in their hometowns or remote places not covered by CGHS were sorted out with the cooperation of collectors and district treasury officers.

TARNAKA WELLNESS CENTRE

Members of the Advisory Committee of Wellness Centre 13, Tarnaka, Hyderabad, brought their concerns and difficulties regarding cramped accommodation and limited facilities to the attention of the Additional Director of CGHS. The association used its good offices and contacts with the Ministry of Health and Family Welfare in Delhi and the DG of Survey of India and successfully secured spacious accommodation at the Indian Institute of Surveying and Mapping in Hyderabad.

13

Godavari Knowledge Society

A Non-Profit Organisation called Godavari Knowledge Society (GKS) was registered to impart skills for personnel development and local entrepreneurship based on local resources duly integrated with the latest technologies through global knowledge channels from many nations of the world. It was started by S Shankar Prasad, a highly qualified and experienced technocrat who had worked abroad. Distinguished persons from different walks of life were founder members of the society. The first President was the late Justice SN Phukan, a former Judge of the Supreme Court, and had eminent technocrats and financial experts on its board.

I was Chairman of the Advisory Board, which consisted of senior scientists, technology business incubators, bio-information experts, and founders of start-up companies. It also had former Heads of the Department of Science and Industrial Research (DSIR) as well as professors from the UK and USA.

Among the objectives of the society were utilisation of plentiful agricultural residues, extraction of valuable pharmaceutical ingredients from algae and seaweeds, training of farmers and science students, guiding entrepreneurs to deploy science and technology to solve local problems and taking up new activities for better incomes besides creating employment opportunities. Dr. Mohan Kanda, IAS (Retd.), former Chief Secretary of the AP government, was its Chief Mentor.

The objective of the society was to serve as a facilitator for government, academic institutions, and the private sector to develop sustainable technologies to achieve the Millennium Development Goals. It was specifically interested in food and agriculture, biotechnology, marine biotechnology, pharma biotechnology, as well as renewable energy, environmental improvement, waste management, etc.

GKS organised the first International Conference, 'Bio-Andhra 2014', with the assistance of the Jawaharlal Nehru Technological University (JNTU) at Kakinada on agricultural and marine pharma biotechnology to unlock the blue potential of the sea. It received active support from the government of AP and the Ministry of Science and Technology of the Government of India. Eminent scientists, engineers, industrialists, and entrepreneurs attended the three-day conference. Delegates from the Federal Research Institute of Microbiology and Biotechnology, Russia, University of Brighton, UK, London School of Pharmacy, and several other institutes participated in the conference and offered a joint research programme with GKS. The Directorate of the Department of Science and Industrial Research extended its support for the creation of Biotechnology clusters in AP.

An incubation centre was set up at JNTU Kakinada, and MoU was signed with IICT Hyderabad to support biotechnology efforts. GKS set up Lepakshi Biotechnology Park in April 2016 in Anantapur district, and N Chandra Babu Naidu laid the foundation stone.

A skill development activity called '*Pratyancha*' was started as a pilot study in cooperation with AP State Skill Development Corporation in 2017- 18 as a 6-month program. The success of this program led to its adoption in other universities in AP. An agro-cum-horticulture cluster was set up at Chintoor in East Godavari district with the support of the Union Ministry of MSME to benefit 700 tribal families in the region. A solar-based mobile cold storage facility was developed and set up for the project.

Non- profit organisations can help in fostering new ideas, mobilisation, and training of entrepreneurs. They need support from the government to grow and serve the cause of the rapid spread of technology, and in particular, biotechnology knowledge to increase income levels and fully utilise vast resources, both on sea and land, by eliminating wastes, reducing pollution, and recycling materials. In short, generate scientific temper in rural areas.

14

A.P. Telaga, Kapu Balija Sangam, Hyderabad

The word Kapu is a generic term in the Telugu language denoting a "cultivator-soldier- protector." The Kapus in Coastal Andhra, Balijas of Rayalaseema, and in the old Madras Presidency area were classified by the British in the 1920s as educationally backward and eligible for reservation quota for educational and employment opportunities in Government jobs. In the Telangana region, Munnuru Kapus whom the Nizam invited to settle in Hyderabad State were included in the Backward Classes list of both the State and Central Government.

Andhra State was formed in 1953, and Andhra Pradesh State in 1956. The reservation benefits granted to Kapus and Balijas was withdrawn by the A.P. State on the advice of a Government Committee. The Kapus and Balijas agitated to secure the past benefits of reservation in government and re-inclusion of the community among the Other Backward Classes.

Some elders of the Telaga, Kapu, and Balija communities in Hyderabad, with Talari Ananth Babu, a leading advocate of Hyderabad (later Advocate General), and some senior serving and retired officials set up a Sangam (Association) to protect their educational and employment reservations in the new State of AP. They decided to set up the A.P. Telaga, Kapu, and Balija Sangam and registered it at Hyderabad in 1959. It purchased land and opened its office at Lower Tank Bund Road, Hyderabad.

It also set up a Government Aided Intermediate College on its premises, named after Dr. Brahmarishi Raghupathi Venkata Ratnam Naidu, a Kapu Educationist and Brahmo Samaj Leader, who later became the first Indian Vice-chancellor of the Madras University. I was President of the College for a long time. Office bearers of the Sangam were mostly retired Judges or retired officers who looked after the interests of Kapus in Hyderabad and honoured the deserving persons of the community with awards, besides Celebration of festivals and hosting Get-togethers. At the request of the Sangam, I instituted three Awards to be given for Best Entrepreneur, Best Educationist, and Ideal Mother.

Government decided to prune the number of aided Junior Colleges and withdraw grant-in-aid schemes in urban areas. The Sangam Junior College was asked to stop recruiting vacancies for retiring teachers. As the number of teachers fell, the enrollment of students declined. Over time, the teaching staff and student admission numbers declined. Consequently, the Government shifted the remaining teachers and staff to other junior colleges in rural areas. We had to close the college, which had served the needs of education for over fifty years.

The Sangam submitted several memoranda to the State and Central Government and OBC Commissions for the continuation of the backward classification of Kapus and restore earlier concessions which they had been enjoying from the 1920s till 1956 in Andhra and A.P. State but withdrawn later by the AP Govt. After a number of agitations and Court cases, the government included the Kapu community as eligible for limited educational facilities and employment opportunities in Government. This did not fully meet the demands of the community, which continued its agitation to secure all facilities available to other backward classes. A three-man commission was appointed in 2016, which, considering the backwardness and population of Kapus, recommended a Special Reservation of 5% from the OBC quota exclusively for the Kapu community, enabling them to receive some educational and job concessions after a lapse of fifty years. It earmarked funds for the Kapu Welfare Corporation, which was set up to provide for the academic and economic needs of deserving Kapus. Funding for the Corporation has since decreased.

In the meantime, the Government of India created a separate category of Economically Backward Classes (EBC) and provided 10% of job reservations from the 50% open category in the Government. By this, the Government of India, for the first time, recognized economic backwardness and not only caste as a criterion for classification in addition to social, educational, and cultural backwardness. Such a classification led to protests by Other Backward Classes (OBC), who believed that their opportunities for employment and economic benefits above their entitlement under the open category would be curtailed. The debate on the criteria for identification of backward classes, their classification, and criteria for eligibility and reservation quota on an economic basis still continues. Political parties are now clamouring for the conduct of a Caste census.

Anantha Babu, my Professor at Law College, Hyderabad, who had spearheaded the setting up of the Kapu Sangam at Hyderabad, constructed Hall in memory of his father, Late Talari Govindarajulu Naidu, a senior Government official, and another Dining Hall in memory of his wife Srimathi Talari Manikyamba in the Sangam premises. As I had retired, he requested that I take over as the President of the Kapu Sangam and chart a new direction for it. I reluctantly accepted the position and was elected for a term. The Executive Committee reviewed the Sangam's activities, which were confined to the twin cities of Hyderabad and Secunderabad. A limited number of scholarships were given to poor students for higher education. Suggestions ranged from establishing the Sangam as an apex body and affiliation of all Kapu Sangams in A.P. and other states like TamilNadu, Karnataka, Orissa, Maharashtra, and Delhi, where Kapus in search of employment had settled in fairly large numbers. During my tenure, we introduced Awards for outstanding Educationists, Entrepreneurs, and Illustrious mothers. A Marriage Assistance cell was set up, and scholarships were given on a merit cum means basis.

ORIGIN OF KAPU EDUCATIONAL TRUST

The Managing Committee of the A P Telaga, Kapu Sangam at Hyderabad felt that very few All-India Service Officers were selected from among Kapus due to educational and economic backwardness, lack of awareness, mentorship, and guidance. A serious attempt was required to encourage Kapu candidates to appear for All India Services examinations. Such officers after selection and during their long careers could be role models to guide students by encouraging them to study and clear the Civil Services Examination and other professional examinations and get good jobs. Later, entrepreneurship support could also be given.

KAPU EDUCATIONAL TRUST

As a senior IAS Officer- and probably the first direct recruit Kapu IAS Officer after independence- I was requested to take on the responsibility of setting up Kapu Educational Trust (KET) with a specific mandate and focus on guiding aspirants and enabling them to appear for the Civil Services examinations and guide them for interviews and selection. I registered the KET as the Settler of the Trust by contributing Rs.5 lakhs and became the first Lifetime Managing Trustee.

As I was earlier delivering lectures at IAS Coaching Institutions in A.P. and other places, we conducted Mock Interviews for candidates. With intensive coaching of candidates for Interviews, the success rate rose.

Coaching institutions in Karnataka, Delhi, and Kerala used to invite me for mock interviews conducted by them.

KET built up a small corpus through donations from Kapus. It got in touch with Kapus WhatsApp groups to spread the message. Several aspirants who visited KET for advice and guidance were given financial and other support and were selected for IAS/IPS and other central services. KET organized lectures for candidates and provided advice and mentorship. It felicitated successful candidates.46 Kapus were selected for IAS, IPS, and the Central Services, between 2013 to 2022. This led to more Kapus preparing and appearing for UPSC and State PSC examinations. However, the number of Kapu candidates selected is still small in proportion to the numerical strength of the community or potential. It is also not comparable to that of educationally and economically advanced communities.

Meanwhile, Sangam has proposed to demolish the existing building and construct a four-storied building to provide more accommodation and earn some rent to meet the expenses and continue its activities. I was invited to lay the foundation for the new building on 31st March 2023. I am now not actively associated in view of my age.

INDIAN INSTITUTE OF PUBLIC ADMINISTRATION (IIPA)

To improve the standards of Public Administration and management in India, Dean Paul H. Appleby of the United States conducted a study and recommended the setting up of the Indian Institute of Public Administration. The Government of India set up the Institute in 1954 in Delhi to train Civil Servants for research and extension work to improve standards of governance in India.

I joined the Institute as a Life Member in 1964. I was associated with it as Honorary Secretary of the Shillong Branch in 1967 and later as Chairman of the Hyderabad Regional Branch for both Andhra Pradesh and Telangana states. It has Local Branches at Warangal and Karimnagar in Telangana and Visakhapatnam and Tirupati in Andhra Pradesh. It has done research and published some books. It conducts Seminars and Lectures for the benefit of administration and management students.

HYDERABAD MANAGEMENT ASSOCIATION (HMA)

HMA was established in 1964 in Hyderabad and is affiliated with the All India Management Association in Delhi. I became a Life Member in 1972 and was associated with drafting its Memorandum and Articles of Association, besides delivering lectures on various Management topics. In 1988, I received the "Manager of the Year" Award for Godavari Fertilizers, the "Member of the Year" Award, and the "Lifetime Achievement" Award from the Vice-President of India.

An Award for "Best Women Manager" has been instituted by me in HMA in honour and memory of my mother.

INDIAN NATIONAL TRUST FOR ART AND CULTURAL HERITAGE (INTACH)

'INTACH" was set up in the year 1984 in Delhi as a non-profit membership-based non-government organization. Its objective is to create nationwide awareness, and knowledge, of India's Natural, Built, and Living heritage and culture. It documents cultural, historical, and cultural resources. It has been recognized as a "Centre of Excellence" and received a grant from the Government of India. It has 231 chapters spread all over India. I am a Life Member and have been the Convenor of INTACH for its 8 chapters in Andhra Pradesh and 4 in Telangana state, with headquarters at Hyderabad. I have served two terms on the Central Council and as a member of the Executive Committee.

15

Rural Development Foundation

Non-Resident Indians in the US from Telangana in 1996 set up the India Rural Development Fund. One of the main objectives was to start schools in Telangana. The Errabelli family from Parvatipur Mandal of Warangal district took the lead and donated their ancestral mansion with adjacent land at Kalleda village to set up a school. E Ram Mohan, an office bearer of an NGO called Rural Development Foundation (RDF) with headquarters in Hyderabad, met and briefed me. The NGO was set up to promote rural development through education by setting up and running good quality non-sectarian schools in Telangana, which was very backward due to poverty, illiteracy, child marriages, unemployment, and poor facilities for education. Girls' education did not receive proper attention in rural areas. He requested me to join as Chairman of RDF to guide and give a push to their activities. They had formulated the,

Vision: To promote education as a vehicle for rural development.

Mission: To make a lifelong difference in the lives of rural under-privileged girls and boys through holistic education.

Goal: To Educate, Engage and Empower rural girls and boys.

KALLEDA HIGH SCHOOL

I paid a visit to Kalleda village with Ram Mohan and his wife Vandita. I was impressed by their dedication to educating children from low-income families in villages in and around Kalleda, with an emphasis on girls' education. I interacted with the schoolteachers to understand their difficulties and find out what help they expected from RDF and the government. I agreed to join RDF, where I was elected Chairman.

MATENDLA HIGH SCHOOL

RDF had a policy of setting up schools in backward areas – not covered by government schools – where students had to walk 5 to 7 km to reach school. It identified a village called Matendla, which was around 4 Km from Jakkampur in Chinnakodur mandal near Siddipet. I visited Matendla with Ram Mohan and met the Gram Panchayat President, who welcomed the idea of setting up a school and spontaneously decided to give one room in the panchayat office to start the school. He shifted the panchayat office to a nearby unused bus stand. Such was his commitment to the cause of education. The school began by appointing a devoted teacher-cum-headmaster, and classes were held in that makeshift room or under trees. A temporary structure was raised inside the panchayat office compound to accommodate classes from nursery onwards. We had a problem of motivating parents and weaning away children from their work of herding cattle or goats or working as farm hands. Slowly, children started joining to study. To encourage them, RDF provided uniforms, textbooks, and notebooks and provided mid-day meals to students free of cost. Noticing the keen interest of the Sarpanch,-head of the Village Panchayat- the headmaster, students, and parents, we decided to build a model school to meet the growing requirements.

K. ANJI REDDY OF REDDY'S LABORATORIES HELPS RDF

On return to Hyderabad, I spoke to K. Anji Reddy, CMD of Reddy's Laboratories, whom I knew, and sought his help for the school in Matendla. He recollected that I had helped him get over his financial difficulty long ago, which had put him and his company on the growth path. They would like to repay that act. He said he would render all help to construct a model school like the one in the US and meet the entire expenditure. I was surprised at his munificent gesture of helping a good social cause. I told him that the school building may cost about Rs. 10 – 15 lakhs. He said that he would meet the entire expenditure of the building, pulled out his cheque book, and asked me to fill up the details. The building was constructed at a cost of over Rs.20 lakhs, and K. Anji Reddy contributed the entire amount. Matendla villagers and the school must remember the munificence of a person who probably remembered his school days in the Guntur district when he donated the amount.

RDF SCHOOLS EXCEL IN EDUCATION AND SPORTS

I used to visit both Kalleda and Matendla schools to address teachers and students separately on their duties and, later, parents and villagers. I talked about the importance for both boys and girls to not only excel but achieve their life goals but also become good citizens. I told them the formula for success was – Home work, Hard work, Smart work, Teamwork, and Network" and that '*work*' was essential to achieve success. RDF took a special interest in imparting not only education but values as well as skills.

The students were encouraged to do useful work like kitchen gardening, helping elders and parents at home, and participating in games and sports events. The emphasis on sports and games led to securing support from Tata Sports Institute and the All India Archery Association, which sent coaches to train students intensively. RDF built facilities required at their schools. The students have 'excelled' themselves in sports and athletics and have participated in national and international tournaments. It is a matter of pride that our students represented India at the Beijing Olympics for archery. Two girls and one boy were selected under the US Youth Exchange Study Program to study in class X in an American school through the help of Synchrony Financial. The strong focus on primary, secondary, and girls' education has paid good dividends. It is hoped that in the future also, every year, the students will get admission through this program.

The schools provide a healthy and stimulating learning environment due to collaboration with educational partners, committed volunteers, continuing education, and training its rural staff and teachers. Mid-day meals are provided for students, and doctors conduct annual medical check-ups. RDF believes that **"when you educate a boy, you educate a family,"** but **"when you educate a girl, you educate not only the family but the entire community."** This is in line with the Telugu idiom, which says a girl is the link between **'Puttinillu'** and **'Mettinillu'** and helps both the parental home and village where she is born and the in-law's house and village which she steps into, adorns, and serves.

We had a perennial problem of paucity of funds. To seek funds, we had to organise contributory dinners and request help from philanthropists both in India and the US. We received a good response and were able to extend the activities of RDF by setting up two other schools in the Redlawada and Rollakal villages of the Warangal district. In 2007, RDF, thanks to the local Pai family's contribution, opened Vanitha Achutha Pai Junior College at Kalleda at a newly built campus. Kapil Education Trust (KET) constructed a new building in Matendla to provide facilities for more students. Value Labs, an IT firm, constructed a building for Kalleda School on the junior college campus. INFOR Company constructed new school buildings in Redlawada and Rollakal schools. The Junior college used to host the Village India Program every summer in collaboration with Washington University in St. Louis, USA, until 2012. Tech Mahindra Foundation, in 2013, adopted government schools at Bahadurpally in Hyderabad district and requested RDF staff to train and guide teachers to embed our values of education, play, learning, creativity, and sports. Both schools have been awarded prizes as best schools in the district in 2016. The RDF continues to provide quality education thanks to the support of AMS, CFBT, Silver Oaks International School, Synchrony Financial, and The Global Edge School.

The alumni of the schools are now engineers, lecturers, doctors, and pride of RDF. Presently, RDF caters to the education of more than 2320 students, and its results and reputation are excellent.

We were lucky to receive the active support of retired principals, college lecturers, and the British Council for Teaching English. Several IT companies and banks have donated computers and sent their staff to conduct training classes for our teachers and students at our schools to provide us with the latest tools, techniques, and technology. Teachers and voluntary students of higher classes in the US visit RDF schools and stay as our guest lecturers for a couple of months.

I conducted sessions for Headmasters and teaching staff at school premises and, later, took classes for them during the summer holidays in Hyderabad. Smt. Vandita was in constant touch to keep me apprised of the developments in RDF and invited me to take classes for their teaching staff during the summer holidays. In fact, this led to many requests from her friends in other schools to talk to teachers and students.

RDF has set an example of how committed, forward-looking citizens can help awaken the social consciousness of society, secure funds, and properly use and account for results. The succession of able Chairmen and Executive Committee members of RDF has ensured that the focus on its vision, mission, and goal is kept in mind at each step in building the succeeding generation to be better than the present generation. The dream of its founding members has translated into visible results. RDF has, by its commitment, made the impossible possible through its determined efforts. We should be particularly happy that RDF has put into practice the ancient saying that work done with *education, faith, contemplation, and commitment,* taking into account attendant circumstances, is the unfailing formula for success.

RDF needs to be complimented for its *Kalpana* (vision), *Sankalpana* (determination), *Parikalpana* (plan of action), *Karya Nirvahana* (execution of the plan) leading to *Sadhana* (fulfillment) – that of making education the instrument of social, cultural, economic and political awakening, action and progress. We wish RDF and similar organisations many more dreams, continuing good results, and path-setting trends. RDF rejoiced in the success of its teachers, students, and parents, which gives it the greatest joy and happiness. Let more such good dreams and better actions provide durable results all over India.

Shrimathi Vanditha and E Rammohan Rao were honoured in 2023 by the Yudhvir Trust of Hyderabad for their social service and given a cash prize of Rs. One lakh. May their tribe increase!.

16

My tryst with Civil Services

In the 1940s, matriculates and graduates aspired for an army or a government job as a career for a good life. It was my mother who, when I was 10 years old, regaled me about the charms of the Collector's job, its prestige, status, and glamour. Hailing from a family of officials, I aspired to become an IAS officer.

I was selected as a direct recruit Probationary Deputy Collector at the age of 21 and joined duty at Guntur in AP. When under training, I appeared for the IAS Examination in 1961. There were no coaching institutions at that time. There was only one examination centre for Civil Services in AP at Hyderabad. Candidates had to study on their own and seek advice from seniors and mentors. They used to make a beeline to the libraries for books. I could get advice on 'what' to study and 'how' to study from Collector GVS Mani and Narayana Reddy, Librarian of Guntur District Library. IAS probationers in the district gave me advice and suggestions. I figured out the subjects to choose and devoted time to study.

I used to wake up at 5.00 am, a calm time to study without any distractions. It helped me to concentrate, memorise, remember, and recall what I had read by writing down **keywords** or sentences. I devised my own acronyms to easily recall what I studied. This method got embedded in my memory and later helped me become a good speaker.

SCHEME OF THE CIVIL SERVICES EXAMINATION

Several committees have examined the examination scheme due to the increasing number of candidates appearing for the examination and the plethora of subjects and services. The scheme has been evolving to meet present and future needs.

Around 4 lakh candidates appear for the examination in India and go through the rigorous stages of qualifying Preliminary examination, which broadly tests the aptitude of candidates. Candidates who clear the first stage have to appear for the Mains Examination. Those who pass the Mains are called for the Optional papers and Interviews where the emphasis is not on knowledge that has been already tested but on the personality' ' of the candidate, suitability, and utility for service – one in two candidates called for interview gets selected to the All-India Services like the IAS, IPS, IFS and Central Services. The range of subjects and intense competition for the Civil Services examination makes it one of the toughest in the world. Selection accords the stamp of merit, and even if one is not selected, it shows the aspiration to pass the test.

AGE LIMIT

The original eligibility age band of 21-24 years, when I appeared, has been raised to 30-35 years to accommodate the needs of reservation and social equity. The present age band has led to uneven competition. Many candidates write the examination as many as 5 or 6 times in a bid to improve their prospects or to move to a higher-rated Civil Service job. The age differential goes against the concept of "Catch them Young" and mould them "to the nuances, ethics, values and needs" of the Services.

CIVIL SERVICES AS A CAREER

Civil Service is an interesting, fulfilling, and rewarding career. It provides opportunities for service to the nation and participation in India's socio-economic development. The career enlarges the scope and perspectives of officers and opens avenues for growth. It provides good pay, promotions and prospects, scope for further study abroad, and interesting assignments. The job scope is such that there is never a dull day, nay even a dull moment! Additionally, it improves the marriage prospects of unmarried young candidates!

Communication skills - oral, written, and presentational - are essential to succeed in life and career. The charms of the service are such that it provides a 360-degree view of the needs of citizens, the scope for redressal, and perspectives of Governance and Government. It provides for active interaction with the Government, the market, and civil society. The officers play a key role in a democracy in ensuring equal opportunities for all and making a huge difference in citizens' lives through contributions in formulating proper policies and execution of the policies; they are Change Makers and leave a lasting legacy of achievement.

The scheme of the Civil Services examination is vast and inclusive, enabling graduates from several disciplines to appear and compete. Candidates write an essay paper and answer four compulsory and two optional papers, selected from among 26 subjects. It enables candidates from various disciplines and professionals like engineers, doctors, chartered accountants, advocates, and liberal arts etc. to compete. Over 60% of the intake to the service comes from engineers, professionals, and the rest from liberal arts stream. Candidates from IIMs and IITs appear to have an edge. A welcome sign is that the number of successful women candidates has been increasing. They have, of late, been securing the highest ranks and marks. Kudos to them!

COMMON CHALLENGES FOR CANDIDATES

Candidates must carefully study the prospectus and scheme of the examination. They need to understand the purpose, process, and practice required to pass the competitive examination.

With careful study of the strategy, candidates can learn to Confidently answer, face competition, and succeed.

Disillusioned with the repetitive, drab, and unchallenging nature of their work, many engineers take a furlough to attempt the Civil Services. The number of engineers selected is currently about 63% of the intake. The trend is clear – India is becoming technology-oriented and services more professional in their attitude and work ethos. Digitisation of records and increasing use of computers is helping to maintain records and provide timely good governance.

One of the major causes of failure is lack of guidance, leading to some candidates giving up midway. It is advisable that they first seek a competent guide or a mentor who can recommend the most practical way of study. The mentor must become a 'Guru' who assesses not just *who you are* but *what you can be* and shows you how to do so.

Many candidates think that a coaching course will help them understand the nitty-gritty of preparation, get tips about likely questions, and help them focus on important issues. Candidates tend to seek, accept, and adopt advice and suggestions from colleagues at coaching classes and seniors. The problem is that there is too much information and too little thought and focus on individual needs. Each candidate needs to form a strategy based on his personality to have the best shot at clearing the exam. It is the mental preparation that distinguishes successful candidates from hardworking ones.

The examination requires perseverance, which must come from self-inspiration and aspiration. Many students lack basic writing skills -thanks to computer usage- and are out of touch with handwriting. They should regularly practice writing fast, which will be helpful in writing the answer within the time given.

HERE IS MY 10-POINT FORMULA FOR ACING THE CIVIL SERVICES EXAMS

1. STRATEGY

Strategy for clearing the Civil Services must be realistic, time-bound, practical, and meet individual requirements. Your dream or "*Kalpana*" to get selected must be followed by Sankalpana or firm resolve and determination, and "*Parikalpana*" or Plan of Action. That plan requires "*Karya Nirvahana*" or assumption of responsibility and work performance. Only such action leads to "*Sadhana*" or achievement. The axioms are "Plan the work – Work the Plan" and "That day's work must be done that day itself." Keep a diary to note points for action and monitor action.

Get the prospectus and course of coaching from reputed institutions for a comparative study and selection of the institution to join. Prepare your framework of study and time allocation – Practice the 'Writing Skills' required for essay writing and answering other papers on time.

2. TIME MANAGEMENT

Strategy needs Time Management, which, if not followed, becomes the root cause of failure. The IAS exam requires a psychological cum technological approach. Candidates should carefully study the scheme of the examination, gain basic knowledge of compulsory and optional subjects, and practice writing. Candidates should follow NCERT books, which provide background knowledge of subjects and the scope of the exam. Buy standard textbooks and study previous question papers to become familiar with and confident about the topics.

A SWOT (Strengths, Weaknesses, or Constraints-Opportunities and Threats) Analysis will help to decide on time allocation for Prelims, Mains, and compulsory subjects and writing the essay. Consult and decide on your 'optional' subjects and seek assistance where necessary-The focus must be on studying to gain knowledge and mastery and not merely to pass.

It is advisable to find a good mentor who can counsel you, clear your Doubts, and guide you.

3. BOOKS TO REFER

Buy standard books prescribed by UPSC or coaching institutions for your study. The latest Yearbook of the Government of India can update you on many matters, which will help you in the Mains and Interviews. Decide on books to purchase for Compulsory and Optional study.

It is difficult to get standard books on Ethics & Values. It is recommended that you read short versions of Ramayana, Mahabharata, Gita, Bible, Quran, Buddhism, etc., and also autobiographies of leaders and civil servants. A visit to Ramakrishna Math Bookshop will be useful.

4. MENTAL PREPARATION, INTERNAL MOTIVATION

The exam is like performing a "*Yagna*". You must be devoted and have a strong desire to achieve your goal. Do not ever doubt: Can I Do? Instead, you must affirm to yourself every day: 'I CAN DO' or 'I CAN PASS'. It is an extremely powerful mantra that helps you become strong in your determination, intelligent preparation, commit to memory and writing skills. Keyword study for recall will help you to focus. Your attention, concentration, observation, memorisation, and imagination must be focused on your goal with steadfast resolve. Maintain a daily journal to note each day's work to be done and tick off completed tasks.

5. PLACE OF STUDY

One can join a coaching institution with facilities, faculty, and a library that provides for the practice of essay writing. Faculty must have and devote time for interaction with students to clear their doubts. Study and practice can be done at home or in a rented study room with a definite time schedule. The requisite books, earlier notes, and question papers for practice must be organised on your desk or shelf. It will save you time looking for the material you need when you sit down to study. Note down important points while reading. Allocate more time for difficult subjects. Practice writing Essays on various topics. It will help you to write the essay or answer in the given time. Women usually prefer this method of study, which helps with remembering.

6. TIME REQUIRED

At least one year of intense study is required. Time has to be provided for Prelims and Mains examinations depending on candidates' level of knowledge and confidence. Faculty can guide regarding the selection of subjects, books, methods of study, and clear doubts. Practice writing short notes and keywords on topics for easy recall and revision of notes. Answering model question papers helps you gain confidence and determine your own self-assessment of competence and confidence. Candidates with engineering backgrounds usually choose optional subjects that are easy to understand, like Anthropology, Sociology, Geography, Public

Administration, Indian Polity, International Relations, Indian Economics, etc., for quick comprehension and expression.

7. STUDY SCHEDULE

One should get at least 7-8 hours of sleep to feel refreshed and welcome each day for invigorating study and gaining knowledge. Candidates would do well to get up early in the morning and devote at least 2 hours between 5-7 am to study difficult subjects. That time in the early morning is conducive to comprehension, understanding, and retention with the help of short notes and keywords. Candidates should read for about 6 to 8 hours a day besides attending coaching classes. As commute might take considerable time, it should be minimised. Time can be spent in the evening for games or relaxation. 7 pm to 10 pm should be for study.

8. NEWSPAPERS

Read a minimum of two newspapers – a regular and an economic daily to update yourself with current affairs – the editorials and important national and international events must receive attention, and short keywords and notes must be prepared.

While reading, concentrate on the clarity of concepts, context, content, clarity, and communication. While writing, remember that lucidity, brevity, and euphony win the day

One final word – Be Alert, Bold, Confident, Disciplined, Determined, and Enthusiastic to achieve your goal – Remember three powerful words – Your mantra for success is "I CAN DO".

9. DRESS

Dress conservatively like an officer in formal attire at the Interview. Keep all certificates, awards, papers, and interview call letters in a brief or folder for easy handling.

10. THE INTERVIEW – THE ULTIMATE HARD TARGET

Candidates who have cleared the Preliminaries and Mains have one final important hurdle to clear – the Interview - for it determines your rank, service, and lifelong prospects in the Civil Services.

My foray into coaching candidates began with conducting Mock Interviews for a candidate in Assam in 1963, about 60 years ago, when I was undergoing Survey training at Guwahati. He is Madan Bezbaruah of the 1964 IAS batch! After retirement in 1997, UPSC enlisted me to participate as an Expert for UPSC Interviews in Delhi. I continued mentoring at coaching institutions in Hyderabad, which requested that I address aspirants on the study of compulsory and optional subjects. I used to advise candidates about preparation for the Preliminary and Main examinations, books to read, practice essay writing skills, the study of Ethics & Values, and how to appear for Mock Interviews. I delivered a series of lectures on current topics, life in the IAS, and personality development for some coaching institutions.

At Mock Interviews, I tried to give candidates a realistic simulation of the UPSC type of experience. Many questions are from the DAF particulars submitted by the candidate. After noting the performance, we gave them comprehensive feedback and advice about correctable mistakes. We emphasised that candidates must be psychologically prepared and answer confidently. Word spread that I was a patient interviewer who corrected mistakes, cleared doubts, and guided candidates according to their needs.

Civil Services coaching institutions at Hyderabad, Delhi, Vijayawada, Visakhapatnam, Kakinada, Guntur, Trivandrum, etc., invited me to participate as a member and chair Mock Interviews. Aspirants who had attended UPSC Interviews but were not selected sought my help. I entertained such requests and conducted interviews at home for a limited number of candidates by pointing out their 'correctable' mistakes, instilling 'confidence,' and teaching them how to listen carefully, formulate the answer, and answer to the point. It has become a part of my social service work.

The final ranks of the candidates are decided on the combined marks obtained in written papers, and the Interview; Candidates are allocated to different services in accordance with choices and reservation policy. Hence, primacy must be accorded to prepare with a positive mind set and present yourself confidently for the Interview at UPSC, Delhi.

The Interview is not a test of knowledge but of personality, responsiveness, integrity, empathy, aptitude, and suitability for appointment and allocation to the Service. Your manner of response to questions, Awareness, Knowledge, understanding of current affairs, basics of technology, level of proficiency, and confidence are tested. You will be assessed on both aptitude and attitude. This often determines the 'altitude' to which you can rise in service and life!

You may recall what the Sanskrit Shloka says: "*Vastrena, Vapusha, Vacha, Vidyaya, Vinayena cha, Maanava Gouravam Prapnoti*" – A person gets respect by his Dress, Personality, Speech, Knowledge and Humility. The Interview is akin to the 'One Day or Two-Twenty' cricket match – Your strategy, timely and crucial batting, or bowling wins the game - You must present your best all-round personality without showing off. To do well in the Interviews, be Prepared, Punctual, Positive, Patient, Poised, Polite, and Professional in your replies.

To put it briefly, an Interview is a test to assess various aspects of your personality, i.e., Physical Quotient (PQ), Intellectual (IQ), emotional (EQ), spiritual (SQ), and your overall interests in life – It is a simple assessment of your Listening, Reading, Understanding and Speaking skills – Be brief, to the point and if you do not know, say so, but do not act smart or show off – DO NOT BLUFF. If you do so, you are 'off' the list!

Interview is an assessment of your general awareness of current affairs, level of confidence, willingness to accept challenges, clarity of thinking, comprehension, and communication. Do not be nervous but be confident during the Interview. Attend Mock Interviews to gain confidence.

The Interview tests the range and depth of your interests and understanding of India, its history and standing in the world, and the role of Civil Services in providing good governance for rapid socio-economic development. The Interview assesses your general understanding, ability to work under stress and tackle socio-economic problems and emergencies, like Disaster Management, Law and Order situations, and the like – Civil Servants are 'Change agents' and expected to bring about transformational change for the better - Civil Servants have and are expected to be Indian in outlook, Civil in conduct and good Public Servants. Service to the nation is the real 'Yagna' that a Civil Servant performs during his career. Remember that the motto of the Services is "*Yoga Karmasu Kaushalam*"

– One has to move from Proficiency to Efficiency to Effectiveness. Effectiveness in work comes from attentiveness combined with the calm equanimity of the mind. Interview is the final test for selection. On an objective, fair, and impartial assessment by UPSC, you have done well and come quite far and near the goal.

One out of two called for the Interview gets selected for a Service. Be confident that you are that one. Do well, and success will crown you – Godspeed to you.

Follow the 3 E Rule for success Excel yourself; Exceed expectations of your parents, teachers, and friends; Expand the scope for achievements Success favours the brave and the bold - Be bold in the Interview, show what you have been and are now, and what you can be with your potential. With best wishes for your success in the examination and life.

17

About the Author

M. Gopalakrishna, born on January 12, 1939, a 1962 batch retired Indian Administrative Service (IAS) officer is a Mentor and Management Guru for aspiring and serving civil servants and a father figure for many NGOs.

A graduate in Science (B.Sc.) and Law (LLB), he did the Advanced Management Programme (AMP) at Banff School of Management in Canada. Cracking the Civil Service Examination (IAS) on his first attempt, he achieved a record 100 percent in the Law Examination for IAS probationers.

An ace administrator, trouble shooter and consultant, his advice is highly sought after. Erudite speaker on diverse topics like ethics and values, science and technology, management and public administration. His lectures on Management, Ethics & Values are currently under publication.

The book covers his career and work as a Karma Yogi in the Civil Service and post-retirement life. It is a memoir that reflects on his six decades of experiences and is an inspiration for civil servants and aspirants.

In Assam, he had an impressive record as Commissioner, Home, Secretary, Industries and Health departments, District Magistrate of Sibsagar and Mizo Hills District, where his contributions are fondly remembered. In Andhra Pradesh, he was Special Chief Secretary for Industrial Promotion; Secretary, Major Industries, Commissioner Visakhapatnam Steel Plant, and Commissioner of Commercial Taxes. As the Founder Managing Director of Godavari Fertilizers and Chemicals Limited (GFCL), from concept to commissioning, he built the plant ahead of schedule and within the estimated cost. It is now a case study in Project management.

In the Central Government, he served as Chairman and Managing Director of the Rural Electrification Corporation (REC) and Chairman of SCOPE, Additional Secretary, Ministry of Mines and Regional Iron, Steel

Controller in Hyderabad. He has chaired several Government Committees on various matters.

He served as Vice President of the International Lead Zinc Study Group of the United Nations Organisation (UNO) and has presented papers at many International Conferences on Energy, Minerals and Rural Development.

He was a consultant for the United Nations Development Program (UNDP), KFW, Asian Development Bank (ADB), and Department for International Development (DFID) of the United Kingdom.

Post-retirement, he was Director of Institute of Public Enterprise and Chairman, AP State Financial Corporation, which was turned around as a profitable entity. Gopalakrishna has extensive corporate experience, having served as Director in Government, Public listed, and unlisted companies.

A Guest Faculty at the Administrative Staff College of India and National and State Level Institutes, he is actively associated with many social, cultural and heritage organisations.

About 400 Awards, trophies, and mementos jostle for space in his house. These include the *Dean Paul H. Appleby Award* for distinguished services to Public Administration, the *Lifetime Achievement Award* of NHRDN in 2019, the *Best Manager Award* from the Hyderabad Management Association, the *Bharat Shiromani Award* from the Institute of Economic Studies, the *Marketing Man of the Year Award* from IMM, and the *Rajiv Gandhi Sad Bhavana Award* for communal harmony.

His personal library includes books on philosophy, religion, management, and a special edition of the calligraphed copy of the Indian Constitution.

Gopalakrishna's passion is mentoring civil service aspirants, to clear the examination and be battle-ready for interviews. His philosophy is one of "Excel Yourself", "Exceed the Expectations," and "Enlarge your horizon be ever in the Pursuit of Excellence". His life is an inspiration for civil services aspirants, bureaucrats, management students, and anyone interested in good governance.

I. FAMILY

1. Grandfather Dr. Govindarajulu Naidu with wife Pushpavenamma

2. Grandfather Dr. Govindarajulu Naidu as Rajayogi

3. Father Late (Shri) M. Narayana Swamy Naidu

4. Mother Late (Smt.) M. Bramaramba

5. Childhood Family Photo-1946

II. EDUCATION

6. At. Wardlaw High School Ballari-1952-53

7. Mahabub College, Secunderabad
Inter-Science 1953-55

8. As Secretary Students Union,
Law College, Hyderabad 1959

9. Winner-Inter College
Elocution Contest 1995

10. LLB Degree 1960

III. AT LBS NATIONAL ACADEMY OF ADMINISTRATION, MUSSOORIE 1962-63

11. On Horseback at Mussoorie

12. Banquet at NAA, Mussoorie

13. In Arunachal Pradesh, Bomdila 1963

VI. AS SDO GOALPARA 1964-66

14. Goalpara Sainik School 1965

15. Flag Hoisting at Goalpara 1966

V. In Mizo Hills 1966-67

16. With Dubashi Pu Sanglira Mizo Hills

17. Mizo Hills 19

18. Mizo Hills 1967

19. Mizo Woman

VI. IN SIBSAGAR DISTRICT (1968-70)

20. At Gormor Satra Mazuli, Sibsagar

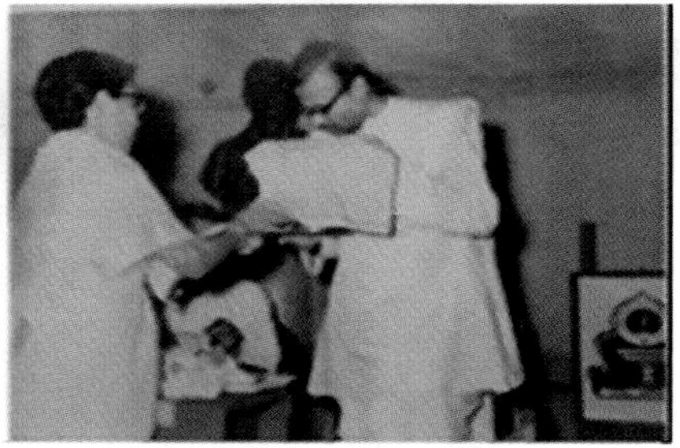

21. Honoured by Assam Sahitya Sabha, Jorhat

22. Flag Hoisting as DC, Jorhat

23. Receiving Mrs. Indira Gandhi at Jorhat Airport 1970

VII. Marriage Photos (1974)

24. Marriage 1974

25. Vengalarao, CM at the Marriage Reception March 1974

26. Marriage Photo 1974

27. At Tajmahal, Agra 1994

VIII. GAMES & SPORTS

28. National Kabaddi Championship, Hyderabad 1988

29. As Vice President of Hanuman Vyayamasala 1976

30. Weightlifting Winners 1985

IX. GODAVARI FERTILIZERS

31. Signing of MoU with IFFCO by GFCL in 1984

32. Godavari Fertilizers & Chemicals Plant 1987

33. Presenting Fertilizer bag to temple

34. Shri N Rama Rao, CM & Shri R. Prabhu, Union Minister of State for Fertilizers (1986)

35. GFCL Meet at Jubilee Hall, Hyd 04-04-1984

X. PHOTOS ABROAD

36. Outstanding student Award at Banff School of Management, Canada-1992

37. As Delegation leader in Vietnam 1993

38. In Morocco 1995

39. Signing of Agreement in Korea for IT Collaboration -2001

AS CMD OF REC

40. REC – Transformer Initiative

41. In Australia -1996

42. Inauguration of Sub-station of HZL at Visakhapatnam

43. With MoS Power at Vemulawada, Karimnagar Dist. 1995

44. Min. of Mines 1991

XI. AS CHAIRMAN APSFC (2002 – 2006)

45. With Shri V.K. Chopra, CMD, SIDBI

46. MoU Signing Cermony

47. Awards Presentation by Minister
Shri K. Vidyadhara Rao

48. Golden Jubilee Celebrations
of APSFC on 01-11-2006

XII. GLIMPSES OF LECTURES

School of Management Studies (HCU):

49. With Shri Rangarajan, at HCU

50. HMA Meet on Women Empowerment

51. Seminar on Galfan

52. As Chief Guest, RBI Reg.Branch, Hyderabad

XIII. AWARDS

53. Army Calls him "Scholar-Warrior"

54. Award from Sri Pranab Mukharji

55. HMA-Best Manager of the Year 1988

56. Receiving Award from
Sri Manmohan Singh, Then Finance
Minister of India

57. Receiving Gold Medal from
Shri S.D.Sharma, President of India

XIV. POST RETIREMENT

58. All India Services Pensioners Association

59. As INTACH State Convenor for AP & TG